Reappraising
an Empire

Harvard Studies in American-East Asian Relations 10

The Harvard Studies in American–East Asian Relations are sponsored and edited by the Committee on American–East Asian Relations of the Department of History at Harvard University.

edited and with an introduction by

PETER W. STANLEY

*Published by the Committee on American–East Asian Relations
of the Department of History in collaboration with the
Council on East Asian Studies, Harvard University.*

*Distributed by the Harvard University Press
Cambridge (Massachusetts) and London.   1984*

Reappraising an Empire

New Perspectives on
Philippine-American History

Research and writing for this book were made possible by the Henry Luce Foundation, Inc., through its Luce Fund for Asian Studies. The Foundation also contributed to the costs of publication.

Designed by Adrianne Onderdonk Dudden

Library of Congress Cataloging in Publication Data
Main entry under title:

Reappraising an empire.

(Harvard studies in American–East Asian relations; 10)
Bibliography: p.
Includes index.
1. United States—Relations—Philippines—Addresses, essays, lectures, 2. Philippines—Relations—United States—Addresses, essays, lectures. 3. Philippines—History—Insurrection, 1896-1898—Addresses, essays, lectures. 4. Philippines—History—Insurrection, 1899-1901—Addresses, essays, lectures. I. Stanley, Peter W. II. Series.
E183.8.P5R4 1984   959.9'03   84-15825
ISBN 0-674-74975-8

C O N T E N T S

Introduction

PETER W. STANLEY

As relations between the United States and the Philippines enter a new and challenging phase, the study of Philippine-American history takes on new importance. This is so because the traditional belief that a "special relationship" unites the two countries rests primarily upon an appraisal of the period when Americans ruled the islands.

The official mythology is that the American empire in the Philippines did credit to us both. Opinions differ as to the reason for the admittedly brutal beginning in 1899; but the traditional view is that, when William Howard Taft became Civil Governor and introduced his policy of "attraction," a corner was turned. The United States began an enlightened policy of development and "benevolent assimilation" from which it seldom thereafter deviated, except to strengthen its commitment to eventual independence for the islands. Roads, hospitals, and, above all, schools and democratic political institutions were the symbols of this new era; the willingness of both sides to debate their differences within the political system, its cement; the peaceful achievement of independence in 1946, earlier than any other Western colony in Asia, its fulfillment.

That is the myth: The Americans were liberal tutors, the Filipinos receptive students. The myth implies what the jargon of the 1950s or 1960s might have called partnership for progress. Critics on the left, of course, have always dissented, arguing that schools, hospitals, and political devolution were nothing but a sentimental cover for the exploitation of another people's country. Their counterparts on the right have contended equally firmly that political liberalism was all too real, an abdication of responsibility and the cause of lost opportunities. Still, the myth has embedded itself in both scholarship and popular political culture.

Now, however, a new critique of the American record in the Philippines is beginning to emerge, a critique that finds the American impact upon the Philippines—either for better or for worse—much less substantial than previously imagined. Taken together, the essays in this collection show that it is a hubristic illusion for Americans to imagine that, in the colonial era, they liberalized, modernized, or, for that matter, exploited the Philippines in any large, systemic, or lasting way. Even when individuals and interests tried to do so—as the abaca merchants of the nineteenth century and the Protestant missionaries of the twentieth assuredly did—they accomplished little. Underestimating the resilience of Hispano-Philippine institutions and the social and economic rhythms of Philippine life, overestimating the power of their own example, Americans achieved much less than they said they did. Sometimes progressive and sometimes not, the American empire was above all naively pretentious in its self-evaluation.

Filipinos have always understood this, and some of them have known how to turn it to their own advantage. Manuel Quezon, the first President of the Philippine Commonwealth and the leader of the Nacionalista Party in the 1920s and 1930s, probably did more than any other person except Taft to set the tone of political relations between Filipino and American leaders. Quezon built his political career upon the twin rocks of nationalism and early political independence. On the hustings, his rhetoric was fiery and absolutist: "I would prefer a government run like hell by Filipinos," he used to proclaim, "to one run like heaven by Americans." So much for tutelary benevolence! In private, however, Quezon and most of the political elite of the Philippines took a much more complex view of the relationship with the United States. "Damn the Americans!" he once mused to a confidant. "Why don't they tyrannize us more?" Quezon's seemingly anomalous question—Why not more tyranny?—is a useful starting point in any reexamination of Philippine-American history.

In the beginning, such a question would have been inconceivable. The questions absorbing both Americans and Filipinos in 1899 and the years just after were questions of conquest, justice, responsibility, and grand strategy. The self-evident reality was that American soldiers *were* tyrannizing the Philippines. The question for Filipinos then was whether to fight, collaborate, or go limp. And the question Americans had to face was whether the advantages of conquest and annexation—economic, strategic, and, many of them would have said, ethical—offset the ghastly cost to their self-respect in terms of atrocities committed and principles violated.

The real roots of Quezon's question lie in the collaborative compromise that emerged in the first decade of civil government and became institutionalized in the second. In the 1960s, the term for this type of relationship was *co-optation,* and many scholars waxed eloquent about co-optation of the Filipino elite through Taft's policies of attraction and conciliation. Since it was equally clear that the Filipino elite had co-opted the American administration, however, the word turned out to lack something in precision. *Collaboration,* with its quisling overtones, was a word most scholars reserved for the Japanese occupation during World War II. Now, thanks to the English historian Ronald Robinson, we have at least the beginnings of a general theory of imperial collaboration.[1] This helps to establish an international context for what many of us have long concluded was not so much an American empire in the Philippines as a Fil-American empire located in the archipelago.

Many people find this a distasteful—even an immoral—notion, one that confuses the issue and obscures the culpability of the imperialist aggressors. Others, from the opposite perspective, resent any theory that dilutes what they take to be the singular benevolence of American imperialism. These are both reasonable objections: Collaboration was, at best, only part of the story.

But the fact remains that no foreign power has ever governed the Philippines without the collaboration of local and regional elites. This was a transaction that worked two ways. On the one hand, neither the United States nor Spain could have retained political control of the islands by force alone: it was beyond the strategic and geopolitical capacity of Spain and beyond the political endurance of the United States to rule the Philippines that way for any length of time. (Japan never got a chance to test its capacities in peacetime.) They needed authoritative mediators to intercede with the mass of the Filipino people and organize the peaceful continuance of daily life. On the other hand, it is equally clear that elements of the Filipino elite, shaken by the class and sometimes racial animosity that had threatened their control of society during the fighting against Spaniards and Americans at the turn of the century, needed help to stabilize authority patterns and quiet the countryside. Originally the provincial elites of the islands tried to dominate the resistance movement against the United States. They decided to collaborate only after American power had been demonstrated and rural violence had begun to threaten their own interest in maintaining social order and economic productivity.

There is no need to dwell on what the United States got from this bargain: It got a governable colony that was never again an important issue, let alone embarrassment, in American politics. It got a chance for the advocates of retention to try for the various benefits they had envisioned—few of which, as we now know, actually materialized. And, however speciously, it got a clear conscience. Americans could say that Filipinos were participating actively in every branch of their government, cooperating in development programs, attending schools, and increasing their commerce. By 1916, even independence had been conceded in principle. In this light, the Quezonian question—Why not more tyranny?—had for Americans of the era between the wars a delicious, self-congratulatory irony. The most enlightened and humane of imperialists had fastened upon its colony a rule so light that the natives were asking for more! If the object of collaboration is to achieve a suitable economic and political environment at the lowest possible cost, the Fil-American empire is surely a prime illustration of the phenomenon.

For the Philippines and the Filipinos, however, the cost has been substantial. Not in terms of lives, to be sure, and not really in economic terms, either, but in terms of the integrity of the polity and the social fabric. Once in office, conservative Filipino politicans became, in effect, the fulcrum of Filipino-American relations and used their position between the two major power blocs, the Americans and the mass of their own people, for narrowly self-serving ends. On the one hand, they arrested the few significant reform programs contemplated by the American government that might have narrowed the gap between rich and poor. On the other, as the political leaders of the country, they took over the campaign for Philippine independence and used nationalist fervor to deflect criticism of their social and economic power. For almost the whole first half of this century, it was impossible for a Filipino to criticize the landlords, industrialists, and professional men who monopolized the wealth and power of the Philippines without attacking in the same persons the leaders and symbols of the struggle for the "National Ideal." This was the bottom line of what Filipino politicians used to extoll as "the discipline of the independence movement."

The United States thus became a double sanction of elite rule—buttress and target simultaneously. It protected and institutionally legitimized the class interests of the indigenous elite, while simultaneously providing a safe—and largely spurious—external reference point against which members of the elite could mobilize the populace behind their leadership.

Seen in this light, the Quezonian question points in quite a different direction—toward the cynically manipulative underside of the collaborative empire. Given the liberality and political permissiveness of American rule, and given also the confidence early arrived at that independence would be granted someday, probably in their own lifetime, Filipino elite politicians had everything to gain and almost nothing to lose by exacerbating anti-American feeling. In effect, they took a legitimate issue— nationalism and the desire for political independence—and misappropriated it as a vehicle for purging Philippine politics of social and economic content.

To say this is not to apologize for American imperialism or to minimize the earnestness and breadth of the popular desire for independence. It *is* to say that, just as syncretism was the price paid earlier by the Spanish religious empire for its collaboration with *indio* elites, so the dual sanction was the price paid for collaboration by America's political empire. And it is also to say that, in a political culture where all the really vital concerns of life are local and familial, a national symbol was manipulated to discourage the articulation of basic issues.

The "special relationship" of the American and Filipino people rests, therefore, upon a foundation of self-delusion. It has corrupted and vitiated Philippine political life, set back the cause of socio-economic equity in the islands, and misled three generations of Americans with a mythology of developmental benevolence.

Historians perpetuated this myth—which corresponded to the self-image of many Americans prominently involved in the imperial venture—because they followed their sources too closely. The extraordinarily rich evidence in the National Archives and the Library of Congress in Washington, the National Library in Manila, and the personal papers of various former officials faithfully reflected the participants' belief that Filipinos and Americans shared an interest in the political and economic development of the colony under American tutelage. It revealed their earnest efforts to build schools and roads, eradicate disease, promote export agriculture, and increase Filipinos' participation in all levels of the Islands' government. Superficially, particularly when parts of it were viewed in isolation from the rest, it suggested an all-encompassing politicization of public life, rooted in nationalist conflicts; but, seen in the whole, it actually described a dialectical progress toward the condition of guided independence, economic preference, and strategic interdependence that was institutionalized in 1946.

This great cooperative venture, with all its ambiguities, ironies, and convolutions along the way and the rainbow at its end, made an absorbing story; and until recently it captivated most of the small circle of historians working in the field. To break the mold they would have needed a different conceptual base—Marxists and their disciples, for example, always considered American-sponsored development and devolution a sham—different evidence, or a redefinition of the nature of colonial historiography. By the late 1960s and the early 1970s, when most of the contributors to this volume began to study the Philippine-American relationship, the requisite changes had occurred; and a new sense of the Philippine-American encounter began to emerge.

As the American role in developing countries, generally, and Southeast Asian countries, in particular, came under gathering attack, the misappropriation of nationalism by self-serving elites stood out in bold relief. So also did the ambiguous role of Westernized collaborators. This reinforced a growing skepticism in scholarly circles toward developmental modernization and what came to be known as reform from above. In this climate, scholars scrutinized more critically the relevance and suitability of Western models to developing, non-Western societies. What had once seemed the "failure" of Asians, Africans, and Latin Americans to maintain inviolate the institutions left by colonial rulers or to replicate the behavioral norms Westerners find essential to good government and ordered life now appeared, in a different light, evidence of the resilience of indigenous patterns. Naive assumptions about progress and growth fell before a resurgent sense of the pluralism of life; and even political development officers took to quoting Kipling on the fate of those who would change the East. Questions of exploitation aside, anyone coming new to the subject in this intellectual environment had at least to ask whether America's developmental benevolence was anything more than myopic arrogance.

At about the same time, the evidentiary base for the study of Philippine history dramatically and—to most people—unexpectedly deepened. For many years, historians had believed that the sources for the study of provincial and local history were inadequate to support sophisticated analyses. But, during the 1960s,

Edgar Wickberg and John Larkin, among others, demonstrated that materials in the then almost unexplored National Archives of the Philippines, in parish registers, diocesan records, the archives of the major religious orders, and the business records of foreign merchant houses permitted the writing of rigorous, modern provincial and regional histories. This, in turn, made it possible to treat traditional historical accounts, based primarily upon the political view from Manila or Washington, as hypotheses and test them against a growing knowledge of events in the countryside, where most Filipinos lived and where the indigenous bases of wealth and power were located. In addition, it gave fresh impetus to the study of social and economic history, since one could now get behind the rhetoric, policies, and macrostatistics of the central government and national leaders to examine what actually happened on the ground. Most such studies suggested a shallowness and impermanence in the American impact difficult to reconcile with the traditional image. Even the Americanization of Philippine popular culture may have to be reexamined, as Ronald Edgerton's supple discussion of the cowboy culture of Bukidnon in this volume suggests.

The historiography of imperialism underwent a complementary change that also affected the study of Philippine-American history. The classic emphasis upon imperialism as a political, economic, and strategic phenomenon led to a preoccupation with issues of conquest, exploitation, nationalism, and political independence. It resulted in a concern with the making and administering of policies, the devolution of authority, the provision of infrastructure, the evolution of tariffs, the significance of the colony in naval strategy, and the like. The social, cultural, and psychological sides of the encounter, on the other hand, were often neglected. Traditionally, most of the Filipinos engaged in the study of Philippine-American history have been political and institutional historians; many of the Americans, diplomatic historians. Increasingly, however, the new and interesting questions have required the interdisciplinary bent of the area-studies specialist, the hard methodologies of the quantifiers and modern political scientists, and the theoretical sophistication of those on the interface of the humanities and social sciences who can study intercultural and psychological history with creativity and control. The most plastic of disciplines, history, has responded to this new situation. And, as the axis of the field swings away from the political and diplomatic, the centrality of political nationalism declines and one can see through and beyond the old formulations.

The chapters in this volume reflect these new beginnings. The stories they tell and the interpretive analyses they provide are, in most cases, new and arresting; certain episodes and problems in Philippine-American history will never again look quite the same as they did before the appearance of these essays. But the primary aim of the volume is exemplary: It is meant to expose the themes and methods through which the subject is being recast, not to retell the story in all its parts. The authors are, for the most part, young historians who matured professionally in the period of intellectual ferment I have just described, although senior scholars such as Frank H. Golay, Bonifacio Salamanca, and Richard E. Welch, Jr., have also lent their perspectives. The book grew out of a workshop and a seminar convened at Harvard University in the summers of 1977 and 1978 to promote communication and intellectual exchange among people who were often quite independently remaking the field. In addition to those who have contributed to this volume, several other scholars took part in one or both of the summer meetings: Theodore Friend, Milagros C. Guerrero, John A. Larkin, Alfred McCoy, Michael P. Onorato, Shiro Saito, David Joel Steinberg. The participants would want me, I know, to express their special sense of gratitude to Dorie Friend, who both stimulated and unified the 1978 seminar through his wise (and sometimes playful) commentary and his transcendent good will.

Perhaps the most valuable single product of all this activity has been the preparation by Shiro Saito of an extraordinary bibliography of primary sources in the United States for the study of Philippine-American history.[2] This bibliography, arranged alphabetically by individual, institution, and, where necessary, subject, and cross-indexed also by chronological period and by geographic location, is the first reasonably complete guide to the subject. Its inclusiveness, descriptive annotation, and logical arrangement will revolutionize research in the field.

The workshop and seminar, related research activities, and both books have all been made possible by the support of the Henry Luce Foundation through its Luce Fund for Asian Studies. All of us who participated in this project wish to thank the Foundation—and particularly its past and present Executive Directors, Martha Redfield Wallace and Robert E. Armstrong—for their generosity and faith.

PART ONE

From Conquest to Collaboration

CHAPTER ONE

The American Soldier and the Conquest of the Philippines

STUART CREIGHTON MILLER

It is tempting to read history backwards and perceive the conquest of the Philippines at the turn of this century as an earlier version of America's intervention in Vietnam. There are many differences, however; and none is more striking than the attitudes of the Americans who fought these two wars. Young men marched off eagerly to the Philippines. Conscription was unnecessary, indeed never even considered.

Americans of that time had matured in an era of intense nationalism. Unaffected by the spectre of nuclear holocaust or ecological disaster on a global scale, they thought little of the interdependency of nations and peoples. Nothing in recent national history burdened them with the sort of doubts provoked in Americans of the Vietnam era by such American setbacks in Asia as the "loss" of China and the humiliating stalemate in Korea. The almost childlike innocence, unabashed patriotism, and "gung ho" spirit of these "volunteers" would have embarrassed the average "grunt" in "Nam."

As Professor Stuart Creighton Miller of San Francisco State University shows, however, these two generations of soldiers did share a racist hatred for "Gugus" and "Gooks" that rendered their victims less than human. Although many Americans at home came to feel shamed by the conduct of the Philippine-American War, there was little sense of guilt among the men in the field. The "special relationship" began not with the recognition of Filipinos' "little brown brotherhood" but with a war that had much in common with the subjugation of the North American Indian.

The recent intervention in Vietnam has rekindled considerable interest in an earlier, almost forgotten war fought in Asia by Americans to suppress the national aspirations of Filipinos. Similarities between the two wars have invited historians to construct some historical analogies. Both conflicts degenerated into "dirty" guerrilla-style struggles that soon blurred any distinction between enemy soldiers and civilians. Both struggles bitterly divided the American people over the issues of imperialism and the nature of warfare. War critics forced debate on these issues in domestic elections, though with far less success in 1900 and 1904 than was realized seven decades later. But the analogy also breaks down in many ways, most dramatically in the vastly different attitudes of the men who fought the two wars.[1]

A surprising number of private and public letters, diaries, marching songs, camp newspapers, and an occasional literary effort from the Philippine campaign have survived the vagaries of time. While not a "sample" in any technical sense, there is sufficient evidence to support some conclusions about the Americans who served in the Philippines. Volunteers for the most part, and recruited largely from western and southern states, these men were lured to combat by both patriotism and a desire to escape dull routines on the farm. While the reality of guerrilla warfare dulled any romantic illusions about combat, it never diminished their ardent patriotism.[2]

THE OCCUPATION OF MANILA

There were abundant complaints, to be sure, aimed at army life, the conduct of war, the natives, and the Islands in general. But they sound much like those common to all wars, and heard, no doubt, by Leonidas at Thermopylae. Rather than expressing qualms over the "dirty" war being waged, the soldiers complained most commonly about the lack of significant combat to relieve the boredom of garrison duty in the "boondocks." They had signed up to fight a war, and to cover themselves with glory before returning to the farm. There was no glory in fighting mosquitos, or in chasing an unseen foe, who sporadically fired a few badly aimed shots before disappearing into the jungle.

Even before the war began on 4 February 1899, there were standard gripes about the quality of the food, the necessity of wearing dress whites, difficulties in finding accommodating females, and, above all, insults endured from Filipino soldiers on a line that encircled the American positions at Manila. These volunteers were bitter that they had missed all the action in Cuba. The assault on Manila in August lasted a few hours, and was too transparently rigged to be satisfying. If there was to be no showdown with their Filipino tormenters, they wanted to be relieved by regulars and returned in time for spring planting. Of course, they vowed repeatedly that they were "just itching to get at the niggers"* before leaving "these damned islands." Their officers were equally eager. Lt. Frederick Sladen, the young aide to Governor General Elwell S. Otis, wondered just what it would take to get these "insolent natives to fight," following a series of provocative American maneuvers and demands designed to incite the Filipinos to warfare. "The fun begins now. Will the Aguinaldo party come off the perch or will they wait for us to take them off? " Sladen wondered.[3]

Contrary to official accounts, American soldiers did not "grin and bear the insult and abuse heaped upon them" by their native

---

*Historical actors, I believe, should speak for themselves as much as possible, even when their terminology might prove offensive to readers of another generation. Racial epithets are quoted repeatedly in this chapter, because the men with whom I am concerned wrote, talked, and thought in such terms. In their time, it was not unusual to do so. Editors, political cartoonists, and even President Roosevelt used terms such as "nigger" casually and insensitively. My purpose in reproducing the terminology here is not to imply that the Americans of Scots-Irish or German descent who fought in the Philippines were more racist than other Americans or than other white Westerners engaged in colonial warfare. Nor do I wish gratuitously to offend readers. My intent is simply to convey what was said.

counterparts. A more sensitive American observed that "almost without exception soldiers, and also many officers, refer to the natives in their presence as 'niggers' and the natives are beginning to understand what 'nigger' means." Filipino soldiers crossing American lines into Manila were knocked down with the butt of a sentry's Springfield merely for seeming "surly." A Minnesota sentry shot a civilian just for "looking suspicious." A Filipino captain was gunned down without warning for approaching a sentry while armed, even though his sidearm was safely strapped into its holster. A native woman and child were "accidentally shot," Otis reported. Pvt. William Christner of the "Pennsy Vols" wrote to his father before the war: "We killed a few to learn them a lesson and you bet they learned it." During this same period, one American was killed and two wounded in a single incident behind Filipino lines. General Emilio Aguinaldo explained to his outraged American counterpart that the three soldiers had shot each other in a drunken argument over cards. Otis apparently accepted this explanation and dropped the matter.[4]

THE SCRAMBLE FOR GLORY

The "glorious Montana yell," and a "fearless Nebraska charge" on the morning of 5 February wiped out all the petty whining, at least temporarily. But, once they were unleashed, the volunteers refused to halt their wild scramble for glory. During most of the preceding night, they had demonstrated a total lack of fire discipline, shooting "wildly into the night and wasting ammunition," a regular officer complained of the "green Dakotans." Major William Kobbe, who commanded the only regular outfit in the northern sector where it all began, had retired early, believing "it was another false alarm brought about by the excited confusion of the volunteers." Only when his 3rd Artillery was ordered to join Dewey's naval batteries in softening up the Filipino lines as the first light silhouetted them did Kobbe realize that the war had begun. American artillery was so effective that the charging volunteers found mostly dead Filipinos in the conquered trenches, so they simply continued on after the retreating enemy. Colonel Frederick Funston led the Kansans so swiftly past their assigned objective on the coast that he came under fire from the USS *Charleston*. By the day's end, the American line was "so greatly extended that any civilized foe could break it," Sladen recorded with contempt.[5]

Over the next few weeks, the letters home were euphoric. "With a good old Pennsylvania yell, we charged up the hill," Christner recounted. "I hardly think that I was born to be killed by a nigger," he reassured his parents. A cavalry unit pierced the line so fast that it crossed the Pasig River ahead of the retreating Filipinos in the only boats available. This trapped swimming enemy soldiers in a murderous crossfire by the Washington and Idaho regiments. "From then on the fun was fast and furious," with the native dead piling up "thicker than Buffalo chips," Sladen wrote. One jubilant lad confessed that picking off Filipinos in the water was "more fun than a turkey shoot."[6]

The mood changed with the realization that, although there would be no more pitched battles, the war was far from being over. "Well, I guess the niggers are whipped at last," Pvt. Hugh Clapp bragged that February. By April, he was complaining that "you have niggers you can't see shoot at you until you get close enough to shoot at them and then Mr. Nigger tears off to another good place and shoots again." Equipped for more traditional combat, the Americans could not keep pace with the lightly armed and lightly clad Filipino. When trapped, the Filipinos buried their weapons and blended with the local peasantry—a "cowardly" ploy that infuriated the over-eager volunteers. Finally Clapp's dream of one final battle was shattered along with his leg by an unseen sniper. His last letter from a hospital was bitter—not because he had been ordered to fight an unjust war, but because he was returning to Nebraska with little glory and no victory.[7]

THE STATE VOLUNTEERS RETURN

All summer long, the state volunteers passed through San Francisco, one regiment at a time, for mustering out at the Presidio. Anti-imperialist editors were eager to gather from them any resentment over having to fight a colonial war of conquest. A Pittsburg *Post* reporter was at hand to greet the 10th Pennsylvania

Volunteer Regiment. He ambitiously interviewed 600 veterans, and his editor gleaned from his notes sufficient evidence that these men agreed with their late commander, Colonel Alexander Hawkins, who had once declared, "Any attempt to hold these islands as a colony is a menace to American institutions and not worth the cost of conquest."[8]

Editors were highly selective in reproducing comments by Philippine veterans. For example, a letter written by Sgt. Charles Burrett of the Wyoming Volunteers made the editorial rounds. In San Francisco, the anti-imperialist *Call* abstracted from it criticism of Otis's leadership and the sergeant's doubts over the potential value of the islands. This was ignored by the imperialist *Sun* in New York, however, whose editor managed to ferret out Burrett's tirade against the war's critics:

> Every soldier in the Eighth Army Corps understands that the responsibility of the blood of our boys rests on the heads of Hoar, Gorman & Co. . . . I don't like to call these fanatics by the ugly name of traitor but when I think of the four brave boys of my company, whose lives have been lost by this disloyalty to the U.S., it is hard indeed, to be charitable toward these men for their mistakes if they are mistakes. The soldiers in this army call them crimes.[9]

Unwittingly, Edward Atkinson undermined the desired anti-imperialist effect of the *Post* survey by publishing a less severely edited version for the Anti Imperialist League. His rendition indicated far less support for the testimony of one officer that the Pennsylvania "regiment sympathizes with the native fighting for a liberty as dear to him as an American's is to him." While 62 percent of the officers and 93 percent of the men were highly critical of the war, they were unanimously opposed to American withdrawal before the Filipinos were "whipped first," or "made to knuckle." Even the few professed "anti-expansionists" were careful to make the same stipulation. "I have always been opposed to this expansion idea," Lt. George Gordon testified: "While I, in common with nearly all the regiment, believe that the Filipino must be whipped now, I also believe that the United States will do well to get rid of the islands as soon as possible with honor." Corporal John Findley agreed that the country "should get out as soon as it can with honor," but only "after we've beaten them into submission." Sgt. James Stickel explained that "most of the men think the natives must be whipped before there is talk of withdrawal." Corporal Moses Smith corroborated this oft-repeated impression: "Now I don't believe there is a soldier or American but believes the Filipinos must be whipped thoroughly. After that we can give them independence under an American protectorate." Only Pvt. John Kenney's suggestion that, "if the United States can drop the hot chestnut without burning its fingers, it should," came close to hinting that withdrawal might come without an American victory. And Kenney realized that he was in a minuscule minority, explaining that, "if blood had not been shed," this might not be the case: "If their comrades hadn't been killed, the men of the volunteers would have been ready to withdraw and let the Filipinos try their hand at governing themselves. Now they believe the job must be finished."[10]

But, contrary to Kenney's assertion, few of his comrades thought the Filipinos were capable of governing themselves. All thought they were "not fit to be American citizens," agreeing with Pvt. Samuel Hays that "we have negroes enough in the country without hunting more trouble." Probably Pvt. Edward McKnight came the closest to expressing the consensus of the volunteers when he told the *Post*'s reporter: "You can put me down as despising a Filipino and opposed to any annexation of them or their islands." If this was anti-imperialist sentiment, it was the type voiced by Senator "Pitchfork" Ben Tillman or Samuel Gompers. A popular marching song summed it up:

> Damn, damn, damn the Filipinos!
>   Cut-throat Khakiac ladrones!
> Underneath the starry flag
>   civilize them with a krag
> And return us to our beloved home.[11]

Even the criticism of the war voiced by veterans in the *Post* survey can be misleading. Most of it was directed at General Otis and his alleged "semi-conciliatory policy." Pvt. Loman Tucker declared:

This thing of letting "amigos," really insurgent soldiers pretending friendliness, through our lines has resulted in the deaths of many Americans. As long as Otis is allowed to carry on his grandmotherish system, I can see no end to the war. [12]

But Tucker was being coy. The need to end the "half-hearted tactics" of "coddling 'amigos,'" and "to soundly thrash the natives" were disguised demands to drop all civilized restraints in waging warfare against "savages." In short, they wanted to wage "Injun warfare." A Kansas veteran stated it more directly: "The country won't be pacified until the niggers are killed off like the Indians." Howard McFarlane agreed: It was necessary "to blow every nigger into a nigger heaven." Adapting an old frontier adage, another veteran explained that "the only good Filipino is a dead one. Take no prisoners; lead is cheaper than rice." [13]

Otis's failure to adopt officially such tactics provided these veterans with a convenient rationalization for their return without a victory. A favorite ditty mocked their commander:

> Am I a man
> or am I a mouse?
> Am I a governor general or a hobo?
> This I would like to know
> Who is boss of this show—
> Is it me or Emilio Aguinaldo? [14]

THE WAR IN PRESS RELEASES

Army press releases announcing another "final battle," or claiming periodically that the war was over, were particularly ludicrous to the men in the field, who failed to appreciate the public relations dimension to modern warfare. Press clippings mailed from home were a source of irreverent amusement. "I do hope the idiotic newspapers haven't had you worried to death about the heavy engagements at Calocoon. 'Battles' out here are greatly exaggerated. This rebel is like a flea that you can't see," Lt. Samuel Powell Lyon warned his wife. "Every paper brings the information that the 'backbone of the revolution is broken,' that 'Aguinaldo is sueing [sic] for peace,' etc., etc., whereas we are no nearer a conclusion of hostilities than we were three months ago." As for the silly proclamation that only "bandits" were left, Lyon cautioned his wife that "there will be lots of 'outlaws' in Luzon for years to come."[15]

These men attributed some of the overheated accounts of the war to other publicity-conscious generals, whose histrionics were designed more to impress correspondents than the enemy. J. Franklin Bell leaped out of a rowboat to reconnoiter, while swimming, suspected enemy defenses. "The newspapers featured this, ignoring the fact that from the level of the water his view wasn't nearly as good as it would have been with a good glass on one of the ships or even in the rowboat," Lyon wrote to his wife. On other occasions, "Bell would pick out some small and inoffensive village, ride into it waving his sword and calling on the town to surrender, which it immediately did." Such "valor" rarely occurred in the absence of reporters.[16]

Ex-Lt. John Hall revealed that Funston kept officers and men busy running "an advertising bureau" to aggrandize the Colonel's heroics, and even to create "imaginary deeds" for him. Funston was "a humbug, who never crossed a river under fire," and "a fraud, who advertised himself as the performer of exploits that were accomplished by other men," Hall charged. Nevertheless, such public-image manipulation paid off. Bell and Funston were swiftly promoted to brigadiers. On the other hand, Captain Matthew Batson never made it past the rank of major, and complained to his wife that "brevets and medals" were "being liberally thrown around" to "phony heroes," for acts "of little military merit." *The Soldier's Banner* observed that "publicity is not always the best test of heroism."[17]

WARFARE AGAINST "ASIATICS"

The *Call* continued to poll veterans, as they passed through San Francisco, with remarkably similar results. Its editor was certainly justified in demanding, "Ask the volunteers who stood the first brunt of the fighting in the Philippines if they want the Filipinos as fellow citizens, and their practically unanimous decision is against it." Almost to a man these veterans despised the natives. There were exceptions to the rule, but, in each case, sympathy for the Filipinos and their cause was expressed early

in a soldier's tour, and gave way to increased contempt for the
natives the longer he remained in the Philippines. Capt. Batson,
Lt. Lyon, and Pvt. Walter Cutter best illustrate this process.
Batson was horrified over a reprisal ordered by General Lloyd
Wheaton after two of his companies were mauled in a guerrilla-
style ambush:

One of the prettiest little towns we have passed through is Apolit. A beautiful river—the Rio Grande de Pampanga—passes alongside of it. A nice drive
runs along the river for miles and on this drive were picturesque houses set
off by the tropical plants and trees. I may add that most of the people
living in Apolit desire peace and are friendly to Los Americanos. When we
came along this road, the natives that had remained stood along the side of
the road, took off their hats, touched their foreheads with their hands.
"Buenos Dias, Senors" [sic] (means good morning) or "Aldo ming despu"
(Pampangan). The 17th Infantry came into this place the other night and
literally destroyed it—looted, ransacked, burned it—and we propose to civi-
lize, Christianize, these people. . . . We come as a Christian people to re-
leive [sic] them from the Spanish yoke and bear ourselves like barbarians.
Well I have said enough.

Batson's early letters to his wife praised the natives as "exceedingly interesting people." He even suggested "When you hear
of our people sending missionaries here, tell them they had better put their missionaries to work in New York." He sympathized with Aguinaldo's political claims, and was very impressed
by the Filipino treatment of American prisoners—even the ones
captured wandering in search of loot, whom Batson would have
treated as common thieves. [18]
    As the commander of the newly formed Philippine Scouts six
months later, Major Batson had greatly changed his tune:

The time has come when it is necessary to conduct this warfare with the
utmost rigour. "With fire and sword" as it were. But the numerous, self
styled, humane societies and poisonous press make it difficult to follow
this policy if reported to the world, so what I write to you regarding these
matters is not to fall into the hands of newspaper men.

Batson joyfully described the conduct of his native troops, recruited from the Maccabebes:

I am king of the Maccabebes and they are terrors. Word reaches a place that the Maccabebes are coming and every Tagalo hunts his hole. At present we are destroying this district, everything before us. I have three columns out, and their course is easily traced by the smoke from burning houses. Of course, no official report will be made of everything.

When Batson's close friend was killed in an ambush, he ordered the nearest town annihilated, explaining: "It helped revenge Boutelle."[19]

Possibly Batson was influenced by the Maccabebe hatred for Tagalogs, but Lyon went through a similar metamorphosis with no such influence. Shortly after his arrival, Lyon was labeled a "nigger lover" by his fellow officers, and he expressed wonder that such biased and ignorant boors could have won commissions. Lyon obtained an English translation of Aguinaldo's history of the rebellion, which he shared with his wife, along with his own doubts about the war he was being asked to fight:

Between you and me Molly, I think we (the U.S.) are making a big mistake in taking the Philippines. I believe it would be a mistake to annex them if they wanted, and I think the mistake becomes a national crime when we force them by superior strength in numbers, enormous financial advantages and mental supremacy, to become subjects of our republic. . . . There is no saying where the new policy of "expansion" (which really means "conquest") will end—what internal dissensions and what external entanglements may result. It is all very well to say as the exponents of expansion all do, that "it is our duty to elevate the people of the Philippines," etc., but the first duty of a nation is to our people. While the trade of these islands may be, and probably will be, a commercial benefit, to restrain them can only be a source of national weakness.

I don't know perhaps that I should have inflicted all this on you, and of course I have never said such things to anyone else—I am an officer of the United States and the politics of the government is no affair of mine but I cannot help thinking. I don't know that you ever told me how you stand on this expansion business. I should like to know. I would like to make a speech in the House or Senate on my side of the question (that is after the war is over, before then no one ought to attack).

I am disappointed in the United States but it is still my country. I am sure the American people will see the right thing to do sooner or later. I only hope they see it in time.[20]

Lyon did have one experience in which he felt trust had been violated by a native. His "muchacho," whom the Lieutenant treated "as a son," attempted to assassinate him while he slept, claiming that he was cleaning the officer's gun when it went off accidentally. Within a year, Lyon dismissed all Filipinos as "treacherous gugus." He confessed to torturing prisoners for information: "I fear that I will have to give the insurgent officer a touch of high life by means of a little water properly applied. The problem of the 'water cure' is in knowing how to apply it."[21]

Cutter's transformation is even more difficult to explain in that he experienced no combat. His literary talent confined him to a desk, editing *The Soldier's Banner*. But only months after his arrival, he jettisoned his initial sympathies for the natives, explaining this change of heart in his diary:

I am forced to conclude that my first estimation of them [Filipinos] was not justified. They are not to be trusted in public positions, no matter how much we might like them in private life. The agitation for independence is fomented by the educated class, who want to cut the melon of public graft; while the poor and uneducated classes are led to support their specious claims under pretext of patriotism.

The final step in Cutter's conversion was his insistence that counter-terror had to be directed at all Filipinos, because "knowing the Malay character" was to understand that a "humane" distinction between "insurrectos" and civilians would be "worthless." He compiled a lexicon for green replacements that carried the same message. *Amigo* was "a 'friend,' sarcastically applied to natives who wear white clothes and conceal guns and bolos beneath them for the benefit of Americans." The commands, *siggie, siggie,* and *vamose* kept *amigos* at a safe distance, particularly when accompanied by the thrust of a bayonet. But "nothing is better than a well placed shot while the 'gugu' is still 200 yards away to keep from being bushwacked by him," Cutter instructed. A young lad in one of Cutter's skits ignores such advice while standing guard for the first time. He offers a cigarette to "a brown brother" he had befriended. He even puts down his rifle to light it for him. The play ends with the anguished cries of the Corporal of the Guard over the body of the recruit: "Amigo be damned! I hate the very sight of their black hides."[22]

THE SOLDIER AND ANTI-IMPERIALISM

Possibly Batson, Lyon, and Cutter simply capitulated to enormous peer pressure to accept the military's conventional wisdom about the Filipinos and their national aspirations. It is also possible that the paternalism implicit in their earlier attitudes had to sour sooner or later. But one thing is clear: They were not influenced by the propaganda of the war critics at home. Only ten days after expressing anti-imperialist sympathies, Lyon wrote:

The Filipinos just now are keeping things stirred up as much as they can, in the hope that the "anti-expansionists" will win out. It would surprise you what a close watch these people keep on American politics—every disloyal sentiment uttered by a man of any prominence in the United States is repeatedly broadcast through the islands and greatly magnified. While Congress is on the fence [debate over the Philippine Bill] there ought to be some way of muzzling these traitors. If Congress comes out decidedly for holding the Philippines—the insurgents will perhaps accept the hopelessness of further struggling. [23]

Cutter caricatured anti-imperialists in his unpublished war novel. His hero, Hank Harkins, rips down a poster telling soldiers that they "are engaged in the task of enslaving a helpless race, whose only crime is a love of liberty. They are brothers and this work must stop." Searching for the "descendant of copperheads" responsible for this "despicable treason," our hero finds "a professional-looking man in linen duster, broad brimmed hat and sporting a beard," surrounded by angry soldiers. Spotting shiny, new stripes on Hank's sleeves, this fussy, bookish and pedantic "agitator" appeals for protection against the "uncouth language and menacing gestures" of his audience. Feigning anger, Corporal Harkins orders the men "to escort this well-meaning gentleman" to the railroad station, and "see that he gets a *good start* for the next town!" Delighted, the soldiers lead their victim toward a deserted back street, while poor Hank laments that his recent promotion precludes his "joining in the fun." Cutter's diary made clear his contempt for war critics, "who, in the security of their homes, have set themselves up as judges." [24]

Comments on anti-imperialism by other soldiers were generally critical. "I wish Bryan and his friends would come over here and talk to the soldiers. I think that they would last just as long as a snowball in H---. I would like nothing better than to string them up," Pvt. A. E. Hambleton wrote. Senator Albert Beveridge, a bombastic defender of the war, was wildly cheered by the troops as he toured the combat zones. Responding to a copy of Beveridge's speech upon his return to the Senate, Hambleton told his father: "I have read it carefully and I think from what I have seen and heard since I have been here that he is right." It was not lost on Hambleton that no anti-imperialist had toured the islands to find out what was happening "first hand."[25]

War critics were also vilified in song. In one ditty, a soldier from Dixie confesses that all the "argufyin'" is "confusin'":

McKinley is our President
    An' as far as I can see
The old flag's just as sacred
    As it wuz in '63
An' his soldiers in the Philyppines
    —True an' loyal men—
Deserve the same encouragement
    That Lincoln's boys did then.
So if Davis, Lee an' Johnson
    An' we who wore the grey
Were traitors to our country then
    Will someone kindly say
What Bryan, Hoar and Atkinson
    An' others of such fame
Expect to find in history
    Writ opposite their names?[26]

Any mention of the election at home in 1900 invariably supported the McKinley/Roosevelt ticket. Presumably most southern and many western soldiers should have favored Bryan, but, according to Sgt. Beverly Daley, even the "howling Democrats" favored McKinley. "Of course there are some boys who think that Bryan is the whole cheese, but they don't say too much," Hambleton explained. Batson testified that McKinley's reelection was "a great satisfaction to most of the men, as Bryan's election would have been disastrous to us here." Such sentiment helps explain the wildly enthusiastic receptions both

McKinley and Roosevelt received from veterans. Their raucous cheering particularly embittered the *Call*'s editor, who insisted that it only "seems to be a unanimous endorsement of imperialism" by the men who fought in the Philippines.[27]

LAWLESSNESS AND ATROCITIES

One shocking characteristic of these soldiers—especially the volunteers—was their lawlessness. Military leaders tried to pass off looting and senseless destruction as "souvenir hunting." Since officers, sometimes ranking ones, were involved, discipline in the ranks was out of the question. Colonel Funston helped loot a Catholic church, and personally desecrated its sacred precincts to amuse his men from the Bible Belt. Funston may have set the lawless tone before the Kansas Regiment ever left San Francisco. Leading his men down Market Street in a July 4th parade, Funston charged, and narrowly missed with his sword, a spectator, who had thrown a firecracker under his horse.[28]

Some soldiers complained of the behavior of their comrades. D. M. Mickle of the Tennessee outfit wrote: "You have no idea what a mania for destruction the average man has when the fear of the law is removed. I have seen them . . . knock chandeliers and plate glass mirrors to pieces just because they couldn't carry them off. It is such a pity." Another soldier observed of his regiment: "Talk of the natives plundering towns: I don't think they are in it with the 51st Iowa." But many others bragged about their loot and wanton destruction. Captain Albert Otis entered a house in Santa Ana that contained five pianos: "I couldn't take them, so I put a big grand piano out of a second-story window. You can guess its finish." San Franciscans got a taste of this lawlessness when some drunken Wyoming Volunteers at the Presidio used a schooner entering the bay for target practice. Thereafter the volunteers were disarmed before leaving the Philippines.[29]

This lawlessness made it easier for soldiers to commit atrocities against natives, who had already been dehumanized by racial hatred. On top of this, widespread stories of Filipino mutilation of American captives helped raise the soldiers' blood lust. "They cut their ------- off and put them in their mouths. That is the kind of people they have here," Hambleton reported to his brother. For every soldier who protested that "we came here to help, not to slaughter, these natives," there were dozens who justified atrocities; many professed to enjoy committing them:

Soon we had orders to advance, and we . . . started across the creek in mud and water up to our waists. However, we did not mind it a bit, our fighting blood was up, and we all wanted to kill "niggers." This shooting human beings is a "hot game," and beats rabbit hunting all to pieces. We charged them, and such a slaughter you never saw. We killed them like rabbits; hundreds, yes thousands of them. Every one was crazy. . . . No more prisoners.

Another soldier explained that, "when we find one that is not dead, we have our bayonets." Because the Filipino "is so treacherous," even "when badly wounded," he has to be killed, Sgt. Leman insisted, asking, "Can you blame us?" One soldier thought it hilarious when some "Tennessee boys" were ordered to escort "thirty niggers" to a hospital, and "got there with about a hundred chickens and no prisoners."[30]

Again, officers set the example. Funston not only ordered the Kansans to take no prisoners, but bragged to reporters of personally stringing up 35 civilian suspects without a trial. He even offered to repeat the chore for leading war critics in the United States. Corporal Richard O'Brien testified that Captain Fred McDonald ordered every native killed in La Nog, save a beautiful mestizo mother, whom the officers repeatedly raped, before turning her over to enlisted men. Major Edwin Glenn did not even deny the charge that he had 47 prisoners kneel and "repent of their sins" before he ordered them bayoneted and clubbed to death. The court-martial acquitted Glenn of murder when he cited the orders of General Adna Chaffee to elicit information from natives, "no matter what measures have to be adopted." It is an error, however, to believe that American soldiers reluctantly obeyed unlawful orders, as some anti-imperialists argued. Sgt. A. A. Barnes reflected the sentiments of too many of his comrades when he described the slaughter of "1,000 men, women and children" after "one of our boys was found shot and his stomach cut open," and confessed, "I am probably growing hard-hearted, for I am in my glory when I can sight my gun on some dark skin and pull the trigger." A Utah volunteer testified that such feeling was widespread:

The boys will say that no cruelty is too severe for these brainless monkeys, who can appreciate no sense of honor, kindness or justice. . . . With an enemy like this to fight, it is not surprising that the boys should soon adopt "no quarter" as a motto, and fill the blacks full of lead before finding out whether they are friends or enemies. [31]

The most damning evidence that the enemy wounded were being murdered came from the official reports of Otis and his successor, General Arthur MacArthur, claiming 15 Filipinos killed for every one wounded. In the American Civil War, the ratio had been 5 wounded for every soldier killed, which is close to the historical norm. Otis attempted to explain this anomaly by the superior marksmanship of rural southerners and westerners who had hunted all their lives. MacArthur added a racial twist, asserting that Anglo-Saxons do not succumb to wounds as easily as do men of "the inferior races." [32]

TROOP MORALE

The war critics had long insisted that a high price in troop morale had to be paid for fighting this kind of war. They cited low reenlistment rates, and high rates for drunkenness, insanity, and self-inflicted wounds, along with some desertions to the enemy, as indices of low morale. In spite of a $500 bonus, Otis was able to persuade only slightly more than 10 percent of the state volunteers to remain in new national units. Anti-imperialists also contended that Otis had ignored a unanimous vote by the Pennsylvania Volunteers shortly after the war began against remaining in the Islands another six months. According to Christner, however, the Pennsylvania Regiment refused to vote on such a sensitive issue: "We did not want to vote either way, nor do we intend to. We are ready to come home when they are ready to relieve us"—a contention more consistent with the strong patriotism expressed elsewhere by these soldiers. Because all of the nation's other wars since the Civil War have been waged with armies conscripted for the duration, there is no comparative data. One can only wonder how many veterans of up to eight months of combat would elect to remain in the field for another two years in any war. How many fliers in the more popular World War II volunteered to continue beyond their fiftieth mission? Given the contempt felt for Otis, the widespread belief that the volunteers were kept in the field while the regulars enjoyed Manila's brothels, the conditions of guerrilla warfare, the climate, sickness, and boredom of remote barrios, it seems amazing that 10 percent did reenlist. As for those who elected to go home, it was clear that none wanted to depart before being "properly relieved." They had done their duty, and felt it was simply another lad's turn to carry on. In song, they explained:

> I came and did my best, sir,
> And, General, taint no harm,
> I'm intending when I ask, sir,
> Can I go back to "Marm"?
> And so, General, as my duty's done
> Don't think I mean any harm
> When I tells yer I've a duty
> ter perform for Dad and "Marm."

And like so many veterans of other conflicts, they made it clear in song that this was their last war:

> Ah, all may sing the glory great of being a volunteer
> But when again the country calls, we'll all be deaf, I fear
> We'll climb up on the street car roof the sucker for to see
> And as they pass we too will yell: "Just give them hell for me."

Such sentiment pertains to any war—its disillusioning lack of glamor, or, more simply, the dreary restrictions of army life— and is not peculiarly a product of the Philippine War.[33]

Drunkenness was a serious problem for the Army, as it was not confined to Manila's red-light district, but also occurred in the field. Fresh out of West Point, and the son of a general himself, Lt. Guy Henry, Jr., was shocked to discover drunken sentries in combat zones. His "cure" for this was to sneak up on the befuddled culprit, fire several rounds over his head, and then station him at the most forward and exposed post. "Most of the men were fairly well cured after about three weeks there and did not need a second tour," he testified. The best description of the problem was a fictional one in *The Soldier's Banner.* After days of chasing an elusive enemy, the captain decided to spend the night in a friendly barrio. Cooked food was purchased, and, unfortunately, so was liquor—surreptitiously from the ubiquitous Chinese peddler who slipped in under cover of darkness. The author assured his readers that what followed would be "familiar to every soldier who served in the field":

That night there were several strange scenes that must have given the natives a strange idea of the civilization we wish to foist on them. Drunken men struck at each other in frenzy and smashed each other's heads on the ground, with sickening oaths, for no reason whatsoever, except their own distorted imagination.

The inevitable occurred. A drunken soldier raped a girl, and her boyfriend slit the American's throat as he slept off the booze. "With the natives, down there, their justice is 'an eye for an eye.' Indeed, amongst a civilized mob it is not much further advanced." Once they discovered their dead comrade, the soldiers burned the already deserted village, and gunned down any native foolish enough to get in their sight.[34]

The rates for insanity and self-inflicted wounds were deliberately inflated by anti-imperialist editors for propaganda purposes. The 347 mental breakdowns listed in the Surgeon General's report for 1900 covered a period during which approximately 100,000 men had served in the Islands, making the rate infinitesimal. Nevertheless, his report provoked misleading headlines, such as "Awful Record of Lunacy." Victimized by his own paper's propaganda, a *Call* reporter was on hand to greet "thousands of insane soldiers" rumored to be "in chains" aboard a transport from the Philippines. To his chagrin, he found only 64 unmanacled mental patients.[35]

"Self-inflicted wounds are so frequent . . . that General Otis has been compelled to issue instructions directing that a strong investigation be made in each case of this character," the *Call* reported. This was never corroborated, but Otis did protest that most of the sick soldiers filling up his hospitals, when he desperately needed them in the field, were "malingerers shirking their duty." Wounding oneself and feigning illness have been traditional means of avoiding combat. There was so little real action in the Philippines that such ruses there may have been more a path back to Manila from some God-forsaken outpost.[36]

The record is not clear, but, at most, 15 American soldiers, about half of them black, did accept commissions from Aguinaldo. Given the racist extremism at home, it is surprising that more Negro soldiers did not desert to the enemy. They left for the Philippines amidst race riots in Chicago and San Antonio. Headlines warned that a "War of the Races Is Threatened." The anti-imperialist *Call* even featured a front-page minstrel-style cartoon depicting "Colored Volunteers" dancing, rather than marching, up the gangplank to a transport. Negro features and speech were grossly caricatured. "Jes' one mo' smack at dem cherub lips," a soldier with ludicrously distended lips and bulging eyes begged his equally distorted girlfriend. The caption explained that, "when dat coon ban' played de cakewalk," each soldier "danced away for dear life." Once in the Philippines, whites refused to salute black officers, jeering instead: "What are you coons doing here?" On a higher level, Otis protested sending black troops whose loyalty in fighting other non-whites would be suspect. Governor William Howard Taft complained that black soldiers got along "too well with the native women," leading to the latter's "demoralization." He recommended returning "colored" regiments to the United States as soon as it was feasible. The Secretary of War ordered that black soldiers marrying natives be discharged and sent home.[37]

Apparently, "Los Negritos Americanos" did get along better with Filipinos because, as one soldier explained, "they do not push them off the streets, spit at them, call them damn 'niggers.'" Some blacks expressed uneasiness over fighting men of "our own hue and color," but others adopted the white prejudices, calling natives "gugus," and insisting that they were only "half civilized" and "savages." Chaplain George Prioleau accused them of "untruthfulness, idolatry, stealing, and every crime in the decalogue," vowing that "the indolence and laziness of the Filipino must not and will not retard American progress." Only a handful of Negroes deserted out of the four black infantries and the famed regular 9th and the volunteer 10th Cavalries, which served bravely and with distinction. "The dusky fellows of the 25th are fierce fighters," conceded a white editor. These soldiers and the Filipinos were racially and culturally so vastly different that the assumption of an instant mutual attraction and loyalty based on racial affinity has to be utterly romantic, and possibly racist.[38]

It appears that morale was lowered because of boredom and a lack of combat to interrupt the tedium of garrison duty in isolated villages. "We haven't done anything but 'wait around.' I don't like it. The 25th is getting in bad shape," Lyon complained. He opened each letter home with "nothing new in the 'war' today," and closed it with "another long stupid day is gone." In between Lyon described numerous breaches of discipline: fistfights, drunkenness, bored pickets imagining attacks and "firing hundreds of rounds at nothing." The single casualty in Lyon's platoon was the bugler, who suffered a heart attack sounding "another false alarm." A real battle was just the elixir needed. When they captured 26 Filipinos with their rifles and stockpiles of ammunition and rice after a genuine firefight, the men joked, sang and shouted "Rah for the 25th" all the way back to their base. Lyon confessed that he had never seen them "so jubilant and happy." That evening, the heavy drinking was distinctively more festive than escapist. Lyon discreetly retired to write a letter: "They are kicking up an awful row. Scared the natives half to death about eight o'clock tonight by sending up a couple of big rockets from the plaza." Other officers commented on the galvanic effect that real combat had on sagging morale. It was rehashed for weeks after, and suddenly their sojourn in the Philippines had meaning. They would have some war stories for their grandchildren after all. As Lt. William Connor explained it, "The American soldier is a mighty poor 'peace soldier,' but more than a mighty good 'war soldier.'"[39]

Their marching songs belie the alleged demoralization of this army. They eulogized "the raggedy man from Kansas," whose "Yankee yell" and "fearless charge" won "jayhawk glory." They were maudlin over their flag, mother back at the farm, and "the fallen sons who never returned." They sang the official faith that Americans were "fighting side by side in the burning Torrid Zone against the right to loot and slaughter burning through the Malay creed," bringing "liberty and justice . . . leading savage minds to light." Often the songs ended with "three cheers for the red, white and blue."[40]

MARTIAL PATRIOTISM

Very few ever altered this patriotic view of the war. No veterans organized against the war, and few joined the Anti Imperialist League. John Hall spoke for the League only after Washington ignored his attempt to discredit his former commander, General Funston. The only residue of bitterness was the government's failure to acknowledge that they had fought a war, which meant the loss of extra pay and other benefits. One song warned that they had "stood with true Yankee grit," on food "that would kill a hog," to fight "in mud up to our chins," and "never questioned for a moment if the cause was wrong or right"; but "some cold November morning," the "defeated candidates will say: 'O that they never meddled with a soldier's travel pay.'" In 1922, veterans' benefits were quietly bestowed on the remaining survivors of the 8th Army Corps. In 1960, Secretary of State Christian Herter turned down a plea by his friend, Ambassador Carlos Romulo, to recognize formally that the "insurrection" had in fact, been a Philippine-American War.[41]

In the final analysis, the American soldier fought this "dirty" colonial war as readily as did his British counterpart in India or South Africa. It was for both, of course, an era of intense nationalism. But possibly there is another more peculiarly American explanation as well. The proponents of imperialism had hailed the Philippine Islands as "America's new frontier," and, appropriately, the volunteers brought with them a frontier spirit steeped in an individualism that easily degenerated into lawlessness. Virtually every member of America's high command in the Philippines had spent most of his career chasing Apaches, Comanches, Kiowas, and the Sioux. Some of them had taken part in the massacre at Wounded Knee. It was easy for these commanders to order similar tactics in the Philippines when faced with the frustrations of guerrilla warfare. But their young charges, many of whom were descendants of old Indian fighters, carried out such orders with amazing, if not surprising, alacrity.[42]

Private Presher and Sergeant Vergara: The Underside of the Philippine-American War

GLENN A. MAY

In recent years, members of the "nationalist school" of Philippine historians have contended that the Filipino war effort against the United States was mass-based. The Filipinos lost, they argue, because the resistance was undermined by indigenous elites: Aguinaldo, the commanding general of the Filipino army, was self-serving and incompetent; other prominent Filipinos actively collaborated with the United States. The real heroes of the war, according to this view, were the Filipino people themselves, who fought on in spite of the odds because they were wholeheartedly committed to the goal of independence.

The following essay by Glenn A. May of the University of Oregon focuses on one theater of the war—the province of Batangas, located just to the south of Manila, the scene of some of the hardest fighting and worst atrocities of the conflict. In part, May simply attempts to reconstruct what the war was like for two enlisted men, one American and one Filipino. His case study of the American soldier, Frederick Presher, clearly echoes themes from the previous essay by Stuart Miller: the relish of fighting, the boredom of garrison duty, the drinking, the moral insensitivity, the contemptuous attitude toward Filipinos. More important, however, May's essay implicitly challenges the nationalist school's analysis of the Filipino resistance. It suggests that some lower-class Filipinos were unenthusiastic about and even uninterested in the war against the Americans and that some may have been unwilling participants in that struggle.

Historians seem to be preoccupied of late with the "underside" of history: the unhappy marriage of a simple woman in seventeenth-century China, the revolutionary tendencies of eighteenth-century American seamen, the chiliastic visions of peasants in nineteenth-century Italy. Students of the Philippine past have shared the preoccupation. Guerrero, Ileto, Kerkvliet, McLennan, Sturtevant, to name only a few, have provided important insights into the lifestyles and *Weltanschauung* of Filipino peasants, and more studies on like themes are in progress.

What follows is an effort to examine the "underside" of a landmark in the history of Philippine-American relations: the Philippine-American war. Two individuals of insignificant stature are the protagonists of this story—Frederick Presher, a private in the American army, and Emilio Vergara, a sergeant in the Filipino. Both served in (and Vergara was actually a native of) the province of Batangas, where fighting between Americans and Filipinos took place between January 1900 and the middle of 1902. Neither was especially heroic or cowardly; neither fought in a major battle; indeed, neither apparently killed anyone during the conflict; but their experiences enable us to gain important insights into the nature of the Philippine-American War.

Two caveats are in order at the outset. This examination of the experiences of Presher and Vergara is meant to be suggestive, at most illustrative. Presher was one American soldier out of several thousand who served in Batangas; Vergara was one Batangueño out of 300,000. Their combined field of vision encompassed only two towns out of twenty-two in the province. Some scholars might argue that the minor atrocities Presher described were relatively rare. Some might also argue that the majority of Filipino soldiers fought for reasons other than the one cited by Vergara. Still, if Presher and Vergara do not tell the whole story, they tell a large part of it: Many of the men who took part in the fighting in Batangas had experiences similar to theirs.[1]

The second caveat concerns the sources. Authors normally discuss their sources in the footnotes rather than in the text, but, in this case, because of the controversial nature of one of the sources, it seems appropriate to alert the reader to the potential problems. The principal source on Private Presher's wartime experiences is the soldier's own diary. Since diarists ordinarily have no reason to dissemble and since, like most diarists, Presher made his entries only a short time after the events described, that diary would be considered by most historians to be a fairly reliable source. The major source on Vergara is an interview conducted with that man in July 1976—that is, approximately seventy-five years after the events described. The interviewee was, moreover, a nonagenarian. One might reasonably assume that a man of such advanced years, attempting to remember events that occurred so long ago, might be able to recall only a fragment of the past, might be fuzzy on details, and might distort some of the events.[2] As a source, therefore, the interview with Vergara must be considered much less reliable. But it should not simply be discounted. An old man with a good memory can recall, in general terms, what his duties were during a long-ago war. Furthermore, on occasion, an interviewee, however old, can answer questions that written sources often do not answer. In Presher's diary, we only rarely get a glimpse of the soldier's motives and feelings, since he was not very introspective. Vergara, on the other hand, tells us a good deal about such things.

THE PRIVATE FROM WANAMASSA

On 1 May 1900, 19-year-old Frederick Presher was plowing a field on a truck farm in Wanamassa, New Jersey. Presher decided on that day, as we learn from his diary, that he was bored with farm life. So he set down his plow, packed his bags, went to New York City, and enlisted in the Army.[3] Presher's decision to enlist eventually took him to the town of Bauan, in the province of Batangas, where, as a member of the 1st Cavalry, he served for almost two years.

In some ways, Presher was typical of the American soldiers who fought in the Philippines: young, recently recruited, relatively uneducated (Presher, for one, had received only a few years of formal schooling). Many, like Presher, were motivated by considerations other than patriotism. Solomon Kenyon of the 38th Volunteer Infantry and William R. Allen of the 46th Volunteers joined because they sought adventure. Georges Le Vallée, a Canadian, enlisted in the 6th Cavalry to escape from his overbearing father. Allen Mummery of the 30th Volunteer Infantry joined up for essentially the same reasons as Presher— in Mummery's own words, "to get away from the farm and to see some of the world."[4]

What distinguished Presher from most of the others, however, was that he kept a diary of his Philippine experiences. If a diary is a reflection of the person who keeps it, Frederick Presher was not an especially thoughtful, insightful, or curious individual. His diary entries were invariably simple descriptions of what he had seen or done. It was rare for him to reflect on the meaning of events or to express opinions. But his diary, for all its shortcomings, provides a unique, unbowdlerized view of the American army's activities in southwestern Luzon during the Philippine-American War.

After enlisting, Frederick Presher proceeded to Fort Slocum in New York where he received drill instruction; next to Fort Keogh in Montana for a modicum of cavalry training; and then, in late July, to Seattle where he boarded an army transport and set off to join his assigned unit, Troop K of the 1st United States Cavalry. Presher apparently was not sure of his ultimate destination. He and the other enlisted men knew only that the ship would stop briefly in Japan and then would proceed either to China or the Philippines. Apparently, they had no preference. He wrote in his diary:

This was their profession, to fight anywhere, any time, any place, the more fighting the happier they were. It is the dreary duty of garrison work that the soldier detests.

Such men had no interest in the *mission civilisatrice,* the commercial and strategic possibilities of the Philippines. They simply wanted to fight. The transport did, in fact, refuel in Japan, and then, on 7 September, it arrived in Manila Bay. Two weeks later Private Presher was on duty with his unit at its station of Bauan.[5]

Bauan, located on Batangas Bay, had a population of approximately 39,000 in 1900. The town had been prosperous before the war. Sugar cane was the principal cash crop cultivated in that part of Batangas, and, with the ever-increasing worldwide demand for sugar, the owners of sugar estates in the environs of Bauan had begun to acquire modest fortunes. They built large homes in the *población;* they imported furniture and the latest fashions from Europe; their sons attended schools in Manila. But the war had badly scarred the land around Bauan. "Now the fields are deserted and the [sugar] mills are in ruins," Presher wrote shortly after his arrival.[6]

American troops had first entered the province of Batangas in January 1900, when Brigadier Generals Theodore Schwan and Lloyd Wheaton led an expedition into southwestern Luzon. Before that time, the U.S. army had concentrated on quelling Filipino resistance in the area north of Manila. The interval had given Miguel Malvar, leader of the Filipino forces in the provinces of Batangas and Tayabas, an opportunity to organize to resist the Americans. Still, his troops were green and poorly armed, and, when Schwan's column entered Batangas, town after town fell quickly to the invaders. The Americans proceeded to garrison the major towns in the province, including Bauan.[7] The Batangueño commanders, now aware of their inability to defeat the Americans in set-piece battles, began to engage in guerrilla warfare. For the most part, they restricted their offensive operations to ambushing small units and escort parties and conducting hit-and-run raids on the American posts. All the while, many of the Batangueños who lived in the garrisoned towns assisted the guerrillas by supplying them with money, food, and weapons.[8]

During Presher's first months in Batangas, he learned about the frustrations of fighting a guerrilla enemy. In early December, for example, a scout reported that he had seen some Filipino soldiers, so the troops at Bauan saddled up and galloped off in pursuit. But, when they arrived at the place where the enemy had been spotted, they found only a group of farmers working in the fields. Presher suspected, but could not prove, that the farmers were actually enemy soldiers. "They are 'quick change' artists in changing from insurgents to ordinary hombres," he wrote in his diary.[9] Other soldiers in the Philippines made similar observations. Colonel Robert Bullard, who also served in Batangas, even witnessed a "quick change":

From Santo Tomas hill I could with glasses see this transformation going on. It was wonderful and fully explained the ease with which our friends, the enemy, have, when beaten, been able to escape destruction at our hands. He has not marched away and escaped the fierce American. He has shed all signs of the soldier, grabbed a white flag and some agricultural tool and gone to work, hard, in the nearest field and shouted "viva America" when the hot American soldier again comes in sight. I caught many wearing two suits, one military, the other, underneath, civilian, so as to be ready for the quicker transformation.[10]

Most of Troop K's expeditions were both exhausting and abortive. In order to flush out the Batangueño guerrillas, the American soldiers regularly set out on "hikes" into the bush. Presher described one which took place in mid-January 1901:

. . . after going up the Bauan-Taal road for about 5 miles [we] turned left and went over a trail towards the hills near the coast. There was no road, only a trail that was sometimes hard to find. The country here is very rough, surprisingly so, for where the surrounding country appears almost level when viewed from a distance a closer view shows deep fissures in the earth's surface, not gradual slopes but deep gashes in the earth's surface some many feet deep, some of them having sides almost perpendictular [sic].

To traverse such terrain, the men dismounted, and then horses and troopers, on their own, maneuvered as best they could. After a while, well up in the hills, the troop came to a small barrio, which they decided to search. Presher's unit followed a set procedure in searching a barrio. They rode as close to it as they could without running the risk of being spotted and quickly surrounded it; then the captain, first sergeant, and trumpeter rode into the barrio; and, if those three encountered no resistance, the troop conducted a house-by-house search. On that occasion, the plan of operation was not particularly effective. As the troopers were in the midst of their search, a man suddenly ran out of one of the houses and dashed for the bush. Presher was certain that the man was a "gugu" (the term he and many other American soldiers used to denote the enemy, although on occasion Presher used the word to refer to any Filipino). Sergeant Niemier fired at the man, but evidently missed because, according to Presher, "the 'gugu' kept on going and dived into a clump of bushes headfirst and disappeared." The troop then resumed the search, but found no other evidence of the enemy. In the end, tired and dirty, the soldiers made their way back to Bauan with nothing to show for their efforts.[11]

Presher participated in other hikes in the first four months of 1901, and all with an equal lack of success. In fact, his troop did not make contact with the enemy until 5 May, when 63 men commanded by Lieutenant John Hartman encountered a force of approximately 250 Filipino soldiers near the southern end of the peninsula between Batangas and Balayan Bays. The Filipinos fought for an hour, but then ran out of ammunition (a common occurrence for them) and scattered. The result was a victory for Hartman and his men: The Americans killed one enemy soldier, wounded a few and captured three others; they lost two horses. Presher, however, learned about the fighting secondhand; he was on guard duty that day and missed the battle.[12]

Presher did take part in the troop's most successful operation, which occurred about eleven weeks later. On 25 July, Daniel Farol, the American-appointed Chief of Police of Bauan, informed the post commander that he had discovered the location of a company of Filipino soldiers. Farol, the most open collaborator in Bauan, was running a considerable risk by helping the Americans. In the previous year, Filipino soldiers had killed three inhabitants of the town who had been friendly with the Americans. Why Farol, formerly a schoolteacher, collaborated is not clear. Perhaps he expected to receive favored treatment from the Americans if they won the war. In any case, early in the morning on 26 July, Hartman and 52 of his men, acting on the information provided by Farol, surprised and captured 34 soldiers of the Flying Column of Bauan at barrio Polong Cupang. One of the captured soldiers was the company commander, Captain Bernabe Magbohos.[13]

Another of the captured men, a corporal named Tomas Diocampo, proved to be especially useful. According to Presher, Diocampo had some grievance against his former comrades (Presher did not know exactly what the grievance was) and consequently was willing to cooperate with the Americans. He immediately led them to a place where 22 serviceable rifles were hidden, and, in the next two months, serving as both a spy and a guide, he assisted them in rounding up members of the Batangueño army and tax collectors for Malvar.[14]

Tomas Diocampo eventually paid the fixed price for collaboration. On 28 September 1901, Basilio Leynes, a lieutenant in the Filipino army, hacked him to death with a bolo while Diocampo was shopping in the fish market of Bauan. That murder angered Presher and his troop, and they were also incensed because the people in the market who had witnessed the event refused to provide them with information. In retaliation, General Sumner, commander of the district, ordered the garrison at Bauan to burn the market and the surrounding buildings. Hartman, who was in charge of the detail assigned to do the burning, was evidently too enthusiastic in carrying out the orders, because in a few minutes the fire began to burn out of control. Hartman and his men did not make an effort to extinguish it until the flames came uncomfortably close to their own barracks. In the end, they had destroyed fourteen buildings. Presher was not at all regretful about those proceedings. The burned buildings were only "flimsy structures of bamboo and nipa," he remarked.[15]

Presher's diary touched on other aspects of the campaign in Batangas. In October 1901, a company of Macabebe Scouts arrived in Bauan to assist Troop K. The Macabebes, mercenaries from southeastern Pampanga, had the reputation of being cruel, at times barbarous. Presher's diary entry for 8 October demonstrates that some of the Macabebes deserved the reputation. On that day, Presher's troop went to Alitagtag, a barrio of Bauan, which, according to intelligence reports, was a headquarters for the Batangueño forces. The Americans surrounded the barrio, and the scouts then searched every home. The Macabebes could find none of Malvar's soldiers, but that did not discourage them. They then proceeded to torture the inhabitants of Alitagtag in order to learn the whereabouts of the enemy:

The Tagals were kicked and beaten but no information was forthcoming. One was knocked senseless by a blow from the butt of the scout's carbine and another was tied up by his thumbs, but the officers would not allow that so he was cut down in a few minutes.

At that point, the Macabebes decided to administer the "water cure," which Presher described:

The victim is laid flat on his back and held down by his tormenters. Then a bamboo tube is thrust into his mouth and some dirty water, the filthier the better, is poured down his unwilling throat.

Normally, the Macabebes had considerable success in extracting information by such methods, but, in this case, the torture victim suddenly broke away and escaped into the bush. "The Macabebes are good soldiers and loyal to the government," Presher commented.[16]

To be sure, Presher did not record in his diary every aspect of the Philippine-American War in Batangas. He did not, for instance, discuss at any length the extracurricular activities of the men in his troop. When they were not performing military tasks, the troopers participated in five principal types of recreation: they played sports, especially baseball; they gambled at poker and craps; they whored; they drank liquor; and they fought with each other. The last two activities are particularly well documented, since the men who did either in excess appeared before summary courts-martial, and the records of the cases tried in Bauan have survived. Those records tell us, for example, that Private George Cusack of Troop K was drunk on 25 January 1901, and again on 1 February, 11 June, 29 September, and 9 November. (On two of those occasions, in fact, he was drunk while in the field!) Private Marion Lindsay was drunk on 15 March 1901 and got in a fight with three other men who were also drunk; was drunk and disorderly on 9 November; and on

10 December was simply drunk. Private James McBride enjoyed his own peculiar kind of recreation· He liked to urinate in the troop's water barrel.[17]

The climax of the war for Presher and his troop came in the period November 1901–January 1902. On 12 November, Hartman, now a captain, received a report from scouts that there was an enemy concentration at barrio Lagnas, so he and 53 men went out to investigate. They encountered a force of approximately 400 led by Majors Francisco Castillo and Geronimo Leynes and engaged them in pitched battle. Again the Filipinos were low on ammunition, and, when they exhausted their supply, they were forced to retreat. Two Americans were wounded in the engagement. The Filipinos, on the other hand, suffered severe losses: 22 killed and about 75 wounded.[18]

In December 1901, the U.S. Army stepped up the pace throughout southwestern Luzon. Until late November, the commander of the American troops in that district had been Samuel Sumner, a brigadier general of considerable experience and limited ability. Major General Adna Chafee, in charge of the Division of the Philippines, finally decided that Sumner was not up to the job and replaced him with Brigadier General J. Franklin Bell, reputed to be a vigorous commander. Bell quickly set out to subdue Malvar and his following. In order to prevent the civilian population from supplying the guerrillas, he introduced his "concentration" policy in Batangas and Laguna. In each garrisoned town, the troops created "zones" where all residents of the *población* and the barrios were required to remain. Outside these areas, in the free-fire zone thus created, Bell ordered the post commanders in his brigade to pursue the enemy relentlessly:

Subordinate officers and young officers of experience should not be restrained or discouraged without excellent reason, but should be encouraged to hunt for, pursue, and vigorously operate against armed bodies of insurgents wherever they may be found. . . . Except when the advantage in position and numbers is overwhelming on the side of the enemy our troops should always assume the offensive and advance on and pursue them vigorously.

He personally told one squad as it prepared to move out on a hike, "I want action and not reports."[19]

Presher's troop clearly complied with Bell's orders. In the month of December 1901, they conducted 44 separate expeditions against the enemy—34 more than in the previous month. They captured enemy soldiers far up in the hills; they imprisoned inhabitants of the town whom they suspected of assisting the guerrillas; they burned barrios which they suspected of harboring enemy soldiers. As the Americans applied more pressure, the Batangueño soldiers still in the field grew increasingly weary of the war. In addition, the Americans now began to receive cooperation from the elite residents of Bauan, most of whom had earlier sympathized with Malvar. [20]

With Bell in command and with the officers in his brigade able to operate with few restraints, there were, inevitably, unsavory incidents. Presher took part in some, and recorded them in his diary. On 26 December, two detachments left the post, one led by Captain Hartman and the other by Lieutenant Arnold. Presher went with Hartman's party. Hartman was also accompanied by about 50 prominent citizens of Bauan who rode on ponies. Hartman's own telegraphic report of the day's activities was brief:

Lieut. P. W. Arnold 1st Cav. with 6 men Troop ⋏ captured 1 serviceable Mauser and 4 Remingtons and 1 unserviceable Remington with 260 rounds ammunition near Mt. Solo today. Many uniforms, bolt of uniform cloth, and 3 seal stamps pertaining to Col. Dimaculangan were captured. Presidente, Chief of Police, Treasurer and numerous other natives accompanied expedition. [21]

It should be noted that Hartman's account did not mention that he also led an expedition on 26 December, and furthermore that Hartman conveyed the impression that the men of Bauan accompanied Arnold's party.

In his diary, Presher described what took place on the expedition led by Hartman:

Our objective seemed to be a deep ravine near Durangao in which a number of rifles was supposed to be hidden and altho' the ravine and the surrounding vicinity was searched, the native volunteers assisting, not a rifle was found.

Finally one lone gugu was found hiding in the long grass near the trail. He was taken before the Captain for questioning but he could not or would not talk so the Captain told Sergt. Hufeld, Pvt. Baylor and myself to take him and see if *we* couldn't make him talk.

According to Presher, they took the Filipino down to the bottom of the ravine where there was a pool of dirty water, threw him in and held his head under water. The Filipino would not talk so they ducked him again and again until he nearly drowned. Every time they allowed the man to come up for air, Sergeant Hufeld would ask "Quiere habla?" But the man would not speak. Finally, the sergeant gave up, kicked the Filipino in the rear and told him to leave. The Filipino staggered away, and, to hurry him along, the sergeant fired a shot over his head.

And that was not the only unsavory aspect of the day's activities. Hartman's detachment and its train then hiked toward the town of San Luis. During most of the war, no American troops had been stationed in that town, and the townspeople had regularly supplied and sheltered Batangueño soldiers. Presher's diary tells us what happened when he and the others reached that place:

... then the "prominent and respected" citizens of Bauan got busy. They first looted and then burned every shack in sight and shortly the ponies had a much heavier load than they started out with, for as fast as a native gathered his loot he tied it to his pony—chickens, rice, clothing, blankets, pictures, in fact, anything they could lay their hands on.

Finally, Hartman, his detachment, the prominent men of Bauan, and their loot-laden ponies returned to Bauan. That was not the end to such expeditions, however. Two days later, another detachment of troopers and leading citizens hiked to, looted, and burned the barrio of Balabag. [22]

Why did the men from Bauan accompany Hartman's detachment, and why did they burn and loot San Luis and barrio Balabag? The first question can be answered with some confidence. During the final stages of the Batangas campaign, Bell authorized American commanders in every town to punish severely all priests, officials, and other community leaders who refused to assist them in capturing Malvar's troops and in identifying supporters of the resistance. The men from Bauan who accompanied Hartman probably did so in order to help the Americans locate

Malvar's forces and thereby to escape punishment. But that does not explain their actions in San Luis and barrio Balabag; nor does Presher's diary, since the young private was not inclined to speculate about their motives. Perhaps the most obvious explanation is that the men from Bauan looted and burned because they wanted to. Disputes between families, factions, and towns were givens of Filipino life, and it would not have been surprising if the leading citizens of one town took advantage of the circumstances to plunder the homes of people they disliked.

The actions of Hartman's detachment on 26 December 1901 were not major atrocities on the scale of My Lai, or for that matter, on the scale of other incidents that took place in Batangas during the Philippine-American War. To some, it might even be tempting to explain away the events of 26 December. After all, guerrilla warfare is a messy business: The line between combatant and noncombatant is often unclear; soldiers subjected to the strain of such a war are bound to commit a few excesses. It might be argued, furthermore, that there is a considerable difference between the events at My Lai and those at San Luis. But the difference is essentially one of degree, not one of kind. A minor atrocity may be less atrocious than a major one, but it is still atrocious.

Presher's account of the Hartman expedition raises other questions. The private's diary makes clear that Hartman told only part of the truth in his official report. The captain did not report that his troops were guilty of abuses in their treatment of noncombatants, nor that he had allowed burning and looting to take place in San Luis. How many other American officers falsified their reports? How widespread were such abuses on the part of American troops? If nothing else, Presher's account should alert us to the existence of a hidden Philippine-American War—a war characterized by atrocities, big and small, not recorded in the official reports of the American Army's actions.

Although Malvar continued to resist the Americans until mid-April 1902, his forces in the vicinity of Bauan had resigned themselves to defeat by the beginning of that same year. On 4 January, the police of Bauan captured Majors Francisco Castillo and Geronimo Leynes. On 6 January, Major Arcadio Villanueva surrendered; on 11 January, Captain Miguel Cuevas; and finally, on 13 January, Lieutenant Colonel Jacinto Dimaculangan. At the end of January, Captain Hartman reported to his superiors that "all insurgent forces pertaining to Bauan have either been captured and confined or have surrendered."[23]

In fact, Presher's troop did not again fight the enemy after 1 January 1902, and the men spent less time in hiking and more on garrison duty. Furthermore, gradually, the town of Bauan and its environs began to recover from the war. "This part of the province is beginning to look prosperous again," Presher wrote after returning from a short patrol in early May. "The barrios are being rebuilt better and larger than before. The land is being cultivated to some extent for the first time in years so it looks as if peace is coming to the Philippines." Frederick Presher remained in Bauan until September 1902, then served several months more in the quartermaster's office at Batangas, and finally, in April of the following year, he left the Philippines for home.[24]

Frederick Presher, was, of course, a minor figure in the history of the Philippine-American War. He did little to affect the course of the conflict, won no medals. As a diarist, moreover, he was not very insightful. His diary provides no evidence that he learned anything about the country in which he served or the people in whose midst he lived for almost three years. At the end of his tour, as at the beginning, Filipinos were to Presher simply "gugus." What is more, throughout the war, Presher seemed to be unaware of—or at least, untroubled by—the moral implications of torturing civilians to extract information. Nor did it ever occur to Presher that in burning barrios he and his fellow soldiers might have been harming innocent noncombatants. At bottom, Private Presher did not question the correctness of what he and his countrymen were doing in the Philippines. He had left the farm to pursue adventure, and in the Philippines he had found it. For Presher, his superiors' orders posed no moral dilemma; he simply followed them, and he apparently enjoyed doing so.

THE SERGEANT FROM MATAASNAKAHOY

I did not know what to expect from my interview with Emilio Vergara. In that summer of 1976, I had already met with a dozen other "veteranos" of the Batangas campaign, and several of those meetings had been, to say the least, unproductive. There had been one poor, senile man in San Luis who could tell me only the names of his parents and his wife. And there was a delightful but decrepit fellow in Nasugbu whose mind could not always distinguish clearly between the Philippine-American War and World War II. After hearing of his experiences in the Philippine Revolution against Spain, I asked him to describe his feelings and actions at the time of the American invasion of Batangas in 1900. "We greeted the Americans," he stated. "You greeted the Americans?" I said with amazement. "Yes," he insisted. "We greeted the Americans. They were kind. They gave us food and candy. After the war, they gave us their jeeps."

I met with Emilio Vergara on 27 July 1976 at his home in Mataasnakahoy.[25] Today Mataasnakahoy is a separate municipality, but at the turn of the century it was merely an outlying barrio of the town of Lipa with a population of about 2,500.[26] Vergara's house, which he shared with his much younger wife (she was in her eighties) and several grandchildren, was a solid structure with concrete walls and a galvanized iron roof. It was not the type of building a peasant normally inhabited. I remarked at once that it was a fine house. His children had built it for him, he told me proudly.

The house was located by the side of a well-traveled road. Throughout our four-hour interview, trucks and buses constantly passed by, changing their gears and honking their horns whenever Vergara would begin to make an important point. There were other sounds that intruded on our conversation: the crowing of cocks, the barking of dogs, the crying and chatter of Vergara's grandchildren, the kibitzing of Vergara's wife and a dozen other people who came by to watch and listen when they heard that an historian had come all the way from the United States to interview old Emilio. "I am going to be famous in Texas," Vergara told each new visitor.

Although he was over 90, Emilio Vergara had the physique of

a man of 50. His arms were still muscular. When he walked there was even the trace of a bounce in his step. Vergara was a short man—perhaps an inch or two under five feet. His eyes were bright, his mind alert. While he might err on details (the first names of various individuals, the month in which a particular event took place), his memory was, on the whole, extraordinary. He seemed to recall the Philippine-American War as if it had happened yesterday. It was, I later surmised, the most important period in his life, and he had probably spoken often to his children and grandchildren about his part in the war.

Emilio Vergara was born in 1883 in Mataasnakahoy. His father, Valerio, was a tenant on the land of Claro Recinto, one of the wealthiest landowners in the barrio.[27] Valerio Vergara was a poor man, and he needed his son to help him with sowing and harvesting, so Emilio received only a few years of primary education.

In 1896, as a boy of 13, Emilio Vergara had his first taste of war. Shortly after the outbreak of the Philippine Revolution, he participated in a battle at Talisay as a member of a battalion commanded by Colonel Valentin Burgos. Vergara described how the Spanish troops at Talisay, after several days of being besieged, attempted to escape but were captured. It was one of the few significant victories of the Filipinos during the Revolution.[28]

"Why were you fighting the Spaniards?" I asked when Vergara had finished his narrative of the events at Talisay. His reply was brief but revealing. "I was drafted," he said. "They lacked soldiers, so they made me go with them." As it turned out, "they" included Julian Recinto, the eldest son of Claro Recinto (the landlord of Emilio's father) and an officer in Burgos's unit.[29] Vergara made clear that he was not fighting because he wanted to free the Philippines from alien rule but because his "pangulo" (leader) forced him to fight.

Those statements by Vergara deserve comment, since they make an important point about Philippine society and the Philippine-American War. Over the years, there have been a number of scholarly studies of patron-client ties in the Philippines, the dyadic relationship between superordinate and subordinate in which each provides services for the other. So, for example, a landlord provides loans and seed to his tenant; and the tenant, in exchange, provides labor services and gifts of food to the landlord.[30] Vergara's relationship to Julian Recinto was, in fact, that of a client to his patron (since Vergara and his father lived on the land of, and worked as tenants for, Julian's father). What is more, it is apparent that the ties were extremely strong, since Recinto was able to demand military as well as purely economic services from Vergara. Thus, Vergara's statements suggest the importance of the patron-client relationship in understanding the recruitment of common soldiers in the Philippine Revolution and, as we shall see, in the Philippine-American War.

One should not conclude that Filipino peasants fought only because of pressure exerted by patrons. Some enlisted because they wanted to free the Philippines from alien rule; others because they believed—naively, as it turned out—that military life would be glamorous. Furthermore, one scholar has argued, forcefully, that peasants fought not to gain mere political independence but rather to effect millenarian goals: to bring about a radical change in society, to create a world in which men attained a high level of spiritual purity and loved their fellow men.[31]

This conflicting evidence on motives underlines a simple truth: The Filipino peasantry was not a monolith. In spite of what "nationalist" historians like Teodoro Agoncillo and Renato Constantino tell us, not all Filipino peasants were enthusiastic supporters of the Philippine Revolution and the Philippine-American War.[32] Some were supporters; some were not. Of the supporters, some were enthusiastic, and some were not. Filipino behavior varied from town to town, barrio to barrio, and house to house; and, not surprisingly, Filipinos had a variety of reasons for behaving as they did. One such reason—in my view, an important one—was patron pressure, which up to now has been largely ignored as an explanation for peasant participation in the Filipino army.

I asked Vergara a few more questions about the Revolution, and then moved on to the Philippine-American War. "What were your feelings when the Americans first invaded the province?" I asked. "I don't remember having any feelings about them," he replied. "I just left the place. Everybody left the place. No one knew what was going to happen. It took some time, maybe a month, before the people returned to their homes."[33] It was apparent that the major concern Vergara remembered from January 1900, the time of the American takeover of Lipa, was survival.

"Did you fight against the Americans?" I then asked. "Oh, yes, many times," he announced. No, he could not recall exactly how many times, but he took part in frequent hit-and-run raids as a member of a 7-man group led by Macario Gonzales, also a native of Lipa. Their primary object, he explained, was not to kill Americans but rather to disrupt their operations and to demoralize them. His group specialized in attacking wagon trains and small patrols. The commander of the battalion to which he belonged, Antonio Mandigma, organized several other groups which conducted like operations. Vergara then described one of his group's actions: an attempt to ambush a wagon train, escorted by a small party of foot soldiers and cavalrymen, just outside the town of San Jose. The unsuspecting Americans walked and rode right into the trap, and the Filipinos fired three rounds at them. But Vergara and his unit inflicted no damage, and, once the Americans regrouped and assumed the offensive, the Filipinos retreated in disarray. Vergara related that he was lucky to escape. The cavalrymen spotted him and chased him through a forested area and into a field of tall cogon. Vergara, now out of breath, hid in the cogon. The Americans searched the field but were unable to find him, although at one point one of their horses almost stepped on him.[34]

Again I returned to the question of motivation. "Why did you fight against the Americans?" I said. "I was drafted that time, too," Vergara answered, and then he described for me the process of conscription.[35] When the Americans had first entered Lipa, Vergara had hidden in a thickly forested area north of Mataasnakahoy. After several weeks in hiding, he decided to return to his home. Shortly after his return, a group of Filipino soldiers appeared at his home and told him that Antonio Mandigma, then a captain, wanted to see him.

Mandigma, like most leaders of the Batangueño resistance, was a member of the local gentry—socially prominent, wealthy, relatively well educated. His father's house in Mataasnakahoy, made of stone and galvanized iron, was assessed at 600 pesos in 1890. True, by Lipa standards, it was not a mansion, but it was one of the best in the barrio. Mandigma's family owned much of the cultivable land in Mataasnakahoy and had many tenants. Furthermore, Antonio Mandigma had attended the prestigious secondary school of Sebastian Virey in Lipa and then completed his secondary education at the even more prestigious Colegio de San Juan de Letrán in Manila.[36]

Emilio Vergara immediately left with the soldiers to see Mandigma, who asked him to join the Filipino army. Vergara explained to me that it was possible for a man to avoid conscription if he had a valid excuse, if, for example, he was in poor health or if another member of his family was already a soldier. Vergara had no such excuse, and, what is more, he was frightened of Mandigma, so he joined up. I pursued the matter. Was he not at all interested in freeing the Philippines from foreign rule? "No," he said, "that was secondary. We were fighting because our officers told us to fight. We obeyed our leaders. There was no alternative. If we did not obey, we would be punished." Although, once again, patron-client bonds largely explain Vergara's participation in the fighting, his use of the word "secondary" should be noted; evidently some of the men had more than one reason to fight.

We explored many other aspects of the war in Batangas during our four hours together. What did he and the other soldiers in Mandigma's command do when they were not ambushing the Americans? "We hid," Vergara told me. Mandigma, who eventually rose to the rank of major, had three well-concealed headquarters in the forests around Lipa, and he and his men moved frequently from one to another in order to avoid capture. What was Vergara's estimate of Mandigma as a commander? "He was a good leader," answered Vergara. Yet, when he elaborated on his commander's approach to warfare, it was apparent that Mandigma's most praiseworthy characteristic, from Vergara's point of view, was that he did not run risks: Mandigma tried whenever possible to avoid contact with large bodies of enemy soldiers, to hide. His leader was not a coward, Vergara assured me, but he recognized that the Filipinos, with inferior weapons and insufficient ammunition, were hopelessly outmatched. If that was the case, I queried, why then did they continue to resist the Americans for more than two years? "The leaders told us that, if we held out long enough, the Americans would get tired and go home," he replied, and there was just a scintilla of sarcasm in his voice.

The documentary evidence on the campaign in Batangas indicates that the guerrillas regularly received money and supplies from the civilian population.[37] I asked Vergara about that support. "In whatever barrio we went, the people hid us and gave us food," he said. In addition, he asserted that the leading men of Lipa were particularly interested in providing money and supplies. According to Vergara, until the introduction of the "concentration" policy by General Bell, the men in Mandigma's battalion were reasonably well fed and well clothed. They even had a monthly ration of cigarettes.

Vergara also discussed the activities of the Macabebes in the Lipa area. (He did not remember exactly when they arrived, but, according to the documentary evidence, a company of Macabebes was assigned to the Lipa garrison in October 1901.)[38] Vergara's recollections squared with Presher's descriptions of Macabebe behavior in Bauan. "If they were asking you questions, and they thought you were not telling the truth, they would torture you," Vergara maintained. He remembered one torture technique the Macabebes used often: They would suspend the victim by his thumbs or by his legs from a branch of a tree until he provided the sought-after information. I had read in official reports by American officers that Macabebes were guilty of raping Filipinas, and I asked Vergara if such things had occurred in Lipa.[39] No, he said; to his knowledge, there had been no actual rapes in Lipa. However, he went on to relate a story he had heard about an attempted rape in Mataasnakahoy. Several Macabebe Scouts had entered a house, tied up the men, and were on the point of raping the women. But one of the women began to scream, and the Macabebes, fearful that their American officers would hear the commotion, had stopped and run away. Vergara conjectured that the Macabebes wanted to rape many of the women of Lipa, but they had resisted the temptation because they were afraid of being punished by the Americans.

Here Vergara touched on an important point. As Presher has already told us, the Americans were not above torturing noncombatants and burning buildings. Yet, apparently (and a large number of documents support Vergara on this point), the U.S. command was absolutely unwilling to tolerate the rape of Filipinas. Why? Was rape so despicable because the U.S. officer corps was wedded to Victorian ideas on sex? That seems unlikely, since many of the officers had Filipino mistresses or availed themselves of the services of prostitutes. Perhaps the prohibition against rape had more to do with military considerations than with sexual hangups. When the troops burned villages, they often destroyed enemy supplies; when they tortured civilians, they occasionally extracted information about the location of enemy troops. On the other hand, if the U.S. command allowed its own troops or its Filipino allies to rape women, the men would only be distracted from the objective of defeating the enemy. To permit rape was to run the risk of prolonging the conflict.

Vergara and I talked finally about the "concentration" policy and the last stages of the war in Batangas. He remembered clearly the establishment of the *zona* in Lipa and the forced relocation of the barrio people into the *población*. He viewed that policy as at once cruel and effective. It was cruel because it resulted in widespread suffering of the civilian population confined to the zone; in Lipa alone, Vergara stated, hundreds died of starvation and disease.[40] It was also cruel because the Americans, free to operate virtually without restraint, burned barrios at will. Mataasnakahoy, for one, was completely razed.[41] Yet, it was effective in ending the war in Batangas. No longer supplied by their civilian allies, Mandigma's men were virtually starved into submission. Vergara recalled that, during his last two months in the field, he went without food for two or three days at a time. Furthermore, because the Americans stepped up their patrolling and hiking, Mandigma and his men were constantly on the run. After being subjected to such pressure for several months, Mandigma decided finally that continued opposition to the Americans was futile and so he announced to his men that he was going to surrender. On 6 February 1902, Mandigma and the remnants of his battalion (5 captains, 4 first lieutenants, 3 second lieutenants, and 67 enlisted men) surrendered to the American commander at Lipa. One of the men who turned himself in that day was Emilio Vergara, not yet 20 years old, a veteran of two wars, recently promoted to the rank of sergeant.[42] Vergara was glad it was over, he told me. He wanted to return to farming, and he did.

THE SIGNIFICANCE OF THE "UNDERSIDE"

What do these two views from the "underside" tell us about the campaign in Batangas? First of all, we learn a good deal about the seamy side of the Philippine-American War. In a monograph, published about a decade ago, John M. Gates described the U.S. army's program of pacification in the Philippines as "benevolent," and even characterized Bell's operations in Batangas as "a credit to the American army in the Philippines and a masterpiece of counter-guerrilla warfare."[43] Presher and Vergara make clear that the campaign in Batangas was nothing of the sort. Rather, it was a campaign in which Macabebes and Americans tortured noncombatants, in which Americans burned barrios at their pleasure, in which looting took place with the knowledge of American officers, in which American officers wrote misleading reports of their operations, in which civilians suffered and died in zones of concentration. But, to be sure, the Americans were not alone guilty of such behavior. While neither Presher nor Vergara discussed Malvar's tactics at any length, we know from other sources that the Batangueño army tortured captured enemy soldiers, killed many Filipinos who appeared to be too friendly to the Americans, and often compelled noncombatants to give them money, rice, and weapons. It was, on both sides, an ugly guerrilla war.

Presher and Vergara also tell us something about the nature of the two armies that clashed in the Philippines. The Philippine-American War might be viewed as the convergence of rural America with the rural Philippines. Both Presher and Vergara were farmers of a sort, as were most of the common soldiers who fought on both sides. But the world views of those two men, and of those two sides, were strikingly different. Presher had been a farmer in a developed country—one that had an interest in overseas expansion and enough resources to undertake such adventures. Presher was aware of the world outside Wanamassa, and he took advantage of an opportunity to explore it. Vergara, on the other hand, had a much more restricted field of vision. Compared to the United States, the Philippines was underdeveloped; and the rural masses had little contact with, or interest in, the outside world. Vergara's world was his barrio and his town. He had no concept of, or loyalty to, a nation-state; his only loyalty was to local authority figures like Julian Recinto and Antonio Mandigma. The difference in world views helps explain a fundamental difference in the two men's attitudes toward the fighting. Presher, aware that there was a more exciting world outside Wanamassa, wanted only to escape from the drudgery of farm life; Vergara, with a narrower field of vision, wanted only to return to it.

Finally, we should pay particular attention to what Vergara tells us about his motives for fighting. Here was a man who was not interested in fighting, who was not especially interested in Philippine independence, but who fought all the same. Why? The answer lies in the nature of his society. He fought because he was a client and his patrons asked him to fight. Many peasants, no doubt, fought for different reasons; but it should be emphasized that others too fought because of patron pressure. In a sense, the patron-client link was the real "underside" of the Philippine-American War.

The Politics of Collaboration in Tayabas Province: The Early Political Career of Manuel Luis Quezon, 1903-1906

MICHAEL CULLINANE

The Philippine-American War ended not only because the Americans won in the field but also because leaders of the two peoples found collaboration with each other a better way to pursue their goals. Americans first perceived the possibility of a collaborative empire during the early days of the war, when the Schurman Commission, hearing testimony from conservative Filipino business and professional men, realized that the interests of such Filipinos complemented those of the Americans in many respects. "The very thing they yearn for is what of all others our Government will naturally desire to give them," the Commission reported, having in mind such matters as infrastructure, law, and governmental institutions.

But Philippine politics, even more than their American counterpart, turn upon personal and familial issues, not grand abstractions. Collaboration was an attractive alternative to a doomed struggle for many Filipinos, especially if it yielded relative prosperity and liberalization; but collaboration really took hold on the Filipinos' side because two important groups of people could turn it to their advantage. The existing elite of the Islands could use collaboration with the new rulers as a way of solidifying control of their own society and economy, and politically ambitious men could use American patronage as a way to rise in politics and business. Manuel Quezon and Sergio Osmeña, who dominated Philippine politics during the America era, raised collaboration almost to the level of art, using it with virtuosity to advance personal, political, and national interests.

In this essay, Michael Cullinane of the Center for South and Southeast Asian Studies at the University of Michigan describes the origins of Quezon's political career and shows how, through American patronage, he was able to achieve increasing stature as a nationalist leader.

An important but overlooked area of early Philippine-American interactions is the direct impact of Americans on Filipino local politics. As Americans in the provinces became familiar with local conditions and personalities they understandably reacted more favorably to some than to others; and, when opportunities arose for political involvement, many seized them with vigor. Some Americans even ran for office themselves.[1] Although civil service regulations forbade involvement in politics, the supervisors of provincial and municipal affairs even more often supported or opposed emerging Filipino political figures. This involvement was rarely interpreted as meddling; it was more frequently viewed by the participants as a part of their duty, for they were confident they knew what was best for the Filipinos.

The tradition of direct American involvement in Filipino politics had been well established under the military regime (1898–1901) and immediately thereafter by the Taft Commission. Before 1904, appointments were carefully awarded to Filipinos (usually to members of the Partido Federal) who had declared their adherence to the new rulers. Though many may have been angered by this favoritism, few Filipinos were surprised, for such prerogatives of power were well understood from the past regime. That the Americans would actually permit their favorites to be voted out of office took longer for many to realize.[2]

In the Spanish period, control over appointments had been one of the most effective powers reserved by the central government. The scarcity of Americans in the provinces opened up to Filipinos positions that had previously been occupied by Spaniards. For those Filipinos who had come to accept the new

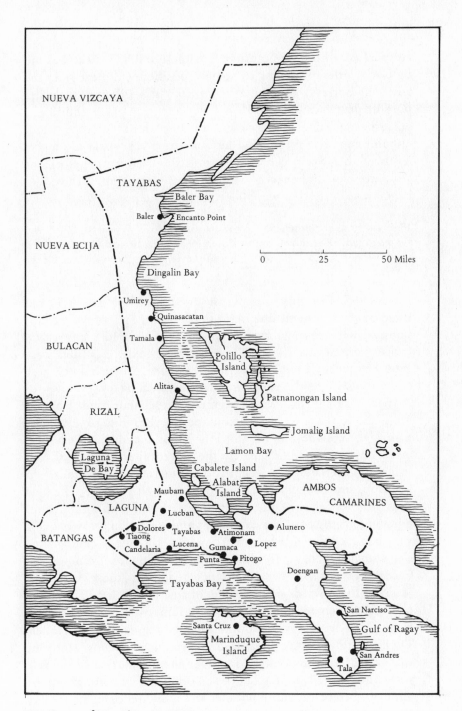

Province of Tayabas in 1900

colonial condition, appointment to these public offices was initially the primary means to achieve position and prestige in the emerging society. But the appointment of a Filipino to an important post meant more than the recognition of his abilities to perform a particular job or the securing of a salaried position; appointment also meant that he had strong backers at the higher levels of the government. The correlation between appointment and later electoral success was high in the early years; thus, William Cameron Forbes was able to boast:

First elections for provincial governors were held in February, 1902, and the good judgment shown by the Commission in its first appointments was demonstrated by the fact that many of the appointees were elected by the voters.[3]

Until 1907, the only post at the provincial level that was not filled by appointment was that of governor. Much of the earliest political activity was, therefore, centered around competition for key appointive offices. The most sought-after positions were generally those of judge of the first instance, provincial attorney (fiscal), justice of the peace, and provincial secretary.

In the provinces, many of the earliest Americans seem to have developed a greater attraction to the younger elements among the collaborators than to the older, incumbent Federalistas. The latter, tending to fit the stereotypes of Spanish bureaucrats, seemed less receptive to American institutions.[4] In addition, few of them owed any particular allegiance to the new American officials. Their debts were to the Philippine Commission and the Manila Federalistas and American army officers who had recommended them. Then, too, the future belonged to the younger men. By the end of 1902 in Cebu, for example, the Federal Party had nearly disappeared; only those who had received the rewards of office could still be labeled "Federalista." What emerged instead was a whole range of socio-recreational clubs, each with obvious political and nationalistic overtones. Typically, these were organized by young *ilustrados,* many of whom had been uninvolved in either the Revolution or the war with the United States.[5] The co-optation of this group of younger, ostensibly more popular and more nationalistic leaders posed a real challenge to the provincial Americans.

At the same time (1902–1906), these youthful *ilustrados* were beginning to object more openly to the monopoly on public appointments the Federalistas enjoyed under Taft and his immediate successors. The Americans in the provinces were the first to recognize that most of the so-called "radicals" were conservative at heart and driven as much by a desire for recognition and position as by abstract ideals. As some of the young radicals realized the value of provincial Americans as an alternative route to political power, specifically appointive offices, the outlines of a new political alignment emerged.

Through encouragement, advice, assistance, the removal of obstacles, the exchange of favors, and numerous other acts in their behalf, Americans facilitated, even participated in, the ascendence and later the consolidation of the political power of Filipinos at all levels of the government. By interaction with representatives of the new colonial regime, certain Filipino politicians verified their legitimacy as recognized leaders and provided themselves with patrons at the higher levels of government. The influence (real or imagined) that some American authorities claimed over dominant Filipino politicians was equally beneficial to their own rise within the colonial administration. In this way, the relationship proved mutually, or reciprocally, beneficial.

It contributed greatly, for example, to the promotion of Harry H. Bandholtz to Director of the Philippine Constabulary in 1907. Bandholtz's promotions in the Constabulary were based on his political, rather than his military, achievements. His most outstanding accomplishments as a soldier resulted more from his personal and political skills than from victories on the battlefield. Bandholtz had shown himself to be exceptionally adept at influencing local affairs and was particularly successful at getting many of the younger Filipino politicians to "play the game." His most prominent protégé was Manuel Quezon, with whom he maintained a long and close personal relationship.[6]

On the other hand, Manuel Quezon's rise to political prominence, both in his home province of Tayabas and later at the national level, was greatly facilitated by his association with influential Americans, the most important of whom was Bandholtz. Because of the significant role Quezon came to play in the collaborative relationship between the United States and the Filipino people, the circumstances surrounding his early political triumphs reveal a great deal about the nature and origin of the "special" Philippine-American relationship.[7] In most accounts of Quezon's life, the details of his early political career remain obscure; in 1906–1907, he simply appeared on the political scene (with Sergio Osmeña) as one of the natural leaders of the Filipino people. His foremost biographer, Carlos Quirino, even suggests that he emerged as a "champion of the masses."[8] No one, however, simply appeared in Filipino politics; success generally resulted from considerable bargaining, maneuvering, and manipulation. This was certainly true of the appearance of Quezon. His "meteoric" rise had little to do with the support he may or may not have had from the masses. To be understood it must be viewed within the context of the changing colonial environment and his remarkable ability to adapt to new conditions; but, at the same time, it must also be viewed, as it will be here, within the context of the collaboration Quezon enjoyed with Bandholtz.[9]

TAYABAS: THE PROVINCIAL ELITE AND THE AMERICANS, 1900–1903

By any standards, Tayabas at the turn of the century was not a progressive province. Although its emergence as the Philippines' largest producer of copra lay just ahead, in the first decade of American rule, this mountainous, typhoon-plagued province still produced little of commercial value. Rice was the main staple, but the lack of extensive lowland plains deterred the development of large-scale production. Most of the agricultural products of Tayabas were consumed within the province and very few found their way to markets outside. The scarcity of arable land on the one hand and the abundance of mediocre land on the other may explain the small number of large landholdings (less than 61 farms over 100 hectares in 1903), the high percentage of small owner-operated farms (81 percent less than 5 hectares), and the relatively small percentage of tenancy (9 percent of the farms and 28 percent of the cultivable land).

Nearly three-quarters of Tayabas's population (1887: 109, 780; 1903: 150,262) lived in the southern part of the province, mainly along the coastal areas of Tayabas Bay, inland from the bay along the southern and eastern slopes of Mt. Banahao, and on the Isthmus of Tayabas. This part of Tayabas was a long-settled area which possessed the best lands, the oldest parishes, and the most active commercial centers; it was clearly the provincial heartland, the area described by Quezon as having "the richest and gayest places in the province." Most of the eastern littoral of Tayabas was sparsely populated, having been inhabited in more recent times by settlers expanding out of the more productive agricultural areas flanking it. Tagalogs predominated in most of the province, but part of the eastern fringe was occupied by Bikolanos. In 1903, Tayabas consisted of 23 mainland towns, each incorporating a varying number of dispersed barrios linked to one another and to somewhat more developed *poblaciones* by little more than foot-paths. The only significant road system in existence passed around the base of Mt. Banahao, linking the towns along it to those of the neighboring provinces of Laguna and Batangas. The most prominent center along this road was the town of Tayabas, which, during the Spanish period, was the provincial capital and most populous municipality (1887: 16,058). Preferring a capital along the coast of Tayabas Bay (for easier communication with Manila), the American authorities, in early 1901, prevailed upon the provincial elite to move the government seat to Lucena. At the time, Lucena was a rather young town, possessed a small population (1887: 5,497) and was located off the main road system; nevertheless, it was only a short distance from Tayabas (less than 10 miles), was a modest trade center for "native craft," and had a "well-built" *poblacion.*

The rugged terrain and general inaccessibility of much of Tayabas resulted in its sprawling interior becoming a refuge for dissident elements, criminals, "social bandits," religious pilgrims (to the slopes of Mt. Banahao), or people simply escaping the ills of the colonial society. Tayabas had long been troubled by banditry. Nevertheless, the *poblaciones* of most of heartland Tayabas exhibited characteristics similar to communities found throughout the Christian Philippines. In each town, a small elite, which Quezon later referred to as the "directing class," controlled the highest municipal offices, possessed the best lands and houses, and tended to play a leading role in the major social and economic activities of the province.[10]

Although these *principales* of Tayabas were generally uninvolved in the Katipunan uprising of 1896–1897, many actively participated in the rebellion after the return of Emilio Aguinaldo to the Philippines with the Americans in May 1898. By June, local leaders had emerged, and military and political organization was taking place under Aguinaldo's agents. Provincial elections were conducted in August, and soon afterwards the local Spanish regiment surrendered to the Filipinos. In September, one of the leading *ilustrados* of the province, Sofio Alandy, from the wealthiest family of the municipality of Tayabas, was chosen as a delegate to the Malolos Assembly. Another *ilustrado,* Quirino Eleazar, became the first Filipino Governor of Tayabas under the Republic.

American troops did not arrive in Tayabas until late January and early Feburary 1900, nearly a year after the outbreak of hostilities between Filipinos and Americans. In Tayabas, the Americans encountered a fairly well-armed Filipino army of over 1,000 soldiers organized into 9 independent companies, each supported by numerous local militia groups. Gradually, as American military might was demonstrated and the principal towns garrisoned, most of the townspeople returned to their homes and livelihoods. Although banditry and sporadic outbreaks of "insurgency" in the form of guerrilla activities continued to be a problem for some time, most of the leaders of the Tayabas forces surrendered or quit the war by the end of January 1901, well before the capture of Aguinaldo; by May, the war in Tayabas was declared to have ended.[11]

As the leaders of the resistance army withdrew from the continuing struggle and accepted political positions in the American garrisoned municipalities, the *poblaciones* became isolated strongholds surrounded by potentially hostile hinterlands. While the municipal elites were depicted generally as enthusiastic collaborators by 1901, fear was expressed that "the people of the barrios," who were "very ignorant and superstitious" and "easily imposed upon," were still supplying men and supplies to the guerrilla units under General Miguel Malvar of Batangas and to local *ladrones,* some of whom were allegedly posing as "insurgents." Impressed by the sensible attitudes of the "fairly well educated and informed" Filipinos of the *poblaciones,* the American governor, Colonel Cornelius Gardener, attributed the continuing unrest to the "densest ignorance" of the barrio dwellers and to the increasing number of "outrages" being committed against the populace by American troops. Gardener insisted that the harsh tactics of the American military in parts of the province were at best unnecessary and at worst "sowing the seed for a perpetual revolution." "True loyalty and contentment," he stressed, "can only come under a benign civil government."[12] These views were strongly opposed by the American military, whose representatives in the area continued to insist that Tayabas was as much a part of Malvar's resistance as Batangas, and that Gardener was either poorly informed or deceived.[13]

In reality, the situation throughout the province was quite complex and varied considerably by time and place. Regardless of the desire of most municipal leaders to establish peace and order and return to the pre-war status quo, there were towns where such efforts were almost impossible. This was particularly true in the towns nearer the center of continued resistance, especially in western Tayabas along the Batangas-Laguna border.[14]

On the other hand, the municipal elites of most of the towns of central and eastern Tayabas engaged in a deepening collaboration with American military authorities. Being less susceptible to punitive action from Malvar's guerrillas and protected by more substantial numbers of American troops, the leaders of these communities were the models for Gardener's enthusiastic appraisal of the response of local elites to "benign civil government." Most of the leading residents of these towns were seeking accommodation with the new colonial rulers, whose most influential local representative was Colonel Gardener. Some fifty years later, local residents of Sariaya, one of the towns in central Tayabas, recalled:

On Feb. 1900 [*sic*] the American Colonel ordered that the people may go back to their homes in the town. The latter part of that month was a period of suspense and uncertainty. The American forces gradually increased and as time went on, the town people became friendly to them. They came out from their hiding places for fear of the bandits. They returned to their homes in the town and those whose houses were burned began to build new ones. The Americans helped the town people materially and financially. And the bandits who dragged on the conflict finally surrendered to the Americans.[15]

For his part, Gardener was a rather remarkable military officer. His first report from Tayabas (February 1900) stressed that a "policy of attraction" would be the most effective way to bring an end to the "insurrection," and his early association with local leaders convinced him that most of them were willing to cooperate with the Americans in bringing peace. He established fairly close personal ties with many of the members of the provincial elite in the heartland towns of Tayabas and, as Taft himself observed, Colonel Gardener was "popular with the people."[16]

In preparation for the visit of the Philippine Commission in mid-March 1901, the leaders of many of the major towns organized local branches of the Partido Federal. When Taft and the Commissioners arrived at Lucena and later at Tayabas to inaugurate civil rule and to set up the provincial government, they were greeted with decorative arches, American flags hanging from most of the houses, and "native bands" playing "The Star Spangled Banner." The school house at Lucena prominently displayed a large photograph of President William McKinley. Only thirteen towns sent delegates to meet with the Commission, but most of the larger towns from the heartland area (comprising two-thirds of the population) were represented. When the time came to appoint the provincial officials, Taft declared that, although it had been his custom to name a "native" as governor, "in this case the people, by their petitions, had themselves chosen Colonel Gardener." The appointments of Gardener as Governor, two American lieutenants as board members and two prominent Federalistas (Sofio Alandy and Gervasio Unson) as fiscal and provincial secretary, were each met by "a round of applause."[17] By July, all the towns (with one exception in the west) "had been organized into municipal governments." There was every reason to believe, as Gardener did, that most of the province was making a successful transition to peaceful civil administration. Gardener was, therefore, greatly disturbed by what he viewed as military atrocities spilling over into Tayabas as a result of the army's accelerated campaign against Malvar in late 1901.[18] Shortly after his criticisms were made public, Gardener became a controversial figure and appears to have resigned.

Taft evidently agreed with Gardener's assessment of the situation in Tayabas, however; and, rather than permit the province to be returned to military rule, the Commission proceeded with its plans to hold general elections there in February 1902.[19] When the ballots of the municipal councilmen from all the towns were tallied, the winner and new governor was another American, Major Harry H. Bandholtz, "the only Army officer who was chosen by the people of a province to represent them."[20] The elite of Tayabas had clearly demonstrated its conservative tendencies and its willingness to cooperate with the American authorities. With the surrender of Malvar in April 1902, Bandholtz was able to reduce considerably the unrest and banditry in the province. By the end of the year, Tayabas was a pacified province dominated at the top by Americans and local Federalistas, or, as Bandholtz preferred to call his Filipino counterparts, "Americanistas."

MANUEL QUEZON, THE BEGINNINGS OF A PUBLIC LIFE

Manuel Quezon was born in August 1878 in Baler, a small isolated town (1887: 2,307) along the eastern coast of Luzon. He was educated at home by his Spanish-speaking parents, at the local *convento* by the Franciscan priests, and at the Dominican-run Colegio de San Juan de Letran in Manila; he owed his formal education to the charity of Spanish clergymen. In 1894, he was enrolled in the law course at the University of Santo Tomas, where he first met Sergio Osmeña, his co-boarder and classmate. When his classes were disrupted by the Revolution (August 1896), he returned to his home town where his family remained loyal to the Spanish administration. He resumed his studies when peace returned to Manila. During the war with the United States, the young Tagalog intellectual joined the army of the Philippine Republic, engaged in relatively little fighting, and ended his military career in April 1901 as a guerrilla major in Bataan. Following his surrender, he was imprisoned in Manila for about six months, until finally released around October. As peace was gradually restored, the schools began to reopen; by mid-1902, Quezon had renewed his study of law. In early 1903, special permission was given for students whose studies had been disrupted to take the bar exam without completing their course work; by the end of April, Quezon was a licensed and practicing lawyer in Manila.[21]

Quezon was an outsider in the political society of Tayabas. He had been born in distant Baler, which, during the Spanish regime, was part of the district of Principe; it was not incorporated into Tayabas until the coming of the Americans. As the first official American guide of the archipelago described it, "There are no roads and but a few trails . . . ships seldom visit the coast on account of the lack of trade."[22] Quezon himself recalled that "there had been no intercourse whatsoever between Baler and Lucena . . . I knew no one there."[23] He visited Lucena for the first time in late 1903; two and a half years later he would be the Provincial Governor.

Quezon's family background seems to have contributed little to his future political career in Tayabas. His father was not a native of Baler or Tayabas; he was a Spanish mestizo (Tagalog) who had migrated from Manila after a career in the Spanish army of the Philippines.[24] His fluency in Spanish, in a town where few spoke the language, seems to have provided him with some prestige. He became the *maestro de niños* and married the local *maestra de niñas,* a Spanish mestiza of unclear origin.[25] Quezon's parents owned little land ("a rice paddy of some two acres"), though Quezon claimed that it "had supported my family." Nevertheless, he added that "we were considered the number one family," by virtue of being the only residents able to communicate with the local Spanish military personnel stationed there and with the Franciscan friars who administered the parish.[26] The family was neither wealthy nor poor; what prestige it had seems to have derived more from its contacts with locally prominent Spaniards than from its links with other Filipinos. This is hardly the kind of background one would expect to find for the Filipino for whom the province of Tayabas would eventually be renamed.

Initially, the most important thing Quezon had in his favor, other than his intelligence and personality, was his education. Thus, in late 1903, he was the only young *abogado* in Tayabas province. The energetic mestizo immediately attracted the attention of the two most influential Americans in the small provincial capital, district judge Paul W. Linebarger, and Constabulary commander Colonel Bandholtz. Recalling their first encounters, Quezon later wrote:

[Colonel Bandholtz] immediately befriended me. He invited me to his house, presented me to Mrs. Bandholtz ... He made me feel at home in his company and asked me to come to him whenever I was in need of his advice ...

Judge Linebarger became fond of me and placed much reliance upon my knowledge of Spanish substantive law and procedure.

[Bandholtz] was kind and courteous, he became deeply interested in my career, and very soon we were friends.[27]

As will become apparent, these two Americans, and particularly Bandholtz, played significant roles in Quezon's rapid rise to political prominence.

Paul W. Linebarger (1871–1939) had come to the Philippines as a soldier, though he was already a practicing attorney with considerable experience abroad (mainly in Europe). He was among the earliest Americans appointed district judge and was apparently assigned to Tayabas province (with jurisdiction over Marinduque and Mindoro) sometime in 1902. As Judge of the Court of First Instance, with its judicial seat eventually in Lucena, Linebarger wielded substantial influence in the region (in the tradition of the Spanish magistrate). Although little is known of his unofficial activities in Tayabas or of his relationships with the Filipino provincial elite, he was close to Bandholtz and had a number of Filipino friends.[28]

Substantially more is known of Bandholtz (1864–1925). A career officer and graduate of West Point (1890), Bandholtz first arrived in the Philippines in 1900, at the age of 35, as a captain in the 7th Infantry, having served previously in Cuba. His first assignment was Marinduque, but in mid-1901 he began his long association with the province of Tayabas, when he became quartermaster and intelligence officer at Lucena. As he pursued *insurrectos* and later *ladrones* around the region, assisted the Philippine Commission in setting up municipal governments, and gathered information on General Malvar's supporters in heartland Tayabas, Bandholtz acquired a genuine popularity among the municipal elites, especially in central Tayabas.[29] Bandholtz "had learned the Spanish language well," Quezon recalled, "and knew a few words of Tagalog."[30] In February 1902, as noted, the municipal officials of Tayabas elected him Governor to replace Colonel Gardener. He held the post for a little over a year, resigning in April 1903 to become colonel and commanding officer of the Philippine Constabulary's 2nd District in southeastern Luzon. Bandholtz's fame became widespread in late 1903 when he negotiated the surrender of the notorious rebel leader, Simeon Ola, in Albay province.[31] Though his jurisdiction included the whole region from Sorsogon to Tayabas, Bandholtz, his wife, and their son continued to reside in Lucena; it was here that he met and entertained Manuel Quezon.

Bandholtz was a man of extreme self-confidence and unique personal qualities.[32] Within the framework of "benevolent assimilation," Bandholtz, like Gardener before him, had been exceedingly successful in his dealings with the "better class" of Filipinos. Winning the cooperation of local leaders through judicious applications of both the stick and carrot, he engineered a relatively non-violent pacification of "his territory." He was, as Dean C. Worcester later insisted, "first, last, and all the time a politician."[33] Tayabas, more than any other province, was *his*. Concerned that it remain peaceful, progressive, and loyal, he carefully cultivated working relationships with municipal and provincial officials and familiarized himself with the sociopolitical factions of most of the important communities. The "Bandholtz regime" in Tayabas was a benevolent rule characterized on one hand by much pomp and ceremony and on the other by strict adherence to the wishes of the "despot."[34] Because of Bandholtz's long experience in Tayabas, he naturally exerted influence on less-experienced officials such as Judge Linebarger. (His penchant for giving advice to anyone, including judges, is revealed in his later correspondence.)[35]

When Bandholtz resigned as Governor of Tayabas, Ricardo Parás, a prominent Federalista and former Governor of Marinduque when Bandholtz was still in that sub-province, took his place. There can be little doubt that Bandholtz was instrumental first in Parás's appointment and later in his election and had a significant influence on the direction of provincial affairs during his administration.[36] When Quezon arrived in Lucena with a letter of introduction to Parás, the Governor lectured him on the advantages of the American regime and introduced him to Colonel Bandholtz.[37]

In September 1903, not long after Quezon's arrival in Tayabas, Judge Linebarger offered him the vacant post of Provincial Fiscal of Mindoro. Quezon, who claimed he still harbored much resentment against the Americans, recalled that he was at first reluctant to participate in the colonial government. After a 24-hour struggle with his conscience, he accepted the offer. Linebarger then asked Commissioner Trinidad Pardo de Tavera, at the time on tour in Tayabas, to convey the recommendation to the Philippine Commission. Before the end of September, Quezon was appointed Fiscal of Mindoro.[38] As he recollected in his autobiography, his ill feeling for Americans had been greatly reduced by his association with Parás, Bandholtz, and Linebarger; and, with the aid of hindsight, he added that this unexpected opportunity "may be the starting point set by fate for a greater service that I may render to my people."[39]

Quezon's performance at his first bureaucratic post was not altogether praiseworthy. In a little more than six months as Fiscal of Mindoro, nine formal charges were filed against him, including malfeasance in office, rape, and assault.[40] By the time these charges were formalized and the testimony gathered, Quezon had been promoted to Fiscal of Tayabas.[41] In spite of the charges against him, Quezon had established a reputation as a good lawyer and an effective prosecuting attorney. For him it was satisfying to return to Tayabas to be among "old friends," especially Governor Parás and Colonel Bandholtz.[42] It was probably at this time that Bandholtz developed an unusually deep interest in Quezon and his future. Although they communicated well in Spanish, Bandholtz "then insisted that I should learn English and offered to be my teacher . . . presenting me with an

English grammar."[43] Bandholtz perceptively saw in Quezon the potential for greater achievement and meant to harness it in the "right" direction.

Shortly after taking over the post of Fiscal of Tabayas, Quezon became the prosecutor in the well-publicized case against Francis J. Berry, Manila attorney and owner of *The Cablenews-American*, who had been involved in several illicit land and property transactions in Tayabas.[44] Amidst threats and insults, Quezon pursued the prosecution with vigor. Fortunately for Quezon, there were as many Americans against Berry as there were in his favor, and the Fiscal had the complete support of the Constabulary commander (Bandholtz) and the Attorney General's office in Manila. Berry was convicted and Quezon enjoyed great acclaim; in later years, he attributed his "popularity in Tayabas" and his "election as provincial governor" to his role in the Berry trial.[45]

Nevertheless, seven months after he took office in Tayabas, Quezon resigned as Fiscal when the charges against him from his Mindoro days finally surfaced.[46] Although it caused Quezon some embarrassment and the loss of his official position in Tayabas, the "Mindoro affair" had no effect on his political future in Tayabas or on his relationship with most of his American friends and supporters. Most Filipino historians—and this must have been generally true also in Tayabas in 1904—have viewed the case against Quezon as a plot instigated by his enemies, allegedly the friends of Francis Berry.[47] This view was reinforced by Quezon's continued close relationships with the most influential Americans in the province. The two cases had even provided Quezon with the opportunity to expand his contacts with other high-ranking Americans. For instance, the assistance he received from the Attorney General's office in the Berry case led to a lasting friendship with the Supervisor of Fiscals, James Ross, who, by January 1905, had been promoted Judge-at-Large of the Courts of First Instance.[48] His friendship with Ross and Bandholtz "became even stronger" after the traumatic events of 1904; Quezon recalled that "my friend Judge Ross" had even advised him not to resign his post.[49] It was at this time that Quezon later admitted, "I was already a convert to the policy of cooperation with the Government of the United States."[50]

QUEZON'S ENTRY INTO POLITICS

After his resignation, Quezon remained in Tayabas and established a lucrative law practice: "Within six months I had clients from the remotest towns of the province."[51] These legal clients would soon contribute to his emerging political career. Quezon has been characterized as "the consummate politician," and yet his autobiography is almost devoid of information on his first political struggle. Regarding his election as Governor in February 1906, Quezon simply noted in passing, "I decided to run for governor and easily defeated my two other rivals for the office."[52] In reality, however, Quezon's entry into politics was anything but smooth.

In October 1905, Bandholtz was promoted to command of the Constabulary's 1st District (central and southern Luzon), which had its headquarters in Manila. There his authority quickly increased—by November he was the officer closest to Constabulary Director Henry T. Allen—and, with it, his ability to influence the central government.[53] A trusted friend, Colonel James G. Harbord, was assigned to command his old district and to reside in Lucena. Although Bandholtz's influence in Tayabas remained strong, and he continued to involve himself in provincial politics and to give advice to local leaders, Harbord eventually developed a very close—perhaps deeper—friendship with Quezon:

Colonel Harbord [Quezon later wrote] was a different type of man from General Bandholtz. I make no comparison of the two men who became very dear friends of mine . . . . But I must say that no American in those early days had as much influence in forming my high conception of public duty or gave me a better idea of American manhood than the then Colonel Harbord. General Harbord is, in my opinion, one of the greatest men I have ever met.[54]

Bandholtz was "deeply interested" in the gubernatorial race in Tayabas province. To prepare Harbord for his new post, he sent him a 17-page memorandum "in regard to the people of your district." This is the first concise picture we have of the political situation in Tayabas on the eve of the 1906 election for governor. The province was said to be divided into three political factions, with the leader of each seeking the governorship. Juan Carmona of Lucena ("somewhat over middle age . . . an Americanista and one of the best presidentes in the archipelago") was Bandholtz's pick for governor. Close behind Carmona in his favor was Alfredo de Castro of Atimonan (a "young mestizo" who was "in a mild way . . . the cacique of the entire Pacific coast of Tayabas"); as Bandholtz lamented, "it is difficult to decide between the two." The third faction, headed by Sofio Alandy of the town of Tayabas ("not entirely bad, yet he is a fanatic"), was clearly the one Bandholtz wanted to defeat ("I was opposing his election not urgently, but nevertheless energetically"). The incumbent Governor, Ricardo Parás ("a highly toned, well educated, honorable Filipino, sincerely earnest but fatally lacking in energy") was thought to be retiring in favor of Juan Carmona.[55] And what of Manuel Quezon? Bandholtz at the time was not yet considering his young protégé for the governorship though he recommended him highly to Harbord:

[Quezon] is one of the most intelligent and influential natives in the archipelago, is a born orator and has been of great assistance to me on many occasions, is young and is liable to commit mistakes at any time, for this reason it is well to keep a paternal eye upon him to keep him from going astray, he had trouble with [Governor Robert S.] Offley in Mindoro which I do not consider to have been of a very serious nature, by proper handling he can be of more value to you than almost any one else in the entire district.[56]

Harbord was pleased to receive these insights and informed Bandholtz that they "have been a great service to me [and] I practically memorized them."[57] Four days later, however, Harbord was already beginning to perceive that significant changes were occurring in the political arena and that Quezon was rapidly moving onto the center stage. Not sure about what it all meant, Harbord relayed his feelings to Bandholtz:

I like little Quezon but I do not feel quite sure that I am reading him accurately yet. In this Governorship race something makes me feel that possibly he is not dealing above board with Carmona, though the latter has confided to me that he is sure of it if Quezon stands by him and the latter has promised to support him. Did it ever occur to you that Quezon might be doing the dark horse with an idea of coming out himself a little before the election? He says he could not afford to give up his law practice, and for my own part it looks to me like he would be foolish to do it.[58]

Harbord found himself in the thick of provincial politics, but was not at first anxious to get entangled. He politely refused a request by Carmona to accompany the new Constabulary commander on his tour of the province: "I discouraged it, not caring to take a gubernatorial candidate around on government transportation or to appear to be lending his canvass official sanction."[59] Instead, he was accompanied by "little Quezon," whom he conveyed to Atimonan. There Quezon met with Alfredo de Castro and promptly negotiated a whole new political alignment for Tayabas.

Although running for governor had occurred to Quezon as early as 1903, when he arrived in Tayabas, he enjoyed few of the advantages that would lend support to his poltiical aspirations: He was neither wealthy nor socially established in Tayabas (he was still single), and he had few personal ties with municipal officials. He did have a difficult-to-assess "popularity" derived from his reputation as Fiscal and a widely acclaimed skill in politics. He was a captivating orator in Spanish and Tagalog and a "master of political intrigue."[60] He would surely need more than this, however, to win in the sprawling province of Tayabas.

The break Quezon needed came when, shortly after Bandholtz left the province, Governor Parás inexplicably decided to back Alandy. The only way to defeat Alandy in this new configuration was to unite the followers of Castro, Quezon, and, it was hoped, Carmona. Why Quezon, the least of the three, should have emerged as the candidate of such an alliance is not clear; but, during his tour with Harbord, he won Castro's agreement to support him against Alandy—and, if need be, Carmona. "Quezon and myself," Castro vowed, "can fight against the Alandys, the Paráses and against everyone."[61] Quezon, Castro, and Harbord then traveled, separately, to Manila to consult Bandholtz.[62]

The result of the Harbord-Bandholtz meeting was a controversial letter to "nuestro amigos Tayabenses," urging the *modernos* (or *modernistas*) "to unite upon Quezon as the candidate to defeat Alandy."[63] Both men regretted having to turn on

Carmona; but, in Bandholtz's words, "it would never do to allow the province to fall into the hands of the clique of Tayabas town."[64] Harbord carried the letter back to Lucena, where he showed it to Quezon and Castro and lent the latter an unsigned copy to show to Carmona's supporters.[65] Apparently, Carmona decided at this point to withdraw his candidacy.[66]

But, at precisely this juncture, the American Principal of the Central School of Lucena, R. H. Wardall, intervened vigorously in Carmona's behalf. Carmona was clearly the favorite of the resident American community, and, as noted earlier, even Bandholtz had backed him for governor until the "necessary" realignment occurred.[67] Wardall, who was at the time Acting Division Superintendent of Schools and thereby a member of the Provincial Board, persuaded Carmona to "stay in the race." Then he called a meeting of American teachers with Quezon, Castro, and Carmona in attendance to publicize the developments; confronted Harbord with the matter; criticized Bandholtz ("but for the influence of the teachers [Bandholtz] would probably not have been made Governor"); attacked Quezon's "personal character"; tried to get Castro to withdraw his support from Quezon; and pronounced his own support for Carmona ("the whole province will very soon know that the Education department are strong for Carmona").[68]

Ostensibly, this division within the American ranks arose from differing political analyses. Wardall contended that "the modernos could not be united in favor of Quezon."[69] Bandholtz, on the other hand, insisted that, while Carmona could not win, Quezon could and "would make a far better governor than Alandy."[70] At a deeper level, however, it may also reflect the Filipinization of provincial Americans—their absorption into highly personal and familial alliances within the elite of heartland Tayabas—and the rivalry for power and influence between the two most numerous groups of Americans in the provinces, the teachers and the Constabulary. In an exchange of letters after the blowup at Lucena, Wardall accused Bandholtz of masterminding provincial politics, and Bandholtz, in reply, reminded Wardall of "the explicit instructions issued from the Bureau of Education relative to teachers actively participating in municipal and provincial elections":

While in our capacity we, as a rule, do not mix in elections either, [he continued] yet our instructions are more elastic and not only at times permit but may require us to participate to a greater or less extent.[71]

For the next nine months, Bandholtz and Harbord, angered by his "mischief," tried to have Wardall transferred from the province, in order to teach what Harbord called "the obvious lesson."[72]

Prior to 1907, provincial governors were elected indirectly by the municipal officials of the province. Campaigning at the time consisted mainly of maneuvers to obtain the backing of enough town councilors to be elected. The councilors, in turn, were elected on the basis of a very limited suffrage, making politics at all levels an elite preserve. If disputes arose over the qualification of voters or the certification of councilors, they were settled by the provincial boards, which had direct supervision over the towns.

After the municipal elections in December, the town officials were invited to attend a general assembly the following February at the provincial capital, where they were lectured on responsible government and called upon to cast their votes for the new governor. Arranging for the transportation, housing, and feeding of all one's own supporters was one of the major tasks of any gubernatorial candidate and his allies at the capital.[73] Failure to comply with these social obligations could cause supporters to switch their loyalty and partake of an opponent's hospitality. Such occasions, though festive, were charged with the dramatic undercurrents of local rivalry and veiled competition and maneuvering.

The municipal elite who assembled at Lucena in early February 1906 knew that those Americans in Tayabas who opposed Quezon were mainly teachers and minor employees with little real influence. Few electors doubted whom Bandholtz and Harbord, the most powerful and influential Americans, were backing. As Quirino concluded, "A distinctly friendly attitude towards the young candidate emanated from Constabulary headquarters, in spite of civil service rules and regulations that prohibited its participation in political matters."[74] This knowledge, confirmed by the famous letter, convinced many that

Quezon should be the next governor. Further American support for Quezon was verified when it came time to transport municipal officials to Lucena for the provincial election. Quezon's resources were too meager to compete with opponents who had "their own ships and a fleet of carromatas." But "Quezon was a good friend of the army quartermaster, Lt. Hunter Harris, who mobilized the U.S. Army transport system in the province to help bring his supporters to Lucena at no personal expense."[75] At the least, Bandholtz heartily approved of this action; at most he arranged it through his friend, Colonel E. B. Robertson, U.S. Army commander at Lucena. "The Army officers," Quezon later boasted, "made it easy for me to win my election as governor of the Province of Tayabas."[76]

Other Americans, however, also became involved in Quezon's electoral struggle. The Provincial Treasurer, Eugene Garnett, and the Division Superintendent of Schools, J. C. Muerman, both members of the Provincial board of Tayabas, were pro-Quezon, or, more precisely, pro-Bandholtz. In a revealing letter, Garnett, only recently arrived in the province, informed Bandholtz:

I was sure you were for Quezon and accepted that as sufficient guarantee that he would be a proper man for the place and although I did not express myself openly, I did all I could for him on the "Board," and it probably amounted to more than the efforts of some people who did a lot of talking. There were several cases before the "Board" for the approval of councilmen needed by Quezon and I saw to it that they were approved although the Governor and Wardall (acting for Muerman without right as we ascertained later) were against Quezon.[77]

"You acted in this entire matter along the proper lines," replied Bandholtz.[78]

In spite of all his support from the representatives of the colonial government, Quezon's victory was hard won. None of the candidates obtained a majority in the first day of balloting.[79] From this point on, the outcome depended on the young lawyer himself, and, as Bandholtz observed a few days later, "Little Quezon must have worked like a Trojan and shown a great deal more ability than his opponents credited him with possessing."[80] When at last the assembly voted a majority to

Quezon, the fight was still not over; his opponents promptly filed protests against the qualifications of many pro-Quezon electors. As the protests became more threatening, Harbord cabled Bandholtz: "Suggest you keep in touch with [Arthur W.] Fergusson [Executive Secretary to the Governor General] and head off effort for new election which will undoubtedly be made."[81]

The field of action now shifted to Manila. By the second week of February, Quezon was in the capital, staying (as usual) with Bandholtz, who was now occupied in obtaining Quezon's confirmation. He must have perceived that his own prestige and authority in Tayabas were also at stake in the Tayabas election. As the situation appeared to worsen, Bandholtz asked Garnett and Colonel Robertson to send to the Governor General letters of reference regarding Quezon's gentlemanly character, to counteract the personal attacks of his opponents.[82] On 21 Febuary, the Governor General confirmed Manuel Quezon as Governor of Tayabas, and Bandholtz immediately sent his congratulations. Quezon's confirmation amidst alleged irregularities did not go unnoticed by the American press. *The Manila Times* chose to criticize the affair on its front page, but in later numbers the issue was dropped.[83] Six days later a somewhat relieved Bandholtz wrote to Garnett:

I think, now that the gubernatorial conflict is ended, my old Tayabas friends will settle down to business and drop politics. It will be up to you to keep careful watch on Quezon to prevent his heart running away with his head. He oozes good intentions from every pore and his main defect is his youth which is more than counterbalanced by his great mental capacity. He has a high opinion of you, and between Muerman and your self on the Board and Colonel Harbord in the District, I predict for Tayabas a prosperous and progressive two years of government.[84]

CONCLUSION

Politics in Tayabas at the start of the twentieth century was the almost exclusive reserve of the municipal elites who had emerged from the socio-economic realities of Spanish colonial rule. Politically inexperienced and disunited and intellectually out of touch with late nineteenth-century developments in Manila and its environs, the *principales* of heartland Tayabas found satisfaction in early collaboration with the Americans, who soon came to play an active role in provincial politics. By 1902, much of the political power in the province was concentrated in the hands of one man, Harry Bandholtz.

From the outset, the collaborative relationship suited the desires of both the Americans and the local elite. The Americans wanted a body of Filipino leaders who were willing to restrain their quest for independence, maintain public order, and participate in the long process of "political education." The Filipino "directing class" wanted to retain its position, acquire some political influence, and avoid, as much as possbile, outside interference in its local affairs. The "Bandholtz regime" in Tayabas successfully balanced the immediate objectives of the colonial government with many of the aspirations of the "better class" of Filipinos.

The success of Bandholtz at controlling Tayabas was no accident. He quickly came to understand the dynamics of power at the local level and was soon playing the "Filipino game" as much as the Filipinos were playing his, though he always remained dominant and confident of his cultural superiority. Political power for Bandholtz was something that was achieved through careful negotiation, manipulation, and the exchange of favors and concessions, as well as by the occasional application of punishments; it was maintained through constant attention to the details of personal relationships. Bandholtz rarely interfered with (and often gave support to) municipal leaders who were loyal to him and his followers, even when these leaders were involved in irregularities or pardonable misdeeds. Thus, for the elite of Tayabas, the earliest lesson in "political education" under the Americans was a blend of benign despotism and patron-client politics. Bandholtz, the politician, was, more than anyone else, Quezon's first teacher in the art of politics. Quezon, for his part, was an exceptional student and a worthy successor.

Quezon's rise to political prominence through American backing should not detract from his reputation as a master politician. Though an outsider to the provincial elite of Tayabas, in little more than two years Quezon had maneuvered his way to the top of that society; his contacts with influential Americans provided him with an additional element to guarantee victory. There is no doubt that Quezon was endowed with remarkable talents within the context of his own society; he possessed the qualities necessary for political success and had the intelligence and sense of timing necessary to take advantage of the opportunities that presented themselves under the new regime. It was precisely these traits that made him so attractive to Bandholtz. Bandholtz did not select Quezon for his docility; it was, in fact, the lack of leadership qualities (such as intelligence, energy, decisiveness, strength, confidence, and the like), that led Bandholtz to abandon his colleague Parás ("fatally lacking in energy") and to oppose the longstanding "Americanista" Alandy ("a trifle weak"). The initial concern of Bandholtz was that Filipinos establish a loyalty to the colonial government through him. Once an individual was "playing the game," Bandholtz looked for other qualities in him. He was genuinely impressed with the young attorney from Baler. Fully aware of Quezon's youthful failings, Bandholtz recognized his potential and gave him his wholehearted support. By 1906, Bandholtz had no doubts regarding Quezon's loyalty or his credentials for future leadership.

The early stages of Quezon's political life clearly exemplify what Peter Stanley in the Introduction to this volume has called the "manipulative underside of the collaborative empire."[85] His Tayabas experience was the foundation for his later career, wherein the contradictions inherent in the "special" Philippine-American relationship were more obviously exhibited: Quezon was for many the "embodiment of Philippine nationalism," while at the same time he was considered the "best asset" of the colonial government.[86] But, above all, Quezon was a politician. The colonial institutions and the issues and rhetoric of the colonial condition served as the milieu for the refinement of his political skills and for the realization of his ambitions. The maintenance of his political power was the primary motivating force in his long career. Once in power in Tayabas, his political instincts grew and matured, and, although he continued to collaborate with and seek support from Americans for the rest of his life, he did so from a position of increasing independence, confidence and strength. Over the years, he masterfully exploited his relationships with American colonial administrators, presidents, congressmen and anti-imperialists, as well as with Filipino colleagues, followers and enemies, to become and to remain the leading figure in what has been rightly called the "Fil-American empire."[87] Manuel Quezon was the most outstanding legacy of the early years of Filipino-American collaboration and "political education."

Orators and the Crowd: Philippine Independence Politics, 1910-1914

REYNALDO C. ILETO

The politics of collaboration and the evident popularity of the nation-building programs in education and public works in which Americans and many Filipinos shared an interest give most of the American era in the Philippines a temperate and progressive appearance. In this light, the inflamed rhetoric of the independence movement and the calculatedly visible advocacy of nationalist leaders can be dismissed as cynical posturing. Few today take seriously the "old history" that chronicled a heroic and resilient struggle to achieve *el ideal*, the national ideal of independence. On the contrary, the ambivalence of Philippine leaders and the eventual achievement of independence without an armed struggle have led many to allege that the country lacks a revolutionary tradition. The vestiges of Philippine-American collaboration trouble Philippine relations with other Third World nations to this day.

In the following essay, however, Reynaldo Ileto, of the Department of History and Political Science, De La Salle University, Manila, argues that a

revolutionary tradition infused by religious imagery simmered just below
the boiling point during the early American era. This tradition, rooted in
the experience of rebellion against Spain and warfare against the United
States, offered an alternative to peaceful collaboration. The contrast between the pure and energizing conception of *panahon,* a millenarian recognition that "the time" was at hand, and the pedestrian tawdriness of
pulitika, or self-interested bargaining and manipulation, disciplined even
the most daring collaborators. As Ileto argues: "Compadre colonial politics
refers constantly to its radical 'other.'. . . It is not so much that uprisings
happened . . . but that they could have happened, and that so much of
what we now know as colonial politics was shaped by this possibility."

Ileto's argument, which extends the thesis of his book *Pasyon and
Revolution: Popular Movements in the Philippines, 1840–1910,* suggests
the need to refine and revise even the "new" political history of the
Philippine-American encounter. His evidence, though limited principally
to Central Luzon, argues, as does much recent historiography of the Philippines, that cultural continuities all but hidden beneath the surface record
of externally inspired change are more important in the Philippines than
the imperial perspective would lead us to believe.

In May 1911, the town of Lucban, 90 kilometers southeast
of Manila, hosted a visit by Hermenegildo Cruz. Cruz had all
the marks of a radical nationalist: pro-independence, secretary
of the Liga Popular Nacionalista, a labor organizer in Manila. He
was, in addition, a fiery orator.[1] His initial contacts in the town
were of a different sort, however. At a private meeting with
ranking *principales,* he produced a letter from Manuel Quezon
describing the Resident Commissioner's efforts to influence the
American press on behalf of Philippine independence. Fully
convinced of the importance of this approach, the *principales*
took up a collection for the cause. Cruz, they concluded, was
"a fine gentleman and a good politician."

Two days later, however, Cruz adopted a different approach.
At a mass gathering in the town plaza—"ninety-five percent of
those who attended were of the lower class"—Cruz spoke in a
manner which was "in some places strongly socialistic." At
about the midpoint of his address, he said "emphatically and
with all the force of his lungs" that, if Quezon's approach to
obtaining independence should fail, it would be up to the
people themselves to act: *Ibinigay na namin sa inyo ang kapasia-
han. Gawin na ninyo ang gusto ninyo. Kayo ang masusunod.*
(The decision is now yours; you can do as you please. Your will

is our command.) These words "produced an instantaneous effect; the populace at once understood their true significance." The listeners burst into applause; afterwards, they talked about nothing else.

Municipal officials took the speech badly, so much so that one of them reported it in detail to a friend in the Constabulary.[2] "Eminent men" of the Partido Nacionalista—Quezon, Sergio Osmeña, and Vicente Lukban are mentioned—had previously orated at Lucban without ever voicing "subversive, destructive ideas." Such politicians were "temporizers and lovers of harmony with the government or, better said, conservatives in nationalism." Cruz, on the other hand, had exceeded the limits of proper politics. He had "fixed in the minds of all, without their comprehending," the idea that "a revolution was necessary" when legal means had been exhausted. The listeners had been "people who do not reflect." Who knew, reported the informer, what might happen the following (election) year when politicians like Cruz would come around to "make the hearts of the people blacker . . . with very serious consequences." Worse still, this "same old song would be repeated from town to town, from province to province," sowing lawlessness and chaos.

Our anonymous principal's fears seem to have been genuine. He felt that there was something in the "unthinking" masses that might snap, run out of control, given the oratory of men like Cruz. We face a problem, however, in assessing what really happened as a result of the incident. Few of Cruz's audience actually joined revolutionary movements and armed themselves. There are only scattered signs of such activity. Early the following year, "1912" was ominously splashed on the walls of many houses in neighboring towns, just as "1896" had been on the eve of the revolution.[3] In June, the adjacent town of Sariaya was attacked by a brotherhood called Colorum which regarded independence as a sacred goal and had sworn before the spirit of Jose Rizal to rise against the United States.[4]

Perhaps the "Lucban incident" had something to do with the election, in June the following year, of Vicente Lukban as Governor of the province. Like Hermenegildo Cruz, Lukban came from a "more militant faction" of the Nacionalistas and owed his victory (according to his Quezon-backed rival) to his "having been a general in the revolution and having told the electors that Quezon's highly paid labors in Washington would not bring independence, whereas action taken by themselves in the islands would."[5] Cruz, we recall, had said something like this. But his "lower-class" audience was quite different from the purely *principalía* electorate that voted Lukban in. The latter's revolutionary past and pro-independence sentiments were obviously attractive to most townspeople, regardless of class, although some members of the society were probably less willing than others to allow advocacy of "revolution" and "independence" to imply violent challenge to the American regime. The "Lucban incident" seems to lead both ways, then: toward revolutionary movements and electoral victories.

Discussions of Philippine colonial politics have dwelt on the motives of politicians, the factional divisions mediating their actions, internal conflicts, such as that between the Assembly and the Commission, and so forth. What hardly ever fails to be noted, and yet escapes serious discussion, is the phenomenon of public oratory. We know that audiences were swayed by images of approaching independence, accusations of deceit against enemies, recollections of the revolution. But this phenomenon is quickly noted, and focus is then directed onto the events leading to the now-familiar gains of the nationalist movement during the period of American "tutelage." Quezon and Osmeña are successful campaigners, but really significant is their role as political brokers at the helm of the peaceful struggle for increased native participation in government and eventual independence. And they succeed, if somewhat reluctantly at first, in bringing independence closer at hand.

In viewing independence politics from the top down, the problem is what to do with the evidence relating to a rather more chaotic "underside" dominated by the rhetoric of revolution and mass action. We read of "disturbances" that were quickly quelled, "excesses" from below that were contained by the "better classes." We know hardly more than that they happened. The raid on Sariaya by Colorum "fanatics" is one of those obscure "insurrectionary outbreaks or attempted outbreaks" which include the foiled "July Fourth uprising" of

1912, the "Manila plot" of August 1912, the Castillejos (Zambales) raid in August 1913, the "Taytay (Rizal) affair" of February 1914, various "plots" in Samar, Pangasinan, and Leyte, and the "Christmas Eve Fiasco" of 1914.[6] The language of the Constabulary records suggests their scale. Perhaps these "failures" might have been taken more seriously if they had culminated in some major outbreak. But there was no revolution in 1914, just "an abortive armed revolt by revolutionary romantics," to cite Peter Stanley, or, as Grant Goodman puts it, "a poorly organized and badly led demonstration by a rag-tag gathering of assorted Filipino dissidents, most of whom surrendered to the police without resistance."[7] It was, indeed, a "Christmas Eve Fiasco."

There is no way in which these mini-insurrections could have succeeded in winning independence by force. To begin with, they were thoroughly infiltrated by Constabulary agents who worked it out so that communications and timetables were disrupted, organizers quietly arrested, and hidden weapons confiscated. "As you know," wrote Constabulary head Harry Bandholtz to a friend in 1911, "these poor devils are entirely in our hands and can make no moves without our knowledge."[8] Artemio Ricarte, the central figure in these movements, was too far away in Hong Kong to properly organize his *Ejercito Libertador* (Liberation Army); the Japanese weapons he promised largely failed to arrive. In such a condition, to challenge the might of the state would have been folly, and most people knew it. An investigator who interviewed participants in the rash of demonstrations and secret societies in 1912, could not resist remarking: "This is all a passing and comic movement . . . At heart they know that violence would be suicide." In a similar vein, Brian Fegan concludes from what survivors of Ricartista and subsequent movements told him in the 1970s that "the vast majority of branches and members of popular organizations" who were inspired by "millenarian myth" nevertheless opted for "commonsense behavior: no guns, no rising." "Here and there," wrote the acting head of the Constabulary in 1914, "some few of Ricarte's men will be run down, only to find them to be the fools or the loudmouth laughing stock of the community."[9] Fools, perhaps, for having turned to armed struggle at the wrong time: Where were the weapons, and was not Quezon promising independence, too?

Viewing popular radicalism in terms solely of its expression in abortive Ricartist "conspiracies" is in fact a convenient way of dismissing it. To avoid this impasse we might instead look at the mentality that made possible the responses to both Ricarte and Quezon. There is no denying the historical importance of "compadre colonial politics," but it ought to be recognized that this developed in relation to a less visible phenomenon labeled "popular radicalism," which happens to have revealed itself in its most acute form in "Ricartism."[10] Perhaps it was not mere exaggeration for the *Cablenews-American* to assert in December 1914 that about 52,000 men, 30,000 of them "Ricartistas," were active in patriotic societies and receiving military training in Manila and surrounding towns.[11] The Constabulary had kept tabs on numbers attending meetings and mass rallies; at the very least, 52,000 men could have risen in arms. That only a handful did makes no difference to our argument: The politicians knew what was possible and they spoke and at least outwardly behaved in relation to it. The masking of this relationship has had the effect of defining Philippine independence politics in terms of one pole—that which could claim responsibility for such gains as the passage of the Jones Bill in 1916—when, in fact, the "conspiracies," "plots," and "fiascos" of the period are thoroughly inscribed in that pole.

We can begin with the glimpses in Stanley's work of the interaction between compadre colonial politics and an ill-defined popular ground swell. Let us look at some of the examples. In the 1908–1909 legislative session, Osmeña spoke for independence in terms more radical than ever, and carried a motion directing Quezon to petition the U.S. Congress for independence. "Then he walked over to Forbes' office and calmly explained that he had had to give his brothers something with which to campaign for re-election." In 1910, in response to a political threat from a coalition of radical Nacionalistas and Progresistas, Osmeña "moved to the left and escalated his rhetoric," at one rally speaking of the Assembly as the "agent for the fulfillment of the people's revolutionary ideal." During the visit of Secretary of War Dickinson later that year, Filipino politicians "loudly proclaimed their desire for early independence. In most cases, however, independence was invoked for its symbolic and political values; what was sought was something appreciably less." A Nacionalista orator in Albay even sent Dickinson an apology for having made inflammatory remarks that were "politically expedient."[12]

Quezon, the chief protagonist, is portrayed as a political conservative at heart who undertook dramatic moves—such as the drafting of the first Jones Bill in 1912—because this was expected of him and his party of *inmediatistas*. So much of what he said and did in later years is explained by his realization since at least the beginning of 1911 that "liberalizing changes in both the insular administration and its philosophy were essential if a dangerous, potentially violent level of alienation between the government and the people were to be avoided."[13] And, in order to achieve this, it was necessary to engage in radical discourse. Election results pointed to this formula. Furthermore, one had to twist the arm of the colonial administration with portents of a chaotic alternative.

Implied in parts of Stanley's work is that compadre colonial politics refers constantly to its radical "other." But, except for references to the spirit of the past revolution, the contours of popular radicalism are hardly described. In attempting this, we have to ignore for the moment what the archives encourage us to see: The interaction between the colonial establishment and native politicians. The latter's posturing vis-à-vis their constituents is more significant. In this respect, mass assemblies like that which transpired at Lucban are crucial events. In them politicians spoke in terms that their mass audiences could comprehend. Former Commissioner Charles Elliott recognized their importance: "The orator who strikes a heroic attitude and announces some lofty but self-evident sentiment . . . is certain of enthusiastic applause from the galleries. When told of their present ability and capacity to run a government, they readily accepted the views of the orator. It was easy to convince the defeated that the victors were remaining in the islands as oppressors." The problem in Elliott's description is the exaggerated role ascribed to the politician-orator. Was it mere brainwashing by the latter that had "the majority of the people . . . charmed by the magic word *independencia*"?[14]

To explore this question further, let us examine some magnified versions of the "Lucban incident"—the massive rallies that marked the anniversaries of Rizal's death and the start of the Katipunan uprising against Spain. Politicians of all colors used these occasions to rally the public behind their projects. What made these events and the rhetoric that accompanied them meaningful? What new meanings were generated? How was the politics of the time shaped by popular responses?

Let us take "Rizal Day" first. There were at least three major readings of Rizal during this period. It is well known that the colonial government promoted the "nation-wide hero worship of Rizal . . . to transfer Filipino adoration away from the revolutionary heroes towards an advocate of pacifist and constitutional nationalism." President Roosevelt even enlisted Rizal in what Usha Mahajani calls "the negation of independence," and insisted that Rizal's apparent denunciation of the Katipunan uprising applied "with tenfold greater force to those who foolishly or wickedly opposed the mild and beneficent government we were instituting in the islands."[15] Few Filipino conservatives would have gone this far. Nevertheless, Rizal to them remained the symbol of evolutionary change: education before independence, the efficacy of the pen, the rule of law, and service to the nation. They would have turned to other patriots, such as Andres Bonifacio and even Emilio Aguinaldo, for symbols of revolution.

There was also a "subversive" reading of Rizal, however. His execution, or rather martyrdom, by the Spaniards on 30 December 1896 was commemorated in Manila and other major towns from as early as 1898, under the auspices of the Malolos Republic. His mode of death, having remarkably adhered to the model of Christ's passion and death (a story particularly loved by the "lower class"), had transposed religious ideas of sacrifice and change to the area of politics, or at least blurred the boundaries between them. Thus, any public recollection of it was bound to cross lines with thinking about independence politics, leading to such questions as, What had happened to the notion of shedding blood for the redemption of the motherland? And that was not all; having died like Christ, Rizal, it was widely believed, arose from the dead and was hidden in some sacred mountain or embodied in a person of unusual powers. Almost without exception, peasant rebel leaders up to the 1920s claimed to be Rizal or to be in some sort of communication with him.[16] This perception was not limited to adherents of religio-political groups like the Colorum. How else can one explain the great impact of the 31 December 1909 issue of *El Renacimiento/Muling Pagsilang* (Rebirth) publicizing a "prophecy" of Rizal? This stated, as a politician later recalled, that, after separation from Spain, the Philippines would join a "strong nation," not Germany, nor England, nor Russia, but perhaps America. The Philippines would not live with this nation long and would "separate to be independent, finding the nations of the Orient to join forces with."[17] The notion that Filipinos and Japanese could ally against the U.S.—a possibility Quezon would never have even considered—was being ascribed to Rizal.

Since 1909 was an election year, perhaps it was politicians' waxing more eloquent than ever in laying claim to the magical heritage of 1896; an unexpectedly vast number of people attended the Rizal Day parade on 30 December. Whatever its circumstances, the event produced a flood of revolutionary signs. Take its highlight, the arrival of a float carrying a boat manned by a Filipino couple "struggling with the waves and the fury of a confused and tempestuous sea . . . the ocean of difficulties on the road to independence," guided by the light of the nationalist organ, *Muling Pagsilang*. This was a familiar image of the struggle, found in the manifestos of rebel leaders from Apolinario de la Cruz in 1840 right up to the Katipunan.[18] Even if the Assembly was officially the vehicle of the struggle, nothing prevented the spectator from allowing the imagery to mean something else. In various public plazas that day, a few speeches were more explicit: Imitate Rizal; don't be afraid to spill your blood.[19] Rizal Day 1910 was equally rousing. In 1911, the traditional parade even saw the participation of units of Ricarte's secret army, the largest contingent displaying the banner of the Pampanga organization Anak Pawas (Sons of Sweat; Toilers).[20]

The efforts of the various colonial administrations to promote a conservative, political-assimilationist image of Rizal were sometimes met with subtle resistance. In order to make Rizal Day 1912 specially significant, somebody conceived the idea of having his remains interred in the new monument on the Luneta. Even though official plans had been made for the transfer of Rizal's bones from his family home, Felipe Buencamino Sr., then a radical Nacionalista, managed to persuade Rizal's sister Trinidad to take the remains first to a Masonic lodge hall, much to the chagrin of the Church. At about the same time, there was a movement instead to form a Filipino pantheon in which Rizal's remains would be placed side by side with the likes of Macario Sakay, Cornelio Felizardo, and, if his remains were ever found, Bonifacio—all patriots whom the *ilustrados* and the Americans would have preferred to tag as *ladrones* (bandits). It took some official persuasion to convince the Rizal family to give up their rights to decide on the matter.[21]

By the end of 1912, then, Rizal had his own shrine, presumably intended to highlight the "approved" meanings of the national hero. But such a move was futile. The very blessing that the colonialists gave Rizal was exploited; his birth and death anniversaries were very much the scene of the "other politics." Buencamino made this point during a speech in Tondo on the night of 30 December. "The government," he said to his predominantly working-class audience, "favors the cult which we render to the martyr of Bagumbayan, and we ought to take advantage of this very propitious occasion to preach to everybody that man ought to die to defend his liberty. If the *juramentado* Moros are terrible, it is because they know how to kill and let themselves be killed. Let us, brothers . . . swear to die as Dr. Rizal died and we shall secure our independence."[22]

Commemorative occasions like Rizal Day enabled orators and their audiences not just to remember and pay homage to the past, but to relive its intensity as well. Tagalog oratory captivates, often makes people forget the particular circumstances they are in. Because people came together and their sentiments were focused on certain themes, "disturbances" were likely to occur on or close to such commemorative dates. In a 1915 report, 30 December (Rizal Day) is listed as a date when "occasionally . . . there were rumors for the most part entirely unfounded, but in some cases with conspiracies behind them." "Sometimes," these occurred on the 4th of July, "frequently" on 30 May (Labor Day), and "almost every year" on 13 August.[23] Obviously, the latter date was particularly potent. As a matter of fact, the whole of August—when, in 1896, the Katipunan uprising began—was a critical month. Its central event, properly celebrated in Rizal Day fashion, was Andres Bonifacio's "Cry of Balintawak" on the 26th.[24] Unlike Rizal, Bonifacio was not the sort of personality that could be appropriated by the colonialists and the "better classes." Even Aguinaldo, the President of the Republic of 1898, would have preferred a lot less fuss over the man he had ordered executed in 1897. The day of the "Heroes of '96," celebrated in Manila and certain towns with a revolutionary past, stood for popular participation, if not the use of force, in obtaining independence.

Following the series of uprisings in 1914, a "prominent Filipino" interviewed by a Manila news daily blamed the administration itself for allowing "survivors of the old Katipunan movement to go out to Balintawak where the revolution of 1896 began and there render homage to Andres Bonifacio . . . This worship of Bonifacio and the bolo has done more to cause such trouble as this than anything else."[25] What exactly was so provocative about this event? Let us take as an example the 1911 celebration. The plan was for everyone to appear in a *camisa* (a native shirt) with a bolo (a bladed weapon) tied to the waist. The Constabulary forecast a riot. The organizing committee was warned that neither they nor the police "could control 25,000 bolo men if they had any patriotic speeches of the usual type poured over them." The danger was ascribed to the effects of the "usual" oratory. Realizing that they were "playing with fire," the committee backed off, counseled moderation, and abandoned the carrying of bolos. Quezon later told the Governor General that the Constabulary's quick action "had saved the government from one of the bloodiest catastrophes in the history of the Islands."[26]

The demonstration, nevertheless, was a momentous event. Without their bolos, of course, between 35 to 40 thousand people flocked to Balintawak dressed in native shirts, many in the red trousers of the Katipunan. There were groups of workmen with the banners of their guilds and mutual-aid associations who "shouted nothing but the words *Panahon na!* (The time has come!). Rich and poor, men and women, old people and children," all chanting *Panahon na!*, marched to the central point, a newly constructed statue of Bonifacio.

Then the speeches began. Having been forewarned, the orators were not as provocative as the audience perhaps expected. But the signs were there of meanings in excess of the "official" limits. Some groups were heard to exclaim, "Even without arms, five thousand enemies would not be enough for us!," to which an upset Doctor Bernabe Bustamante of the Liga Popular Nacionalista shouted in reply, "Do not be imprudent!" Bishop Gregorio Aglipay of the Philippine Independent Church must have had ruffled feelings when he declared in fiery Tagalog:

We should not be contented with the excessive salaries that the Amerian government pays and we ought always remember what happened in 1896 in this idolized motherland when the revolution broke out against the government of Spain. The arm (showing his arm to the audience three times) is the only factor that really counts in the time of war.

How the audience might have reacted to this can be gauged from the comments of a Constabulary agent who was listening intently: "The people who were near me said, 'That is true. What we need now is not politics but arms (human) to secure the independence we long for.' Those people appeared not to be educated."[27]

The following year's celebrations were no less dramatic. Among the highlights was a demonstration by the Dimas-Alang (a mutual-aid association organized along Katipunan lines) and workers of the Katubusan tobacco factory, which nearly developed into a riot. On the night of 24 August, despite the fears that the affair might be branded seditious, the famed Katipunan rendezvous of San Juan del Monte was again inundated (as in 1896) by the rhetoric of rousing speeches. The rally had been planned to "help . . . the campaign sustained by the Hon. Quezon in America," but how could such a project remain within bounds with orators harping on the theme "that the people should not forget the first shout of emancipation because only with this memory can a people obtain their independence"?[28] Patricio Belen, a cigar-maker and head of the Dimas-Alang, soon had problems of control. His association, originally set up to harness mass support for Quezon and Osmeña, was composed mainly of "the lower and more ignorant classes," who had little inkling of what went on in the highest circles of leadership. They had joined what seemed to be a replica of the Katipunan, complete with initiation rituals. Many of its members were also admirers of Ricarte. It is not surprising, then, that lower-level leaders and other "hotheads" (to cite Belen) were inciting members to rise on the 26th. Belen was all over Tondo and Gagalangin on the eve of the planned uprising counseling people that the time was not yet ripe. Lope K. Santos, the socialist writer-turned-Governor of Rizal province, "worked all night to stop the people, insisting that it was not yet the hour designated, and visiting Tondo, Gagalangin, Paang-Bundok and Balintawak," all places with a Katipunan heritage. According to Bandholtz, a mass uprising was averted "by warning the ringleaders that if anyone got hurt they would be the first ones."[29]

Things were very much the same in August of 1913 and 1914. Rumors of war, heightened expectations, and tension on the part of the American community always preceded Balintawak Day. Servants would be heard repeating rumors of grand celebrations and the approaching hour of conflict. The Constabulary would be busy monitoring secret societies, often nipping uprisings in the bud. Ricarte had problems with some of his commanders in Manila who wanted to synchronize the new revolution with the time of 1896; he had to constantly remind them of the saying *Ang lumalakad na matulin, kung matinik ay malalim* (The thorns stick deep into the feet of him who walks fast). When, after at least six postponements, the uprising eventually took place on Christmas Eve 1914, Ricarte was not in control. When it looked as though this would fail, predictably, "persistent rumors [kept] flying about of another attempt, Rizal Day night."[30]

Quezon himself could not resist emulating the other orators on Balintawak Day, delivering "one of the most fiery of the many speeches . . . ever delivered at the foot of the Bonifacio monument," boasting that, "while he could not wave the

Katipunan flag in the Philippines," he always kept one spread in his office in Washington."[31] But, for all this fanfare, Quezon's motive was to channel the people's sentiments in a "responsible" and legal direction. These were critical times for him. In late 1911, newly arrived from Washington and having just missed the threatened riot on Balintawak Day, Quezon "inside of 48 hours . . . got next to the Ricarte conspiracy and verified everything that [the Constabulary] had." The result was a thorough police hold over Ricarte's movement. Not long after the threatened uprisings of 1912, a disappointed Col. Bandholtz wrote him: ". . . it has been painfully evident that all your efforts to keep the Dimas-Alang Society in order were futile."[32] Obviously, Quezon was playing the game in order to contain it.

We can generalize further. On each of those occasions when politicians took to the stump, they played to sentiments in the audience that normally were suppressed or hidden in the course of everyday life. Through oratory, popularity and votes were won, and the people's desire for independence was demonstrated to the colonial administration. But, as Elliott pointed out, Nacionalista politicians mouthing independence propaganda as "a popular party shibboleth" had, in many localities, to deal with situations that "got beyond their control." Soon after the discovery of some Rizal Day plots in January 1913, the American press reported how "the insurrection . . . got away from the leaders" to the extent that "much bloodshed and disorder were expected."[33] The perception is undoubtedly alarmist, but it gives us a sense of how "control" was crucial in a style of politics that thrived on mass euphoria. It is not so much that uprisings happened (and few there were of any consequence) but that they could have happened, and that so much of what we now know as colonial politics was shaped by this possibility. The "menace," as Col. Taylor put it, was Sandiko (another radical Nacionalista) and men like him, "firebrands who live on excitement and the applause of the mob. The small portion of the population which such men control could do great harm and might start a flame which would extend to other parts."[34] What was the thinking behind the mob's enthusiasm and the possibility of its spread? What were the meanings of the "the revolution," "the times (panahon)" and "politics (pulítika)"?

Mass patriotic rallies were an outgrowth of the revolution. During the centuries of Spanish rule, mass assemblies had been held mainly on religious festivals, particularly those of patron saints and during Holy Week. The Republic of 1898, as we saw, made 30 December a national day of mourning for Rizal, but the latter was, after all, widely revered as the Filipino Christ. During the American regime, so much of the popular perception of time was still shaped by the church calendar and "Biblical time."[35] This is the context in which we must view the slogan *Panahon na!*, The time has come! There were different ways of saying it, but the perception of imminent change can be found in nearly every mass rally of the period. Without a powerful undercurrent of beliefs about the *panahon,* the speeches would have lost their punch. What were the conditions that made the crowds receptive to the notion of *panahon na?*

We can argue that compadre colonial politics was itself responsible for creating such an atmosphere. The years 1909, 1912, and 1915 were Assembly years, and the coming of independence was always a powerful feature of campaign rhetoric. Whether for election purposes or not, this was bound to resonate with ideas of *panahon,* of the approach of a new era heralded by signs and, possibly, conflict.[36] The Resident Commissioner's movements and speeches abroad and the introduction in the U.S. Congress of various bills or petitions calling for some kind of eventual independence, provided grist for the rumor mills; news of such invariably "spread through the populace in exaggerated form."[37] The Commissioners were partly to blame; why, we might ask, did Pablo Ocampo, who had just completed his stint in Washington, have to say publicly in February 1910, ". . . the day of the redemption of the Philippines is very near"?[38] Quezon had even more flair, with predictable consequence. In July 1910, barely two months after his plea in Congress for complete and absolute independence, the following reaction was observed: ". . . nearly all the populace, even the pessimistic Katipuneros of '96, have become optimistic. They think they see very near at hand the advent of independence, generously granted by the ruling country."[39]

Democrat Woodrow Wilson's presidential victory in 1912 brought independence even nearer to hand. Ten thousand people paraded through Manila's streets, and 20,000 gathered on the Luneta to hear Osmeña, Quezon, and Aguinaldo speak of the event's significance. The Manila newspaper *La Vanguardia/ Taliba* (successor to the suppressed *El Renacimiento/Muling Pagsilang*) was quick to put it in "proper" context: Wilson was a modern Moses who would "preside over our triumphal entrance into the Promised Land after redeeming us from the long captivity to which the imperial Pharaohs reduced us."[40] Given such publicity, Bandholtz's observation of February 1913 is not surprising: "The little people are firmly convinced that as soon as President Wilson assumes office, independence for the Philippines will be one of the first things that is turned out." There was a "serious" situation, however, caused by the uncertainty of U.S. action.[41]

In October, the new Governor General, Francis Harrison, fueled the fires of expectation when he publicly announced on the day of his arrival: "People of the Philippine Islands, a new era is dawning. We place within your reach the instruments of your redemption. The door of opportunity stands open and under Divine Providence the event is in your hands."[42] The triumph of light over darkness, the approach of a new *panahon,* redemption, the opened gates, divine blessing, personal participation—Bonifacio had done no better in 1896! The colonialists themselves provided so many signs that the appointed hour was approaching.

We might perhaps wonder why even the Americans indulged in such bombast. Could they have been playing to a sentiment that was already there? The notion of *Panahon na!* is, in fact, implicated in another series of events that begins with Japan's victory over Russia in 1905. All over the colonies of Asia, Japan became the source of inspiration for a relatively new generation of nationalist intellectuals and politicians. "Like the same class in India and Egypt," wrote Elliott in 1917, young Filipinos, many of them *pensionados* educated in the U.S., "joined with the radicals, and the work of educating the masses to demand independence was commenced under their directions."[43] The editors of *El Renacimiento/Muling Pagsilang* belonged to this group. As an example of their activity, on 19 November 1909 *Muling Pagsilang* carried an editorial arguing that America was the "Russia of the Orient" and would suffer the same fate. "In a vague manner, using words of double sense, the people were advised to sharpen their wits to put themselves on the side of the better (Japan) . . . the one who will unquestionably come out victor in this war." This message, naturally, was branded by the police as "pernicious for the popular masses, who read this publication with true faith and satisfaction." Soon after its appearance, it was reported that people were "saying in all the meetings of workmen that the United States [would] not conquer Japan."⁴⁴

It is common knowledge that every discussion of independence among the *ilustrados* and the Americans entailed consideration of the looming Japanese presence in Asia and the Pacific. Less obvious but equally important is what an examination of hundreds of Constabulary reports from 1908–1913 tells us about popular responses to such news. Colonel Rafael Crame introduced the subject well in his preface to a volume of reports: "The rumors of war between America and Japan and the inclination of the Filipinos in favor of the latter, have so increased in the last two months that they are the subject of conversation, both among the educated and ignorant classes of Manila and the provinces."⁴⁵ From 1909 to 1913, at least, the advent of a "great war," a repetition of the revolutionary wars still fresh in people's minds, was endlessly talked about, with consequences for prevailing conceptions of the *panahon*. A whole study might well be devoted to the rumors that floated about, the signs that were interpeted in terms of the approaching cataclysm. We can mention a few: the appearance of strange warships off the coasts; routine maneuvers by the U.S. Army; the influx of Japanese spies masquerading as gardeners, peddlers, and the like; news reports of Japan's occupation of Korea. Fegan points out that the Japanese emblem of the rising sun eventually got caught up in ideas, derived from religious rituals, about the "light in the east," the coming of a redeemer and source of *liwanag* (light). Governor General Harrison claimed that European war news and pictures were a cause of unrest in late 1914.⁴⁶ Rumors betray the structure of past events: The Philippines was sold by the U.S. to Japan, with delivery promised in 1910—a repetition of 1898! But the greatest link between the past and the present was Ricarte, the intransigent revolutionary general who, as we shall see, was believed ready to return with the aid of the Mikado's armies.

In late 1909, the influential *espiritistas* or spirit mediums based in Malabon and Caloocan were spreading the word that "a greater and more terrible war than the two past revolutions would take place in 1910." By the following year, *espiritistas* all over the country were repeating the same prophecy, said to originate from the spirits of Rizal and Bonifacio, that, in the war between Japan and the U.S., the Philippines would gain her independence if she sided with Japan.[47] Adding a convincing note to such forecasts was the appearance of Halley's Comet in mid-1910. People were heard to say that the very same comet that "announced the birth of the Son of God to the Wise Men . . . today announces to the Filipino people the proximity of independence."[48]

Such was the comet's impact that George Zwack, a Jesuit priest and secretary of the Philippine Weather Bureau, hastily published a short monograph "to furnish some notes on Halley's Comet which would help to quiet the fears of such persons as might anticipate trouble from its approach to earth." There were, said Father Zwack, too many "wild rumors circulated by ignorant or malicious persons, setting forth in glowing colors all the horrors which the 'comet' is going to bring upon us poor mortals. It is even stated that these irresponsible mischief-makers are already at work in some sections of Manila."[49]

As a matter of fact, the comet was partly responsible for the peasant unrest that shook central and southern Luzon in March and April of 1910. Felipe Salvador, the proclaimed King of the Philippines, the Liberator just returned (contrary to fact) from Japan, is rumored to have said, "Just as soon as the comet shines in all its spendor, the era of the happy emancipation of the Philippines will be born."[50] Indeed, the dramatic entrance of his forces into Arayat, Pampanga, took place on 17 April, two days before the comet's pass. Salvador, in a sense, was the orator tapping ideas of the *panahon* to mobilize central Luzon peasants. But no less active were Nacionalista politicians in Manila—including such names as Ramon Diokno, Timoteo Paez, Fernando Maria Guerrero (former editor of *El Renacimiento*), and Hermenegildo Cruz—who exploited the comet's effect by "visiting houses, streets and districts, preaching that the hour [was] approaching for the independence of the Filipino people, and that the only thing lacking [was] an effort on the part of the people in response to the call for everyone to sign a message addressed to the American government and people."[51] Salvador may have called for armed rebellion, and the radical Nacionalistas for the mere signing of a petition, but for all parties a condition of popular response was the sense of the changing *panahon*.

After Salvador's capture on 24 July 1910 and eventual execution, his role as a focus of popular expectations was assumed by Ricarte, who had reappeared in June. Jailed for sedition since 1904, Ricarte had served his sentence and won his freedom but, true to form, refused to salute the American flag and was promptly deported to Hong Kong. On 2 February 1911, he announced the formation of the Consejo Revolucionario de Filipinas, a government-in-exile which demanded, among other things, "immediate and complete independence and the equalization of wealth."[52] Implicit in the mass rallies from 1911 to 1914 is the public awareness of this alternative to compadre colonial politics, whatever individuals might have thought of actually joining Ricarte's army. It is hard to imagine Rizal, Bonifacio, and the "heroes of '96" being remembered without the intrusion in people's minds of "El Vibora," a part of that past who still carried on the struggle.

The "politically active Filipinos" of the period, says Stanley, had lived through the revolution, many having fought on or sympathized with the Filipino side. Their goals were basically those of the Republic of 1898; their rhetoric, that of the Katipunan. In short, as so many works have shown, the revolutionary heritage was a "given" in the politics of the times. Quezon, the dashing major in the republican army, and his superior, General Aguinaldo, have been the best known competitors for the hallowed blessings of the past. It is a puzzle, then, to be told by Goodman that there was an "obvious lack of any serious support for Ricarte himself who was even in 1914 becoming a somewhat remote figure already relegated to the historical past."[53] Lack of massive support for poorly armed and organized "conspiracies," yes, but the remoteness of a figure like (though not necessarily limited to) Ricarte?

A veteran of the first Katipunan rising against Spain, Ricarte had an edge over Quezon. He had fought alongside the original "heroes of '96" and had adopted a stance second only to martyrdom: the refusal to acquiesce to U.S. rule. However, during the whole period of American rule, Ricarte was absent: in Guam (to 1903), in prison (1904-1910), in Hong Kong (1910-1915), and in Japan (1915-1942). This creates a problem for those who wish to assess his impact on domestic politics. He was, to be sure, very much in people's minds. In May 1910, just before his release, Assemblyman Macario Adriatico was addressing an independence rally in Manila when he rhetorically pointed in the direction of Bilibid Prison where patriots of the past revolution were still languishing. "On hearing these statements the public immediately said among themselves that the orator referred to Artemio Ricarte, Villafuerte, Carreon and others."[54] The problem is that Ricarte's attractiveness was mainly to the "lower-class" imagination, about which the sources are fragmentary. The membership of his revolutionary army, "like that of all those established by [him], was extensive only among the lower and more ignorant classes of the people ... [and] like that of the society founded by A. Bonifacio, was composed of domestics, cooks, cocheros, muchachos, and such like."[55] Writing in the 1920s, Serafin Macaraig said that "the Spirit of the Revolution [was] personified in the sacrifices of its leaders who are remembered and idolized" and that Ricarte, in particular, "was capitalized by some of the ignorant classes" who joined the numerous "Vibora" societies throughout Manila.[56]

From 1911 to at least 1914, Ricarte had a profound effect on popular perceptions of the *panahon:* His banishment to Hong Kong was almost immediately followed by rumors that he had promised to "return ... in January 1911, to define and solve the critical situation of the Philippines."[57] Indeed, in that year the Constabulary had its hands full dealing with reports like the following by an *ilustrado* who had toured the Ilocos region: ". . . Ricarte's name is greatly respected in Ilocos and the people believe he will return and are prepared to serve him with their lives."[58] In October, Patricio Belen read to an assembly of peasants in Bataan a letter that proclaimed, "Ricarte is with the Japanese and is the only one who can save the Filipino people and is the one who can lead the Filipinos to their desired independence."[59] In mid-1913, amidst rumors of war, residents of Rizal province were said to be whispering among themselves: "If war breaks out, Ricarte will again come to defend the rights of the people."[60] To rumors and conversations about coming independence and a great war must be added that of the Liberator who would return from overseas.

"Alas, Jose! All the people here ask about you and pin their hope on you ... It seems that they consider you the second Jesus who will liberate them from misery!"—so it was in 1889; Rizal was expected to return with the aid of Bismarck's navy.[61] Bonifacio, it was thought, had the backing of Japan, if not that of the legendary King Bernardo Carpio who would descend from Mount Tapusi with a liberation army.[62] The popular mentality during the revolution was, as Isabelo Artacho, an *ilustrado*, once stated with scorn, inhabited by "the personages of Philippine legends and comedies": chivalrous knights, kings, sorcerers and messiahs.[63] Things could not have been much different a dozen years later, despite some inroads of the American educational system. To Bulacan peasants even up to the 1930s, notes Fegan, Ricarte's actions embodied the myth of the returning hero.[64] And Ricarte himself was quite aware of the potential value of such thinking. Having managed to slip into the country in November 1903, "wherever he went, Ricarte impressed upon his hearers, both those he called upon and those who went to visit him that he had been 'liberated'!" He even said that he had arrived in a flying balloon.[65] It is not surprising that, on Balintawak Day 1911, "the rumor was current that Ricarte had gone to attend that festival and that he was dressed in the uniform of a Japanese admiral and that a person of very high rank in the Mikado's government was with him." It was the "plebeians" who repeated the rumor, said Ricarista leader Juan Villarino, and "we should not contradict it in order not to injure the faith of lovers of revolution."[66]

But, if Ricarte could do it, so could the politicians. Take, for example, the following account of the the 1909 electoral struggle

between rival Assembly candidates Justo Lukban and Dominador Gomez in Manila:

. . . when the people gather in a place for a meeting and before the speakers
have arrived, it is heard in whispers that war is approaching, and that it is
necessary that a Gomez triumph because he is brave . . . [or] a Lukban because he has a brother in Japan, and Lukban, more than anyone else, will
be the one called up to appear by the side of his brother. For this reason
each party tries to get more proselytes, even though they may not be
electors, to the extent that in the meetings the greater part of those present are illiterate laborers, sympathizers either of Gomez or Lukban.

A contest between rival candidates involving masses of people
who cannot even vote? A close reading reveals, among other
things, how electoral politics could easily get caught up in
thinking about an impending war and the requisite liberator,
such as Lukban's brother in Japan, or Gomez who, having recently emerged from prison, fancied himself a hero.[67]

There was, of course, Ricarte's alter-ego at that time—
Quezon. The Resident Commissioner's almost total absence
since 1910, his travels to a foreign land to seek that elusive
independencia, enabled a web of myth to be likewise spun
around him. The beneficial effect on his political career of his
campaigns, leading to the successful passage of the Jones Bill
in 1916, is well known. But what form did this popularity take
at the level of worker-peasant associations such as the Dimas-
Alang? In Zambales, a near insurrection was caused by the cir-
culation of a letter, falsely attributed to Quezon, stating that,
if he failed to obtain independence, he was giving the people
"permission to do as they pleased." If they decided to fight,
he would seek the aid of Japan and other nations. If independence was not declared on the 4th of July 1914, the people
should go to the mountains and notify him of their whereabouts. According to the police, "Quezon's" letter had a great
impact on the "ignorant people" of the Dimas-Alang, and this
was a technique used by the leaders (who were far from anxious
to revolt) "to keep their followers worked up to a condition of
mind where they are willing to contribute funds."[68] Quezon,
who was in touch with Dimas-Alang leader Patricio Belen, probably knew what was happening. While visiting Ricarte, he ap-

parently intimated (and this was relayed to Ricarte's lieutenants) that, if his efforts in America failed, he would return to Hong Kong to join Vibora "and the two [would] come to the Philippines to join the revolution."[69]

When orators spoke of the *panahon* and the revolution, there were all of the above meanings floating around which Ricartistas, Progresistas, Nacionalistas of all colors, and other parties sought to appropriate. But there were also limits to what compadre colonial politics could absorb, hence the ever-present threat of rallies and movements getting out of control. In mid-1912, a Dimas-Alang orator was telling his peasant audience in Norzagaray, Bulacan, that the Dimas-Alang was the same as the old Katipunan, that its goal was to "redeem" the country. He went on to say: "Ricarte is the present chief and is abroad arranging for arms for the Philippines. . . . Today [he] needs a little money for his expenses and the rich Filipinos pay no attention to him. Thus it is that we poor people have to aid him, because we, and not the rich, are the people."[70] It is likely, as colonial records insist, that the speaker meant only to agitate the masses so as to solicit contributions. Whatever his motives, however, he was speaking in terms comprehensible to his audience that therefore deserve a closer look.

Quezon's campaign was predicated on the fulfillment of America's promise to grant self-rule to the Philippines. He was merely hastening the process, making America set definite dates on which concessions were to be granted. But memories of the revolution were still potent during this period; the earlier arguments for separation from Spain could readily be called upon to question Quezon's approach. Manifestos from the 1914 uprisings reveal the following patterning of events: It is time to awaken from a long period of darkness and slavery, because America has not fulfilled her obligations.[71] Compare this with Bonifacio's appeal. Spain had made a pact with the early Filipinos. She had promised "increased betterment and awakening of our minds"; the Filipinos had responded in good faith, giving the Spaniards everything they wanted, even defending them from the Hollanders and the Chinese. But, wrote Bonifacio, "as their fulfillment of the promise to awaken us to a better life [*sic*], they have only blinded us more." And so the need to

awaken and to separate by force of arms.[72] The revolution of
1896 then, had been a reaction not only to Spain's deceitfulness but to the Filipinos' own self-deception (blindness) in
thinking that *kalayaan* would come without effort.

"Deception" was a theme that could not but creep into perceptions of compadre colonial politics. The unrest of 1912, particularly the Balintawak Day disturbances, was attributed to
the fact that a great number of Dimas-Alang members, although
instructed by Quezon to remain calm and obey the government,
had started to doubt the promises of Quezon and Democrats.
In April 1913, at a festival in honor of the Katipunan patriot
Emilio Jacinto, Isabelo de los Reyes told a receptive crowd that
the independence platform of the Democrats was a myth, while
Cipriano Nicolas recalled Taft's empty words, "The Philippines
for the Filipinos," and maintained that Democrat promises
would likewise remain empty.[73] In 1914, the Sandiko-led Nacionalista left wing joined forces with former officers of the
revolutionary army in the Partido Democrata Nacional, attacking Nacionalista stalwarts Osmeña and Quezon as well as the
colonial administration. Notably, its organ, *Consolidación,* announced that the New Era of Governor General Harrison had
become an "Era of Deceit." Even Rizal, interviewed by the *espiritistas,* said that "the Filipino politicians [were] deceived by
the American politicians."[74]

Ricarte merely presented in a clear and uncompromising
form an interpretation of events already floating around in the
concern about "deceit." His open letter of 1911, for example,
deals with America's deceitfulness and lack of honor. He re-
minds his countrymen that, in 1898, Dewey and Pratt promised
Aguinaldo independence, "and yet they not only broke their
agreement but now President Taft and his followers allege . . .
that the Filipinos are unfit for self-government until after
several generations." Now that Japan is threatening war, should
Filipinos come to the aid of the Americans? Well, Ricarte argues, if the Americans need help, "let them begin by keeping
their old promises before making new ones, for one would have
to be very guileless to trust again a delinquent debtor. . . . Let
them first pay us the 1898 account. . . . Until they do so, we
ought never to trust the promises of men who, like the imperial-

istic Americans, have no word of honor."[75] The argument would
be sustained in later years. Ricarte's lieutenants in Manila argued in early 1913 that even "the promise of independence
contained in the Jones Bill [was] only to deceive the people."
The leaders of the Christmas Eve Fiasco said the same thing at
their trial: They had rebelled "because the United States had
promised independence but had failed to keep its promise."[76]

The recognition of deceit must be followed up on by a recourse of bloodshed—we can see the logic, or part of it, behind
the Ricartist "conspiracy." But a narrow group must not take
the credit for this notion. Shedding blood for individual and
social renewal was already implicit in the rituals of Holy Week,
which were part of the masses' experience; the Katipunan
merely transposed such notions to a nationalist framework. It
is not surprising, then, to find in accounts of mass rallies the
appeal and receptivity to bloodshed. Even Osmeña's speech of
May 1910 hinted at this as he dwelt on the following comparison: "A child is born and sheds tears; people also weep for their
independence, but their tears are of blood." No wonder his
audience was brought "to a state of great excitement."[77]
Stanley notes that Democrata orators at a rally in 1914 even
"hinted at a return to armed rebellion, winning wild applause."[78]
It was always like this on Rizal Day and Balintawak Day, or at
any time and place that orators spoke of the revolution.

"The Philippine independence which the Democrats promise
is a dream, because without blood independence is not possible"—this argument was heard again and again in Cavite, the
old revolutionary heartland, specially from people unhappy
with Aguinaldo's involvement in politics.[79] For, while politics
was claimed to be a way—the only legal way—to gain independence, past experience facilitated a contrary argument. During
the campaigns prior to the 1911 Assembly and Municipal
Board elections, the public was told to place its hopes in Quezon and the U.S. Democratic party, but in less open gatherings
(to avoid arrest) orators—Assembly candidate Hermenegildo
Cruz among them—spoke of the need to obtain independence
not through "politics" but "by means of blood."[80]

What did "politics" mean, in the first place? Gregorio Aglipay
and Hermenegildo Cruz, among the orators we have mentioned,

used the Tagalog term *pulítika,* and contrasted it to the use of force. *Pulítika* is the perception of politics as a process of bargaining, with implicit self or factional interests involved. The interaction between the colonial power and its native wards was *pulítika.* At another level, it refers to the practices by which leaders cultivate ties of personal loyalty and indebtedness to them, or simply attract votes. In a sense, as numerous studies of Philippine political culture have shown, *pulítika* holds the society together; the interests of both leaders and followers are ultimately served. But Aglipay and Cruz were speaking of *pulítika's* limits. The electoral candidate sways the crowd through his flowing rhetoric. There is exhilaration and hope in the event. But, as usually is the case, promises are not kept and thus the cynical, oft-heard comment: It was all *pulítika.*

Spain was perceived to have been guilty of *pulítika,* and America was beginning also to appear guilty. Now Filipino leaders had to be careful lest they themselves become implicated in the logic of their anti-colonial rhetoric. As we have seen, Quezon's name could be dragged into denunciations of U.S. deception.[81] His effort to appear on the side of immediate independence, contrary to his personal inclinations, was a matter of political survival. In harping upon the theme of deceit and hinting at a return to armed struggle, the Democrata attack on the Nacionalistas was true to form.

Ricarte merely pushed the critique to its limit, condemning all political parties for their insincerity, for merely "working to secure for their members the best paid positions under the American administration." He pointedly refused a stipend and the rank of "Superior General-in-Chief of the Filipino Army" offered by Quezon. Had he acquiesced, he would have had to return the favor, gradually sinking into *pulítika.*[82] Ricartistas and Democratas spoke the same idiom in their attack on compadre colonial politics. Ricartistas, however, went a step further in actually rising in a revolt. When Governor Mariano Melendres, trapped in the Navotas municipal hall held by some 200 Ricartistas, appealed on patriotic grounds for his release, his captors "replied, almost in one voice, 'That is all politics' or deceit."[83]

"The people are sovereign; the people are composed of the plebeian class; they are the true heroes and patriots. If they

want and if they do, there are no rich nor wise who will not respect them"—such were the contours of an "alarming rumor"
current in Rizal and Laguna provinces in late 1911. Hardly surprising. We have seen how close orators like Cruz, Belen, Aglipay, de los Reyes, and even Buencamino came to voicing such
sentiments. Daniel Tirona, who reported the rumor, knew that
there were grounds in the recent past for its existence and
spread.[84] Governor General Forbes himself made generous references to the elite's alleged fear of an outbreak of anarchy
following an American withdrawal.[85] A group of prominent
Manila Americans, soon after the 1914 uprisings, concluded
that the "unrest among the tao class" was based not so much
upon anti-Americanism as upon "an envy of the official Filipino,
. . . the latter largely recognized as an ex-insurgent who has
graduated from the Tao class and prospered by reason of his
political activity as an insurrecto."[86] Could the "official Filipino" have been Quezon himself? This somewhat puzzling
statement confirms at least that Modesto Victorino, a Ricartista
leader, was not alone in his stated desire to "capture all the
great Filipinos . . . at work with the American government."[87]

Victorino, of course, never got his wish fulfilled. He was arrested for sedition in August 1914 and thrown in jail; other
Ricartista leaders were rounded up after the Christmas Eve
Fiasco at year's end. But that is only one outcome of the story.
There were many more who shared Victorino's sentiments but
thought it foolish to rise up in 1914. And joining Ricarte's
army was only one of the options of the crowd. While the Constabulary was busy monitoring and generally messing up the
"conspiracies," the politicians were promising to obtain immediate independence from America. We have seen how Quezon
and Osmeña tapped memories of the revolution and perceptions
of the *panahon. Independencia,* or its more potent Tagalog
counterpart, *kalayaan,* was another one of those terms whose
meanings could be invoked or appropriated.

The Ricartistas, very much like the peasant movements that
challenged the 1898 Republic, promised that independence
would include equalization of wealth and distribution of public
lands. Other parties, while perhaps intending a lot less, spoke
of independence in such glowing but vague terms that the public

only had to add the specifics: alleviation of poverty, abundance of rice, lower or no taxes, ownership of friar lands, a new Eden and no more politics.[88] Hamilton Wright describes one extreme use to which *independencia* appeals were put. An "educated but low and cunning politician," intending to drive a poor farmer off his land, presents the following argument:

Your stomach is empty. What you need is independence. Then you will have many carabaos and fields, and your stomach will be full. I am a great leader, a general; I am going to secure the independence of the Philippines and make myself emperor of the Republic, and I will reward you; but if you do not follow me, we will come here and burn your house and kill all your cattle.[89]

In the contest to win the hearts of the majority, the Nacionalistas won out. After 1914, the top leadership of the Ricartista movement was broken up, and the Viper himself was forced by British authorities to flee to Japan. Meanwhile, says Stanley, the abortive uprisings and the outbreak of the European war "produced panic and a retreat to the security of proven leadership" even among Osmeña's critics.[90] Rallies were held calling for support of the Jones Bill, which Quezon was nursing through the U.S. House of Representatives and Senate, as the vehicle for national liberation. It was a mild piece of legislation, calling for moderate reforms with a pledge of eventual independence. But that is not exactly how the public perceived it, as the following report suggests:

The natives of this city (Iloilo), and, I am told, of the whole province, are impatiently awaiting the passage of the Jones Bill, and the belief is general among the plebeian class here that the passage of the Jones Bill will be the granting of independence. This circumstance should not cause any surprise, for I believe that this opinion is general throughout the archipelago.[91]

When the Jones Bill became law in 1916, it was greeted with mass euphoria. After years of campaign work for independence at Washington, Quezon came home in September 1916, "with the glory of a conquering hero."[92] The subsequent years would see cabinet crises, independence missions, political rivalries, and agrarian discontent, with Quezon apparently weathering the storms. On the other hand, the story of the Tanggulan, Colorum,

Sakdal and other popular movements of the 1920s and 1930s evidences the continuity of perceptions of the *panahon*, the revolutionary past, peasant leadership, and independence, which we have discussed. How much of compadre colonial politics after 1914, we wonder, continues to speak of its radical "other"?

PART TWO

Cultural Interactions

"The Voice of Worcester is the Voice of God": How One American Found Fulfillment in the Philippines

PETER W. STANLEY

PETER W. STANLEY

To administer an empire, one needed a colonial service, people willing to make a career of the colony. Compared with what Philip Woodruff tells us of the British colonial service in India, we know relatively little about the Americans who staffed the government of the Philippines. Even the "Thomasites"—the American teachers in Philippine schools—remain largely an abstraction. What motivated Americans to travel to the other side of the earth and devote their lives to work in a foreign culture and, for most, an inhospitable climate? In an era newly oriented toward professional careers, a time of growth and challenge at home in the United States itself, what drew these people from the center to the periphery? To answer such questions is to explore the psychology of empire.

In this essay, Peter W. Stanley, Program Officer in charge of Education and Culture, The Ford Foundation, New York, examines the psychology and structure of the Philippine career of Dean C. Worcester, a prominent official of the colonial government for fourteen years.

Worcester's experience suggests that, for some, the Philippines served as an extension of America's recently vanished frontier, an environment in which authority, once established, had about it heroic, almost magical properties denied to those working within more settled institutions. The enlightened tyranny of the civilizers, their totemic power over both the "natives" and people of their own kind, is, of course, one of the great themes of *The Tempest*. Prospero, however grievously wronged by others, holds imperial sway over Caliban, his own daughter, and the very island itself. But Prospero had not chosen his fate. For that, one turns to Joseph Conrad and *The Heart of Darkness*.

Today, as in his own time, Dean C. Worcester seems larger than life. Part of the reason for this is the physical image of the man himself and the photographic record of it that survives. Like many of his American contemporaries in the Philippines—one need only mention William Howard Taft—Worcester was a big man among a small people. In his case, moreover, a special interest in the "wild men" of the Philippine back country led to regular contact with the shortest and slightest people in the archipelago. An avid photographer, he left numerous pictures of himself among them, often showing several adults standing upright beneath his outstretched arms or dozens clustered around his massive form, peering avidly at whatever he was doing. In one memorable photo, used on the cover of the program at a testimonial banquet to him in 1913 and again seventeen years later as an illustration in Ralston Hayden's biographical portrait of him, Worcester sat alone astride a magnificent horse on the very edge of a vast and rugged mountain panorama, a modern colonial counterpart to James Fenimore Cooper's image of the solitary horseman, the Natural Man.[1]

The image is not altogether misleading. Worcester played a towering role in the first fourteen years of America's colonial experience in the Philippines. Already an acknowledged authority on the islands, he arrived as a member of the Schurman Commission shortly after the outbreak of fighting in 1899, and, with one brief exception, remained a senior official of the insular government until the advent of the Wilson Administration in 1913. Apart from education, transportation, and the original modification of Philippine legal codes, Worcester had responsibility for every key program of the American civil government. Public health, public lands, agriculture (until 1910), ethnic and religious minorities, forestry, mining, fisheries, and even government laboratories and the implementation of the American Pure Food and Drug Act fell under his authority. Worcester himself liked to say that these included most of the flash points in relations between the American government and the Filipino people. They were also the fields that offered Americans some of their most promising opportunities to make good the rhetoric of progressive imperialism and contribute to the health, happiness, and prosperity of the Filipino people. For an evaluation of the imperial legacy in the Philippines, Dean C. Worcester may be the most important American of all.

Worcester was right in emphasizing the controversial character of his career, but misleading in attributing this to the nature of the work itself. Much of his reputation both then and now has centered upon his volcanic personality. Testy, truculent—gratuitously outspoken, but also a master of intrigue—Worcester seemed always to be fighting someone. Even his characteristic figures of speech bespoke a sense of struggle, competition, and ultimately anxiety.[2] His contempt for the competence and aspirations of Filipino nationalist leaders has become legendary; what is less well known is that he was equally scathing toward many of the Americans in the islands. In a government ostensibly dedicated to attracting and winning the cooperation of Filipinos, and in the midst of a white colonial society whose favorite idiom was "to play the game," Worcester stood out as not only a powerful official but an "original," a rogue elephant endangering a precarious ecological balance.

His friends preferred a different metaphor. They called him, affectionately, "the Old Bear."[3] But even admirers wondered occasionally whether he was not "temperamentally unfit" for public office. The *Philippines Free Press,* in an editorial calling for his resignation, offered a balance sheet on the man: "Honest, earnest, well-meaning, and hard-working, he is nevertheless a stumbling block. Owing to his rough and unfortunate manner he walks with spiked boots over Filipino prejudices."[4]

Worcester's contributions to specific aspects of the Philippine-American encounter have been studied and appraised by others, including contributors to this volume, and idealized by Worcester himself in his 1914 book, *The Philippines Past and Present*. The man himself remains something of a mystery, however. What follows is an exploration of the personal meaning of Worcester's Philippine career.

THE ROOTS OF A PHILIPPINE CAREER

Dean Worcester was born 1 October 1866, in Thetford, Vermont, the son of a local physician whose New England roots dated to 1638. It was a family with a tradition of earnestness, willfulness, and commitment to public service. Several members had been clergymen; others had been literary figures or minor public officials. Dean's uncle, the missionary Samuel A. Worcester, won enduring fame by siding with the Cherokee Indians against Andrew Jackson and the State of Georgia—and going to jail rather than compromise his principles. Dean fit the family mold. A cousin, memorializing him for a family reunion in 1924, concluded: "It was facts and not suppositions that interested him. He was, perhaps, deficient in imagination and playfulness. These are Worcester deficiencies. Seriousness, rather, is our inheritance."[5]

Evidently the family was not affluent. Rather than apply to Dartmouth—12 miles away—or another New England private college, Dean saved money by attending the University of Michigan, where he had a relative. The choice of Michigan led Worcester ultimately to the Philippines and probably strengthened the habits of mind he had inherited from his family. The university was, at the time, self-consciously dedicated to the Germanic ideal of science, one of whose tenets was that the systematic accumulation of particulars would lead to the discovery of objective, verifiable Truth. Long fascinated with collecting and stuffing animals, Worcester gravitated to the zoology courses of Professor Joseph B. Steere and picked up, along with the new scientific attitude, Steere's excitement over the potential for both scholarship and adventure in uncivilized parts of the world. When Steere sought student volunteers to accompany him on a zoological expedition to the Philippines in 1887, Worcester borrowed the necessary money and took a year off to do so. After graduating in 1889, he and a colleague on the Steere expedition, Frank S. Bourns, obtained funding from a Minneapolis philanthropist and returned to the Philippines between 1890 and 1893. On the second expedition, he and Bourns traveled to parts of the Philippines seldom, if ever, before seen by an American.[6]

The second expedition launched Worcester on what might have become a career in biology. On the strength of the preliminary report (1894), he was appointed assistant professor of zoology and curator of the university museum in 1895. More important in the long run, the expedition established Worcester— and Bourns, had he cared to exploit it—as a unique American authority on the Philippines. Upon the outbreak of the Spanish-American War, he began a lengthy and profitable series of public lectures, produced articles on the islands for *The Independent* and *The Century,* and, in six weeks of intense work with the help of his sister, converted letters written to his family from the Philippines into a popular book, *The Philippine Islands and Their People.* [7]

The book foreshadowed the emphases of Worcester's later career. Juxtaposing the corruption, sloth, and decadence of the Spanish colonial regime against an extraordinary potential for agricultural and mining development, it suggested implicitly that progress and profit could go hand in hand: "Should the islands come under the control of some progressive nation, great opportunities will open before the capitalist who has patience and enterprise." Of the Filipino people, there was only a fragmented picture: "There are more than eighty distinct tribes, each with its own peculiarities. They are scattered over hundreds of islands." Yet, already, Worcester was sure that the real Filipinos were the minority uncompromised by regular contact with Spain. "One who would really learn to know something of the country and its people," he informed his readers, "must . . . leave cities and towns behind, and turning from the beaten path, push into the almost unexplored regions where the wild tribes are to be found."[8]

This notoriety brought Worcester to the attention of the federal government, which was then seeking advisors on Philippine matters. In the apparent absence of other Americans who knew the archipelago outside its cities and commercial regions,

Worcester was a natural. Moreover, he was beginning already his lasting practice of using his knowledge of the back country to overawe others. Having obtained an interview with President McKinley, ostensibly to alert him to the nation's special responsibility to care for the primitive people on the Philippine frontier, Worcester peppered the President with questions designed to show his own mastery of Philippine geography. What, he asked, would be American policy toward the "Calamianes Islands? In Palawan? In Tawi Tawi? In Sulu? In Basilan and Mindanao? In the Tablas-Romblon-Sibuyan group?" McKinley, one recalls, liked to say that, at the time of Dewey's victory, he could not have come within two thousand miles of the whole archipelago on a globe! Already committed to retaining the Philippines, he must also have been impressed with Worcester's sympathetic political views. "Insurgent leaders:" reads one of Worcester's questions for the President, "To what extent if at all have we been already compromised?" [9] So striking was Worcester's performance, in fact, that the President's initial response was to make him his own personal representative in the Islands. After time for reflection, he settled for appointing the young biologist one of the five members of an investigatory mission to be sent to the archipelago under the leadership of the President of Cornell University, Jacob Gould Schurman.

Appointment to the Schurman Commission altered Worcester's life. From a struggling junior faculty member without advanced degree, he abruptly became a highly paid senior official of the United States government. With a starting salary of $15,000, complemented by endless perquisites ranging from military salutes and clothing allowances to reduced fares for the finest shipboard accommodations, he achieved overnight what might never have come to him in a full lifetime of academic work. Returning from the islands in November 1899, he launched still another profitable lecture series. [10]

This was not only upward mobility on a grand scale, but also salvation from a scientific career that had entered the doldrums. Worcester's expeditions to the Philippines had been dramatic, extroverted affairs—very physical and adventurous. By all accounts, he was good at this sort of thing. Returning to Ann Arbor, however, he retired to the world of the museum and the microscope. With his nervous, vigorous, combative temperament, Worcester can have had little relish for such work. Under the loose direction of the department chairman, Professor Jacob E. Reighard, he launched a microscopic study of the behavior of the centrosome in coregonus (a type of North American whitefish). "Tinkering away at the centrosome," was his own way of describing the study.

Evidently the work was going nowhere. In the summer of 1898, in the midst of lecturing and preparing his book, Worcester wrote to Reighard that he was "finishing up" the project.[11] Nevertheless, what he left behind when turning to Philippine affairs for good that winter was, in Reighard's term, merely "fragmentary." "For some reason," he wrote to Worcester, "we can make very little out of [the notes and slides]. . . . I can find no statement of the points that you proposed to make."[12] From the opposite side of the world, Worcester replied, largely conceding the point:

I . . . had thoroughly satisfied myself that [the centrosome] went through periodic variation in size. . . . Its fate during metakinesis I had not settled to my own entire satisfaction. . . . I think that the persistence of the centrosome as a cell organ might be settled for this material, but, as I said, did not settle it to my own satisfaction. . . . There was much to be done in the matter of cytoplasmic structure, formation of spindle and astro-spheres and the mechanics of cell division; but I had been working on centrosomes and chromosomes and had not done much with the other matter. . . . I had not satisfied myself as to the origin or fate of the centrosome during [maturation and fertilization]. . . .

The photographs were, I think, pretty good, but I was in a fair way to secure better ones. It always makes me sick when I think of the way that piece of work was left, and I might as well stop talking about it.[13]

Not the least abashed, however, a few years later Worcester wrote as Philippine Secretary of the Interior to offer Reighard a job as one of his subordinates, Chief of the Bureau of Fish and Fisheries. "I should very much like to see you out here," he wrote to his former chairman, "and if you were to come I believe you would promptly find yourself dealing with much weightier problems than any you are likely to encounter while you are in your present position."[14]

The financial and psychological rewards of his Philippine

career—along, of course, with the satisfaction of the work itself—
gave Worcester a unique commitment to the Islands. Almost
alone among senior American officials, he had no desire to use
the Philippines as a stepping stone to something else. William
Howard Taft, returning from Manila to the Cabinet and the
Presidency, had set the model in this respect; and almost all
Worcester's contemporaries, except the multi-millionaire W.
Cameron Forbes, pursued—often unsuccessfully—a small-scale
version of the same career line. Governor General James F.
Smith, for example, returned to a federal judiciary appointment;
Vice-Governor Newton W. Gilbert was angling in Indiana politics; Secretary of Commerce and Police Charles B. Elliott in-
trigued from Manila for a seat on the United States Supreme
Court. Except for Gilbert, all of them promptly left the Islands
when leaving office. Worcester not only took less leave of absence than he was entitled to—and much less than any of his
colleagues—he chose to remain in the Philippines as a businessman after leaving the government.[15]

A PLACE AT THE CENTER

Once in the Islands, Worcester built his Philippine career upon
two foundations: the creation of a secure base of power at the
center, on the governing Philippine Commission; and the definition of a territory, both geographically and figuratively, that
was his own. The position at the center grew out of Worcester's
decisive, unambiguous attitude toward both the Filipino people
and the ethical issue of conquest, his superior contacts and
sources of information, his affinity for self-dramatization, and
his mastery of intrigue.

Many Americans had ambivalent feelings about the prospect
of an insular empire, conquered by force. They had doubts as
to whether a republic could ethically and constitutionally incorporate others against their will, doubts as to the wisdom of adding to the "colored" population of the United States, doubts as
to the consequences of entering the strategic equation in East
Asia, even doubts that the Philippines could be a paying proposition economically. Above all, they faced unanswered questions

about the character, competence, and ethnic identity of the Filipinos.

For many of those sent to the Philippines, moreover, these uncertainties were intensified by the sense of remoteness and cultural shock induced by the long journey out to Manila: five or six days in a train crossing Canada, followed by twelve to fourteen days at sea on the barren, lifeless expanse of the North Pacific, and then the encounter with Asia, beginning in relatively Westernized Yokohama, deepening in Kobe and Nagasaki, where Westerners still drew a crowd of curious onlookers on the streets of the city, and finally coming to fulfillment as the ship steamed slowly up through the sea of mud to the anchorage at Woosung and disembarked even transient passengers in Shanghai. There the venturesome would strike out from the European city for a tour of the Chinese city, a scene, as Worcester put it, of "filth and degradation," of stench, crowds, disease, and dead bodies decomposing in the gutter. Jacob Gould Schurman, President of the first Philippine Commission, spent the entire tour with a handkerchief over his nose and still felt unwell two days later. After Shanghai came Hong Kong, citadel of British imperial power, its bay filled with warships and merchant vessels from every part of the world. Then the invariably turbulent crossing to Manila, when even seasoned sailors were often confined to bed, culminating in a slow progress up the bay into what was usually a steamy, thick haze gathered over the squat city on the muddy banks of the bay and the Pasig River.[16]

Worcester was spared the disorientation this experience caused in many others. He was, in a sense, going home: he had been there before, at a time when the voyage was more uncomfortable and Manila more alien. He had friends waiting for him, notably Frank Bourns, back in the Islands as an interpreter on the staff of General Francis V. Greene and shortly to undertake intelligence and liaison work with the Filipinos for both the Army and the Commission. And he had settled views about the Filipinos.

As a people, Worcester insisted, Filipinos were ignorant, impressionable children.[17] "Utterly incapable of believing in moderation," they had "wholly misunderstood" American

"forebearance" during the interregnum after the Spanish surrender of Manila. Seizing upon this, "ignorant natives, mere
military leaders, who had nothing to hope for under any rational
system of administration," had displaced the responsible conservative leaders of the islands and launched a "perfect reign of
terror" to coerce their own people. Becoming "insolent" toward the American occupation force in Manila, their followers
had then "provoked" hostilities, expecting to "drive our troops
into the sea." A product of mass ignorance cynically manipulated by the ambitious, this was also a tribal aberration with
few, if any, roots outside the Tagalog provinces of Central Luzon. Even though their heads were "filled with the most incred-
ible and preposterous lies," ordinary Filipinos would welcome
Americans in "some of the northern and all of the southern
provinces of this island [Luzon] today, while from various parts
of the Visayan group word comes that they are looking forward
to our coming as they do to heaven." First, however, the back
of the "insurrection" would have to be broken: "Nothing but a
smashing defeat will bring these people to their senses." General
Elwell S. Otis, the American commander, seemed to Worcester
"if anything, *too* [*sic*] humane to cope with a situation like
this . . . he hates to kill a man or burn a house, even as a military
necessity."[18]

Worcester's confidence arose not only from his experience in
the past and his initial observations upon returning in February
1899, but from the briefings given him by Frank Bourns. As
early as August 1898, Bourns had concluded that the insurgent
army was little more than a rabble bent upon looting Manila.
Regarding Filipinos as irresponsible children, he blamed their increasingly hostile behavior upon their leaders. These he subsequently identified as a small group of rootless, middle-class men
on the make, an unscrupulous and unrepresentative group, manipulating the emotions of the masses. "If their chiefs could be
disposed of," he wrote, "there would be little trouble with the
masses of the people." This superficial analysis, along with
Bourns's view that the Filipinos had provoked the hostilities
the following February, complemented Worcester's own views;
and he took it over as his own. "If we could get rid of half a

dozen men," he announced within weeks of his arrival, "the bottom would drop out of the whole affair in a fortnight."[19]

The Worcester-Bourns analysis, whatever its shortcomings, was clear and unambiguous; it provided the sort of imagery that could motivate Americans to fight a war or govern an empire. It also offered a neat solution to the problem of the Filipino elite. In Manila and other parts of the archipelago, Americans were encountering a number of highly accomplished Filipino professional men and landowners. Schurman, for one, thought some of them quite impressive. It was hard to sustain the argument that Filipinos were incompetent to govern themselves in the face of such human evidence. The Worcester-Bourns analysis, however, defined such people as aberrational. For one thing, the very existence of the sort of revolution described by Bourns and Worcester demonstrated that the conservative elite did not control political society. Even more important, the "real" Filipinos lived in the back country. Seen in this light, Schurman's efforts to identify competent provincial leaders was a sign of his superficiality. "He is doing exactly what [sic] was supposed he would and looking for capable Philippine statesmen," Bourns wrote scornfully, "and what is more, he is finding them in abundance in all the towns." When the semi-autonomous government established in Negros by a group of the "best" Filipinos, acting with American approval, subsequently collapsed, Worcester was actually pleased. It proved conclusively, he said, that Filipinos needed American supervision.[20]

The concomitant of this appraisal of the Filipinos was Worcester's strong emotional affinity for fighting and for the American military. The formal panoply of power thrilled him, whether it was the spectacle of British naval power at Hong Kong or the advance of a formal line of American troops on the attack. Like Congressmen trooping out to Manassas, he and his friends would hurry out from Manila at the prospect of action to see the fight. Sometimes this civilian demand was so great that the American military could not satisfy it: "Otis always hates to begin a fight," Worcester lamented.[21]

Even before the turn to guerrilla tactics and the spread of atrocities, however, the Philippine-American War was a hard struggle to celebrate. Worcester understood why. Untrained in modern warfare and unfamiliar with the sighting mechanism on modern rifles, Filipinos fought bravely but ineffectively. Usually they shot much too high. American troops, often advancing in parade-like order, suffered few casualties; while Worcester and his friends, watching from a church tower, were sometimes in danger of losing their lives. "The insurgents have a most remarkable faculty for shooting high," he wrote to his wife. "Had they known how to shoot, the attacking force would have been simply annihilated." Yet the picture-book aspect of the war was part of what fascinated him. "That advance," he wrote of one such maneuver, "was the finest thing I ever saw, or expect to see." "Nothing will stop these men of ours. They have no idea of going any way but forward, and are ready to do it whenever asked, against any sort of fire." Whatever the reason, he was forever underlining his repeated injunction to "hit them *hard*."[22]

Knowledgeable, decisive, emotionally attuned to the conquest of the islands, Worcester, with the help of Bourns, came to dominate the Schurman Commission.[23] He did so by outmaneuvering Schurman and co-opting two of the remaining four members. General Otis, the military governor of the Islands, was too powerful and erratic ever to be taken for granted; but Worcester had special access to him through Bourns, who was his chief intelligence and liaison man with the Filipinos. Recognizing Otis's resentment toward the Commission and his irritation at the demands it made upon his time, Worcester and Bourns hit upon the tactic of isolating the General in his military role. While defending his prosecution of the war both in public and in the Commission,[24] they simultaneously worked to define areas of exclusive civilian control. The culmination of their efforts was a proposal to establish a wholly civilian government in regions already pacified. This two-track proposal piqued the General's pride, since it would have meant the elimination or reduction of his role as military governor; but, increasingly harassed by the problems of the war and out of sympathy with the efforts of Schurman to arrange an early truce and devolve authority upon Filipinos, he succumbed to Worcester's tactics. Although testy and unreliable wherever his own prerogatives were involved, Otis became a sure ally in the struggle for power within the Commission. By June, he and Worcester had become "chummy" and were trading "secrets."[25] Colonel Charles Denby, former United States Minister to China and a pompous, aging nonentity in his own right, fell into line more easily. Emotionally attuned to Worcester's black-and-white judgments, his affinity for the military, and his view of the "oriental mind," Denby allowed himself to be seduced by Worcester's personal attentions. Worcester was the only high-ranking American in Manila who took the old man at all seriously. Since Admiral George Dewey seldom attended the Commission, this left the nominal President, Schurman, in a minority of one.[26]

While undercutting Schurman, Worcester was simultaneously reaching out to cultivate allies of his own among the conservative Filipino elite. Worcester's argument with Schurman—to the extent that it was substantive and not merely a power struggle—was not over the need for Filipino collaborators, but rather over the identity of those collaborators and how much to give them. Building upon Bourns's spy network, Worcester quickly got in touch with a group of highly hispanized landlords and professional men who held the Aguinaldo government and the mass of the Filipinos in much the same disdain as he did. T. H. Pardo de Tavera, Benito Legarda, and Felipe Calderón, among others, had left Aguinaldo's government over issues of policy and personal ambition. Having alienated the revolutionary leadership, they had little choice but to seek protection and power through the Americans. Some of these men inspired genuine respect in Worcester. Cayetano S. Arellano, for example, he found "absoluely honest . . . universally admitted to be the brightest native or mestizo in the islands." Others, such as Calderón, were merely allies of expediency.[27]

Having such allies was, at best, a mixed blessing. All of them wanted to influence American policy and ride their American connection to positions of power in the new colonial government. Some, such as Pardo de Tavera, quickly involved Worcester in their personal feuds.[28] On balance, however, they were an asset in deepening his reputation as an expert on the Philippines. Appointed to the Second, or Taft, Philippine Commission in 1900 after the disbanding of the Schurman Commission,

Worcester cited "my old Filipino friends" along with his knowledge of Manila and the Spanish language as factors making him particularly valuable to the new Commission. The relationship had a characteristically Filipino element of reciprocity. All the original Filipino appointments to the Taft Commission—Pardo, Legarda, and Jose R. de Luzuriaga—were, as Worcester put it, "intimate friends of mine."[29]

A PLACE OF HIS OWN

It was generally agreed that Worcester was not a good administrator. Intensely personalistic, he trusted his friends and lieutenants too much, everyone else too little. Morever, his interest in projects was mercurial. A creative man, he conceived many useful undertakings, only to neglect them until a crisis arose. The government's work in public health affords an example of this. No one surpassed Worcester in mobilizing the resources of the government to fight an epidemic or clean up questionable practices in the Philippine General Hospital; but, between these crusades, disease and scandal alike germinated without much interference from him.[30] The tribal peoples—or, as they were called at the time, non-Christian peoples—and the territories in which they lived were the one striking exception to this. Not everyone agreed that the tribal peoples deserved the attention Worcester lavished upon them: Governor General Forbes removed agriculture from the Department of the Interior in order, as he said, to place it under a secretary "without distracting hobbies."[31] For better or for worse, however, this was the work to which Worcester gave his heart. In 1912 and 1913, as the Taft era drew to a close, both he and many of his critics suggested that he retire from Interior to a new and smaller position with exclusive, full-time responsibility for the tribal peoples.[32]

The back country of the Philippines genuinely fascinated Worcester. Interesting, exciting, often extravagantly beautiful, the country and the people contrasted happily with his image of the hybrid culture of Manila. This was so from the very beginning. The rural passages of his 1898 book—based, one recalls, upon actual letters written during his zoological expeditions—have a naive sense of exhilaration, risk, and discovery, whereas the pervasive imagery in the sections on Manila and the Spanish regime is that of decay, corruption, and sloth. The Filipino people interested Worcester in the back country: His descriptions of them are colorful—perhaps inventively so—and show a range of human emotions. In Manila, the Filipinos in his pages are background, the chorus in a poor opera, noted but not clearly perceived.

This orientation extended even to parts of the Islands Worcester had not seen; it was more than just the parochialism of a man who had been someplace unusual. Invited to give a lecture under the auspices of the National Geographic Society in 1899, he ferreted out "a Spanish monograph on the manners and customs of many of the wild tribes with which I never came in contact," and asked permission to give two lectures, the first devoted entirely to "the pagan tribes" and the second to the Christians and Muslims comprising 95 percent of the population.[33]

The authenticity of Worcester's attraction to the back country and the tribal peoples was continually evident throughout his Philippine career in the freshness and vigor of even his private comments upon them. The journal he kept with the help of James LeRoy in part of 1900 and 1901, for example, is a tissue of repetitious—and often brief and sarcastic—comments on his dealings with both Filipinos and Americans over the major issues of the period. It is broken, however, on 27 January 1901, by a detailed, scrupulously objective nine-page account of a visit to a Negrito fiesta in Bataan that clearly absorbed Worcester. Culturally, ethnologically, even biologically, such encounters symbolized to him a health and integrity lacking in the rest of his surroundings. "There are no mosquitos nor white ants," he wrote of his original viewing of Benguet. "Malarial fever is unknown, and persons suffering from the diseases peculiar to the tropics promptly recover under the stimulating influence of the climate. . . . The country is perfectly beautiful. . . . The Igorrotes, or natives of Benguet are savages, but they are perfectly harmless and peaceful, and they are furthermore honest and truthful, which is more than can be said of their civilized neighbors in the lowlands."[34]

The tribal people had another appeal, as well. They were, in a political—but obviously not anthropological—sense, *tabulae rasae*. Condemn the Spaniards as one might, it was still true that they and the Filipinos and Chinese of their era had left a powerful imprint upon the organization of lowland society. This greatly reduced Americans' ability to make an original and creative impact, whether economic, political, or cultural. Nothing epitomizes this more clearly than the dependence of the imperial regime upon Filipino collaborators such as Pardo de Tavera in the early period and Manuel Quezon and Sergio Osmeña after 1907.[35] The political and economic organization of the tribal peoples, on the other hand, was so weak and inappropriate to modern life as to give Americans something approaching carte blanche. That their homelands happened to be regions thought to be rich in mineral wealth and agricultural potential added a profit motive to the psychological rewards of power and initiative.

Worcester's contributions to peace and order, health, education, and ease of communication and transportation in Mountain Province and parts of Mindanao, Mindoro, and Palawan are well known.[36] So is the story of the successful business career he and some of his former lieutenants enjoyed in these regions after leaving the government. Notable in themselves, these achievements became positively heroic as recounted by Worcester. The motif was invariably the same, one of vision, endurance, and raw courage: Worcester, the "white Apo," dominating both the savage little "wild men" and the brutal, dramatically beautiful terrain. Worcester the superman of the mountains, both stronger and wiser than any other white.[37]

Worcester relished this role and the special kind of recognition it brought him. Actually called *apo*—or sometimes, to distinguish him from other colonial officials on the frontier, "the Big Apo from Manila"—by the tribal people, he preferred to translate this as "god" rather than "ancestor," its literal meaning. By the final years of his career in government, he was spending almost as much time on tour in the non-Christian provinces as in Manila. So awesome had his authority become, that even men on the spot in remote corners of Mindanao or Mountain Province wrote to him in Manila or Baguio for advice on the particulars of their own region or people. "If you put up a good stiff fight for what is really right," Worcester wrote to his successor in Mindanao and Sulu, ". . . you can make a name for yourself which will endure . . . win lasting fame, and gain the love, devotion, and loyalty of a very interesting group of backward peoples who know mighty little of laws, and still less of politics, but have no difficulty whatever in sizing up individuals."[38]

"The truth is," he said, on another occasion, "that in spite of hardships and dangers the work for the wild man gets a strangely firm grip on us."[39] And so, one might add, did he upon it. Worcester seems to have had a powerful sense of territoriality. Although physically courageous, he was easily threatened emotionally and intellectually. He was a man who needed lots of space, clear boundaries, and unchallenged authority within his sphere. We have noted already his discomfort with ambiguity, his black-and-white judgments, his reluctance to draw meaning from the particulars of his scientific scholarship, his drive to dominate the Schurman Commission and bend it to his own will. It is a reasonable inference that his endless truculence was at least partially defensive. The "wild men" and their country provided Worcester with the space he needed, and he made it his own. Although he liked to claim that the work was his by default—"this work, of which no one but myself knows or seems to care very much"[40]—he fought with bitter intensity to keep other parts of the government out of his terrain. (Ronald Edgerton recounts one such instance on pages 178-181.) Alongside the motif of endurance and courage within his domain, he created another motif of eternal vigilance along its borders. In defense of the "wild men" and of sound policy, he struggled successfully to subordinate the Constabulary within "his" provinces, and to keep out the United States Army, the Philippine Assembly, and ordinary hispanized lowland Filipinos.[41]

THE VENDETTA AS AN INSTRUMENT OF POWER

When Worcester fought someone, he usually won. This was so partly because a lot of reckless charges were made against him. An irascible man in a sensitive post, he made a deceptively easy target for critics of the American regime. As many learned to their sorrow, however, there were no cheap gains to be won by attacking him. An American Congressman who had accused him of maladministration bordering upon land fraud had to eat his words; a Filipino newspaper, *El Renacimiento,* which rashly impugned his integrity, was silenced by the libel suit he brought in response. The fact is that Worcester liked to fight and was good at it. This was one of his bonds with the tribesmen of northern Luzon, who, laying down their spears at the end of a battle, would sometimes say to their opponents, with satisfaction, "We had a good fight."[42]

An effective polemicist and a punishing infighter, he characteristically overwhelmed his opponents with volumes of densely factual argumentation, and continued to press the attack long after everyone else had been exhausted or had lost interest. Even bureaucrats shrank before the onslaught, the sheer weight of paper. Contemplating one of his lengthy rejoinders, accompanied by seventy pages of "exhibits" running back over seven years of charge and countercharge with one of his subordinates, the Chief of the Bureau of Insular Affairs recommended capitulation as the only way to staunch the flow of words. Worcester, he concluded, "has taken what is usually considered a woman's privilege—the last word."[43]

No one can fault a man for documenting his case. In retrospect, however, one of the striking aspects of a typical Worcester brief is the ancillary or irrelevant character of much of its contents. Worcester tended to fight line by line and word by word, often filling pages over remarkably small and petty matters that by themselves did not greatly advance his case. Often he digressed at great length and questionable relevance. For whatever reason, the bulk of the supporting evidence was usually spun out by reproducing the complete written record on the question, including even the perfunctory endorsements of officials through whom documents were sent. As a result, the whole of a Worcester brief was generally less than the sum of its parts.

What gave Worcester his sting as an infighter was his use of *ad hominem* arguments and his liberal reliance upon red herrings. From the very beginning, Worcester had been privy to Frank Bourns's spy network and had used his access to secret information as a lever of power. When Bourns was assigned temporarily to the Visayas, Worcester even took over "all of his odd jobs." By 1901, sources were providing him directly with secret information about the Manila resistance and underworld.[44]

Somewhere along the line, Worcester started accumulating evidence and even unsubstantiated rumors that could be used to discredit other Americans and Filipinos in the government. An enormous quantity of it exists to this day in Volume XXI of the Worcester Philippine Collection at The University of Michigan Library. It extends from criticisms of the drinking and smoking habits of James H. Blount to reportage, speculation, and even plots concerned with the sex life of Manuel L. Quezon. A substantial amount of this information was evidently copied from government files—under whose authority one cannot tell; some of it was solicited from government employees in the field; some may have been volunteered by sources who thought Worcester would be interested.

Possession of such information gave Worcester extraordinary power, and he used it cunningly. Having established a reputation for knowing the worst about people, he could often bluff other people down simply by intimation or veiled allusion. This amounted to a kind of totemic power, a manipulation of mysteries to enhance his own authority and dominate others. Having completed a reasonable argument against Governor General Forbes's desire to appoint Dr. R. P. Strong Director of the Bureau of Science, for example, he added cryptically: "Altogether apart from this, however, there are other considerations, of which I assume that Mr. Forbes has no present knowledge, which in my opinion render Dr. Strong absolutely ineligible for this place and which would make it entirely out of the question for me to accept him as a bureau chief of the Department of the Interior."[45] Again, to relieve the pressure upon two of his lieutenants, he threatened the Governor, Treasurer and third member of the Provincial Board of Misamis with prosecution through "use of evidence which I held against *them*" [*sic*].[46] The use of innuendo and the absence of a specific charge made such tactics peculiarly vicious. A powerful and intriguing, if vague, insinuation was written into a man's official record; and he had no way to respond to it and clear his name.[47]

Worcester used his reputation knowingly, manipulating his public image to add to his power. Seeking to confirm malpractice charges against a government doctor who was a protégé of Forbes, he called in the young man and confronted him. "I had before me a somewhat formidable pile of documents, and as in connection with previous examinations of Dr. Gregg and others, I had held in my possession documents which gave me the 'dead wood' on each of them, I suppose he thought that I held documentary evidence against him in this connection, which was not the case. At all events under close examination he promptly and irrevocably committed himself, leaving me amazed, sick at heart, and utterly disgusted."[48]

Such bluffs worked only because, when called upon to play his cards, Worcester was often able to deliver. There was a striking incidence of sexual red herrings in his attacks upon Filipinos and lower-ranking Americans. One is not concerned, today, with the accuracy of the charges, but rather with the use made of them. Worcester had a way of using sexual charges to smear his enemies and to throw others off the track. A lengthy investigative memorandum on Quezon's alleged rape of a girl in Mindoro, for example, suggests no remedy or prosecution, but proceeds in a non sequitur to recommend Quezon's suspension as Governor of Tayabas, a different province, on other grounds altogether.[49] Worcester's report on the extremely embarrassing irregularities that had existed at the Philippine General Hospital for more than a year digresses in the middle into an enormously lengthy, captious, and detailed discussion of the discovery that a certain physician treated prostitutes. In both length and heat, the section on the billing of medical fees for prostitutes overwhelms the serious problems of maladministration—faulty food storage, dirty operating rooms, incompetent staff, unreliable ambulance service—affecting the whole hospital. All these reflected at least indirectly upon the Secretary of the Interior and his Director of Public Health.[50]

This tendency to argue by insinuation, red herrings, and character assassination is all the more notable because Worcester was not an inherently vengeful person. In the abstract, when issues were not personified in such a way as to challenge him directly, he could be as compassionate as the next man. Indeed, more compassionate than many. Denouncing vigorously the obligatory penalty imposed by the insular civil service upon government employees discovered ever to have committed a criminal act, he wrote to Governor General James F. Smith: "Shall a man, who at some stage of his career, and perhaps in his early youth, has been guilty of some act of folly or dishonesty be eternally damned . . . ? It would seem, from his attitude in this matter, that the Director of Civil Service must believe in a hell burning with fire and brimstone and rejoice over the torments of the damned! But let us not, in obedience to his wishes, endeavor to anticipate and supplement here below such provisions as may have been made for the future punishment of those who have been wicked. It is believed that this matter may safely be left in the hands of the Almighty."[51]

Worcester was a belligerent man, quick to take offense. An inner compulsion drove him first to seek power and then to defend it, inch by inch, word by word. He fought with relish, and, some said, unscrupulously, but never recklessly or with abandon. Considering himself beleaguered both by problems and by enemies, he perfected the vendetta as an instrument of power.

PERSONAE

Worcester seems always to have felt persecuted and beleaguered in his Philippine work. The magnitude of the self-imposed task before the Commission combined with the indifference or criticism of most Americans and Filipinos left him frustrated. Like a parent confronting ingratitude, a reformer in an unpopular cause, or—let us bring this closer to home—a scholar in a peripheral, little-known field, he had to rely upon his own inner sense of worth in the absence of support and recognition from others. The tension between this inner valuation and the indifference or hostility of others was difficult to reconcile. Worcester recognized the problem right from the start: "We can, I suppose, make up our minds in advance to all sorts of misrepresentation, criticism, and abuse. If we succeed in our undertaking, however, it will be something to have lived for." His initial response, as this statement suggests, was to invoke the psychology of deferred gratification and appeal to the verdict of history. "Probably no situation was ever more thoroughly misrepresented or misunderstood in the United States," he wrote in 1901. "We have been forced to face a good many difficult propositions which the world at large will know little or nothing about until the history of these times is written; but, in spite of these obstacles, we are winning out, and it is a thing well worth having had a hand in."[52]

This provided a serviceable explanation of the situation in which Worcester worked, but it did not account for his own special reputation as the most controversial of all American officials in the Philippines. To do that, Worcester constructed an extremely revealing public *persona.* Mistaking form for content, others emphasized the appearances, style, and symbolism surrounding him. To them, he was, in the imagery of the opening section of this study, the big man among a little people, the imperialistic modernizer, the rogue elephant. Worcester, on the other hand, called himself a "scapegoat" and a "skunk-skinner."

This was not Worcester's everyday image of himself, but rather his last line of defense: the imagery he invoked to explain himself and his plight in the crucial moments when it appeared that critics and enemies might succeed in ending his Philippine career. He used it in 1908, when William Howard Taft intimated that, despite Worcester's talent, he was expendable; and he used it again in an extraordinary, passionate defense of himself at a public meeting in Bontoc before Secretary of War Jacob M. Dickinson at the time of the friar land "scandals."[53] The argument, as he expressed it before Dickinson, was "that a very large portion of the work which, if successfully performed, necessarily brought personal unpopularity on the doer, has fallen to my lot." This included "the disagreeable duty of safeguarding the public health and maintaining an efficient quarantine" over the objections of inconvenienced entrepreneurs and "superstitious . . . profoundly ignorant" Filipinos; organizing the first modern scientific programs in the Islands over the opposition of know-nothings and tight-budget men; protecting the public forests against both waste and rapaciousness; defending the public lands against land-grabbers; administering the politically sensitive friar lands under conflicting pressures to dispose of the land and protect existing occupants; suppressing animal diseases; enforcing the pure food and drug laws; civilizing and bringing under effective government control "several hundred thousand head hunters in northern Luzon." Summarizing the whole catalogue for Taft, he concluded:

What with rinderpest, bubonic plague, cholera, smallpox, the concentration of lepers, the exercise of watchful care over the Sampaloc ladies, the necessity for constant intervention between the provincial and municipal officials and the *caciques* on the one hand and the wild people throughout the islands on the other, and last but by no means least, the ultimate responsibility for the administration of the Pure Food and Drug Act, I sometimes compare myself with that useful but unpopular animal mentioned in Holy Writ, the scapegoat, and feel that if I could but flee away to the *bosque* with a joyous populace in full pursuit, the simile would be complete.

What is remarkable about this picture in retrospect is that, far from having a monopoly on the odious work of the empire, Worcester had charge of most of the really creative programs of the early American period. If public health, science, the administration of the public lands and forests, and the work with tribal peoples were onerous, "unpleasant," and, by implication, controversial, it was largely because of Worcester himself. Where Forbes took a purely utilitarian task—the building and maintenance of roads—and infused it with romance and dynamism, and where all sorts of people took a very controversial and socially disruptive phenomenon—education—and made it the crowning symbol of American enlightened benevolence, Worcester took something everyone values—good health—and made it a bone of contention between the government and various of its constituencies. By the same token, he blew up the protection of tribal peoples into a symbol of confrontation between the tribes, the lowland Filipinos, and the American government, rather than simply a frontier phenomenon.

Perhaps the most revealing part of the whole image, however, is the picture of the scapegoat fleeing to the bosque with the population in hot pursuit. Because figuratively, at least, this is what Worcester did. It is difficult to avoid concluding that, by the last several years of his official career, he saw his position of power at the center primarily as a means to maintain his autonomy in the tribal regions. Faced with Taft's intimations of expendability in 1908 and the likelihood of President Wilson's removing him from the Commission in 1913, he actually suggested giving up the Department of the Interior, and retiring to Baguio, as he expressed it to Taft, "to spend my entire time in work for and among the non-Christian inhabitants of the Philippines at half my present salary."[54]

The reason for this disposition cannot have been either expediency or cowardice: Worcester was not a man to run away from a fight. One infers that, just as appointment to the Commission liberated him from a careerist backwater in academic biology, so the life of a "white Apo" in the back country of the Philippines liberated him psychologically from the constraints of political and bureaucratic society. There are abundant signs that Worcester found in his career among the tribal peoples something akin to what Walt Whitman once called a "free, original life"—a life of emotional authenticity and intellectual spontaneity. After leaving office, he upbraided his successor in the Moro provinces, Frank Carpenter, for having become something less—an administrator, negotiator, and tactician, rather than a creative man of action. By contrast, the imagery that Worcester preferred for himself was dynamic and sweepingly heroic. "Regions were penetrated," he said of his early explorations of northern Luzon, "where no white man had previously set foot." The man who only a few years before had been "tinkering away at the centrosome" wrote proudly to his former department chairman that he "had been making a long horseback trip of some 350 miles through a country inhabited by wild people."[55]

In the Philippines, Worcester found not only fame, power, and scope for his considerable talent and energy, but ultimately psychological sanction for a temperament difficult to encompass within institutions and conventions. The irony is that he had to fight his way to the outermost periphery of America's vastness in order to achieve this, and did so there in the most perilous and unformed social environment under American rule. Ever testing—and perhaps ever doubting—himself, Worcester had finally found a primal encounter that gave meaning to his life. "The wild man," he once said, "is as quick to detect any faltering on the part of the man who attempts to control him as is a vicious horse, and the results in both cases are much the same!"[56] The image of the big man among a small people is, therefore, much more complex than one might imagine. The "scapegoat" of the mediocrities and the politicans found a better identity on the frontier of civilization among the headhunters of northern Luzon and the unspoiled, "natural" men of the back country everywhere. As he rashly wrote in a draft of his annual report for 1911—subsequently expurgated by more politic officials—*his* natives said, "The Voice of Worcester is the Voice of God."[57]

CHAPTER SIX

Protestant Missionaries and American Colonialism in the Philippines, 1899-1916: Attitudes, Perceptions, Involvement

KENTON J. CLYMER

When the United States wrested the Philippines from Spain, sizeable numbers of Americans found their way to the Islands. Some, such as Dean C. Worcester, found fulfillment there as high-ranking government officials. Others made money, or attempted to, as cowboys in Mindanao or as merchants in Manila. And some came to bring the True Religion and make the society pure. They shared much. All saw themselves as pioneers on an exciting, but dangerous, frontier. To some degree they all tried to be "civilizers." They supported the American decision to take the Islands and resisted nationalist designs to weaken American control. The missionaries alone tried to serve as the conscience of the American experiment.

In one sense, the missionaries who went to the Philippines were part of a crusade that had begun some years before to "evangelize the world in a single generation." Their activities in the Islands are part of a nearly global phenomenon. But the Philippines was *American* overseas territory, and newly acquired territory at that. Thus, the missionaries' activities became equally a part of American nationalism and imperial history. A study of their thought helps define the colonial mentality. In this essay, Professor Kenton J. Clymer of the University of Texas at El Paso explores the attitudes and perceptions of the first generation of Protestant missionaries as they related to the American colonial government. He finds that the missionary community was not monolithic, that on some matters it was deeply divided. On balance, however, the missionaries supported the general direction of American policy, while not hesitating to criticize the government vigorously, particularly on moral issues. Their criticism was seldom anti-imperialist in nature, however, for they sought to purify American rule, not end it.

A modified version of this essay will appear in Clymer's forthcoming book, *Protestant Missionaries in the Philippines, 1898–1916* (Urbana, University of Illinois Press).

Among the Americans who ventured to the Philippine Islands in the early years of the American occupation were Protestant missionaries. By 1905 several main-line denominations—Presbyterian (U.S.A.), Methodist-Episcopal, American Baptist, Christian and Missionary Alliance, Christian (Disciples of Christ), Episcopalian, and United Brethren—had established missions. In addition, a small holiness group, the Peniel mission, operated in Zamboanga, staffed by an Apache Indian and a Swede; the Seventh-day Adventists arrived in 1905 and established a permanent mission in 1908. The Free Methodists had one unofficial missionary couple in the islands for a few years, and there were perhaps some Mormons and Christian Scientists working unofficially.[1] Allied organizations, such as the American Bible Society and its British counterpart, were also active, as was the Young Men's Christian Association. Initially the "Y" worked mostly among American servicemen and civilians.

Studies of the missionaries can help elucidate the Phil-American experience from various perspectives. Many of them left extensive records which cast light not only on theological matters but on Phil-American society and government.[2] Nor were the missionaries without influence on the American government and Philippine society. At a time in American history when the missionary movement. attracted considerable support and enthusiasm, even from Presidents like William McKinley and Woodrow Wilson, colonial administrators could not well afford to ignore religious opinion. Governor William Howard Taft, in fact, cultivated missionary leaders in the Philippines. The impact of the missionaries on the Philippines directly is less easy to assess. Only about 3 percent of the present-day population traces its religious roots to the Protestant missionaries, but it is a commonplace belief that Protestants have had considerably more influence at many levels of society than their numbers would suggest.[3] Some observers credit Protestantism with raising the moral tenor of Philippine society, fostering a respect for law and education, and inculcating such "Protestant" values as frugality and social equality. It has even been claimed that Protestantism increased respect for women, the family, and the elderly. But objective studies are scarce.[4]

Just how much lasting influence the missionaries had deserves further investigation. What can be said with some assurance now, however, is that most missionaries of the first generation welcomed the American occupation; supported the American purpose (or at least what they perceived that purpose to be); attempted to influence governmental decisions in order to purify, but not to reduce, America's paternalism; used their influence to infuse American ideals; and tried to reconcile Filipinos to American oversight. They were, in a real sense, allies of the government in what both perceived as a "civilizing" mission.

PROVIDENTIAL EXPANSION

Missionary expansion to the Philippines was part of the larger missionary outburst in the late nineteenth century which, in turn, had its roots in the evangelical revivals of Dwight Moody, John R. Mott, and others. Its objective was to evangelize the world in a single generation. A missionary who embarked for Manila or the provinces was not, therefore, ipso facto, an agent of the national purpose. At least one described himself as an anti-imperialist, and others were indifferent to the secular authorities.[5] Applicants for a missionary position who were ultimately sent to the Philippines often listed the Islands as only one of several preferences.

But, ever since the Civil War, most Protestants had identified the survival and expansion of the United States with the divine plan. "God cannot afford to do without America," a Methodist

Episcopal bishop told a large crowd in 1864.[6] Increasingly, Protestants believed that American-style democracy required an evangelical base. "The August Ruler of all the nations," said the president of Wesleyan University in 1876, "designed the United States of America as the grand repository and evangelist of civil liberty and of pure religious faith. And," he added, "the two are one."[7] Such sentiments were commonplace. As a group of Methodists advised President McKinley a quarter of a century later, "Civil liberty is really found only under the shadow of the evangelistic gospel."[8]

Ideological compatibility between church and state found practical expression in missionary efforts to further the national purpose and in the close relations that many of the missions enjoyed with the government. As early as the 1830s, missionaries in the Oregon country served the nation as well as the church, a fact that caused William A. Slacum, an official emissary from the President, to do what he could to fortify the Oregon missions.[9] Perhaps the closest ties between the missions and the state occurred in 1872 when President Ulysses S. Grant, in a move designed to eliminate corruption and provide more efficient management, entrusted administration of the Indian reservations to the various mission boards.[10] Later in the same decade, Mrs. Rutherford B. Hayes, wife of the President, accepted the presidency of the Methodist Women's Home Missionary Society.[11]

Given the strong belief in the godliness of American institutions, most evangelical Protestant clergymen and many laypersons viewed American territorial expansion in 1898 as divinely inspired. "God has given into our hands, that is, into the hands of American Christians, the Philippine Islands," the Presbyterian General Assembly affirmed only two weeks after Commodore Dewey's victory at Manila Bay. "By the very guns of our battleships," the statement continued, God "summoned us to go up and possess the land."[12]

Though there were dissenters, the large majority of first-generation missionaries in the Philippines accepted the providential viewpoint and rejoiced in America's new imperial destiny. If some missionary applicants listed the Philippines as only one of several preferences for their assignment, others chose to go to the Islands because they were now in American hands. Several missionaries already established in foreign stations when the Philippines were acquired requested transfers to the Islands,[13] for here was a chance for the purest religion (evangelical Protestantism) to join hands with the most Christian of states (the United States) in carrying out the plan of Providence. One woman missionary, for example, was "thrilled" when her ship dropped anchor in Manila Bay, "not because it was my first touch with eastern life, for I had been in many other eastern cities, but because it was my first experience of this kind of life under the Stars and Stripes. I had lived many years in Burma under the British flag," she explained, "and now I was to learn what American rule would do for this branch of the Malaysian race in the Philippines."[14]

So strongly did most missionaries support the American purpose that, like their counterparts in the United States, there was an almost incestuous quality to their thought. Presbyterian James B. Rodgers joined Methodist Missionary Bishop William F. Oldham in appealing for funds "to serve God and the fatherland."[15] Episcopalian Bishop Charles Henry Brent advised Governor Taft that his only motive in going to the Philippines was "to serve the nation and the kingdom of righteousness."[16] Brent even insisted that Episcopalians build dignified edifices and use good equipment because Filipinos "estimated the value of the State through the Church."[17] Homer C. Stuntz, a prominent Methodist, thought that the interdenominational college he was attempting to found would "be a desirable ally of the Government,"[18] while Bruce Kershner cautioned his fellow Disciples missionaries to measure carefully the ramifications before criticizing the government, lest they foster revolution.[19] From such perspectives, not only was the national role to be a Christian one, but the mission's role was to be national in orientation. Few would have contested the chairman of the Presbyterian church's standing committee on foreign missions, when he reminded missionaries in the Philippines that "patriotic loyalty is a cardinal tenet of American Protestantism."[20]

In any event, most missionaries in the Philippines assumed, as a Baptist expressed it, that "the purpose and attitude of our country is absolutely altruistic." They also expected the government to be paternalistic, for, like most Americans of the age, including the most respected social scientists, the missionaries by and large believed that Filipinos and most other non-Anglo-Saxon peoples were culturally, and perhaps racially, deficient and incapable of governing themselves. [21]

One reason for the backwardness of Philippine society, according to the missionaries, was that Spain had done little in her occupation of three centuries to uplift her wards. The brightness and quickness of Filipino children faded as they became older, observed a Presbyterian missionary physician, a fact he ascribed not so much to inherent racial incapacities as to poor Spanish tutelage. "Let them learn under proper conditions and teachers that they are men," he wrote, "and they will in time come to be a nation as capable of self government as the Japanese." [22]

Not only had Spain failed to introduce modern educational, political, and social systems, the missionaries felt, but she had supported a venal, degraded, and politically grasping ecclesiastical establishment that had Christianized the populace in only the most nominal sense. As Methodist Bishop James M. Thoburn wrote several years *before* the American occupation, "These [Philippine] islands present as needy a field for [Protestant] missionary effort as any of those farther south, where Christianity is wholly unknown." [23] Extreme denunciations of Spain's shortcomings may well betray a certain defensiveness about Protestant missionary activity in an already Christian land, and in their more reflective moments thoughtful missionaries credited Spain with introducing important religious truths. But even the most balanced assessments agreed that Spanish Catholicism had weaknesses sufficiently profound to justify a Protestant presence in Spain's former colony. [24]

THE GOVERNMENT AND THE WHITE MAN'S BURDEN: MILITARY CONQUEST

Given the deficiencies of Philippine society, the missionaries believed it was America's obligation to bear what Rudyard Kipling termed "the white man's burden." Just precisely what they expected the government to do was variously, and often vaguely, expressed. But, in general, Philippine culture was to be upgraded by infusing American material and spiritual values and by bringing to the islanders American political and economic concepts and arrangements.

There was a surprisingly strong cautionary note, however. Though not opposed to American rule, some missionaries feared that an unselective and rapid infusion of Western influences might overwhelm and demoralize Philippine society, particularly the mountain people who had had the least contact with the outside world. The popular view that civilization had a regenerating effect on culturally underdeveloped people was illusory, thought the *Philippine Presbyterian*.[25] The Episcopalians, who carried on a significant ministry in the mountains of Luzon and Mindanao, were the most sensitive to the dangers that "civilization" posed. A trip across Mindanao in 1904 led Bishop Brent to comment, "One fears for them [the pagan groups of Mindanao] if, or when, they come under the influence of 'civilization.'" More than most missionaries, the Episcopalians distinguished between Christianity, on the one hand, and American (or Western) civilization, on the other. There was no need to interfere with most Igorot customs, wrote Walter C. Clapp. "Clothes are not the essence of Christianity."[26]

But, with the partial exception of those who were apprehensive about the threat civilization posed to indigenous cultures (and the exception *was* only partial),[27] most missionaries welcomed the government's efforts to change Philippine culture and values. Like other humanitarian imperialists, missionaries were sometimes overly sanguine about the possibilities of effecting meaningful societal transformation and blind to the consequences. But, like Kipling, few expected the effort to be easy or appreciated. The United States, wrote a Methodist missionary, should not expect "to enjoy the sweets of appreciated service"; instead it should "courageously bear the 'white man's burden.'"[28]

One of the difficulties the United States encountered from "unappreciative" Filipinos was armed resistance. Believers in the white man's burden were thus confronted with an immediate and bloody challenge. Yet, those missionaries who welcomed America's assumption of sovereignty, particularly those who believed that it was part of a providential design, could not logically object to the use of force, if necessary, to confirm that sovereignty.

There was, in fact, virtually no missionary opposition to the military purpose. A few extremists thought that God himself directed American operations during the conflict; others argued that America's wars had always been humanely inspired and the Philippine campaign was no different.[29] It was also comforting to think, as most missionaries did, that the resistance was composed of disorganized, marauding bands of common bandits.[30] Insurgent leaders, it was commonly said, were motivated chiefly by "personal ambitions for place and power" and did not enjoy much popular support.[31] Emilio Aguinaldo might be intelligent, wrote the secretary of the Presbyterian board after an extended visit to the Islands in 1901, but he was an "Oriental despot" whose rule, if allowed, would be as bloody as that of the Sultan of Turkey.[32]

Some missionaries, along with some civil and military officials, acknowledged that the resistance had widespread support and that the Filipino forces fought bravely and capably.[33] This view revealed that missionaries were not of one mind and embarrassed the government, which took great pains to deny the popular base of resistance. But varying assessments of the nature of the resistance did not produce differing recommendations, for the missionaries spoke with virtually one voice in saying that the resistance was misguided and must be crushed, regardless of the degree of popular support it enjoyed, so that American beneficence could proceed. "All that the governor, the commission, the school master, the civil judge, and the missionary are attempting," wrote Homer Stuntz in a widely read account, "would have been impossible without the work of the soldier."[34]

The propensity of most Americans (including missionaries) to characterize the armed conflict as an "insurrection" served further to disguise the nature of the Filipino resistance. The term "insurrection" implied an uprising against an already established American regime, which was correct, if at all, only in the Manila area. For the most part, the conflict was objectively an American war of conquest. Whether most missionaries who used the term "insurrection" consciously intended to misconstrue the nature of the resistance may be doubted. But Bishop Brent, at least, understood that "insurrection" had certain important connotations favorable to the American cause, for he once chastised the English writer John Foreman for referring to the "war" in the Philippines rather than to the "insurrection."[35]

The issue of American atrocities during the war troubled the missionaries. Early in 1902, a Baptist in Panay complained, without results, to military authorities that American soldiers had killed a number of innocent people.[36] But that was exceptional. The more common view was that isolated acts of cruelty were unfortunate but inevitable and should not distract attention from the generally praiseworthy conduct of the military. Few missionaries criticized the American version of the Spanish tactic of *reconcentracion,* the herding of civilians into secure enclosures in order to make the elimination of guerrillas easier;[37] and Zerah C. Collins of the Y.M.C.A. even defended the infamous General Jacob Smith, who ordered Samar turned into a "howling wilderness." When President Roosevelt retired the General, Collins surmised he had been punished for political reasons.[38]

Missionary refusal to take seriously the atrocity issue resulted, in part, from the fact that anti-imperialists, whom the missionaries cordially distrusted, made the atrocity question a central one in their critique of American imperialism. The missionaries were reluctant to give credence to anti-imperialist charges.[39]

What criticism there was of military policy tended to be that the army was not aggressive enough. Even those who rejected the optimistic picture painted by American authorities urged new and "vigorous measures."[40] All looked forward to the election of 1900, assuming that McKinley's Administration had restrained the military to benefit his candidacy. Once William Jennings Bryan, the anti-imperialist candidate, was defeated, reasoned Presbyterian J. Andrew Hall, "we look forward for all this to change." The authorities, Hall wrote approvingly, would no longer "be so lenient with those they catch as heretofore."[41] When in fact the President ordered a more vigorous policy after the election, the missionaries were pleased. The new policy "seems to be working like a charm," wrote one, "and the country is coming to its right mind."[42]

For similar reasons, the earliest missionaries deplored the so-called Bates Agreement (or Treaty) of 1899. That agreement, negotiated by General John C. Bates on behalf of the United States with the Sultan of Sulu, was irregular, but apparently legal. Though the agreement served the immediate purpose of neutralizing Muslim areas during the Philippine-American war,[43] it was widely condemned. James B. Rodgers found it "irritating to see the Sultan treated with so much deference for he is a villain," and he considered the agreement another example of the doubtful policy of conciliation. Even more opposed was John McKee of the Christian and Missionary Alliance who, ignoring provisions of the agreement that restricted the movement of Americans and, by implication, forbade proselytizing among the Muslims, preached in Sulu and other Muslim areas in 1900 and again in 1902. "God has laughed at such diplomacy," McKee concluded.[44]

Though the military must have considered missionaries like McKee a nuisance, good relations more normally prevailed.[45] Missionary reports and letters, for example, regularly included accounts of assistance from the military in such matters as housing, transportation, and communication. The Y.M.C.A. enjoyed the closest of relationships with military personnel, since it was a semi-official arm of the government. If "Y" materials are to be credited, in fact, military officers were unanimous in their enthusiastic support for the organization. But the missionaries of other agencies also received encouragement, as well as favors, from the military and in some instances accepted military advice on when and where to begin work. Some missionaries, in turn, offered advice on ways to increase the army's efficiency. In 1899, for example, Bishop James M. Thoburn, who was in Manila when the war commenced, urged the United States to follow the English colonial practice of enlisting indigenous people into the ranks.[46] James B. Rodgers, who arrived a few weeks later, interviewed and evaluated prisoners of war. It is difficult to disagree with a recent scholarly assessment, that "Rodgers was clearly working with the United States occupation forces;

he would have been termed by Marxists an instrument of imperialism."[47]

Just as the missionaries supported the military during the Philippine-American War, those with responsibilities in Mindanao applauded initial attempts to exert military control over the Muslims. For centuries, the various Muslim groups of the south had fiercely maintained a practical independence from Spain, and they were no more inclined to acknowledge American hegemony without a struggle. But, as the fighting became protracted and brutal (it lasted for more than a decade after the official end of the Philippine-American War),[48] Bishop Brent, who had admired the repressive policy of Military Governor Leonard Wood, at first demurred, and then openly attacked the American use of arms. "The Moro is still unsubdued," he said in October 1913, "and I say more honor to the Moro! We can go on with our oppressive measures to the end of time," he added, "but all we can effect is annihilation."[49] Brent's opposition, which was late in developing, was the only significant exception to missionary support of the military's combatant role.

THE GOVERNMENT AND THE WHITE MAN'S BURDEN: IMPROVING SOCIETY

Outside of Muslim areas, overt resistance to American arms had largely ended by the time President Roosevelt declared the "insurrection" at an end on 4 July 1902, and the civil government took over the bulk of the white man's burden. The missionaries applauded much that the government undertook. Improvement in public health and in public works attracted especially widespread favorable comment. The missionaries repeatedly remarked on the transformation of Manila under American rule. Under the Spanish, wrote a Seventh-day Adventist, the capital city "was indescribably filthy."[50] The change was apparent by 1904. When Fred Jansen, a Presbyterian, returned to the city that year after an extended absence, he could scarcely recognize it.[51] By 1909, one missionary insisted, Manila "was fast becoming one of the most attractive cities of the Orient," and two years later another claimed it was "one of the nicest and cleanest cities of the East."[52] Perhaps Methodist Bishop Henry Warren summed it up most colorfully. The Americans, the bishop wrote, found Manila "a pesthole, and made it a health resort."[53]

There were occasional discordant notes. A Y.M.C.A. official admitted that, "in a city where scores of thousands live in wretched nipa shacks on low, undrained land," there was too much truth in the observation that "many if not most of the splendid improvements that are being made in the Islands, are chiefly for the pleasure or advantage of the Americans and foreigners generally." But such criticisms were rare and confined to an occasional private letter—especially in the case of "Y" officials.[54] Most would unhesitatingly have agreed with a United Brethren spokesman that "the American Government is here doing a real missionary work on a very large scale."[55]

Although the missionaries thought the government's purpose deserved support, they sometimes encountered indifference, even hostility, from government officials who did not share their view that the interests of church and state were intermingled. Homer Stuntz recalled that American officials in Dagupan initially "cursed us, and expressed the wish that we would go away and never return."[56] A Presbyterian found that civil employees feared to identify themselves with Protestant causes for fear it would "hurt their prospects of promotion,"[57] while, as late as 1913, the leading Baptist missionary felt that government officials still considered missionaries "a pernicious element in the Philippines."[58] And there were numerous complaints that officials catered too much to the Roman Catholic hierarchy which was, by definition, opposed to Protestant missions.[59]

Among the important officials whom the Protestants viewed with suspicion was James F. Smith, a Catholic who served on the Philippine Commission from 1903 to 1909, including over two years as Governor General (1906-1909). They also found W. Cameron Forbes, who succeeded Smith as Governor General (1909-1913), less than cordial. Though Forbes respected Bishop Brent, served on the boards of some Episcopalian organizations, and contributed to the Y.M.C.A., he was contemptuous of most clergymen. Missionaries, he once wrote, were "usually the most grossly incompetent people that live."[60]

The official against whom the missionaries voiced their

strongest objections was the outspoken and arrogant Secretary of the Interior, Dean C. Worcester. When the Commissioner attempted to block Episcopalian efforts to purchase land in Bontoc for a mission station, missionary Walter C. Clapp could not contain his anger. Worcester, he wrote, was "a despot as merciless and malicious as one would expect to find in the Middle Ages," while Bishop Brent, agreeing with his subordinate, prepared a letter (left unsent) to his friend Theodore Roosevelt asking that the official be deposed.[61] If the missionaries disliked Worcester passionately, they could take comfort in the fact that they were not alone. The Secretary, wrote an official of the Manila Y.M.C.A., was "most cordially hated by his subordinates and Americans generally and . . . is almost universally execrated by Filipinos."[62]

On the other hand, government officials who encouraged mission work more than counterbalanced those who were critical. Expressions of encouragement ranged all the way from polite but meaningless gestures (Governor General Luke Wright once granted an interview to Seventh-day Adventists and flattered them by suggesting that, inasmuch as they took seriously the Biblical admonition to labor six days and rest on the seventh, they could do good service by teaching the Filipinos how to work),[63] to monetary contributions and active involvement in mission work. Especially in Mindanao were government officials solicitous. Peter G. Gowing's statement, that, "beyond the extension of a few courtesies, American governmental officials [in Mindanao] did not actively aid any Christian missionary activities,"[64] underestimates the encouragement and assistance rendered by the officials. Robert F. Black, the first Congregationalist to venture to the Islands, found officials in Mindanao eager to assist him. Black was permitted, for example, to travel on government ships after that privilege had been withdrawn from other civilians. "I hardly think I am going to compromise myself by accepting these favors," he wrote uneasily to his board. "What do you think?"[65]

Government assistance to Black was not merely a matter of courtesy, for officials saw value in his missionary activity. They encouraged Black and other American Board missionaries to expand their work. In 1911, Governor Henry Gilheuser of the

Davao district stated publicly that "the church is one of the strongest governmental agents that we have." The new Congregational chapel that the Governor was helping to dedicate constituted, he said floridly, "another stone in the wall of Americanism which is slowly but surely being built up around these Islands."[66] In 1915, Frank Carpenter, the popular Governor of the Department of Mindanao and Sulu (1914–1920), urged the Congregational missionaries to take charge of a government school in Mumungan (now Baloi), and a few days later he asked Frank C. Laubach to introduce athletics—"base-ball evangelism" Laubach termed it—to the Moros.[67]

Episcopalians, too, found officials on Mindanao eager for them to begin work. Both Leonard Wood, the Provincial Governor, and General George W. Davis, the supreme military commander in the Philippines, agreed that there was "great opportunity" for the Episcopalians on the island. From Zamboanga, a little later, the Episcopalian missionary in charge reported that Wood was "in thorough accord with & will back us in every way." Brent, in fact, was concerned that criticism would develop if it were generally known how candid governmental officials had been in their expressions of support. "This is not for publication or notice at all in print," he once cautioned his mission board, while relaying Wood's words of encouragement.[68]

Those officials who encouraged the establishment of Protestant missions were surely shrewder than those who were indifferent or hostile, for the missionaries were, at least in the short run, a force for reconciliation and conservatism.[69] No one understood better the value of the missions to the government than William Howard Taft.[70] As the first civil Governor of the Islands (1901–1903), Taft established lasting relationships with several Protestant missions. He traveled to the Islands in 1902 with Bishop Brent and later that year sought the Bishop's counsel when President Roosevelt offered him a seat on the Supreme Court.[71] The following year, shortly before he returned to the United States to become Secretary of War, Taft spent an hour with the Methodist leader Homer Stuntz, who had admired the Governor ever since his inaugural address,[72] and hammered out an agreement whereby missionaries could submit names to fill vacancies in the Phil-American government.[73] In future years the missionaries did not hesitate to communicate with Taft, and some became his staunch political supporters as well. [74]

If it is true that in India the British government did its best to inhibit the spread of Christianity and that "never at any time or in any way" did it "identify itself with the missionary cause," [75] the same was demonstrably not so with the American government in the Philippines.

CREATING THE NEW FILIPINO

Of all of the government's undertakings, none was so "missionary-like" as the massive educational effort. In other lands, in fact, a major portion of the missionary's time and resources was devoted to establishing and operating schools. Because, in the Philippines, the government assumed the task of education, the missionaries were left free to engage in other pursuits. This alone predisposed them to praise the schools. But to the missionaries the schools had important cultural advantages as well. To the evangelical Protestant mind of that age, the American public school held a significance far beyond its obvious educational and patriotic functions. Protestants might quarrel among themselves on a variety of issues, but they joined in support of the public school. Support of the public school was, in fact, an integral part of the Protestants' "strategy for a Christian American." Though the American school was officially secular, in practice Protestant values pervaded it. Nationalism and Protestantism were joined in the public school to produce, it was hoped, the highest form of Christian civilization. [76]

The missionaries had great hope, therefore, that the new public schools in the Philippines, modeled after the American school, would help create a new Philippine society free from superstition and outmoded styles of life. The New Filipino, like the American, would be democratic in inclination, questioning in mind, strong in body, and in general capable of contributing to the new society. His value structure would be American and, by implication, Protestant. The schools, wrote a Presbyterian, inculcated "American ideas" and created "a practical American spirit." Finally, he would be pro-American and would reject emotional calls for independence. "By the time they are really ready for independence," wrote Charles N. Magill, "they will not want it. I believe that they will then realize what an honor it is to be a part of the greatest nation in the world."[77]

One very important result of the school's effort to recast Philippine society, to the missionary mind, would be the liberation of the people from Roman Catholic authority, a goal of both religious and national importance, in their view. Frank C. Laubach stood quite literally alone in arguing that the public schools provided no opening at all for the Protestant message.[78] The rest insisted, fervently and often openly, that, as a Baptist missionary expressed it, "every public school can be counted an evangelical force in a Roman Catholic country."[79] By 1911, Methodist missionary Marvin Rader insisted that the public schools had "broken the hold Romanism has upon these students."[80] So frank were the missionaries about the value of the schools in the fight with Rome that government officials, had they read the missionary press, would have been sorely discomforted.

At the same time, the missionaries always feared that Catholics had, or threatened to have, too much influence in the educational system at all levels. As early as March 1899, James B. Rodgers observed that the Catholic church would "make desperate efforts to hold the schools in their power and try to perpetuate the old system,"[81] and throughout the period the missionaries remained ever vigilant. They often found evidence of Catholic efforts to influence educational policy; too often, they felt, the "Romanists" were succeeding. In 1903, Presbyterian missionaries noted the arrival of two Catholic teachers in Dumaguete and assumed that their appointment indicated increasing Catholic influence in high places.[82] The following year, a Baptist missionary in Panay felt that the government was pandering to the "Romanist party," while Methodist Harry Farmer, in Pangasinan province, reported that Catholic teachers and principals taught Catholic doctrines in the schoolroom, required students to attend Mass, and warned them not to listen to the Protestants.[83] In 1907, Homer Stuntz complained directly to President Roosevelt about the "rapid promotion of Roman Catholic teachers."[84] In 1908, a Disciples missionary felt that the Department of Education exhibited "a spirit of fear and subserviency to Roman Catholic opinion," while the following year an Alliance missionary reported that Jesuits had infiltrated the schools of Zamboanga.[85] Complaints of this sort never outweighed the positive aspects of the educational system, in the missionary mind, but, as late as 1915, when Frank Laubach dismissed the schools as essentially without value to the Protestant cause, he pointed to Catholic influence to support his argument.[86]

Some missionaries considered the efforts of educational administrators to remain absolutely neutral in religious affairs as evidence of hostility and/or Catholic influence. Protests of this nature were especially evident during 1901–1903 when Fred W. Atkinson was Secretary of Education. During the Atkinson period, missionaries complained, Protestant teachers and administrators were flatly forbidden to express their religious views, even outside the classroom;[87] if one Presbyterian report is to be credited, teachers could not even entertain a missionary in their homes, "even when there was no other place in the village where he might obtain boiled water and food free from cholera germs."[88] Reports of this sort led one missionary to refer to the "terrors of the Atkinson period" in one of his annual reports.[89]

The missionaries were gratified when David Prescott Barrows, a devout Protestant, succeeded Atkinson as Superintendent in 1903. But, in 1904, James F. Smith, a Catholic, became Secretary of Public Instruction. As Barrows's superior, Smith had ultimate responsibility for the Islands' educational system. A report that the Catholic church in the United States had condemned the unfortunate Smith's supervision of the Department of Education did little to lessen Protestant suspicions. "When dealing with tricky people it is well to be cautious," advised a Baptist publication, adding that few Protestants in the Philippines took the denunciation seriously.[90]

In any event, the basic policy requiring teachers to remain neutral in religious matters and to refrain from influencing the religious views of their students remained unchanged, and some missionaries continued to feel that the policy represented an unconstitutional infringement; furthermore, they complained, the policy was enforced only on Protestant teachers.[91] Observing cases of drunkenness among some teachers, one missionary mused that it would be better for the government to order "its employees to abstain from alcohol rather than from religion." [92]

Complaints about governmental school policy reflected the missionaries' deep concern that a school system that excluded moral instruction would produce a generation of skeptics instead of morally responsible, committed Christians. As early as 1902, Arthur J. Brown observed that, by calling into question the old verities, the schools would be preparing the soil for the "noisome seeds of infidelity and atheism." [93] To the missionaries, this presented grave dangers, for it was from the schools that the leaders of the new society would come. "Educated pagans," to use Laubach's phrase, in leadership positions presented a spectacle too horrible to contemplate. [94] In short, there was a danger that the public school in the Philippines, for all of its good points, would lack the crucial moral component found in the American school. Without that moral dimension, the value of the school as the bearer of Christian civilization diminished.

Nevertheless, many missionaries defended the government's policy as the best possible under Philippine conditions. Arthur J. Brown, who was well aware of the dangerous potential of a secular school, argued with indisputable realism that any other policy would increase Catholic influence. If religious influences were permitted in the schools in a land that was overwhelmingly Catholic, he pointed out, Catholics would benefit more than Protestants. Though the missionaries continued to be sharply divided on the issue, [95] probably a majority eventually accepted Brown's reasoning and supported the authorities. In 1910, for example, the Presbyterian committee on religious liberty concluded that the policy was reasonable, and the mission as a whole concurred. [96]

The religiously neutral school presented an exciting, and generally welcome, challenge to the missions to provide the moral dimension the public school allegedly lacked. The establishment of parochial schools was, in part, a response to the perceived shortcomings of the public school. [97] But, instead of erecting competing institutions, the missionaries more usually attempted to create a Protestant presence near the schools in the form of kindergartens, dispensaries, social clubs, and, above all, dormitories. A portion, at least, of the future leaders might be saved from free thinking, and they in turn would help ensure the success of the American-created, new, Christian society.[98]

Protestant worry about the direction of public education was connected with the larger issue of religious liberty. The freedom of religious expression, in fact, was to the missionaries the most important advantage of American rule. But, especially in the early years, the missionaries questioned whether the government took seriously enough its role as the guarantor of religious freedom. Time after time, the missionaries complained, local officials (usually Filipinos) failed to investigate instances of interference with their religious meetings and of persecution of their adherents. If a case was brought before a justice of the peace, it was too often dismissed on a pretext or technicality.[99] Though appeals to higher authorities (often Americans) might achieve better results, the situation would never be truly satisfactory, the missionaries believed, as long as the government at the highest levels remained inordinately sensitive to Catholic interests.

The Philippine Commission's decision in 1904 to proclaim a holiday in honor of Nuestra Señora de Rosario, the Virgin of Antipolo, was an early example, the missionaries thought, of the government caving in to "Romish pressure," as Homer Stuntz put it in a long letter to Theodore Roosevelt.[100] Three years later, Protestant sensitivities were even more deeply bruised when the Commission deigned to be present while Nuestra Señora was crowned patron saint of the Philippines.[101]

Significantly, the latter action occurred when James F. Smith was Governor General, a period when complaints alleging religious persecution and government unconcern seem to have multiplied. Baptist Charles W. Briggs wrote that "all who have been watching the course of events have noted the decided increase in religious preferment and in persecutions since our present Catholic Governor-General came into office," while a Presbyterian in Cebu went so far as to claim that "religious liberty is a myth."[102] The most celebrated allegations of religious persecution during Smith's tenure, and of the government's ineffectual response, were brought to public attention by the Reverend Harry Farmer, a prominent Methodist missionary. Convinced that affairs in the islands were "very much in the hands of the

Roman Catholics, and to all indications and purposes, Church and State are one,"[103] Farmer filed at least four complaints with the authorities in 1908 alleging persecution in Navotas, Meycauayan, and Vigan. When Farmer concluded that government officials had failed to investigate his complaints adequately, he published the details in a Methodist publication, after which religious magazines in the United States picked up the story. It created a minor sensation for a time and threatened to embarrass William Howard Taft, the Republican candidate for the presidency.[104]

Complaints of religious persecution diminished notably under Smith's successor, W. Cameron Forbes—an irony, given Forbes's contempt for missionaries. The Presbyterian Committee on Religious Liberty received no complaints at all in 1909 and only one the following year.[105] In 1911, missionaries in Bohol reported "a good deal of persecution," but they added that it occurred in "a quiet way." The same year, mission personnel in Camarines observed that persecution occurred "only in outoftheway [sic] places."[106]

THE GOVERNMENT AND MORAL ISSUES

Just as the missionaries were willing to criticize the government for allegedly failing to uphold religious freedom, so too they were not silent when the government pursued policies or sanctioned activities that departed from American Protestant moral norms. They were, in this sense, the conscience of the American experiment.

Even while the Philippine-American War was in progress, some missionaries engaged in sustained attacks on the Army's policy that permitted soldiers to purchase intoxicants on military bases. The missionaries also insisted, especially in the early years, that public officials set a good example by regular attendance at religious services. So vocal did criticism become of members of the Taft Commission for alleged non-attendance that each commissioner felt obligated to file a written statement denying that there was a government policy discouraging church attendance.[107] Bishop Brent dismissed most of these allegations (some brought by his own Episcopalian missionaries) as unjustified.[108] (Taft did not attend at first, apparently because no chair could comfortably accommodate his ample frame, whereupon Brent ordered a suitable chair constructed.)[109] But, like other missionaries, the Bishop believed that public officials had an obligation to maintain high standards of conduct, including church attendance. When Judge Adolph Wislizenus objected to being treated as "a potted palm that can be carried around to decorate a religious festival," Brent shot back, "Attendance on public worship is a public duty."[110]

Another moral issue that attracted missionary attention in the early years was the sale of opium. In particular, the Protestants were outraged when in 1903 the Philippine Commission proposed to regulate the sale of the drug by granting a monopolistic franchise to the highest bidder. The missionaries regarded this proposal as unbecoming to an American government and feared that under the plan the opium concessionaire would not, as he was supposed to do, limit his sales to persons already addicted. Because of strong missionary pressure (Methodist Bishop James M. Thoburn told Secretary of War Elihu Root to his face that the monopoly idea was "bad, and only bad, and bad continually"),[111] the government backed down. President Roosevelt personally ordered Governor Taft not to pass an opium bill until he, Roosevelt, had approved it.[112] In the end, Taft shelved the plan and appointed a three-man commission, which included Bishop Brent (at Brent's own request), to review the entire matter. After a serious investigation, the special commission suggested a solution, involving the gradual phasing out of the opium trade and no government-sponsored franchise, that met with the approval of all concerned. "Our gratitude to God for this termination of the opium debate should be very real and very great," concluded the Methodist Committee on Public Morals.[113]

The missionaries regularly urged the elimination of a host of other evils (including obscene postcards). But the moral issue that most persistently attracted their attention was gambling, something they fervently tried to eliminate or at least place under the most stringent regulation. In 1906, the Methodists took the lead in forming the Moral Progress League, whose primary concern was to suppress "the extensive public gambling that has developed *unchecked under the American administration.*"[114] The League acquired a substantial boost when Bishop Brent endorsed its purpose in a biting sermon that received front-page coverage in the *Manila Times,* in which he accused the Philippine Commission of moral timidity for failing to come to grips with the problem of gambling.[115]

The Moral Progress League had some immediate success,[116] yet, less than two years after the organization was founded, the municipal government of Manila raised missionary hackles by letting a concession for a cockpit, where gambling would be permitted, at the semi-official annual carnival. Although the concession was a local matter, the missionaries suspected that Governor General Smith was really responsible, and they berated him and the Philippine Commission as much, if not more, than the Manila authorities.[117] The Evangelical Union, which represented most Protestant groups, protested to President Roosevelt, and the Reverend Mercer G. Johnston, rector of the Episcopal cathedral in Manila, condemned the authorities in a colorful sermon entitled "A Covenant with Death, An Agreement with Hell."[118] One consequence of Mercer's diatribe was that he gained the lasting enmity of Commissioner Forbes, who rejoiced when a sizeable number of parishioners withdrew from the cathedral in protest.[119]

In fact, the missionaries' anger seems misdirected. Far from instigating or approving of the action of the Manila government, members of the Philippine Commission considered it ill-advised. Forbes thought the municipal board consisted of "fools," and he fancifully suggested that the board be abolished.[120] Forbes and Governor General Smith each offered 1,000 pesos, as did the Evangelical Union, to buy up the concessionaire's permit, without success.[121] But the Commission had no authority to overrule the decision, and the missionaries' inability or unwillingness to understand the Commission's predicament irked Forbes. "If these propositions of the ministers [to cancel the concession] were made to me as a business man at home," he wrote, "the least that could happen to them would be to be taken by the seat of the breeches and back of the neck to the top of the stairs and then to be kicked down."[122]

This time, Protestant objections proved unavailing. The authorities in Washington upheld the Philippine Commission's refusal to intervene, and those attending the carnival that year found the cockpit operating as planned.

THE GOVERNMENT'S FAILURE TO LEAD

A common thread runs through missionary criticism of the government. Whether they chastised it for pursuing a too lenient military policy, for being too susceptible to Catholic pressure, for not encouraging church attendance, or for failing to deal effectively with moral issues, the government stood charged with lacking in leadership ability, with suffering from a failure of nerve. This was even more apparent to the missionaries when they evaluated the government's overall performance as upholder of the white man's burden, of its moral obligations to the Filipinos. For example, the Baptists, more than any other mission group, wanted to eliminate the system of *caciquismo,* which they perceived as exploitative and degrading, something that sapped the very personhood from the peasants. The American regime, they were sure, would root out prevailing practices: "The conditions . . . exist today in an atmosphere where they can no longer thrive. The government system . . . is going to undermine the whole social structure that has so long been dominant."[123] But, within a few years, doubts developed about whether the government really wanted to carry through the kind of social revolution required to dislodge an institution as deep-seated as *caciquismo.*[124]

The government's failure to lead manifested itself even more clearly, most missionaries believed, in the granting of too many concessions to Filipinos, who were as yet ill-suited, they felt, to carry out important responsibilities, especially if these involved the making of policy. This attitude was evident in the skepticism with which the missionary community greeted the establishment of the Philippine Assembly in 1907.[125]

When Secretary of War Taft arrived in Manila to open the assembly, the Reverend Stealy B. Rossiter, pastor of the English-speaking Presbyterian church in Manila, engaged the former Governor in an unseemly debate over the appropriateness of Taft's policy of "The Philippines for the Filipinos," with which Rossiter vehemently disagreed.[126] Similarly, many missionaries threw themselves fervently into the effort to prevent an even worse policy from being enacted under the Democrats, who won the election of 1912. Several of the leading missionaries, including Presbyterian Rodgers, Methodist Oldham, and Episcopalian Brent, involved themselves in the strongly retentionist Philippine Society, an involvement that led to serious repercussions on the mission field.[127]

By this time, missionary opinion was not monolithic. Disciples missionaries Bruce Kershner and C. L. Pickett, for example, were not worried by the prospect of a change in policy and almost welcomed it.[128] In addition, just as the Jones Bill promising independence was being debated, a second generation of missionaries began to arrive, a generation influenced by the almost revolutionary changes just then beginning to take place in missionary thought. The outbreak of World War I added to the growing challenge to missionary optimism and certainty. Representatives of this new group in the Philippines, men like Congregationalist Frank C. Laubach and Disciple Leslie C. Wolfe, had no objection to independence. Even within the retentionist majority there were divisions. Bishop Oldham, for example, advocated setting a specific date sometime in the future for a vote on the political future of the Islands, whereas Bishop Brent opposed the idea.[129] But a majority still felt that the time was not ripe for Filipinos to look after their own destiny and that the American government had been entirely too prone to accede to Filipino and anti-imperialist demands.

In the opinion of these missionaries, the government needed to rule with a steady hand. The government must have "the whip over the door," as one Episcopalian missionary put it bluntly, "for the Malay Willie will not be a good boy nor learn his lessons unless it is in sight."[130] Missionaries of this persuasion were "running scared," genuinely fearful that the American experiment would fail. The Filipinos would "never be able to govern themselves if the government continues its present policy," Brent stated publicly in 1907, much to the chagrin of President Roosevelt.[131] To educate and elevate the Filipinos to the desired level was not the work of a day or even of a few years. It required a dedicated, imaginative, career-oriented colonial civil service working for at least a generation. "If a man like General [Leonard] Wood could be undisturbed as governor for twenty years and be surrounded by men of the same type," wrote another Episcopalian, "the thing to all appearances would be done."[132]

Unfortunately, the missionaries felt, the American colonial service did not measure up. Politics infested it. Administrators, including the Governor General, were replaced all too often. Too many colonial officials despised their surroundings and longed to return home. Too often they remained aloof from Filipino society, exploited the people, and addressed them contemptuously. American *policy* in the Philippines would "never be accused of a lack of imagination," wrote a Baptist medical missionary in a sensitive essay, "but I fear that many who endeavor to execute that policy may be accussed [*sic*] of a lack of *heart*." He explained:

The building of roads, the opening up of the interior, the establishing of new avenues of communication, new and better governmental methods and the maintaining of a splendid school system all accomplished by determination and indomitable energy, will not avail to win the hearts of the people and lead them to a higher life, so long as it is done in a deliberate, calculating way with none or very little heart-felt sympathy. . . . The Islands need men and women who are willing to admit that the spiritual and temporal welfare of the humblest peasant is worth as much as ours or mine. How unfortunate it is to find that the majority of minor governmental officials and some other Americans find it impossible to speak a good word for the Filipino people.[133]

In their efforts to save the government from its own mistakes, a number of missionaries, though by no means all, held out the example of European colonial administrations, notably the British experience in India. Methodist Bishop Thoburn, who had lived for many years in India, alluded to the British model on occasion, as did Bishop Brent, who read and traveled widely in an effort to familiarize himself with non-American colonialism. Though Brent did not entirely approve of British administration, sensing that British colonialists were too self-serving and overly pessimistic about the prospects of eventual native rule, at least the British experience was not characterized by the "instability, superficiality, feverish haste, and unreality" that, he felt, infected the American effort.[134] On the contrary, the

English, Brent thought, possessed a steadfastness of purpose, good government, a sense of duty, a dedicated colonial civil service, and policy-makers who, through long experience, had acquired perceptive insights into the "oriental mind."

This is not to say that the missionaries were completely disillusioned. Few of the first generation, after all, supported Filipino demands for independence, though that was beginning to change. Most would have insisted that the government had pursued an enlightened colonial policy, all things considered, that deserved support. Much as some of them admired the British, they contended that the American vision was more humane, more democratic, perhaps even more Christian. If only America would slow down a bit and professionalize its colonial service, if it would pursue its goals at a "steady jog trot" instead of a "gallop," as Brent put it, American colonialism might yet become the best in the world. [135]

Were the missionaries, then, agents of American imperialism? They defined their task in theological terms: To carry the Protestant Gospel to a land that had hitherto excluded it. Those who could clearly differentiate between Protestantism and Americanism cannot properly be called imperial agents. But an important segment of the missionary community—including the leading missionaries of most churches—consciously sought to infuse American concepts and values along with Protestantism, just as they often did in other lands. [136] And probably most missionaries could not escape, did not even want to attempt to escape, the bounds of their culture. They too served the interests of the state. They viewed the American occupation as providential, or at least as an expression of American benevolence that deserved their support. They accepted the necessity for the military conquest of the Islands. During the war, they deferred to military opinion, and a few gave advice and even direct support to the authorities. In the main, they applauded the civil government's attempts to remake Philippine society, physically and culturally, along American lines. They served as a force to reconcile Filipinos to their new fate. Their sometimes heated, sometimes telling criticisms of the government were intended to purify and make more effective American colonialism; almost none of them questioned the American presence.

Whether the missionaries were effective colonial agents cannot yet be determined in a definitive fashion, but there are some indications that they were. Throughout the colonial period, the churches were organically tied to their American counterparts. American churchmen visited the islands regularly. The most promising Filipino pastors and educators studied at institutions of higher learning in the United States. Only after national independence arrived did the major Protestant churches achieve an independent status, notably with the merger of several missionary-founded churches to establish the United Church of Christ in the Philippines (UCCP) in 1948. Even today, however, the UCCP retains close ties with American church-related organizations, while the United Methodist Church in the Philippines, whose membership equals that of the UCCP, is still officially connected with the American branch. As late as 1973–1974, in fact, an American United Methodist bishop exercised temporary ecclesiastical authority over the crisis-torn Philippine church.

Nationalistic resentments did sometimes erupt against American missionaries, resulting in important schisms.[137] But the bulk of the congregations remained loyal, and a fascination with America was a notable attribute of prominent Filipino Protestant clergymen.[138] Some have even expressed themselves in language resembling that of the early missionaries. Three United Methodist bishops, for example, all active in the 1970s, have written that the American occupation of the Philippines was providential. President McKinley, writes the distinguished clergyman D. D. Alejandro, brought "a new day for religious liberty and freedom of conscience in the Philippine Islands, a country long enslaved by a so-called Christian church, utterly selfish, intolerant and unscriptural in its practices."[139] If Filipino Protestants can accept missionary-inspired notions of providential history, is it not reasonable to assume that they also absorbed important American values?

To be sure, there are today strong nationalistic currents in the Filipino churches. Methodists are seriously considering severing their ties with the American church, and, in all communions, there is a heightened awareness, and rejection, of a "colonial mentality." But is it too much to speculate that the public condemnation of the martial-law rule of President Ferdinand Marcos by the UCCP and other Protestant bodies resulted from the profound attachment of its members to democratic principles, principles that may well spring from the recesses of the Filipino soul or even from aspirations common to all people, but which were most obviously inculcated jointly by the American regime and the missionaries?[140] Perhaps the missionaries were more effective agents of American ideas than either they or the government ever imagined.

CHAPTER SEVEN

Americans, Cowboys, and Cattlemen on the Mindanao Frontier

RONALD K. EDGERTON

The Philippine frontier had a poweful emotional attraction for Americans of the early twentieth century, possibly because they thought it similar to their own vanishing frontier at home. Colonial administrators like Dean C. Worcester sought to replicate the American frontier experience in north-central Mindanao, where they came upon relatively unsophisticated and unhispanicized tribal groups dispersed over a wide plateau of rolling grass-lands reminiscent of parts of the American West. They deliberately set out to fashion this great upland area (called Bukidnon, from the Cebuano word for mountains) in the image of the cattle frontier they had read about as youths, complete with cowboys, ranches, and cattle drives. They did this not just for personal profit, but because they thought it would be beneficial to Filipinos to take on the hard-riding, risk-taking, individualistic entrepreneurial behavior of the American frontier myth.

In this case study, Ronald K. Edgerton of the University of Northern Colorado studies the process of cultural interaction. He analyzes how, where, and with whom the American frontier ethos caught on in a frontier area of the Philippines. Implicitly, he is exploring the limits of cultural imperialism.

When Governor General William Cameron Forbes visited the area of central Mindanao now known as Bukidnon in 1911, he declared it to be "white man's land." It was "an ideal spot" for those possessed of virtues exemplified by the American frontiersman—namely, a willingness and drive "to get to work and cultivate the virgin soil, and undertake other enterprises." Here on the periphery of Philippine lowland society, beyond the line of settler migration, here the American could recreate the frontier society. The great open plateau had all the attraction of a laboratory awaiting an experiment. But there was no time to waste; already north-coast Bisayans were closing in. "If only we can be left alone here," lamented Forbes, "and the present policy be allowed to get crystallized before it is taken out of . . . [our] creative hands.[1]

For Protestant missionaries, too, the Philippine frontier offered a special attraction; when contrasted with the hispanicized and Catholicized core regions of the archipelago it seemed open, untamed, and untainted—a fair field for spreading the faith. Mountain Province was the first peripheral area to receive such attention; Forbes built the road, and the missionaries followed. The non-Moslem region of central Mindanao did not have long to wait. Just as in Luzon, top priority was given to constructing a road up into the interior from the coast. "I can see its empire-making possibilities creeping slowly mile by mile, year by year, opening up a world of wealth, waiting only the opportunity that the road brings to be useful to mankind, order, and happiness," wrote Forbes in his Journal. In its wake, "progress and wealth [would] follow, and poverty, misery, superstition, and danger . . . flee before it."[2] And in its wake, too, the Protestant missionary would follow. Reverend Henry DeVries, a tall, stern, trombone-playing Baptist, organized a church in Malaybalay, the principal town of Bukidnon, almost a decade before the municipality was constituted as a parish.

But the environment of this central-Mindanao frontier gave rise to a unique variant of the colonial pattern in the Philippines.

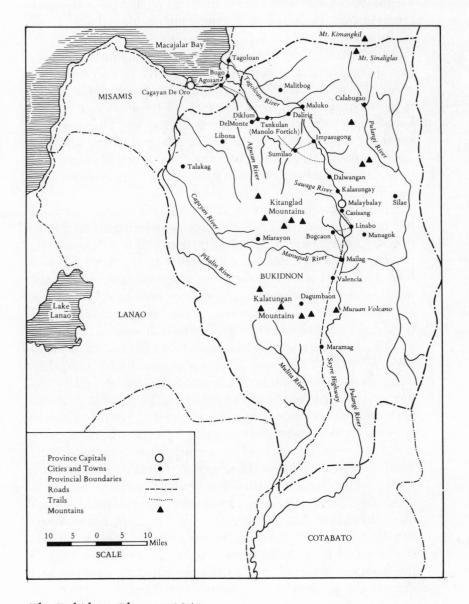

The Bukidnon Plateau, 1941

With its rolling grasslands, jutting mountains, and widely-scattered tribal peoples, this region reminded Americans of the great American West. Tropics or not, this was ranching country! Beginning in the second decade of their colonial rule, Americans initiated here the most productive ranch-cattle industry in the entire archipelago.

Today, some sixty-five years after organized ranching was begun in Bukidnon, the Provincial Governor wears a cowboy hat made of abaca fiber. It is the symbol of the province, but already it is an anachronism. The open spaces have acted as a magnet; land-hungry settlers have made Bukidnon the fastest-growing province in the country (its population grew from 63,470 in 1948 to 630,128 in 1980), and the great sweep of rangeland is now divided into rice and corn fields, coconut groves, and sugar haciendas.

An abaca cowboy hat may still work as a political gimmick, but is it a valid symbol of Philippine-American cultural interaction on the frontier? Americans drawn to this frontier envisaged the emergence of a Filipino counterpart to the American cowboy. Imbued with the belief that rugged individualism, self-sufficiency, egalitarianism, pragmatism and straight talk had typified the American response to the western frontier, they looked for the same response among Filipinos in Bukidnon. They had reason to be optimistic in this regard. Upland people were, as we shall see, open to change in their lifestyle. Lowland migrants, separated from their hispanicized culture, might also prove responsive to American-initiated change. But Filipinos, both upland and lowland, were oriented to a very different system of values than those admired by their American rulers. Uplanders were accustomed to a much more communal social order. Lowlanders, meanwhile, tended to put more store in the family as an institution than in the abilities of any rugged individualist. They were also accustomed to an elaborate social hierarchy rather than the simple, egalitarian living of the American West, and they preferred the use of euphemism to straight talk in social interaction. Would the experience of ranching on the frontier change all this? In the pre-war days when ranching became the principal export industry on the plateau, did ranchers and cowboys there internalize a system of values that

Americans have associated with ranching on the American frontier?

THE MINDANAO FRONTIER BEFORE AMERICAN INFLUENCE

In the 1890s, the Bukidnon plateau was still a wide-open expanse of grassland inhabited by scarcely more than 20,000 "pagans" and perhaps an equal number of Muslims.[3] Extending for hundreds of thousands of hectares, it was so sparsely populated that few traders or priests could be induced to trek inland from Cagayan and other north-coast towns.[4] In the mountains that border the plateau and along the rivers that cut deep canyons through the sea of grass lived the Bukidnon and Manobo peoples, racially similar to the Bisayans of the coast but linguistically and culturally distinct. There existed no concentration of people anywhere from the north coast to the Pulangi (or Rio Grande) River where it flows into Cotabato. Small settlements were dispersed in three widely separated nuclei: Manobo along the middle Pulangi and Mulita Rivers south to Cotabato, Bukidnon along the Tagoloan and upper Pulangi Rivers, and, to a lesser extent, on the upper Cagayan bordering Lanao.[5] No overarching political structure linked the three areas. Although at one time there may have been regional or high *datus* (chiefs) ruling over each, by 1910, the anthropologist Fay-Cooper Cole was struck by the lack of a well-defined political hierarchy in these regions.[6]

The loose pattern of inter-tribal organization was repeated in the settlements themselves where there existed no elaborate social hierarchy. Settlement *datus* held their positions not strictly on the basis of inheritance, but rather by their ability to mediate disputes. As this required a knowledge of customary law and a relatively high level of wealth, datuship often abided in one nuclear family. But it was not uncommon for an eldest son to be overlooked when another tribesman proved more adept at settling disputes.[7]

Below the level of the chief *datu*, settlements of never more than 100 families were divided loosely into freemen (some of whom were recognized as lesser *datus*), and slaves who were the unfortunate victims of raids on other settlements. All but the slaves were interrelated by marriage or blood. Land was held in common, not owned by each nuclear family, and was meted out in swidden plots under usufructory rights by the chief *datu* of the interrelated community. Although a few of these settlements were still clustered around a large house or *tulugan* where the chief *datu* resided, by the turn of the century, most Bukidnons did "not make up a compact settlement," living instead near their dispersed fields in simple houses "within hailing distace of each other."[8]

Mindanao's frontier in the late nineteenth century thus was inhabited by swidden farmers living in scattered little settlements not yet deeply affected by lowland Philippine culture, either Muslim or Christian. But this is not to suggest that it was a society in stasis. In the last decades of the century, the Bukidnons and Manobos were being drawn as never before into the orbit of coastal influence by the arrival of Augustinian Recollect and Jesuit priests, by the extension of Spanish governance, and by the expansion of trading contacts with the coast.

In 1849, Kalasungay, a settlement of 20 houses, became the first recognized pueblo on the plateau, and Malaybalay, Tanculan, Balao, and Impasugong followed in 1877. The Recollect Fathers journeyed inland from Cagayan as early as 1867, and Jesuits began to make visits in the 1870s.[9] The latter set up the first parish ever on the plateau, at Sumilao in 1890, adding another at Linabo in 1894.[10] Under the prompting of these priests, villages, which "in general . . . differed but little from the Bisayan towns along the coast," grew up on the grasslands.[11] Most important of these were Malaybalay (then called Oroquieta), Sumilao, Bugcaon, and Linabo, with populations respectively of 1,439, 1,340, 1,083, and 790 in 1892.[12] In these and other still smaller settlements the Jesuits baptized at least 4,992 Bukidnons by 1900.[13]

In persuading upland peoples to settle in larger villages within the web of lowland influence, Jesuits were aided by Muslim raids on outlying *sitios*. To offer some protection, the Spanish established an outpost of 30 Guardia Civil led by a Spanish officer.[14] Given the choice, more and more upland peoples fled their isolated settlements for the relative security of the plateau villages. There the Jesuit Fathers organized some into

a militia and, with the approval of the Governor General, supplied them with guns and led them against their Moslem enemies.[15]

Pushed on the one hand by Moslems, Bukidnons were pulled
on the other by lowland traders. They grew a variety of crops
which Bisayan and Chinese-mestizo merchants eagerly traded
for sugar, salt, cloth, and liquor. Abaca was their principal export, but American troops who passed through "the center of
a broad belt under cultivation" along the Tagoloan River at
the turn of the century remarked that coffee, rice, cacao, hemp,
and copra were also growing there in abundance.[16] Bukidnons
traded with their Manobo neighbors as well, and the gongs and
brass betel-nut boxes common in their houses evidenced trading
contacts with Moslems south and west.[17] This trade, however,
did not compare in volume with their north-coast ventures. As
Cole noted in 1910, the Pulangi "afforded a possible but seldom
used route to the Moro territory on the Southwest coast." The
chief trading contacts for the Bukidnon people were with Bisayans of the north coast.[18]

THE FIRST AMERICANS ON THE FRONTIER

If the world of north-coast culture began to draw upland peoples into its orbit by 1900, society on the plateau still remained
open to outside influence. It was into this open but fluid environment that Americans marched, pursuing General Nicholas
Capistrano and his 200 troops across the grasslands in the
Philippine-American War. Some American soldiers recognized
the potential of the plateau for development, and one of them,
Captain Eugene Barton, Quartermaster, 40th Infantry, United
States Volunteers, became the first American actually to settle
there. In 1905, having resigned as Provincial Treasurer of Misamis (the province that then included both the coast and plateau
within its boundaries), he settled with his brother in Mailag, in
the valley of the Pulangi River south of Malaybalay. As soon
as he had constructed a house, Barton sent to the United States
for his wife to join him and began conducting a trading business
in which he purchased Bukidnon and Manobo rice, coffee, and
hemp for salt, sugar, and cloth. As his business grew, Barton

established a store in Mailag, and also "a farm where he eventually laid out bananas, hemp, and about sixty thousand coffee trees."[19] But in 1910, when they ran afoul of both local Manobos and Dean C. Worcester, Secretary of the Interior, the Bartons abandoned their efforts and left.[20]

Other Americans lasted longer, although all were gone by 1945. Ole Waloe developed an interest in the plateau area while a member of the Philippine Constabulary, and he became one of the earliest cattle-ranchers there. Frank Gearhart, who had been Chief of the Bureau of Animal Industry, came to the Bukidnon plateau in search of land for ranching, and, upon finding a suitable spot on the northern edge, settled with his brother Rafael until 1941 when both men were murdered.[21] And Frederick Lewis, the first Lieutenant Governor of Bukidnon sub-province, stayed on after his retirement to become a cattle-rancher as well.[22]

DEAN WORCESTER'S IMPRINT

The Bartons, Gearharts, Lewis, and Waloe were among the best-remembered Americans to have settled on the plateau. But it fell to another man, Dean Worcester, to initiate and direct the American experiment in frontier democracy there. Worcester was absolutely fascinated by the Bukidnon territory. When he brought Governor General Forbes there in 1911, they took time to ride out from Malaybalay to the Mailag valley. "I never saw so smiling nor so alluring a country," said Forbes. Mailag looked out on "fertile plains sloping gently up to mountains in the distance covered with a dense growth of grass waist high, with occasional clumps of trees, usually following the course of streams." Forbes and Worcester spent all day "in dreams of conquest of the soil and getting out of the government service to run a big cattle, coffee, cocoanut, and rubber ranch up here. What a glorious life."[23] While Forbes never realized his dream, Worcester returned again and again, and in the end left his imprint on the society of this frontier.

Worcester epitomized the American frontier effort in the Philippines. Not a man to compromise easily, he had come to regard the lowland Philippine elite as adversaries rather than associates, and they reciprocated his feelings. Too proud to engage in what he called "peanut politics," he turned to the frontiers of the archipelago where Filipino nationalist leaders exercised the least influence. To him, befriending lowland politicians and upland people too would be like trying to mix oil and water: the result, "an *emulsion,* not a mixture." "You have the opportunity to become a second Rajali Brooke," he told Frank W. Carpenter, Chief of the Department of Mindanao and Sulu and the man responsible for administrative supervision of "non-Christians" in the southern Philippines. "Honestly, don't you think it would really be worth while to break away from peanut politics and make a good stiff fight to get for the backward peoples under your control the things that they really need?"[24] Thus, just as his missionary uncle had dedicated his life to the defense of Cherokee Indian rights in the American south, so Worcester came to the defense of minority tribes in the Philippines.[25] "While I fully realize that no man is in any sense indispensable," he wrote William Howard Taft in 1908, it would, he warned, be a betrayal of "non-Christians" to replace him as Secretary of the Interior. After all, "not one single measure for their betterment has ever been proposed by anyone but myself."[26]

Attracted to the model of Rajah Brooke, Worcester set out to reserve the governance of minorities in the Philippines for direct American rule. Americans like himself, unhampered by interference from Filipino politicians, would supervise the maturation of these "backward peoples" in an environment of carefully managed growth. In applying these ideas specifically to Bukidnon, Worcester adopted a twofold program. First, he maneuvered to cut off the plateau administratively from Misamis and the coastal elite, making it into a special American-controlled and protected reserve similar to a territory in the American West. Second, he sought to alter the lifestyle and values of Bukidnon people without changing their environment to the point where the plateau would attract large numbers of settlers. To achieve the first of these goals, he created a new administrative entity—Bukidnon province; to achieve the second, he specifically encouraged cattle-ranching as a means of effecting change within the pre-existing ecosystem.

The frontier area known as Bukidnon was literally carved out of the province of Misamis in order to protect the upland peoples there who had "suffered wrongs unspeakable." Hitherto, where "Christian natives" in the Islands had come in contact with "non-Christian tribes," their interest had "almost invariably been confined to working out the most satisfactory and effective system for exploiting them."[27] And probably nowhere "were members of the non-Christian tribes so robbed and oppressed as were the Bukidnon people." These "comparatively industrious" people had for years been compelled to sell their forest products "to the Christian Filipinos at prices fixed by the latter."[28] So, in 1907, Worcester "finally persuaded" his fellow commissioners "to cut out of the provinces of Misamis and Surigao the whole . . . territory inhabited principally by the non-Christians and to form it into a new [special] province" called Agusan, with Bukidnon as one of two sub-provinces.[29] During the next seven years, Bukidnons came directly under American administrative control, from their Lieutenant Governor, Frederick Lewis, to the Secretary of the Interior who had appointed him, Dean Worcester. Then, in 1914, Bukidnon became a full-fledged province and its boundary was extended to encompass virtually the entire plateau. This represented a victory for Worcester's protective policy, not only over the north-coast politicians but also over Brigadier General John J. Pershing who, as Governor of Moro Province in 1909–1913, had considered the plateau south of the 8th parallel to be part of his domain. The victory, however, was vitiated when the Interior Department lost its jurisdiction over the new province to Carpenter and his newly created Department of Mindanao and Sulu.[30]

These administrative acrobatics succeeded to the extent that Filipinos of the north coast were circumscribed temporarily in their power over Bukidnons. But administrative arrangements alone could not protect Bukidnons from an influx of farmer-settlers. It was necessary to develop Bukidnon society and economy in such a way as to pre-empt the land for other purposes. This is where cattle-ranching became so important; Worcester saw it as a necessary adjunct to administrative control. Thus, when he accused Carpenter of attempting to reserve the province's agricultural lands for homesteads, thereby inhibiting the "proposed investment [of] American capital [in] agriculture [and] cattle raising [in] Bukidnon," he was not acting from purely pecuniary motives.[31] Carpenter, knowing of Worcester's anxiety about settlers flocking into his reserve, had "teased" the Secretary's good friend Frederick Lewis, saying he "was inclined to reserve the great plateau . . . and [to] cut it up into homesteads for colonists from the north."[32] Worcester was not amused by such humor. He warned Carpenter that "someone might be foolish enough to believe that as a mature man, charged with very grave responsibilities, and known to entertain views of somewhat socialistic character relative to land tenure . . . you really meant what you said, and that would be unfortunate."[33]

To be sure, homesteading was part of the frontier experience just as much as ranching. But where homesteading meant an influx of lowlanders into a sanctuary preserved by Americans for themselves and their upland wards, it had to be channeled elsewhere, to Cotabato for instance. Worcester made this crystal clear to Carpenter who promised to treat "the Bukidnon plateau [as] negligible from the standpoint of the small agriculturist or homesteader, particularly because of the tremendous areas of fertile land elsewhere."[34] As a result, no effort was made to set up a colony or otherwise to attract homesteaders to Bukidnon. Between 1918 and 1922, there were only 29 homestead applications submitted for all of Bukidnon, while in the same period 719 were submitted for Cotabato. Not until 1925 was the first homestead patent actually granted for Bukidnon, and only 598 such patents were granted for that province before the war.[35]

OPEN LAND AS A LURE TO INVESTORS

Worcester's urge to protect upland tribespeople was manifested in so many of his actions and writings that it almost certainly constituted his primary motive in obstinately opposing homesteading in Bukidnon. It should be noted, however, that his opposition to homesteading also accorded well with investment schemes entertained by himself and other Americans. Clearly

Worcester did not believe that large American-run enterprises represented a threat to Bukidnon's ecosystem equal to that posed by migrant settlers. While, on the one hand, he championed minority interests against those of lowlanders, on the other, he struggled to change the Public Land Act in order to permit corporations to own or lease at least 4,050 hectares of land instead of the 1,024 hectares to which they were limited before 1935.[36] Thus, he denounced Carpenter's aforementioned reservation idea not only because of its probable impact on Bukidnon society but also because it would "cripple the plans of the Bukidnon Plantation Company," a company he directed.[37] This enterprise (which was under the Agusan Coconut Company) occupied some 10,000 hectares of pasture land around the village of Diklum by subleasing from individual lessors.[38] Worcester's own ranch near Mailag also came to extend well beyond the 1,024-hectare limit. Some of its 7,000 hectares were leased in his name, some in the name of his son-in-law, and some in the names of his wife and children.[39]

Other lessors of public lands in Bukidnon circumvented the 1,024-hectare limit simply by pushing their fences out well beyond the legal boundary line. So long as they stayed in the good graces of the Governor—himself a prominent rancher—they had little cause for anxiety until settlers who poured into the province after the war began to question their boundary claims.[40] The best example, however, of an American-run enterprise getting around the limits of the Public Land Law in Bukidnon is that of the Philippine Packing Corporation, a subsidiary of DelMonte Corporation. PPC began growing pineapples along the northern rim of the plateau in the late 1920s. Seeking room for growth, it was able to persuade American Governor General Dwight. F. Davis to turn an expanse of public land west of Maluko into a Naval Reservation. Thereupon, this American enterprise subleased almost 20,000 hectares of plateau land from the United States Navy for the purpose of pineapple production. Then, in 1935, when this land reverted to the Philippines, PPC was able to persuade Commonwealth President Manuel Quezon to declare it a National Development Company lease, and it is from this public company that PPC continues to sublease land now.[41]

THE RISE OF A CATTLE-RANCH INDUSTRY

Rainfall and soil conditions were not conducive to pineapple growing except on the northern edge of the plateau. Elsewhere in the province migrant settler-farmers were, as we have seen, slow to fill up the space. But, whereas farming made little progress in Bukidnon before 1941, ranching boomed. For this industry, not only the plateau's climate but the government's land-lease policy as well contributed to growth. A 25-year lease cost 20 centavos (10 cents) a hectare annually. For ranching, then, "you could almost have land for the asking."[42] Until World War II, when destruction of the herds opened the range to burgeoning settler immigration, ranching thus became the principal method of land utilization on the plateau. Between 1914 and 1941, at least 67 ranches were staked out, and the cattle population multiplied from just a handful to over 100,000. From the northern rim to Maramag in the south, an area encompassing "at least 10,000 square kilometers of good grazing land," "all was cattle."[43] And, between 1932 and 1933, Bukidnon moved ahead of Batangas and Masbate to become the largest supplier of beef to the Manila market of any province in the country.[44]

Cattle ranching on this frontier developed in two stages between 1914 and 1941. In the pioneering stage, when it did not yet involve most of the people of the province, the industry was dominated by Worcester and his American and Filipino associates. In the 1920s and 1930s, when it blossomed into a major enterprise involving people all over the plateau, wealthy Filipino investors in Manila, Cebu, and Cagayan de Oro led the way. But the ranching industry never became simply a back-country variation of the "cacique"-dominated rice and sugar industries of the archipelago. To the contrary, here on the frontier the small rancher, being typically a civil servant with sufficient independence and enterprise to migrate to Mindanao and then invest his salary savings in a pasture lease and a few cattle, played an important and often colorful role.

While there had been cattle on the plateau before 1900, organized ranching did not get started until the second decade of American rule. In 1879, there had been at least 10,039 head in Misamis, most of them very likely on the plateau, ranking Misamis eighteenth in cattle population among the provinces.[45]

And, in 1901, Colonel H. R. Andreas was surprised, while pursuing General Capistrano's troops across the plateau, to discover "tens of thousands of cattle which looked at us without fear." Yet Andreas detected no evidence of any organized ranching there, for the cattle seemed never to have seen riders before.[46] The herds he spotted were all in the north and may have been owned by wealthy north-coast Bisayans. But, if this was so, then the owners did not live on the plateau itself, for Andreas saw only "occasional lean-tos of herders" in the area.[47]

Between 1890 and 1905, these "native" cattle were decimated by rinderpest, which killed 90 percent of the stock in the Philippines.[48] Passing through the herds in 1901, Andreas described how hundreds of head were dying of the disease even as he watched.[49] By 1911, cattle in Bukidnon numbered only 159. Rinderpest and anthrax thus made cattle-ranching a very risky investment. "There are so many diseases here," wrote Worcester, "that cattle raising is not a safe industry for any but men with abundant capital" who could stand "serious reverses." The only safe bet would be to "acquire whole islands" and quarantine them thoroughly.[50]

Ranching became a much better investment when disease was controlled and when new breeds were imported. Worcester and his friend Forbes led the way in controlling rinderpest. Thanks to a vigorous campaign to inspect and control the movement of cattle and to isolate those found to be infected, rinderpest had been eliminated as a nationwide scourge by 1913. Predictions that it had been "practically wiped out" proved premature, but the risk definitely had diminished for investors in ranch cattle, and would continue to do so through the 1920s and 1930s.[51]

Worcester and Forbes also played a leading role in importing new breeds. At first, they encouraged an Australian cattleman, Francis Connor, to begin stocking the plateau with 1,000 heifers and stud bulls from Australia. In 1911, with Forbes's knowledge, Worcester invited Connor to accompany him on his annual inspection of Bukidnon. Connor became, in Forbes's words, "greatly enamored with the Bukidnon country" and proposed "to start an important industry there, stocking the fields ...with cattle, sheep and horses." Plans were laid and conditions agreed upon by the three men, but all came to nought when F. W. Taylor, Director of the Bureau of Agriculture, could not be persuaded (despite Worcester's considerable efforts) that it would be possible "to get cattle from Australia which are free from disease."[52] Eventually, it was Worcester himself who imported the first Nellore Brahmin bulls into central Mindanao, and these remain the most common variety there to this day.[53]

"Among all of the enterprises in which he was interested, the cattle business was probably nearest to Worcester's heart."[54] Upon his retirement as Secretary of the Interior in 1913, Worcester became Vice-President and General Manager of the American-Philippine Company. This company's subsidiary, the Agusan Coconut Company, established a ranch at Diklum which boasted 6,000 disease-resistant cattle by 1920, by far the largest herd on the Bukidnon plateau.[55] Farther to the south, on the very spot where he and Forbes had dreamed of conquering the soil, Worcester set up his own ranch. Known as the "Nellore," it occupied, as we have seen, some 7,000 hectares of prime pasture land near Mailag, and its herd numbered some 2,500 before the war.[56] Having started his own ranch, the former Secretary enticed friends and associates to do the same. In fact, the new cattlemen of the plateau were at first almost all close associates of Worcester. They included his loyal lieutenant, Frederick Lewis, who became manager of the Agusan Coconut Company's ranch; Kenneth Day, his son-in-law; and Frank Gearhart, who had been Chief of the Bureau of Animal Industry when that Bureau was under Worcester's Interior Department, and whose ranch near Diklum covered 3,000–4,000 hectares and grazed 2,000–3,000 head.[57]

More important than any of these American associates in the ranching business was a Filipino Constabulary lieutenant who won the Secretary's lasting support and admiration in 1907 when he first guided him through the Bukidnon territory. Joining the Constabulary from a well-connected Cebu family, Manuel Fortich had helped pacify the north-coast towns after the Philippine-American War. He impressed Worcester tremendously with his energy, fortitude, and resourcefulness. Recognizing his frontier leadership capabilities (his descendants liken him to Theodore Roosevelt), Worcester had him appointed Lieutenant Governor of the sub-province when Lewis became

Governor of Agusan. To the extent that he won Worcester's loyalty, Fortich incurred the wrath of political leaders in Misamis, who attempted to jail him in Cagayan de Oro in 1910.[58] Appointed full Governor of Bukidnon when it became a province, he exercised unparalleled influence over developments there until his death in 1943. At first as Governor, later as Assemblyman-Representative, and always as an enthusiastic rancher and horse-breeder, he vigorously encouraged cattle ranching in the province, himself leasing some 7,000 hectares which supported at least 4,000 head in the years before World War II.[59]

FILIPINOS TAKE OVER

For organized ranching on the plateau the pioneering stage ended and the developmental stage began in 1920–1921 when cattle on the provincial government-run experimental ranch south of Mailag were sold to private investors. Started by Governor Fortich with the strong endorsement of Worcester, the Dagumbaan ranch was intended to demonstrate the profitability of ranching in the interior, far from the coast. It did just that. By 1920, it boasted a herd of about 2,000 cross-bred Nellores and returned dividends of almost 100 percent a year.[60] Thus, when Fortich offered to sell the government's stock in 1921, investors were quick to respond. And, when he decided to sell most of the herd to Worcester for 43,000 pesos ($21,500), they accused him not only of favoritism but of being an "Americanista" as well.[61]

What Worcester and Fortich had begun in 1914, Alejandro Roces, Angel Elizalde, and others developed in the 1920s and 1930s. Roces bought up the 10,000-hectare Dagumbaan pasture lease, hired José Sanvictores as ranch manager, and watched his herd multiply to an estimated 15,000 head by 1941. Elizalde acquired the Agusan Coconut Company ranch in Diklum and then Ole Waloe's spread as well, and his herd grew to approximately 10,000.[62] Teopisto Guingona, José Ozamis, José Sanvictores, and Dr. Mamerto Escaño were still other out-of-province investors.[63] By the mid-1930s, the only big cattlemen left from the pioneering days were Fortich, the Gearhart brothers, and

Worcester's son Frederick who took over the Nellore Ranch when his father died in 1924, and who employed Carlos Fortich, son of the Governor, as his veterinarian. Among the big ranchers, only they, together with Sanvictores, actually lived on their ranches rather than as absentee owners in Manila, Cebu, or Cagayan de Oro. And even Fortich began to drift toward the coast. He built his home not in Malaybalay but in Dalirig, close to Cayagan, married all four of his sons into prominent north-coast families, and, in the 1930s, spent as much time in Manila, Cebu, or Cagayan de Oro as he did on his ranch.[64]

The failure of Americans to remain leaders in ranching can be attributed in part to the economic realities of the industry in the 1920s and 1930s. It simply did not turn out to be profitable enough to attract American investors. A rancher, for example, who sold to a buyer in Bukidnon would receive 10 centavos a kilo for his cattle weighed on the hoof at the coastal site of Bugo. Weighed after having been driven to the coast, cattle rarely brought more than 30 pesos ($15.00) profit per head.[65] A rancher could make more if he could transport the stock himself to Manila, "the main market, on which the industry [was] dependent for its existence."[66] Even here, though, profits were not high. Between 1927 and 1933, wholesale prices dropped from 60 to 35 centavos a kilo for dressed beef. Bukidnon cattle, which averaged 135 kilos of dressed beef after the long voyage to Manila, thus brought between 47 and 81 pesos ($23.50–$40.50) per carcass. But, when slaughterhouse charges and freight, handling, and registration costs (amounting to an average of ₱17.75 or $8.88 per head) were subtracted from this total, the rancher did not have much to show for his troubles.[67] Wholesale prices remained low because demand for beef did not meet expectations. Manila, far and away the most important market, consumed only 9,000 kilos a day.[68] Furthermore, all beef sold in that city had to be butchered in the city slaughterhouse at a charge of 5 centavos per kilo, or 12.5 percent of the producer's gross returns in 1932. Finally, there existed in Manila what *The American Chamber of Commerce Journal* called a "retail beef-dealers' ring" so strong that it was "practically out of the question to market beef independently."[69]

Ranching thus became more and more the business of Filipinos

—either those like Elizalde and Escaño who owned their own cattle boats and hence could make the most of the situation, or those like Santos Cudal and Guillermo Tabios who had migrated to Bukidnon as salaried civil servants and who settled down there to become small ranchers as well.[70] Between these two groups, ranching grew and grew on the plateau. The year from 1932–1933, when Bukidnon became the largest supplier of beef to the Manila market, represented a watershed of sorts. Some 67 ranches, big and small, exported 7,038 cattle that year, and this accounted for 77 percent (₱175,950/₱228,791) of the province's export proceeds.[71]

BUKIDNON COWBOYS

In Bukidnon's burgeoning ranching business, tribal minorities emerged as the lowest status group. Of the province's 51,200 residents in 1933, 92 percent were classified as "non-Christian." And yet, of all the province's ranches, only one was operated by a Bukidnon, Juan P. Melendez of Malaybalay.[72] Bukidnons and Manobos, especially those working on the large absentee-leased spreads, came to have much in common with tenants on rice haciendas elsewhere. They were at the bottom of the ranching social structure; the top was occupied by wealthy absentee-leaseholders like Elizalde and Roces, followed by managers, invariably lowlanders, contracted to oversee the ranches. To the Bukidnons and Manobos fell the job of handling the cattle: of roping, branding, and riding herd. They became, in short, the cowboys of the Bukidnon frontier.

Being a cowboy in Bukidnon might seem to bear little resemblance to being a cowboy in the American West. While the Bukidnon or Manobo cowboy was typically poor, landless, and indebted, his American counterpart is usually pictured as subservient to no man, as in Owen Wister's *The Virginian*. Such a contrast, however, confuses the American folk hero with his flesh-and-blood prototype who, just as often as Bukidnons and Manobos, suffered from poverty, landlessness, and indebtedness. He was, in the words of Lewis Atherton, "a drifter whose work and economic status made it difficult for him to marry and rear a family . . . . In the true economic sense, rank-and-file cowboys were hired hands on horseback, and very unromantic ones at that."[73] The cowboy imagery, in the American West as well as on the Philippine frontier, was preeminently the property of the landlord rancher rather than of the cowboy himself.

Insofar as being a cowboy came to be associated with being Manobo or Bukidnon, it was clearly not held in high regard as a profession. "Anybody could be a cowboy," said former manager Manuel Fortich, Jr., referring to the fact that the eight cowboys under his direction at Elizalde's ranch had all been Bukidnons. One didn't have to be "tough," just able to ride a horse, and even a small boy could do that. "We were not like American cowboys. We could cover our pasture in one day. [While] they stayed outside, we could always stay at home."[74] The Bukidnon cowboy was just a *muchacho,* a boy who was paid from 20 to 30 pesos a month for his labors.[75] Most of them, having no land or even tenancy rights, depended solely on their wages for their livelihood. In a society oriented to the accumulation of landed wealth, it is no surprise that few took great pride in their profession or that few opted to stay in ranching when given the chance to farm. Jesus del Rosario, chief cowboy of the Gearhart brothers, for example, took pains to point out that five of his nine children held college degrees while none had become a cowboy.[76] Teofilo Madula, a former cowboy under Frederick Lewis, remarked that his children had chosen farming over cow-roping. He had himself begun a small farm soon after the war, and he could not remember any cowboy who had wanted his children to follow in his footsteps.[77]

Little of the American cowboy myth appears to have rubbed off on Bukidnons or Manobos. They were "tenant cowboys," not "real cowboys." Neither self-reliant nor especially mobile, most experienced a life of dependence on their manager-patrons. "Before the war, if they were sick, they'd come to us," said Manuel Fortich, Jr., of his ranch hands. "We always gave them rice and food to get over hard times."[78] The single ones lived with the manager in the ranch house, but others had families with whom they would live in ramshackle huts. In either case they often fell into debt to the manager, and thus became even more dependent.[79] A poor, depressed class, they rarely had occasion to experience any of the glamor associated with their profession in the United States.

THE "REAL" COWBOYS

If the reality of being a cowboy in Bukidnon did not often approach the myth, the myth nevertheless exercised a strong pull on some. This was particularly the case after Mr. Brock, an American from a Wild West show, signed on with the Agusan Coconut Company in the late 1920s. Here was a "real cowboy," according to José Fortich—a tall, lean, tobacco-chewing Texan who could stand a rope on its end.[80] To this day, no one remembers his first name, but they remember that Brock taught "natives" the fine points of the business, including how to use a rope and how to pull a steer down without depending on brute strength. After he left in the early 1930s, Patricio Dumayao, a Bukidnon who had been his chief cowboy, passed on the techniques to others.[81]

It was the cattleman and the ranch manager rather than the impoverished cowboy who were able to identify with the romantic cowboy image and adapt it to the Bukidnon frontier environment. One such man was Manuel Fortich, Jr. "If you want a *cowboy*," said one interviewee, "go see Maning." "Yes, yes," all agreed, now there was a "real cowboy."[82]

Manuel was not the only Fortich to be drawn toward a set of values associated with the American frontier. But, more than any other member of the family, he lived the lifestyle his father and brothers admired. "Among us brothers," said José, "Maning was the hardest worker."[83] Never interested in education beyond high school, he had signed on as manager for Angel Elizalde's ranch in 1934. There he picked up Brock's "American style," and there he managed eight Bukidnon cowboys for five years before taking over management of his father's ranch in southern Bukidnon. Described by one of his former employees as a hothead who drank heavily and once rode his horse into a general store, he spent most of the next two decades, including the war years, on the ranch. There he protected the herd from hungry Japanese soldiers and USAFFE guerrillas, and there he matured into an excellent manager and an expert horseman and hunter. To his cowboys he was a tough, absolutely fearless copy of his father, and, like his father, a law unto himself, meting out frontier justice on at least one occasion. Of all the cattle in Bukidnon, his herd alone survived the war. After liberation, he and his brother José managed the Escaño and Ozamis properties as well as the Fortich herd in southern Bukidnon, while earning pocket money selling the carcasses of wild animals they had hunted down. After almost a lifetime of this, he looked back on ranching as "the only way we knew how to live."[84]

The Fortich family, even to its recent political foes, personified the lifestyle of the Bukidnon frontier before the war. Theirs was a life of relatively few luxuries, of hard work, of pride in their self-sufficiency, and of love for the outdoors, for their animals, for riding, and for hunting. Although they can afford more than a few luxuries today, the sons of Manuel, Sr., or Don Manolo as he is remembered, retain a love for the simple life of the cattleman. Not only do they continue to operate small ranches in Bukidnon, but they prefer living on them to staying in the city. Asked where they'd get items they couldn't produce themselves before the war, one answered, "The same place as now," and then, pointing to his boots, said, "Sears and Roebuck, . . . the best!"[85]

The Fortiches typified the majority of Bukidnon ranchers in another way as well: their relations with Bukidnons and Manobos were always colored by their paternalism. To be sure, Don Manolo did stress the virtues of self-reliance, and he encouraged these "non-Christians" to attend school.[86] Furthermore, he compelled them to accept the jurisdiction of American-initiated courts. Thus, he brought to trial one of his own cowboys for stealing a roll of barbed wire valued at 7 pesos.[87] But the paternnalism was always there. Just like Worcester before them, the Fortiches became both tutors of the "natives" and jealous protectors of them against migrants from the coast. Bukidnons came to regard themselves as being perpetually in debt to the Fortiches, and they repaid the debt by providing the votes for a Fortich victory in every election the family contested until 1965.[88]

MIGRANT CIVIL SERVANTS AS RANCHERS

If the Fortiches set the example, the other ranchers who had migrated to the plateau followed their lifestyle. As cattlemen and ranch managers, many Filipinos who first came to Bukidnon as civil servants recreated the cowboy image in their own lives. These civil servants-become-cattlemen typified the small rancher, of whom there were many on the plateau by 1941. As they moved from schoolhouse to ranch house, from clerk to frontier entrepreneur, they also moved from ethno-linguistic separatism toward a shared subculture, that of the ranch-cattle businessman rooted in a social world transcending subnational boundaries.

They came from many provinces but especially from the Ilocos: schoolteachers, sanitary inspectors, nurses, and other government employees needed to operate the new provincial government of Bukidnon with its capital at Malaybalay. It was a small town, Malaybalay, and the newcomers soon met the Governor who ruled over the place—Manuel Fortich. They worked for a few years in the public employ. But very soon, and more often than not "obliged" or persuaded by the Governor, they turned to ranching.[89] At first they leased land at 20 centavos a hectare a year and turned loose on it perhaps no more than half a dozen cattle. What risk they incurred was acceptable because the initial investment required was so low. For perhaps a decade, they would live in town while their herd grew in size to a point where they could begin living off the proceeds of sales. Then most moved out onto the range, built a ranch house, managed a few Bukidnon or Manobo cowboys, and became serious ranchers. Those who continued to combine ranching with government employment usually had small herds of no more than 500. Others who became full-time ranchers possessed as many as 2,000 by 1941. But all enjoyed at least a modest degree of socio-economic mobility, and all came to regard the frontier as an open land of unlimited opportunity.

Santos Cudal was one of these small ranchers. An Ilocano from Pangasinan, he had come to Malaybalay as a vocational-arts teacher in 1909, having studied at Philippine Normal College and Silliman University, where he converted to Protes-

tantism. He quickly became the first head teacher of the Bukidnon Agricultural School, and then married Marcela Abello,
daughter of one of the most prominent Bukidnons in Malaybalay. At one point when he longed to return to Luzon, Fortich
(by then his compadre) insisted that he stay. "No, you must not
go. You will stay here and buy some cattle," he said.[90] Cudal
stayed, raised a family of twelve children (four others died), and
got into ranching. Claiming 600 hectares by tax declaration and
another 900 as pasture lease, he built up a herd of 1,200 from a
beginning in 1918 of 30.[91] There, on the ranch north of Mailag,
he proved to be no paternalistic *hacendero* but rather a tight-
fisted disciplinarian, remembered by one of his children as "a
wonderful father, after he died."[92] A great one for being self-
reliant, he built his own ranch house and furniture, and insisted
that both his own and his wife's relatives (who had come to
stay) work for their keep. A great believer in social mobility
through education, he sold about 60 cattle annually in order to
pay for the tuition of his children. "He thought that forever and
ever we would be getting cattle," and hence reinvested most of
his profits back into the ranch.[93] But the war destroyed the entire herd. When he was mortally wounded by a Manobo during
the war, he told his wife, "No matter what will happen, do your
best to educate the children; send them to school."[94]

Another small rancher, Guillermo Tabios, came from Ilocos
Norte as Senior Audit Clerk for Bukidnon in 1920. He married
Basilia Nazareno from Cebu who came as District Nurse from
the Protestant mission hospital in Iloilo. In 1927, he opened a
store in Malaybalay, and later added a rice and corn mill, the
beginnings of a business that would make him one of the wealthiest businessmen in the province after the war. In the meantime,
he homesteaded 24 hectares and leased another 300 for a ranch,
beginning with 6 head which multiplied into a herd of 300 by
1941.[95]

Among the good friends of the Cudals and Tabios were other
Ilocano civil servants-become-ranchers, including Antonio Alvarez, whose ranch in Mailag had at least 1,000 head.[96] Still
another good friend, Julian Rubio, came from Batac as a teacher
in 1922. Four years later, when he became head teacher in the
tiny village of Alanib, he homesteaded and leased 500 hectares

there, watching his herd grow from 15 to 500 between 1927
and 1941.[97] In 1918, Simon Mamawag, a mixed Ibanag-Ilocano
from Cagayan Province, also arrived as a teacher, settling south
of Malaybalay, where he taught in the Bukidnon Agricultural
School. He too resigned to homestead and begin a small ranch,
which grew to include 500 head by 1941.[98]

Not all the civil servants were Ilocanos, of course. Antonio
Rubin came from Laguna as District Health Officer for Bukidnon in 1918. As a doctor of medicine and captain in the Con-
tabulary he had been assigned to Cagayan de Oro as Medical
Inspector for northern Mindanao. In 1922, he was appointed
Governor of Bukidnon with the blessing of Fortich, yet he also
operated a ranch with a herd numbering 2,000–3,000 before the
war. This made it equal in size to the ranches of two other
Tagalogs, Florentino Cruz, from Rizal province, and Cenon
Paulican, who became Deputy Governor of the province. Still
another Tagalog, Domingo Limbo, came to Bukidnon in 1928
from Batangas. A graduate of the University of the Philippines
School of Agriculture, he taught at first in the Bukidnon Agricultural School. In 1930, his wife, Patricia Mendoza Limbo,
joined him after graduating from the Philippine Normal College. While she taught at the Bukidnon Normal School in Malaybalay, he began a ranch in Maramag which, by 1941, employed
5 Bukidnon cowboys who were responsible for a herd of 1,600
cattle.[99]

Ranching on the Bukidnon frontier thus developed as an important avenue for social mobility among a low-salaried but
highly educated and motivated group of migrants. World War II
proved especially devastating to this group, for their herds were
wiped out, and only a few ever attempted to rebuild their stock
after liberation. Yet, in the years between 1914 and 1941, the
frontier did bring out in them many of the attributes of the
American frontiersman, including a high degree of entrepreneurship, self-reliance, and inner-directedness. For men like Manuel
Fortich, Jr., or Santos Cudal, the reality of their lives became
indistinguishable from that of their nineteenth-century American
counterparts.

THE AMERICAN ROLE

Without American involvement in the region, ranching would not have developed as independently from the north coast as it did. American efforts to protect the plateau succeeded in limiting north-coast influence, especially before the 1930s. To be sure, some coastal families did become involved in ranching too, among them the Ozamis, Chavez, Neri, Roa, and Alquitela families.[100] Their herds, however, were situated (with the exception of the Ozamis') near Cagayan de Oro. The central plateau ranches were, almost without exception, leased and operated by small-rancher migrants from Luzon, by the Manila-based rich like Roces and Elizalde, or by Americans. Cattle from these spreads were driven directly to the coast, where they were shipped from Bugo to Manila. The cattle trade avoided Cagayan de Oro, and the Cagayan elite was deprived of an important role in marketing or buying the product. From ranch to dinner table, the beef was raised, shipped, slaughtered, and retailed without extensive north-coast involvement.[101]

The American role in the development of ranching was not limited to protection of the plateau from the coast; it also operated to encourage and sustain a favorable climate for middle- to low-income entrepreneurship. By isolating rinderpest, importing disease-resistant breeds, training Bukidnon cowboys, and beginning their own ranches, Americans helped get ranching started in an organized way. By placing limits on landownership and instituting a cheap pasture lease policy, they kept the range open and reduced the risks for investors. And, by creating a separate province of Bukidnon with its capital in Malaybalay and then advertising for trained civil servants everywhere, they attracted enterprising small investors from throughout the archipelago.

When, however, we look beyond the economics of the emergent ranch-cattle industry to the cultural matrix associated with it, the American impact is not so clear. The cultural attributes so closely associated with American ranching were transmitted not to everyone on the frontier, but rather to just one group. Members of this group—the managers and small ranchers—already possessed a measure of social and economic security, for they had a relatively high level of education and/or income, and either owned or leased land. Another attribute was their acquaintance with American culture, owing to their direct contact with Americans in the civil service and education. They had at least heard about the cowboy ethic, something that could not always be said of Bukidnons. Finally, these managers and civil servants-become-ranchers came from middle-class backgrounds and viewed themselves as professionals. Instead of regarding the cowboy ethic as a threat to their status positions, they utilized it to legitimize efforts they made to improve their economic position. The cowboy emphasis on self-sufficiency, for example, was adopted by a number of small ranchers as a rationale for refusing to jeopardize their economic mobility by supporting large numbers of would-be dependent relatives. It can be said, therefore, that those who already enjoyed a good basis for social and economic mobility and who had closest access to Americans, did often adapt the cowboy ideals to their own lives. They did so in large part because they realized how such ideals could contribute to rather than detract from their social and economic well-being.[102]

But what of the Bukidnon people? Were they able to take advantage of the new stereotype? Clearly, the answer is "no." Thanks to the fact that they had little familiarity with concepts of land ownership, they neither homesteaded nor leased land in substantial numbers. Instead of becoming ranchers, most of those who participated in the ranch-cattle industry at all did so as ranch hands hired to labor on land controlled by non-Bukidnons. Those cowboys who remained landless laborers enjoyed little prestige in terms either of Philippine or of American society. Those who settled down and farmed tended to encourage their children to become farmers as well. Either way, they had little to gain from living as the Philippine counterpart to the American cowboy.

While the stereotype of the self-reliant frontiersman symbolized by the cowboy was not without any impact, it was found suitable for only a very limited group of people. In families like the Cudals, Tabios, Fortiches, and others, it helped foster a separate identity that remains vital to this day. They became the local apostles of frontier rugged individualism, self-reliance, pragmatism, and straight talk. As José Fortich emphatically told this writer in his ranch house south of Malaybalay, "My father was a pioneer, we all were pioneers, and we still have that pioneering spirit now."[103]

PART THREE

Economics and Aspirations

CHAPTER EIGHT

Americans in the Abaca Trade: Peele, Hubbell & Co., 1856-1875

NORMAN G. OWEN

The economic aspect of the Philippine-American relationship did not begin or end with direct colonial control. Long before the Spanish-American War, Americans were trying to link the Philippine economy with that of the United States. As early as 1796, Nathaniel Bowditch began trading in Manila; and, during the nineteenth century, as Benito Legarda, Jr., has shown, American merchants played a catalytic role in the development of the Philippine export economy. American involvement prior to 1898 is potentially as significant in the total context of Philippine-American relations as anything that came later. Yet, since the pioneering work of Legarda over a quarter of a century ago, no one has studied the American merchants of the nineteenth century in any detail.

Who were these men? What were they trying to do? Perhaps most significant, how much impact did they really have? By concentrating on one generation of a single merchant firm, particularly its purchases of one commodity (Manila hemp) in one region, it is possible to provide answers that

have implications for these larger questions. Dr. Norman G. Owen, Research Fellow in Pacific and Southeast Asian History at the Research
School of Pacific Studies, Australian National University, suggests that,
in this as in other aspects of the relationship, Americans' aspirations and
self-appraisal greatly exceeded their actual impact upon the Philippines.

Among some 5 million inhabitants of the Philippines in 1869
were approximately 200 "foreigners" (American, British, and
other non-Spanish Europeans) in Manila. "It is this small number," one of them noted, "which controls almost the entire
commerce of the islands."[1] Almost thirty years ago, Benito Legarda, Jr., analyzed the critical entrepreneurial role played by
these merchants in the transformation of the Philippine economy from subsistence to export agriculture.[2] Research on the
provincial Philippines over the past two decades has confirmed
the importance of this transformation, and thus by implication
of the handful of men who served as catalysts in bringing it
about. By the latter half of the nineteenth century, for example,
the economies of the provinces of Albay and Camarines Sur
were so well integrated into the world fiber markets by the ex-
portation of abaca (Manila hemp) that the economic cycles of
the industrial West are clearly reflected in the local crop prices,
wage rates, government revenues (including cockfight admis-
sions), and even the rate of marriage.[3] This chapter is an attempt
to examine in greater detail one agent in this transformation,
the American merchant house of Peele, Hubbell & Co. (PHC),
particularly its involvement in the abaca trade between 1856
and 1875.

The significance of these dates is more historiographic than
historical. The papers of three partners of the firm during this
period have survived, providing us with more detail than we
have for any other merchant house or any other time.[4] In the
history of PHC, the years 1856–1875 appear to represent the
precarious pinnacle of their success—building on the pioneering
efforts of the previous generation, not yet declining toward the
bankruptcy into which they fell in 1887. Yet, as this chapter
will indicate, even in the best of times PHC was never very far
from failure. It was an age in which small-scale capitalism involved very real and uninsurable risks.

By 1856 PHC had long since lost all direct connection with the families of George and Henry Hubbell and J.W. Peele, who had founded the firm a generation earlier.[5] Ownership had passed through several hands—mostly Salem merchants, apparently. The current owner, William P. Peirce, left actual management of the firm to three nonproprietary junior partners named in the previous year, Horatio Nelson Palmer, Ogden Ellery Edwards, and Richard Dalton Tucker. After William Peirce's death (in 1859?), these three purchased the "name" of the firm from his widow, and continued as owners through most of the period of this study. Along the way they promoted three clerks to be nonproprietary partners: George Henry Peirce (clerk 1856-1867, partner 1868-1874); Frederick Emory Foster (clerk 1869-1873, partner 1874-1876?); and Rufus Allen Lane (clerk 1871-1874, partner 1875-1887).

These seven men—and for most of this period just five of them (Palmer, Edwards, Tucker, George Peirce, and Foster)—owned and operated the firm. PHC's nominal capital in this period ranged from less than a quarter of a million dollars to over half a million; their annual balance sheets in the early 1870s showed about 2 million dollars each in assets and liabilities; and, in 1881, the only year for which we have accessible statistics, they exported over 4.5 million dollars worth of abaca and sugar, more than 20 percent of the total exports of the Islands. Between 1862 and 1875, a "joint account" of PHC and the other American agency house, Russell & Sturgis, handled over half the abaca exported from the Philippines; in fact, one of their provincial buyers, George Peirce, then age 25, bought for the account about one-third of the whole Philippine crop—and thus of the entire world supply—in 1862-1863.[6] From the correspondence of these men (chiefly with each other) we can reconstruct a picture of who the American merchants in the Philippines were, what they were trying to do, and how well they succeeded in their endeavors.

THE AMERICAN MERCHANTS

> Far behind our glorious country in the march of ideas on
> nearly every good topic is this Philippine region, oppressed by
> arbitrary government.
>
> George H. Peirce, letter to Charles Wyman,
> 27 Nov. 1856, Peirce Family Papers.

So far as can be told, except for a few English clerks, and
some Spanish employees in those positions requiring contact
with the colonial government, the partners and clerks of PHC
were not only all Americans, but also all from one region of the
United States—New England (especially Salem and Boston)
and New York.[7] Nor was this coincidental; when PHC needed
more clerks in 1866, Edwards asked Peirce to "engage two
young yankees," preferably with experience in a country store.
No "silk-stockings" were welcome, however; "we want good
honest fellows," said Edwards, "who come from decent families,
who are willing to work and who are not above doing their
work as they are ordered."[8] Even within the limits of these
qualifications, recruitment was not exactly random; George
Peirce was William Peirce's nephew, E.D. Edwards the younger
brother of Ogden, and William Huntington the half-brother of
Tucker. When there were no suitable PHC relatives available,
the field broadened to include others with connections to Far
Eastern trade: former employees of other Manila houses, relatives of other Manila traders, employees of China agency houses
or relatives of American importers.[9] Family or company connections offered only an opportunity, however, not a sinecure;
the partners were resolute in asserting that those who lacked
the discipline, initiative, or judgment for the trade would be
sent home—"Business is business."

The employees of PHC went to the Philippines as sojourners,
hoping to make enough money to return home and live a "secure" life of some gentility. Most of them arrived with a high-
school education and a few years' experience in some branch
of commerce. All were recruited as bachelors; only those well
established in the business (on the verge of partnership) were
permitted to return home to marry and bring a wife back to
the Philippines, as Edwards did in 1857, George Peirce in 1867,

and Foster in 1873. This made for a lonely and difficult life. George Peirce in particular bewailed his "exile" in Manila and constantly proclaimed that he would return as early as possible "consistent with duty and with my purpose of seeking a settlement in life." Edwards was equally anxious to leave as soon as he could "lay something by for old age and rainy weather." Other partners were less open in their dislike of the Philippines and desire to return to a more "civilized" society and climate, but seemed equally glad to leave Manila whenever possible.[11]

The salaries PHC offered clerks, though substantial by the standards of the time, were not great. They ranged from a starting figure of less than $1,000 per year to $5,000 or more for a senior man with major responsibilities. The real economic attractions of the job were, first, a chance for private speculation (often with money borrowed from the partners),[12] using an insider's knowledge of Philippine produce and of the Manila market for imports, and, second, the hope of eventually being accepted as a partner sharing in the profits of the firm. The gains from private speculation could be substantial. In 1863, George Peirce's total "adventure" (exporting cigars and rattans, importing "carriage goods," and so forth) made over 100 percent profit; in 1866–1867, he made $9,200 (nearly double his salary) on one shipment of abaca on margin, calculating it as 45 percent profit "on an invoice which employed none of my own capital." But there were also risks, and in other years he lost money on such ventures as imported codfish and beeswax (which were delayed in transit, arriving after Lent with the demand for both diminished and the fish spoiled), and exported indigo (which reached the United States just after Appomattox, with the need for blue uniforms suddenly reduced).[13]

Partnership offered even greater profits—and concomitantly greater risks. Besides interest on the partners' funds invested (calculated at 9 percent p.a.),[14] net profits in a good year could run as high as a quarter of a million dollars, divided proportionally among the partners according to their capital invested and the time they spent managing the business in Manila. At one time or another most of the partners could claim a net worth of over $150,000, with Palmer's nominal share in PHC reaching $290,000 in 1870.[15] The losses, however, could be ruinous.

Even in years when commodity prices were generally rising, PHC might lose money through unwise speculation in abaca (1864) or sugar (1869–1870). During the great cyclical depressions of the world economy, which hit the Philippine export trade heavily in 1857–1861 and 1873–1878, all the partners could hope to do was limit their losses. After his first eleven years in the Philippines (1852–1863), the last nine of them as a partner in PHC, Edwards had only $30,000 invested in the firm—an average net profit of less than $3,000 a year. PHC lost hundreds of thousands of dollars during the depression of the 1870s and nearly went bankrupt when Russell & Sturgis collapsed in 1875; it was saved only by a timely moratorium granted by its major creditors. The estate of George Peirce was entirely wiped out at this time, and Edwards, who had hoped he was leaving the Philippines forever when he departed in 1866, was forced to return in 1874 and periodically thereafter. When PHC finally failed in 1887, it ate up every dollar Edwards owned except the money in trust for his children's education.[16] Most other Americans in Manila fared no better.[17] Only a fortunate few, such as two partners of Russell & Sturgis who retired in 1871–1872, and PHC's Palmer, who retired at the end of 1873, escaped from the Philippines with their hard-bought fortunes largely intact.[18]

Nor was financial loss the only risk these merchants assumed. Their health was also constantly at stake. Of some twenty-odd Americans in PHC during this period, four, including George Peirce, died either in the Philippines or as a result of illnesses contracted or exacerbated there. Russell & Sturgis, for whom the surviving records are much less complete, lost at least as many. Although we lack their exact ages, it is very unlikely that any one of these men had reached his fortieth birthday at the time of his death. Among the surviving partners of PHC, Edwards reported notably impaired health ("ruined" by his years in the Philippines), Foster lost an infant son, and Lane wound up an alcoholic.[19] It is little wonder that personnel problems were among the major concerns of PHC during these years; the absence of suitable young men prevented the firm from entering certain branches of commerce, such as the tobacco trade, more vigorously.

The attitudes and values of the PHC partners were generally what one might expect of Yankees of their generation. Edwards and George Peirce, whose letters are the most revealing in non-business matters, were both staunch Republicans, avid Unionists before and during the Civil War, even Abolitionists.[20] They were serious-minded and religious, but they were aware of falling a little short of the highest religious norms of their culture; Peirce's future wife at one point broke off their correspondence because of doubts as to his devoutness, and Edwards confessed he could not read the sermons of his ancestor, the Puritan divine Jonathan Edwards.[21] Save as they were personally honest and expected honesty in others, there is no evidence that their religion ever directly affected their business dealings.[22] Political corruption was abominable to them, and in time they became disenchanted with the Republican Party under President Grant. Edwards even talked of returning to the United States to start a newspaper in favor of free trade, a non-elected judiciary, and an honest civil service.[23] They believed in literature, civilization, and culture, and generally bemoaned the absence of these in the Philippines.[24] One clear example of Western superiority was technology, of which they were typically Victorian in their admiration. Excited by the prospect of a Suez Canal and a cable to China, Peirce asked, "Will not men be better, as well as commerce flourish, from this rapid communication from point to point?"[25]

The vision of a perfectible future, along with the memory of a genteel, pious, and civilized America, contrasted vividly in the minds of these men with the "mean and repulsive" life of the Filipino—the "two footed caribao" [sic] misruled by Spanish bureaucratic "partisans and parasites" and by hypocritical priests "almost all . . . eager for money."[26] They held in contempt almost every aspect of local culture: climate, religion, clothing, indigenous architecture, entertainments, cuisine (they usually hired Chinese cooks rather than eat Filipino dishes), the courts (which offered no justice without money), the "province life of petty interests and mean intrigues," and the alleged indolence and dishonesty of all the inhabitants—natives (who love to gamble, "hate to labor," and "have a peculiar aptness & inclination to deceive") as well as Spaniards ("not a

labor-loving people"—"unscrupulous men, intent only upon
robbing the 'malditos estrangeros,' if they can").[27]

In their own eyes, the American merchants were honorable
men surrounded by cheating and dishonesty: "All men are liars
especially those who deal in Hemp." From the letters of Ogden
Edwards a classic nineteenth-century businessman's ethic can
be reconstructed—the sense of duty, the compulsion to hard
work, the fear (generally unwarranted) of being "too good na-
tured and yielding," the attempt to find the appropriate balance
between strict fairness and generosity toward friends (always in
tension during the periodic renegotiation of PHC partnership
agreements), and the rejection of "tricky" or "slippery" merchants. "Character," he piously affirmed, "is more important
than wealth." The precise dividing line between honest shrewd-
ness and unscrupulous "rascality" in business may be somewhat
obscure to us, but it was totally clear in the mind and conscience
of Edwards and his associates.[28]

Fortunately, perhaps, for the future of Philippine-American
relations, these manifestations of racism, cultural chauvinism,
and moralizing condescension had little impact on either society. The American merchants in the Philippines were not men
of great influence in the United States, although they may have
affected public perceptions of the Philippines indirectly through
their reports as United States consuls in Manila, their hosting of
foreign visitors to the islands, their correspondence with the
"China houses" and with American import firms, and their
contribution to a body of local "expertise" which their associates and successors relayed to the American colonialists in
1898.[29] Such connections are tenuous, however, and there is no
evidence that later Americans were conscious of any legacy from
PHC or Russell & Sturgis. As far as imposing their values on the
Philippines is concerned, the merchants, despite their convic-
tions of cultural superiority and their general sense of duty, had
very little of the missionary about them. "You do not go abroad"
William Peirce told his nephew, "to preach a Crusade against
the existing customs of the people." George Peirce, taking this
advice to heart, later remarked that it was not his business "to
subvert . . . or modify" Spanish rule, however deplorable.[30]

In spite of all their overt prejudices, the partners of PHC were pragmatists, and in the interests of doing business (and, perhaps, of keeping their own sanity) they assimilated themselves quite well to much of Hispanic Philippine society. They often sneered at Spaniards; nevertheless, they attended Spanish dances, ter-tulias, fiestas, and even clubs—at least until the "Casino" split in 1863 over whether members should wear white jackets or black.[31] Like the Spaniards around them, they bought, sold, and rode horses, and entered them in races at the Manila Jockey Club.[32] After deprecating the corruption in Spanish colonial government, they concluded that "between bribing judges and bribing Governors . . . the latter is the cheaper course"; acting on this principle they maintained good relations with, and granted numerous small favors to, Spanish provincial officials.[33] Eventually, despite themselves, some of them developed a real taste for Manila life. "You cannot yet realize," William Peirce wrote George from his home in New England, "how necessary the petty luxuries there enjoyed become and how much one misses them in this cold and inhospitable climate."[34] Only at religion and marriage did PHC partners draw the line, looking with great disapproval on those who married locally and con-verted to Roman Catholicism.[35] Otherwise, they were Hispan-ized, even to the extent of adopting Spanish epigrams as their own: *Vd. cuidado!* (Be careful), *Paciencia y barajas* (Have pa-tience and shuffle the cards).

The American merchants were Hispanized rather than Philip-pinized because it was Spaniards, not Filipinos, with whom they dealt. Both in Manila and in the provinces, a thin but indispens-able layer of Spaniards—far more important than Legarda recog-nized—served as insulation and intermediation between the foreign merchants and the *indios*.[36] The chief provincial agents of PHC were Spaniards, as were most of the sub-agents (*person-eros*) of these agents, the principal independent hemp brokers, their major business rivals (Muñoz Brothers and Nephews) and *their* principal associates, and, of course, the provincial officials and priests who also dabbled in trade. Furthermore, the vast majority of these were *peninsulares* (born in Spain); only one of these Spaniards was identified as an *español-filipino* (born in the Islands).[37]

This is not to suggest that the abaca industry was monopolized

by Spaniards; indeed, I have argued elsewhere that it was remarkable in its ethnic diversity.[38] Although most of its business
was with Spaniards, PHC also dealt with Spanish mestizos,
Chinese mestizos, Tagalogs, even a Bikolano or two, as well as
unnamed Chinese, whose role in the abaca trade of the Bikol
provinces increased gradually during this period.[39] The point is
that the Americans trading in the region had almost no contact
with ordinary Bikolanos.

Though the details are less clear for Manila and elsewhere in
the Philippines, the outlines are the same. PHC had regular dealings with British agency houses, with Spanish employees and associates,[40] with Spanish commercial rivals, and with miscellaneous Chinese competitors and suppliers, but hardly any at all
with Filipinos, save as domestic servants. Apparently no partner
of PHC ever bothered to learn any Philippine language;[41]
Spanish was the regular medium of communication. The firm
ran no haciendas, and thus had no tenants. When they were
forced to foreclose on a Spanish debtor's land in Albay, their
first thought was to find another Spaniard to run it for them.[42]
When they hired laborers for their abaca presses and warehouses,
they did so through contractors; most of these workers seem to
have been Chinese, anyway. PHC made only one brief and unsuccessful foray into importing during this period (1867-1868),
so they had no need to assess public taste or buying power.

American opinions of Filipino life and culture must, therefore, have been derived from superficial observation and from
their Spanish acquaintances. Foster had spent six years in the
Philippines, the last two as manager of the firm, before he first
saw how abaca fiber was actually grown and processed—on a
Spanish-owned plantation. By this time, he had doubtless been
exposed to numerous computations of the cost of production
and the mean living standard of the Filipino, so he saw no contradiction between trying his hand at the "heavy labour" of
abaca stripping (which it surely was) and almost immediately
afterwards proclaiming that "it costs the Indian no more to
make good than bad hemp."[43] Such insensitivity to the human
costs of non-white labor is all too typical of a certain kind of
colonial mentality. But it also reflects, like the endless asser-
tions that the Filipino was an indolent spendthrift, an American

adoption of the Spanish view of Philippine society—even though the Americans recognized that "the Spaniard generally speaks illy of the Indian."[44] This kind of secondhand acceptance of third-rate prejudices was to characterize American thinking right up to the Schurman Commission of 1899, which welcomed as "Filipino" the testimony of numerous witnesses of Spanish or predominantly Spanish ancestry, including the son of PHC's long-time bookeeper, Antonio V. Barretto.[45] Not until the twentieth century would Americans even begin to see the Filipinos through their own eyes.[46]

The same layer of Spaniards that hid the Filipinos from the Americans also served to conceal the Americans from Filipino eyes. Certainly what we know of the events of 1898–1900 suggests that most Filipinos had no recollections of what Americans were like. On the contrary, in Albay, at least, many of their ideas were derived from the anti-American propaganda of those ubiquitous if unloved culture-brokers, the Spaniards.[47] Nor is this really surprising. The residence, decades earlier, of two or three Americans in a province of over 200,000 Bikolanos was hardly more memorable than the passage through it of the German naturalist Fedor Jagor—perhaps less so, because Jagor got out into the countryside and forests, which the American generally avoided. For the significance of American merchants to Kabikolan, and the Philippines in general, we must look not at their backgrounds or prejudices, but at their business.

THE ABACA TRADE

> If you can find out about production of Hemp, and can foretell [sic] anything about same, with any degree of certainty, you will be considered the most intelligent Man known in modern times.
>
> Richard D. Tucker, letter to George Peirce, 9 October 1861, Peirce Family Papers.

In assessing the economic impact of American merchants on the Philippines, it is useful to distinguish between their catalytic role as pioneers of export trade in the first half of the nineteenth century, and their later efforts to control and expand the trade they had helped create. By accepting foreign orders for Philippine commodities, then borrowing local capital and "advancing" it to provincial suppliers, the merchant houses (British and American) had stimulated the rapid expansion of such crops as abaca and sugar. This commercialization of agriculture—a shift in perception and practice from farming for subsistence to farming for the market—was central to a transformation of Philippine society at least as profound as any brought about by direct American rule after 1898. In one sense, American merchants might be held responsible for most of the changes, good or bad, in the nineteenth-century Philippines. It was the merchant houses, Legarda argues, that "formed the nexus between the Philippine economy and the currents of world trade. The rising demand of the Western world for raw materials was transmitted by them to the country in which they operated."[48]

Once this essential "nexus" was established, however, the influence of American merchants was less than they believed it to be or hoped it might become. During the third quarter of the nineteenth century, they still dominated the abaca export trade and began to make serious efforts to control the provincial trade as well. There can be no doubt that they remained at the center of this growing industry they had helped create. But they thought of themselves not only as astute traders, but also as representatives of "Yankee enterprise" within a backward society, potentially capable of making commerce more modern and profitable. Yet a close study of their business operations 1856–1875—even before the bankruptcy of PHC in 1887— reveals certain limitations on their power to control the world in which they operated.

Peele, Hubbell & Co., like other agency houses in Manila, began as, and nominally remained, a firm of commission merchants. Through regular circulars sent to consuming markets, they advertised Philippine commodities available for export and quoted "Prices Current" for them.[49] On receipt of orders from abroad, PHC would fill them at then-prevailing prices (so long as these fell within the "limits" imposed by their clients), arrange for shipping and insurance, and ship goods to the importers at the latter's risk. On such a transaction they would collect a commission of 2.5 percent.[50] Payment was made (in advance) to PHC through bank drafts, usually on a British firm such as Baring Brothers.[51]

In practice, the operations of PHC and other agency houses were much more complex than this simple description suggests. There were ordinary but interminable complications such as juggling exchange rates between the peso (silver) and the dollar and the pound (both backed with gold), arranging for favorable terms for shipping (taking into account such factors as foreign wars and the volume of trade in other Asian ports), and ensuring that the quality of the goods exported conformed to standard grades (which became increasingly numerous and precise during the late nineteenth century). There were also ventures in areas other than trade—cordage manufacture, sugar milling, insurance, banking, steamship operations (including government mail contracts), and so forth—which sometimes seemed to absorb as much time and energy as the export business itself.

Even in export trade, moreover, PHC was never simply an "agency house." They also engaged in "own account" shipping of abaca, sugar, and other commodities to England and the United States. Anticipating a rising market (sometimes because they had reason to believe local production was about to decline), PHC would take on themselves the risk of a shipment of produce for the chance of a substantial profit when the goods reached their destination. This necessarily involved arrangements with import brokers in British and American ports, and, therefore, more commissions and complications; sometimes the shipments would be made "joint account," with PHC and the importers sharing the costs and risk. It is all but impossible to work out the balance between commission and own-account shipping by PHC, but clearly there were many years when the latter was much more important to the firm, responsible for both the great profits of 1866–1868 and the losses of 1869–1870.[52]

Given the great risks of "own-account" trading, why did PHC not content itself with commission business? The answer is twofold. During a rising market, of course, PHC had hopes for higher profits than a mere commission would offer. But during a declining market, commission business fell way off, or limits were imposed below what the Manila market would provide.[53]

The alternative to "own-account" trading then became doing no business at all—and this PHC could not afford. As Legarda first pointed out, PHC in effect operated as merchant bankers, receiving funds at interest (6 to 9 percent), which they then invested or loaned out again. The total obligations of the firm—up to four times its nominal capitalization—created a substantial interest load, which, combined with the fixed cost of salaries, and so on, made it all but impossible for the firm to remain idle, even in the worst of times when "it would have been far better for us if we had not shipped a [picul] of produce."[54] To obtain the regular supplies of produce necessary to sustain an export business, PHC had invested heavily in provincial "advances." In these "advances," most of their borrowed funds were not only illiquid, but were at considerable risk of default—a risk any stoppage of business would increase enormously. The implications of the advance system will be analyzed later; here it is sufficient to note that PHC was chronically undercapitalized and overcommitted. The very measures PHC had taken to stimulate and dominate the export trade had made it all but impossible for them to withdraw from that trade, even in the worst of times. The resulting inflexibility of action markedly limited their capacity to demonstrate "Yankee enterprise" by innovations, technological or commercial, in the abaca industry.

As far as abaca cultivation itself was concerned, the Americans had no effect whatsoever besides their general impetus to productivity. They owned no estates, and thus attempted no technological innovations directly. Nor did they have any indirect effect at this level; agricultural technology, patterns of landholding, and labor arrangements remained virtually unchanged throughout the nineteenth century.[55] Like the Spaniards before (and after) them the American merchants attempted to introduce new hemp-cleaning machines, but all of these failed utterly to displace the traditional labor-intensive but efficient "knife" used by the Bikolanos since the seventeenth century.[56] It remained for the Japanese in twentieth-century Davao to transform the system of abaca cultivation in the Philippines.

Intra-provincial transportation was also unaltered; abaca was carried from the fields to the markets and ports by carabao carts on dirt roads and by rafts down shallow rivers. In the ports, however, PHC and Russell & Sturgis were able to make some changes, beginning with an improved "screw press" for baling abaca, brought to Albay in 1858. This reduced the cost of freight to Manila by a small but critical margin (roughly 1 *real* per picul, equivalent to no more than 3.5 percent of the export price), so that all who would sell their abaca in Manila (rather than to the American agents in Albay) had to pay either a premium on freight or an extra fee for baling in the Americans' screw press.[57]

The second, and more important, American innovation was the introduction of the steamer into the Albay-Manila trade in 1871–1872. From just 10 percent of the abaca trade of Kabikolan carried in 1872, the steamers expanded to carry roughly three-quarters of the trade by 1886. Besides these technological innovations, the American merchant houses were responsible for the building of more substantial warehouses and piers in the region.[58] Thus, within the third quarter of the nineteenth century, there were visible changes in the conduct of the abaca trade in the provincial ports, all apparently attributable to American entrepreneurship. It should be noted, however, that the innovations were not themselves American. The steamers were British, as were the screw presses; and the warehouses and piers were of local construction, with no notable new elements of design. Moreover, the ability to utilize them was not a monopoly of the Americans. Spaniards were regularly operating screw presses in the Bikol provinces by 1859 and steamers no later than 1881 (with occasional single voyages as early as 1872).[59]

It was in business principles and practices rather than technology, however, that American merchants most sharply distinguished themselves from those around them. They felt that honesty, of which they claimed a near-monopoly, would show itself as the most profitable as well as the most ethical policy. They believed strongly in the rules of commerce and sanctity of contract—a faith that often backfired. Again and again, they entrusted large sums of money to men who did not repay them, and in many cases presumably had no intention of repaying them. Again and again, in a demonstration of surprising naïvety, the Americans were furious at this putative betrayal, a violation of basic trust and the most elementary principles of civilized commerce as they understood it. Yet, having given these loans with inadequate collateral (or none), they found that neither moral pressure nor legal sanctions provided adequate redress for nonpayment of debts or even more serious crimes against property. Twice within twenty years, PHC lost $80,000 in the province of Albay through the mismanagement and gross defalcations of their agents there, the Spaniard Juan E. Roco in 1856-1858 and the American J.B. (?) Endicott (Jr.?) in 1870-1873. Yet, when they had recourse to the Spanish courts against these blatant offenders and lesser miscreants, they found only that "the case drags on and the result is very uncertain."[60]

Within the Kabikolan and throughout the Philippines during the nineteenth century, there arose what might be called a "new legalism"—the implementation of a whole array of new rules and regulations regarding landholding, transfers of property, registration, licensing, and taxation. It was most visible in an enormous increase in the volume of notarized records (which for Albay rose from 1.4 books a year, 1844-1866, to 11.4 books a year, 1867-1890) and an explosive proliferation of the colonial bureaucracy, "an uninterrupted contradance of officials that made thousands and thousands of Spaniards pass through the Philippines like trains passing through a tunnel."[61] The Americans played some part in fostering this new legalism through their insistence on contracts and courts. Edwards almost despaired of imposing these principles on one mestizo *personero:* "He has no idea of being bound by a contract except as he gets the benefit[;] he forgets that every bargain has two parties with equal rights." Yet PHC did not give up; a few years later, George Peirce reported that, much as he disliked doing it, "I had to sue an insolent native for a small balance of an old debt."[62] In so doing, the Americans merely reinforced a transformation already in progress, arising from the general sweep of commercialization and from politics in peninsular Spain (combined with vastly improved transportation, by way of Suez). The Americans were a part of a process of change, but not masters of it—as their lack of success at manipulating courts and contracts demonstrated.

The same failure followed them in their persistent efforts to effect two structural changes in the provincial abaca trade—the creation of a monopsony and the abolition of the advance system. For twenty years, these twin themes recur endlessly in the correspondence of the partners in PHC, yet by 1875 they were no closer to accomplishment than they had been in 1856. An overview of these efforts does much to show the limits of American influence in the nineteenth-century Philippines.

It is hard for us, living in a century when anti-trust legislation is taken for granted (if not always enforced), to imagine a time when combinations in restraint of trade were not regarded as inherently wrong. In the nineteenth-century fiber trade, such "arrangements" were assumed to be in the natural order of things, no more to be protested than the weather. The history of the cordage industry in the United States is a history of an almost uninterrupted series of attempts to restrict competition or prevent it entirely. After the collapse of the greatest of these combinations, the National Cordage Company, the judgment of the industry was that it had been inefficient; no one considered (or bothered to say) that it was in any way immoral.[63] Manila merchants generally resented such combinations at the consuming end, but only because they usually did not benefit themselves. In 1868, Edwards suggested that PHC should ship its abaca to Britain through Barings rather than their regular importer, because, since Barings already handled the hemp of Russell & Sturgis, "our consignments will give them a large control of the market."[64]

Within the Philippines, mercantile collusion goes back to the 1840s at least, when Russell & Sturgis told its constituents that abaca prices would remain stable "so long as the collection of it is confined to the Americans who purchase in company and thus avoid a competition fatal to the interests of all." It was competition, not monopoly, that was perceived as the threat to an orderly market—particularly competition from British merchant houses, which seems to have begun that same year.[65] PHC did not object to competition at a distance or in the abstract; George Peirce dismissed Spanish complaints of Chinese competition in the retail trade, pointing out that, if the Chinese could sell goods cheaper, the native consumer would benefit.

But where it affected PHC, particularly in buying abaca in Albay, they sang a different tune: "Something must be done to stop competition."[66]

Through most of this period, the chief obstacle to PHC's dream of monopsony in Albay was the firm of Muñoz Brothers and Nephews, supported by the British houses of Manila. Other rivals included Fred Baker & Co., with whom there had been a brief but expensive "Hemp War" in 1857–1858, and Russell & Sturgis, in the period before the creation of the "joint account" in 1862.[67] In the 1870s, the Americans anticipated a desperate attack from Smith, Bell & Co. on their position as "monopolists" of the abaca trade, but the British firm moved first into the less-developed fringes of the abaca-producing zone (Sorsogon, Leyte, and Samar) rather than into Albay itself.[68] Thus, the major rivals remained the *peninsular* brothers José, Antonio, and Francisco Muñoz de Bustillo, resident in Albay by the mid 1850s, whose polite "enmity" to PHC was felt as early as 1859 and whose competition continued, unabated by all efforts at "arrangement," until the demise of the American firm in 1887.[69]

The best-documented effort of the Americans to come to terms with José Muñoz, head of the firm, occurred in 1864–1865, when abaca prices were rising after a lengthy depression. In October 1863, they had thought they could simply "block him" if he tried to increase his province business, since he could not afford to "run amuck" with them. But, by February 1864, they were hoping to persuade him to collude with them in fixing prices by promising him one-third of all the abaca shipped out of Albay, excluding the port of Tabaco. Muñoz, backed by Ker & Co., did not agree. Edwards could never understand why such a self-evidently beneficial arrangement could not be reached: "If you get a strong opposition going in Albay there will not be much profit in the business." An uneasy truce was concluded in August 1864, when Jonathan Russell and Muñoz agreed to put province prices down together, but by early 1865 the arrangement was breaking down. Another meeting between the American merchants and Muñoz was scheduled in the hopes of preventing a "clash"—"so that we can keep on making money and not making bad debts." By now they were prepared to offer him one-third of Albay's abaca *including* that shipped through Tabaco. A draft agreement on price-fixing and division of output was submitted to Muñoz in June 1865. Its object was "to avoid competition" and the high prices which sometimes slowed down "the good march of business." But Muñoz refused to sign (perhaps he foresaw that abaca prices were about to take a spectacular climb?) and the Americans resigned themselves to cutting their margins rather than be "run off" by Muñoz and be forced to "drop the hemp trade" entirely.[70]

Thus the rivalry continued. In 1867 there was a flurry of activity when Ker & Co., anxious for more abaca, tried to "run" the joint account off again and Muñoz hoped to take advantage of an inexperienced American agent in Albay. The Americans survived that threat, however, and by 1868 the situation seemed reversed. Rumor had it that "Dn Jose Muñoz intends leaving, and the brokers will be much more inclined to fall together with us. At all events I think more Money will be made for white people and less for our Indian and Spanish amigos if a good understanding exist [*sic*]." But Muñoz did not in fact depart. By 1875 PHC had concluded that the only place to shut him out was at the exporting end. If PHC could get Ker & Co. "to bind themselves . . . to purchase from us," all would be solved. Unfortunately, however, it was "altogether Ker & Co.'s policy to support the opposition," even to the extent of taking a shipment of overpriced abaca off the hands of Muñoz at the latter's own price.[71] After this date, the documentation becomes sparse, but enough remains to show that the Muñoz family continued as independent traders and local political bosses in Albay into the 1890s—after the fall of PHC.

The motives behind PHC's efforts to establish an abaca-buying combination in Albay are clear enough. The primary one was to drive down provincial prices, so as to make "more Money . . . for white people." Even without such a monopsony that was a recurrent strategy of PHC. When a new screw press in Tabaco gave them a momentary edge in shipping costs, Palmer immediately wrote George Peirce, "As we now have some little ventaja [advantage] in Tabaco over the buyers I would make a strong effort to get prices down a little."[72] Sometimes the ambitions were more grandiose: "You must keep the

price of Hemp down in Manila and provinces and see if production cannot be curtailed somewhat, as but little profits will result, if large ship[men]ts to continue [sic]." Generally, however,
the firm was glad enough to see large production so long as the
profit margin was substantial. Recurrent efforts to calculate the
minimum price at which production remained marginally profitable to the growers and laborers reflected this viewpoint. It was
partly a question of will: "Of course the native resists low prices
and strict classification, but the question is how long can he
hold out?" But PHC also realized that it might be dangerous to
depress prices below a certain point, because "all the extensive
advances made to producers may be entirely lost if the Albay
& Leyte people are condemned to turn their labor to other
produce."[73]

This was the other advantage of monopsony—it would allow
PHC to establish some control over the advance system, which
perpetually seemed to be getting out of hand. Foster put it
most bluntly: "If the [joint account] does not retain its position
as a 'monopoly', or at least as 'leaders' in the hemp business,
our permanent investments in 'advances' will become poor
property."[74]

American merchant houses had begun "advancing" money to
provincial brokers and growers almost from the time of their
establishment in the 1820s.[75] By the mid 1850s, PHC advances
in the province of Albay alone amounted to nearly $150,000,
increasing to an estimated $200,000 by the mid 1870s, plus
$70,000 more in Leyte. Russell & Sturgis had equivalent in-
vestments in abaca, plus more than $1 million in sugar advances
by 1876. The surviving records do not tell us how much of this
money actually circulated each year and how much was simply
the accumulation of nominal bookkeeping balances, but in
either case it represented a significant investment for firms
nominally capitalized at less than a million dollars. With their
advances in Albay, however, the American merchant houses
were able to control half to two-thirds of the abaca trade in
that province, the average worth of which increased from $1.2
million to $2.2 million between the 1850s and the 1870s.[76]

Through the advance system, PHC became involved in commodity speculation even when they were nominally acting as

commission agents. The firm sent money to Albay through provincial agents, who advanced it to *personeros,* who in turn advanced some of it to sub-sub-agents (*personeritos*) or directly to growers, in return for abaca to be delivered at a slightly later date. Thus, the "joint account" already owned the abaca when it was delivered to them in Legazpi or Tabaco at the province price, roughly one dollar less than the Manila price. They then pressed it into bales, shipped it to Manila, and listed it at the going export price, which in good times would give them a small profit on each bale even after deducting the real costs of pressing, shipping, loading, insurance, and storage. When they received a foreign order, they then bought the abaca (at the export price) from themselves, collecting the usual 2.5 percent commission when they shipped it out. The potential benefits of this practice—an early, if crude, form of transfer pricing—are obvious.[77]

Seen in this light, the advance system was a rational way for Westerners to do business. The merchant houses gained the advantages of a regular supply of export produce and potential profits from processing and transfer pricing. To achieve this they had to tie up (at interest) a substantial amount of their capital, though not nearly so much as direct investment in abaca plantations would have required. If the system had ever worked as PHC felt it should, they would have obtained maximum leverage for their capital in the abaca trade, taking only those risks inherent in any commodity speculation. Yet, their correspondence shows that the system never worked quite as they envisaged it, and the Americans were consistently unable either to make it conform to their model or to escape from it entirely. At the root of their problem was the fact that it was not really an American system; it was essentially an indigenous system in which the Americans participated as uncomprehending partners.

In one form or another, the advance system could be found in almost every Third World society in which export goods were produced by smallholders or by voluntary wage labor. In Southeast Asia, it characterized the rice industries of Burma, Thailand, and Vietnam, the pepper industry of Aceh, various export industries in Java, the sugar and indigo production of the eighteenth-century Philippines, even the sago industry of twentieth-century Sarawak. "A Javanese without an advance," grumbled one

Dutchman, "fades away and dies an early death."[78] In its basic form, the producer of goods or services demanded and received a substantial portion of his payment or wages in advance. (Sometimes this was urged on him by the buyer or employer, but not so often as later critics of the system would claim.)[79] Every middleman in the system—frequently characterized by an extended hierarchy of intermediaries—both provided advances to his agents and suppliers and demanded an advance from the superior to whom he was to pass on the goods or labor. Westerners, raised in the ethic of payment only for work done or goods delivered, often found this system repugnant, but they also found it unavoidable.

The advance, seen from the perspective of an indigenous producer, might have both economic and cultural functions. Economically, its most important function was to filter capital down to the levels where it was needed for expansion of production and subsistence of labor. In the case of abaca, substantial labor was required to clear the forest and plant the trees; then it took two or three years before the first harvesting could take place. Someone had to put up the money for this, as well as for warehouses, carts, rafts, and other capital equipment. Moreover, if the laborers stripped abaca fulltime (rather than combining this with subsistence farming) they had to be fed until they could afford to buy their own food.

This economic rationale, though it had a certain validity, did not by itself explain the ubiquity of the advance system. In prosperous times, the workers of Albay had suffcient funds to gamble at cock-fighting and cards, while the landlords enjoyed even more conspicuous surpluses available for building luxurious homes, buying political influence, and paying for the education of their sons; yet both groups continued to demand advances.[80] Moreover, the continued existence of a competitive commodity market parallel with the advance system also suggests that it was possible to mobilize some productive capacity in the Philippines without recourse to advances.

One cultural function of the system, less understood than its economic function, was the creation of patron-client networks. In the ideal Western scheme of things, each transaction, like each work of literature, is perceived as complete, with a Beginning and an Ending, money borrowed and repaid in full, contracts stipulating exactly how much (or how little) each party must do, no loose ends. But, from the indigenous Asian viewpoint, the emphasis in economics, as in drama, was on continuity. A given transaction was only one manifestation of an ongoing relationship; the very act of exchange implied a future exchange. Thus an advance was a means of creating an ongoing patron-client relationship in which the debt was never totally repaid, nor the mutual obligation totally exhausted. The debtor/client was then committed to providing such goods and favors as the creditor/patron might reasonably request, while the patron owed the client protection and such further loans as might be needed. John Foreman was correct when he observed that "a native considers it no degradation to borrow money; it gives him no recurrent feeling of humiliation or poignant distress of mind . . . . At most, he regards debt as an inconvenience, not as a calamity."[81] But his indignation was misplaced. The advance system, with its perpetuation of a debt relationship, offered certain cultural advantages to both parties, prestige and influence to the giver, security (and the status of being recognized as credit-worthy) to the recipient.

Midway between the capital-providing and the patronage-building functions of the advance system fell a third function, perhaps the most important—that of shifting the risks of commercial enterprise to a higher level in the hierarchy. Since payment was in advance, it was the giver, not the receiver, who was temporarily embarrassed when anything went wrong. It seems to have been understood that, if any disaster befell the cultivator or the crop, or if the market fell, the loan would simply not be repaid until times were better, although the nominal size of the debt would increase. Moreover, the giver of the original advance was often obliged to provide a supplementary advance at such times if he ever hoped to have any of the debt repaid. Otherwise, the debtor might simply disappear, turning "advances . . . into insolvent credits." No contract, written or implied, could resist the fluctations of fortune or supersede the basic indigenous principle of equity that those most able to should bear any loss, since those at the bottom always had a right to survive.[82]

This is not the place to elaborate further on the functions of the advance system or even to enquire how it actually was perceived at all levels of the abaca trade. What is clear is that the Americans understood little of this, appreciated it even less, yet, despite decades of protest and plotting, were quite powerless to change it. Their correspondence shows that PHC regarded the advance system as a nuisance and felt no more than the most perfunctory obligations toward old clients, agents, or suppliers. They gave advances because they could not obtain enough abaca without doing so. They kept giving advances because there was no way to withdraw without losing the money already advanced. But they resolutely resisted the idea that they were bound to anything beyond their contractual obligations.[83]

By 1856, PHC's abaca ventures in Albay were already "rotten" with advances, which led to disastrous losses in the depression which followed the "hemp war" with Baker and the discovery of Roco's defalcations.[84] The partners never forgot this, but neither were they ever able to construct a working alternative to the system. No more money should be advanced, they said, "to the small fry who have swallowed heretofore such large quantities"—but, at the same time, several new advances (of $2,000–$3,000 each) were being made, and larger ones were to follow.[85] By 1864, Edwards, who had been managing partner during the worst years, had begun admonishing George Peirce on the subject, as he was to do regularly until the latter's death a decade later. "Look how your advances grow," he warned. "Little by little those chaps alike destitute of means, or honesty get into you—and your temporary advance becomes a fixed one & your fixed advance a dead loss." Two weeks later he admitted that he knew how hard it was "to retrace steps once taken in this direction. The advance asked as a favor in the first instance, is held afterwards as a matter of right and to call in these advances will create ill feeling to some extent—However it must be done."[86]

But those were years of booming fiber markets, and the job of Peirce and his successors in Albay was to buy abaca, not to stand idle on principle. Four years later, with Peirce now managing in Manila, Edwards continued to complain that Albay advances were creeping up, and suggested that PHC should put a "Yankee" with a strongbox in each of the market towns, paying cash down for every picul. Although more agents were sent to Albay, the system remained unchanged, and by 1871 Edwards was reminded by the large advances outstanding of "the old bad style of business" in the days of Roco.[87]

The situation worsened when abaca began to fall again in the early 1870s and borrowers began to default. By 1874, Foster had come around to the solution earlier advocated by Edwards: "We have got to remodel our Province Hemp business on a cash basis." This was easier said than done, however, as he admitted to PHC's agent in Ligao, Albay: "I appreciate the difficulties of ever getting any money out of those Chinamen, and, of course, if we do not furnish them with money, they are not likely to deliver any hemp, and to run the risk of increasing their debt to us is not to be thought of for a minute." As much as Foster might fulminate that "the advance system is ruinous and ought to be done away with altogether," it continued in existence, and PHC continued bound to it.[88]

Whether or not any exporter could have run an abaca business on a "cash basis" during this period is questionable. Certainly PHC could not, if for no other reason than that they could never afford to try. Cutting off advances would have meant both losing those advances already made and risking having to turn away commission orders because there was not enough abaca for sale on the open market. So long as no arrangement could be made with competitors, such as Muñoz, to cut off all advances simultaneously, most of the crop would continue to be sold before it reached the provincial markets, often even before it was harvested. In order to pay interest on borrowed capital, to keep *personeros* loyal, and to retain customers in the consuming markets, PHC needed to "turn over" their capital rapidly and maintain a constant flow of abaca. Eventually, PHC proposed to set aside a sum of $10,000 in the partnership for "prospective depreciation of province advances," on the assumption that it was better to plan for that steady and inevitable drain than be surprised by it after the losses had accumulated.[89] Although the sum proposed was too small, the assumption was sound, so PHC went on, after all their protests, doing business the Philippine way.

The structural changes that did occur in the Philippine economy had more to do with imperialism as a system than with the American merchants as conscious imperialists. If PHC did not exploit the Filipinos, it was not for want of trying; exploitation, defined as taking from the worker the real value of what he produces, leaving just enough to live on, was exactly what they intended for the abaca cultivators of Kabikolan.[90] But because they never succeeded in establishing the monopoly which they desired, their efforts at such exploitation were inefficient. Levels of living in Kabikolan apparently rose slightly during the nineteenth century,[91] while the American merchants, despite the huge profits they made from time to time, eventually went bankrupt.

While PHC lasted, however, the firm had played an important part in incorporating Kabikolan into an international capitalist economy, characterized by an imbalance of profits and of power between the core and the periphery. Legarda has described how the Americans helped to link the Philippines to world markets— markets that in time would come to control the rhythm of the Philippine conomy. Here we are concerned also with the linkage between Manila and Kabikolan, and the increasing dominance of the former over the latter. Not only were provincial price limits set in Manila, and decisions made there as to fiber quality, collection points, and shipping terms, but the Americans, unfamiliar with local resources, imported into the province the screw press (displacing local devices), the steamer (all but destroying local shipbuilding), skilled labor, even some foodstuffs, mats and rattans for baling, and lumber for repairing godowns.[92] Thus many of the potential "multiplier" benefits of the abaca boom were diverted to Manila and abroad. At the same time, the screw press, steamers, stone warehouses, and private piers made the provincial trade more capital-intensive; the trend toward its concentration in fewer (and usually foreign) hands continued even after the fall of the American firms.[93]

The effect of each of these shifts was to increase the dependence of Manila on the West, of Kabikolan on Manila, and of provincial cultivators on provincial capitalists. Although in the short run such a system might prove profitable to all, in the long run those on the periphery would lose control over their own resources and therefore over their own destiny—a classic result of imperialism. The ultimate consequences of this loss of autonomy are beyond the scope of this chapter, though the persistent poverty of both the region and the nation may be among them.[94] It is clear, however, that once again the merchants of PHC were not so much masters of their fate as participants in a larger process which they comprehended dimly, if at all.

The eventual failure of PHC in 1887 may cast some light backward on the fundamental weaknesses of the American merchants in Kabikolan. The proximate cause of bankruptcy is clear: "Sugar did it." Between 1882 and 1886 PHC all but abandoned the abaca trade to plunge heavily in sugar, which proceeded to suffer a world crisis, precipitated by the rise of government-subsidized sugar-beet cultivation in Europe. The Hongkong & Shanghai Bank, PHC's largest creditor, refused to make any more advances and instead began calling in its loans. A "junta" of PHC's Spanish creditors was unable to save the firm, though they offered a moratorium on their loans, as they had in 1875, and eventually PHC went under, paying 10 to 20 cents on the dollar. The steamer and insurance agencies, the Samar abaca business, and the Manila screw press were picked up by Edwin H. Warner (a British PHC clerk), Earle W. Blodgett (an American), and Charles I. Barnes (formerly of the Hongkong & Shanghai Bank), assisted by Palmer, who also helped them get the San Francisco hemp business, the only American market PHC had managed to retain.[95]

Gaps in the surviving evidence prevent us from tracing clearly the transition from the PHC of 1876, which had survived the failure of Russell & Sturgis and remained the leading abaca exporter in the Philippines, to the PHC of 1886, which had virtually forsaken abaca to plunge wholeheartedly into the precarious sugar business. The explanation for the change may simply be unwise management—errors in judgment comparable to those which had merely cost PHC profits in the generally buoyant 1860s, but were ruinous in the collapsing sugar market of the 1880s. Or PHC's failure to hold its place in the American fiber market may instead be attributable to the incompetence of its import brokers, as Edwards often implied, though that begs the question of why PHC did not switch brokers.[96] Personnel attrition may have enfeebled the leadership of PHC, as bright young men (George Peirce, Huntington, Foster, Ramón Arlegui) died or left the firm, leaving control in the hands of senior partners (Edwards and Tucker, assisted by Palmer) long since tired of Manila and the whole business.

There are some broad parallels with the decline of American merchant houses in China after the extension of the cable to Hong Kong in 1871 and the establishment of British banks there.[97] The former innovation almost eliminated one major commodity the merchant houses had to offer—expert knowledge of (or at least educated guesses as to) both the supply and demand ends of the trade. They had made their living for decades as brokers of information, as well as commodities, between two distant societies; now the linkage was direct, and the brokerage no longer needed. PHC partners realized some, if not all, of the implications of the cable—profits would depend more on volume, less on windfall transactions, and so forth.[98] But the realization itself could not restore their old advantage.

The Chartered Bank of India, Australia, & China opened a branch in Manila in 1872; the Hongkong & Shanghai Bank followed suit in 1875.[99] Their arrival meant, first, the loss to PHC of potentially profitable exchange transactions—"Now that we have a Bank here it is difficult for a private firm to undertake exchange operations."[100] It also facilitated the rise of competition by "the speculative element in commerce . . . fostered by the anxiety of large capitalists to find an outlet for their money."[101] Moreover, the banks soon came to dominate the capital market within the Philippines, so that PHC wound up borrowing more extensively from them, and less from the Spanish merchants, bureaucrats, and even priests who had previously been their creditors. Thus PHC was far more dependent on the Hongkong & Shanghai Bank in 1887 than it had been in 1875, and so was less able to ride out the final crisis after the bank refused to concede further credits or extensions.[102]

Meanwhile, as in China, the agents, associates, and rivals of the American merchants were expanding their activities in shipping and brokerage. There is some evidence that within Albay the continued competititon of the Spaniards, the rising activity of the Chinese, and the direct involvement of the British firms were whittling away at the American lead in the abaca trade, although as late as 1886 Edwards claimed that PHC's agent was still "the principal buyer in Legaspi," while Spanish rivals Muñoz and Aramburu were "pretty much out of the market."[103] In the internal trade of the Philippines, the Americans had no inherent edge; those advantages they had gained by being pioneers could easily disappear whenever adequately financed rivals emulated them.

This is, of course, far from a complete explanation of the failure of the American merchants in the Philippines. Many of the same obstacles faced the British firms which had competed with the Americans for half a century. Indeed, right up to the collapse of Russell & Sturgis in 1875, Foster was arguing that Smith, Bell & Co. was the Manila house most overextended and likely to fail. The later rationalizations that the British firms had better access to capital (through British banks) and greater freedom from bureaucratic harassment (through stronger British diplomacy) are unconvincing. There is no contemporary evidence that British banks discriminated against American merchants (in fact, the agent of the Hongkong & Shanghai Bank in Manila up to 1875 was Russell & Sturgis), nor that bureaucratic interference varied significantly by nationality; and neither of these excuses was mentioned by PHC in 1875 or 1887.[104] The most plausible explanation for the survival of the British houses —other than simply wiser management—was their involvement in the import trade, which the Americans eschewed. This not only spread their risks (and opportunities for profit), but it necessarily linked them with Chinese retailing networks throughout the Philippines. When the Chinese expanded their procurement of export produce during the last quarter of the nineteenth century, it would have been logical for them to have delivered this produce to the British, rather than to the American, houses.[105]

If this chapter has focused on the weaknesses of the American merchant houses rather than their strengths—they did, after all, survive for over half a century in one of the most precarious outposts of the capitalist world economy—it is in part because Legarda has so admirably described their entrepreneurial virtues.

They saw the possibilities of a connection between Philippine supply and Western demand and forged the links themselves, mobilizing local capital to promote production, borrowing abroad to finance shipping, establishing a chain of contacts all the way from Legazpi to London. Most of the Americans also worked hard, followed as best they could good business practices of the day, and exercised prudent mercantile judgment more often than not. They were generally willing to take calculated risks and to postpone temporary gratification in the interest of longer-term profits. They were more "businesslike" than any merchants the Philippines had seen before; when the firms finally went bankrupt, it was because their competitors had caught up to the standards they had pioneered, leaving them no margin for error.

In the long vista of history, however, the American merchant in the Philippines failed to turn American know-how—technological and commercial—into permanent advantage. PHC had introduced few innovations, and failed to monopolize those they introduced. They had played only a small part in the rise of the new legalism and still got bogged down in unfulfilled contracts and unrewarding court battles. They had failed to create the provincial monopsony they had sought for decades, and they never curbed the advance system that so persistently plagued them. Although they had helped incorporate Kabikolan into a global system of imperialism, they had not themselves reaped the rewards of exploitation. In spite of their position as "leaders" in an industry they had helped create, eventually the American merchants could not dominate it. They had believed that it was easy to understand the "native" and that "Yankee enterprise" would always prevail over local customs. Despite their real accomplishments, in these two beliefs they were proved wrong—thus foreshadowing a multitude of later Philippine-American interactions.

The Search for Revenues

FRANK H. GOLAY

Modernization and development of the Philippines were prominent among the shared interests that made possible the collaboration of American and Filipino leaders. Hence their emphasis on roads, schools, harbors, public health measures, and agricultural development programs. For often dissimilar reasons, the two groups also agreed to promote the colony's political development. American conceptions of federalism and Filipino concern for the family and its local bases of power led to a steady enlargement of the autonomy vested in local levels of government. At the same time, Filipinos' power in the provincial and central governments grew, as well.

Recently, historians have concluded that achievements in all these spheres were far more modest than the rhetoric of an earlier age would lead one to believe. Frank H. Golay, retired professor of economics and former director of the Southeast Asia Program at Cornell University, argues that this shortfall can be traced to the failure of American and Filipino leaders to agree upon the governmental priorities behind their policies.

As their power grew, Filipino leaders turned out to have less interest than their would-be mentors in mobilizing Philippine society for development or creating a representative democracy along American lines. The struggle to design and implement a system capable of supplying reliable and adequate public revenues reveals these differing priorities.

In this chapter, Golay marshals evidence to show that development and tutelage in self-government were set back by concern for governmental efficiency, resistance to taxation, and ambivalence as to the distribution of power between local and central governments. The determination of Democrats in the United States and nationalists in the Philippines to press independence above other issues brought to a premature end the developmental policies that distinguished the initial stage of American rule in the Philippines.

As a latecomer to the final scramble for overseas colonies in the last quarter of the nineteenth century, the United States apparently confronted a choice among colonial models. Closer scrutiny, however, reveals that differences in economic aspects of colonial policy and practice were insubstantial. Governments of colonies were expected to be self-supporting and in a few prominent cases provided sizeable subventions to the home governments. There were two departures from this colonial principle. The metropolitan power could not escape responsibility for defense of its colonies and maintained such sea power as the home society was willing to afford for this purpose. Colonial governments also were given preferential access to the capital market of the home country, and savings mobilized by the sale of bonds provided funds for the construction of railroads, street railways, and other "public improvements." These capital projects enhanced the attractiveness of a colony as an outlet for foreign capital and entrepreneurship, which were expected to support economic development in the colony.

Colonial tax systems reflected the priority assigned to productiveness of the tax base and ease of administration. Ability to pay, progressiveness in rates, and sumptuary considerations received little attention. Generally, the tariff was the major source of revenues as the burden could be imposed disproportionately on the indigenous society, and administration was simplified where imports were funneled through one or a few major ports. Substantial revenues were also derived from excise taxes on commodities such as alcoholic beverages, tobacco products, salt, and opium, for which demand was inelastic. Such items could be taxed at high rates without reducing materially the amount consumed. To obtain a contribution to the cost of government from those outside the market economy, poll taxes, the corvée, or obligatory labor service, and, in a few cases, taxes on land were used. Fees for services in excess of the cost of providing the service, stamps required on documents, fees for inspections and certifications, rentals of market stalls, and wharfage charges frequently generated significant revenues.

REVENUE GENERATION UNDER AMERICAN RULE

Americans embarked upon colonial rule of the Philippines confident of the high purpose of that venture and with ambitious plans for the colony which would maintain unrelenting pressure on the financial resources of the colonial government. To shepherd America's Filipino charges along the path to representative self-government and material well-being, President McKinley appointed the Philippine Commission headed by William Howard Taft, a young federal judge and formerly Solicitor General, to govern the islands once the United States Army had suppressed the revolutionary ardor of the Filipinos. McKinley charged the Commission to give the colony enlightened government and an efficient civil service and to extend free, secular, primary education over the Islands.[1] The Commission found other challenges after disembarking at Manila. Within a few weeks, the Commission was busy with plans to transform Manila into a healthy, habitable city and modern port; to build a summer capital to which Americans could flee the hot, dry season; to facilitate development of the colony's resources with all-weather roads and bridges, regional ports, and other "public improvements"; and to modernize and extend public health services and facilities.

On 1 September, four months after arriving in the Philippines, the Taft Commission assumed legislative power in the insular government. The Commission turned promptly to the task of devising a revenue system that would generate adequate financial resources for the colonial administration. To do so, the Commission planned to rely heavily on tariff duties which provided two-thirds of the revenues of the Spanish government of the islands. Taft and his colleagues were eager to demonstrate the superiority of American colonialism, and they intended to organize a government that would provide more and better services than those made available by the Spanish. For this they would need more revenues.

Efforts to raise more revenues from the insular tariff had been under way since the military authorities resumed collection of the Spanish tariff upon occupying Manila in August 1898. Frequent increases were made in tariff rates, and the War Department undertook a systematic revision of the insular tariff which was in process when the Commission arrived in the Islands. The Commission's plans to reform the insular tariff were brought to a halt shortly after they started, however, when the so-called "Insular Cases" reached the Supreme Court.[2] These cases raised the constitutional issue of the power of Congress to legislate for the islands ceded by Spain in 1898. The plaintiffs in the initial cases were importers of Puerto Rican products who protested the payment of United States tariff duties, contending that Puerto Rico had become United States territory, and as such came under the constitutional ban against taxation of internal trade. The Commission was faced, therefore, with the possibility that the Philippines would come within the American tariff wall and the prohibition of duties on internal trade. If this should happen, imports from the United States would quickly capture the Philippine market and deprive the colonial government of revenues from tariff duties. Faced with this uncertainty, the Commission turned to other problems.

To minimize friction with the Military Government, Secretary of War Elihu Root, who drafted McKinley's instructions to the Taft Commission, enjoined the Commission "to devote their attention in the first instance to the establishment of municipal governments in which the natives of the islands both in the cities and rural communities, shall be afforded the opportunity to manage their local affairs to the fullest extent of which they are capable." The Commission was cautioned, moreover, that "in the distribution of powers among governments the presumption is always to be in favor of the smaller subdivision . . . so that in the governmental system the central government shall

The Search for Revenues 235

have no direct administration of matters of purely local concern, and shall have only such supervision and control over local governments as may be necessary to secure and enforce faithful and efficient administration by local officers."[3]

Root's instructions reflected the American experience with local autonomy and the Commission found congenial the emphasis on local government as the instrument through which Filipino charges would acquire experience in self-government. The Commission members also shared the conviction that self-reliant local governments would emerge as communities acquired experience in collecting taxes and providing services which would earn the loyalty of Filipinos to their local governments. To begin the scheme for training Filipinos in self-government, the Commission, early in 1901, enacted the Municipal Code under which the colony was blanketed with participatory governments, each embracing the principal urban community in its area and the surrounding villages, or barrios.[4] To provide financial resources for these governments, the Municipal Code established a tax on land and improvements at the rate of seven-eighths of one percent of their assessed value. The law allocated four-sevenths of the revenues from this tax to municipal governments, of which half was earmarked for primary schools and half for general governmental purposes. The remaining three-sevenths of the proceeds were allocated to provincial governments with one-third reserved for construction and maintenance of roads and bridges.

Meanwhile, the Supreme Court, by a narrow 5–4 majority, decided against the importer-plaintiffs in the Insular Cases. Reassured by the Court's decision that the tariff would be a major source of revenues, the Commission resumed work on a suitable tariff, which was enacted in September 1901.[5] The resulting tariff retained most duties of the Spanish tariff, but many rates were raised and new duties imposed. The tariff was designed to collect a larger share of revenues from imports consumed by well-to-do Filipinos and Chinese and American commercial classes, and reduced somewhat rates on foods and cheaper textiles. The tariff also continued the Spanish duties on exports which produced substantial revenues.

Tinkering with the tariff to increase its productiveness did not cease with enactment of the Philippine tariff of 1901. Limited revisions of the tariff recommended by insular customs officials were enacted by Congress in 1905 and 1906. In 1909, a thorough revision of the tariff designed to minimize the loss of insular revenues expected to result from mutual free trade between the colony and the United States was approved by Congress as a companion measure to the Payne-Aldrich revision of the American tariff.[6]

The final task faced by the Commission in erecting a revenue system for the colony was that of devising an appropriate structure of internal revenue taxes to replace the cumbersome, regressive, and relatively unproductive taxes that evolved under Spanish rule. As the Commission proceeded step by step in erecting a revenue system, its members expected Congress to vest the Commission with ample powers to ensure economic development of the Islands. The Commission members expected to initiate development by creating incentives that would attract American capital and enterprise to the colony. Such development would moderate pressures on the insular government to provide welfare payments and services and, at the same time, generate increasing tax revenues.

The abrasive debate over ratification of the Treaty of Paris in 1899 left Congress deeply split along party lines over policy toward the new Asian colony. Efforts of the McKinley Administration in 1900 to push through Congress the Spooner Bill giving the Commission virtually a free hand to govern the colony were turned back by the Democratic minority. This setback was repeated in 1901 when Senator Spooner attached his measure to the annual army appropriation bill. Threatened by a filibuster in the short "lame duck" session, the McKinley Administration accepted amendments that emasculated the authority it intended to vest in the Commission.[7]

McKinley, who was governing the Philippines under his war powers through the Military Government, expected Congress to approve the Spooner measure and scheduled the transfer to civil government under the Commission in July 1901. The failure of the Spooner Amendment to survive intact, however, left the Commission with powers inadequate to carry out the Administration's plans for the colony. To obtain an organic law or constitution for the new civil government of the colony, Theodore Roosevelt, who succeeded to the presidency when McKinley was assassinated in the fall of 1901, was confronted by a full-scale debate on Philippine policy in the new 57th Congress. Root cabled Taft that Congress would draft such a law and requested the Commission to recommend provisions to be included in the measure.[8]

Concerned to get the Islands' economy moving after five years of rebellion, war, and economic dislocation, the Commission urged Congress to allow American enterprise and capital to play a major role in developing the colony. The Commission proposed that the migration of these resources be induced by permitting American investors liberal access to Philippine public lands, and mineral and forest resources; by empowering the Commission to charter corporations and grant franchises on liberal terms; by permitting the Commission to sell bonds in the United States to raise money to build ports, roads, and other public works; by amending the National Banking Act to permit American banks to operate in the colony; and by granting imports from the Philippines a substantial and nonreciprocal reduction in the American tariff.[9]

To help shepherd the government bill through Congress, Taft was recalled to Washington. In testifying before the Senate Committee on the Philippines, Taft described the system of local governments that had been created in the islands and emphasized the Commission's plans to provide financial resources for these governments. Taft told the Committee that, under the Spanish, "great complaint was made that all the (tax) money went from the provinces to Manila and the result of its expenditure was never seen in the provinces." He then explained that the Commission planned to have no internal taxes "that should furnish revenue to the central government" and that the revenue needs of that government would be met by "customs alone."[10] Encouraged to do so by the election of 1900, which produced enlarged Republican majorities in Congress, Taft and his Commission colleagues assumed that Americans generally shared their enthusiasm for indefinite retention of the colony. Believing this, they assumed that Congress would extend a substantial nonreciprocal tariff preference to the colony while permitting the colonial government to maximize receipts from a revenue tariff collected on insular imports, including those from the United States.

Taft also identified tax revenues the Commission intended to allocate to local governments. In addition to their share of the land tax, municipalities were scheduled to receive the proceeds from licensing of local businesses, occupations and professions, one-half the revenues from the planned excise tax, and one-half the cedula, or poll tax, paid by all adult males. Provincial governments were to receive the remainder of the revenues from the land tax, the excise tax, and the cedula.[11]

The partisan split in Congress was conspicuous in the acrimonious debate over Philippine policy in 1902 and in the rough treatment given the Commission's development strategy in the Organic Act and the Payne Tariff Law.[12] The latter established a tariff preference of 25 percent for imports from the colony and provided that duties collected be turned over to the insular government. This concession proved meaningless, however. Republican administrations following the Civil War raised the wall of American protection to such a level that even a preference of 25 percent in American tariff rates left duties so high as to exclude significant shipments of dutiable Philippine products to the United States. The Organic Act fixed the authority of the colonial government to sell bonds in the United States for "public improvements" at $5 million, a level not to be increased for fourteen years, despite repeated pleas from the Commission that this be done. Congress ignored the banking recommendation of the Commission and established stringent limits on access by individuals and corporations to public lands and other natural resources of the Islands, which severely restricted the role played by American capital and enterprise in the development of plantations, mines, and forest industries throughout the American period. Although every subsequent report of the Commission repeated basic recommendations made by the Commission in 1901, they received little attention from Congress.

When Taft returned to Manila in the fall of 1902, the Commission resumed work on an internal revenue law that had been suspended while Congress debated the ground rules under which

the Commission would govern the colony. With their development strategy a shambles, the members of the Commission
faced fiscal uncertainties they could not assess with confidence.
They could be certain, however, that pressures on insular government revenues would be heavier and, as a result, the Commission radically changed the internal revenue plan that Taft described to the Senate Committee.

The Commission also departed from the structure of internal
revenues of the Spanish period under which five-sixths of internal revenues came from the cedula, or poll tax, the opium
monopoly, lotteries, and the sale of stamps required on documents (Table 1). The draft law established a uniform cedula of
1 peso which produced about two-fifths of the revenue produced by the Spanish cedula.[13] In their search for revenues, the
Commission proposed to tax distilled liquors and manufactures
of tobacco at relatively high rates and to collect substantial
license fees from manufacturers and retailers of these products.
Other major sources of internal revenues in the bill drafted by
the Commission included a percentage tax of 0.5 percent on the
gross proceeds of merchants, manufacturers, and common carriers, and a range of license and business privilege taxes on enterprises, trades, and professions. The Commission proposed to
retain documentary stamps but drastically reduced their cost
as compared to the Spanish period. Torn by the need for revenues, the Commission wrestled with the moral issue raised by
taxation of opium until Congress, impatient with the Commission's vacillation on this question, passed legislation in 1905
banning imports of opium except for medicinal purposes.[14]

The Commission also abandoned its plan to turn all internal
revenues over to local governments. Instead, the draft law
mandated certain revenues for the insular government, provided
that receipts from the cedula would be shared equally by provincial and municipal governments, and allocated fees for licenses to engage in various business activities to the municipality
in which the business was located. All other internal revenues
were to be shared by the three levels of government in a ratio
specified in the draft law. As ultimately approved, the internal revenue law allocated to municipal governments 15 percent of internal revenues shared among the insular and local

TABLE 1 Comparison of Internal Revenues and Customs Collections Under Spanish and American Colonial Rule of the Philippine Islands

(Annual average, P000)	American Period 1907–1909[a]	Spanish Period 1894–1896[b]
Internal Revenue Collections	FY ending 6/30	Calendar year
Cedula or poll tax	2,877	7,018[c]
Excise tax	5,299	
Manufacturers and dealers in alcoholic and tobacco products	503	
Percentage tax on gross proceeds of merchants, manufacturers, and common carriers	1,319	1,690[d]
Licenses and taxes on privilege of doing business or practice of professions and occupations	719	
Documentary stamps	184	820
Lotteries	n.a.[e]	987
Revenue from opium	n.r.s.[f]	548
Revenue from public forests and mining claims	209	155
Miscellaneous internal revenues	52	18
Total internal revenue	11,162	11,236
Customs Collections[g]		
Import duties	13,213	3,412
Export duties	1,830	810
Other customs collections	905	500
Total customs collections	15,948	4,722
Total revenue collected by the insular government	27,110	15,958[h]

governments, 10 percent to provincial governments, and 75 percent to the insular government.[15]

With the important exception of the excise taxes on distilled liquors and tobacco products, the planned internal revenue taxes aroused little controversy within the Commission. The excise taxes of the draft law produced a sharp split between the American members and Benito Legarda and T. H. Pardo de Tavera, Filipino protégés of Taft and leaders of the pro-annexationist Federalista Party, who had been added to the Commission. Legarda and Pardo had major holdings in distilleries and firms manufacturing cigars and cigarettes, and, rather than force the issue to a decision over their opposition, the American majority on the Commission set aside the draft law.

Public hearings on the draft internal revenue law were held intermittently in 1903, but the Commission was still divided when Taft returned to Washington early in 1904 to become Secretary of War. Later that year, the Filipino members of the Commission, together with some three dozen other members of the Filipino *ilustrado* and economic elites, comprised the Honorary Philippine Commission to the Louisiana Purchase Exposition in St. Louis. The honorary commissioners were wined and dined appropriately, but found themselves competing with scant success for American attention with the primitive tribal peoples of the Islands who were on exhibit in their natural state in replicas of their villages. The members of the Honorary Commission, most of whom were Federalistas, were also

---

aGPI, Dept. of Finance, Bureau of Internal Revenue, *Report on the Operation of the Bureau of Internal Revenue Since Its Organization in 1904* (Manila, Bureau of Printing, 1927).

bU.S. War Department, *Annual Report, FY 1900*, Part 10, Report of the Military Governor of the Philippine Islands, 56th Cong.; 1st Sess. H. Doc. No. 2, pp. 32-34.

cIncludes cedulas, Chinese capitation tax, and vassalage of mountaineers and heathens.

dFor the most part, receipts from the "industria." Includes revenue from the "urbana" and small amounts of revenue from miscellaneous taxes.

eNot applicable.

fNot reported separately. Average annual revenue from opium during 1907-1909 included ₱245,000 from the excise tax on opium, ₱85,000 from licenses required of opium dealers, and ₱267,000 from the import duty on opium, a total of ₱597,000.

gGPI, Bureau of Customs, *Annual Reports of the Collector of Customs* for years indicated.

hAdult Filipino males were obligated under the "prestacion personal," or corvée of the Spanish period to contribute 15 days of labor annually on public works.

frustrated upon finding no American interest in annexation as a solution to the "Philippine problem." The Filipino members of the Philippine Commission were in no mood, therefore, to learn while in St. Louis that their American colleagues in Manila had enacted the internal revenue law in their absence.

Taft was inundated with protests against the law: personal protests from Legarda and Pardo, who submitted their resignations from the Philippine Commission; a formal protest signed by virtually all members of the Honorary Commission; a similar petition from Federalista Party leaders in Manila; and a flood of press accounts of the outcry in the Islands against the law.[16] Taft sought to conciliate Legarda and Pardo by promising that their objections to the law would receive "full consideration from himself and President Roosevelt." He finally persuaded them to withdraw their resignations from the Commission and proposed to Luke Wright, his successor as Governor General, that the law not be put into effect until mid-1905. The American members of the Commission stood firm behind the law, however, and Taft ultimately decided to wait until the law had been in operation a year before making a final decision.[17]

FILIPINOS ADAPT TO NEW TAXES

Most of the taxes under the new law, including the controversial liquor and tobacco excises, went into effect in September 1904, accompanied by well-publicized closings of distilleries and cigar and cigarette factories, which had been working around the clock to build up tax-free inventories before the law became operative. Despite the continuing outcry in the islands, Taft took no action, and, after a few months, the accumulated inventories were depleted and the distilleries and tobacco factories resumed operation. As was predictable, the controversial excise taxes were passed on to consumers in higher prices with no visible impact on consumption—or on the profits of manufacturers —and agitation over the taxes quickly subsided.[18]

The first major change in the internal revenue law, an increase in the cedula, resulted from the efforts of Cameron Forbes, who replaced Taft on the Commission when the latter returned to Washington to be Secretary of War. A compulsive builder of roads, bridges, and other transport works, Forbes was impatient with financial constraints he encountered as an administrator and searched for ways to escape them. It was no surprise, therefore, when he turned to the corvée, which had been a mainstay of the Spanish colonial government, and persuaded his colleagues to pass a law obligating all adult male Filipinos to contribute 5 days' labor per year on roads.[19] Forbes was elated with passage of the bill which he considered his "magnum opus" and claimed that the law would make the "difference between good roads and bad, between prosperity and failure."[20] To make the double cedula palatable to Filipinos, provincial boards were empowered to place the law in effect, but not a single board proved willing to do so.

Forbes was downcast but not for long, and, less than a year later, the Commission, again prodded by Forbes, enacted a law authorizing provincial boards to double the cedula with the additional peso earmarked for roads and bridges. To induce provinces to implement the law, the Commission appropriated ₱1.2 million for roads and bridges and voted to reward those provinces doubling the cedula with an increase of 60 percent in the combined share of local governments in internal revenues distributed between the insular and local governments.[21] The scheme was a great success, as the double cedula quickly became a permanent feature of the revenue system. Twenty-seven out of 31 regularly organized provinces increased the cedula in the first year. In the second year, only one province held out, and in the third year all provinces collected the double cedula.[22]

The new tax enacted by the Commission, acceptance of which proved most difficult to obtain, was the land tax provided in the Municipal Code of 1901. The land tax encountered resistance from the start, since the initial assessments were done hastily and aroused widespread criticism. This reinforced the instinctive resistance of Filipino peasants to a tax with which they were unfamiliar. More important was the resistance of local magnates or caciques with large holdings of land in central Luzon, much of which lay fallow because of a shortage of agricultural labor. This leadership class had an obvious stake in subverting the land tax and was capable of organizing the rural population to support efforts to do so. Strikes against the tax were organized, and there were some successful boycotts of public sales of lands forfeited for nonpayment of taxes.

More trouble was ahead for the land tax when rural areas of the Philippines were hit by a series of physical disasters in 1902 and 1903. The wet-season rice crop on Luzon was a relative failure in 1902, and a severe epidemic of rinderpest threatened to decimate the population of water buffalos, the principal work animal in the countryside. These developments coincided with the period of peak intensity in the locust cycle, which added to rural distress. Further complicating the tasks facing the new government was a severe outbreak of cholera which spread over the islands killing an estimated 120,000 before subsiding to minor proportions in 1904. Moreover, rice harvests were poor throughout East Asia, and rice produced in French Indonesia, which customarily supplied the Manila market, underwent a sharp rise in April.

Collection of the land tax for 1902 and 1903 encountered strong resistance, and forfeitures of land for nonpayment of the tax were widespread. The Commission responded by extending time for payment of the tax and remitting penalties for late payment. Four laws extending relief from the 1902 tax to extensive areas and 17 measures extending relief from the 1903 tax were enacted. Within a year, the agricultural sector had recovered from the crop failure in 1902, but pressures for tax relief continued; 26 laws were passed providing relief in various forms from the land tax due for 1904, and 19 such acts covered the tax due for 1905.

Filipino resistance to the land tax created still another problem for the American colonial officials. The prices paid for land forfeited for nonpayment of the land tax were frequently only a fraction of the value of the land sold, a circumstance not lost on American officials scattered over the colony—provincial treasurers, collectors of customs, internal revenue agents, provincial engineers, and Army officers in garrisons. As these officials became aware of the opportunities to acquire forfeited lands at distress prices, a number did so. A damaging scandal threatened the colonial administration when, late in 1906, Governor General Smith issued an order requiring insular officials who had acquired land forfeited for nonpayment of taxes to return the land to the original owners. The Commission subsequently passed legislation authorizing local governments to repossess land sold for nonpayment of taxes and to hold the land in trust until it could be redeemed by the delinquent taxpayer.[23]

By 1905, the fiscal situation facing the insular government had improved markedly. Customs revenues exceeded expectations, and receipts from the Commission's internal revenue taxes were rising. Congress appropriated $3 million in 1903 to relieve rural distress in the colony, and bonds of the insular government and the city of Manila sold in the United States provided funds to construct needed "public improvements." The insular government also received a substantial windfall when the price of silver rose sharply following 1904 and the coins circulating in the islands were reminted with reduced silver content.[24]

Late in 1905, Taft decided to use the improved fiscal situation to conciliate his Federalista Party protégés who still rankled over passage of the internal revenue law and, at the same time, help Federalista candidates in the forthcoming election of Filipinos to the legislative assembly provided in the Organic Act. The prospects of the Federalista Party and its candidates were deteriorating as Federalistas had monopolized appointments of Filipinos to the colonial government and the Party and its candidates had to share the onus directed at the new taxes. Early in 1906, the Commission suspended the land tax for that year and initiated a carefully planned reassessment of land values based on reliable information about prices of land and rentals. The Commission also appropriated funds to reimburse municipalities and provinces for land taxes foregone.[25]

A year later, again under Taft's instructions, the Commission suspended the land tax for 1907 but appropriated only one-half of the estimated land taxes foregone for transfer to municipalities and provinces. The Commission also announced that insular government funds would not be appropriated in the future to replace uncollected land-tax revenues. Subsequently, in its final legislative session before inauguration of the Assembly in 1907, the Commission passed a measure delegating to provincial boards authority to impose or suspend the land tax beginning with the tax for 1908. In other words, the Commission "washed its hands" of responsibility for the enforcement of the land tax after announcing that it would do nothing to replace uncollected or foregone land taxes.[26]

The careful assessment of land values completed in 1906 and 1907, in conjunction with transfer of the responsibility to suspend or collect land taxes to the local officials dependent upon the tax for a substantial part of their revenues, worked a minor miracle. The land-tax "problem" disappeared; thereafter only an occasional provincial board suspended the tax. Throughout the American period, the land tax remained a productive source of revenue of major importance in maintaining local government functions and services.[27]

Reassured that the structure of taxes it had erected was gaining acceptance, the Commission in the legislative session of 1907 also voted to increase the shares of municipal and provincial governments in internal revenue collections shared between the insular and local governments. In fiscal year 1906, the first full year under the new internal revenue law, three-fifths of internal revenues accrued to the insular government. Three years later, in 1909, the ratio in which these revenues were shared had been reversed, with three-fifths going to local governments. The same priority was also evident in the practice of the Commission to make grants and loans to municipalities to build revenue-producing facilities, such as municipal markets. Similarly, the Commission reserved to municipalities productive sources of revenues, such as fishing privileges, locally administered licenses, fees for various services, and locally administered taxes like the cart tax and road tax. By 1909, these locally administered sources of revenues were producing more revenues for municipal governments than the land tax (Table 2).

The years following 1905 saw the revenue system stabilized and administrative problems solved. Once the elective Filipino Assembly was inaugurated and legislative power was shared between the American-dominated Commission and the Filipino Assembly, however, conditions favorable to further revenue-producing innovation evaporated. Having renounced revolution as the means to independence, the Nacionalistas, who dominated the Assembly from the start, had no choice but to go into

TABLE 2   Local Government Revenues, 1907–1909 (Annual Average, ₱000)

	Municipal Governments (Calendar Year)	Provincial Governments (Fiscal Year)
Apportionment from Insular Treasury of internal revenues shared with local governments	1,232	1,204
Cedula	876	1,848
Insular tax receipts retained locally[a]	383	30
Share of internal revenues[b]	2,491	3,082
Land tax[c]	1,183	895
Municipal taxes[d]	29	n.a.
Tax collections, Moro province	n.a.	504
Fisheries privilege	180	n.a.
Cattle registration	244	n.a.
Registration of property and mining claims	n.a.	22
Municipal licenses	320	n.a.
Fines and justice of peace collections	168	n.a.
Net receipts from markets and other enterprises	691	n.a.
Tolls	n.a.	9
Total revenue	5,306	4,512

Source: Government of the Philippine Islands (GPI), *Report of the Auditor for the Philippine Islands,* Part I, 1907, 1908, and 1909.

[a] Internal revenues from business licenses, licenses for weights and measures, opium certificates, cart tax, and road tax.
[b] The share of internal revenues allocated to local governments totaling ₱5,573,000 departs from the share to local governments of ₱5,735,000 reported in Table 4. This discrepancy arises because municipal government data reported by the Bureau of Internal Revenue are reported for fiscal years ending June 30.
[c] Includes payment from Insular Treasury in lieu of land tax for 1907.
[d] Property taxes and local franchises.

opposition to the American executive to pursue the independence to which they were committed. The Nacionalistas—and all other parties and candidates in the Assembly election of 1907—appealed to Filipinos generally by attacking the extravagance of the colonial administration. Contending that the high salaries enjoyed by American administrators and the costly perquisites of their offices caused the "oppressive" tax burden borne by Filipinos, they promised to reduce that burden.

The first session of the new Assembly was a relatively placid one as the Nacionalista leaders—Sergio Osmeña and Manuel Quezon—mastered parliamentary procedure and organized their followers to wield the political power they had won. Thereafter, the Assembly's confrontation against the Commission hardened, and prospects for new taxes and larger appropriations withered.[28]

TAFT AND CONGRESS PRODUCE A REVENUE CRISIS

Taft emphasized "tariff reform" in his campaign against Bryan for the presidency in 1908 and, upon taking office, called Congress into special session to lower the tariff. The Republican majority, split between "progressive" followers of Roosevelt and stand-pat "regulars" led by "Uncle Joe" Cannon, the Speaker of the House, and Nelson Aldrich, Chairman of the Senate Committee on Finance, engaged in a divisive battle over the tariff, which produced some rearrangement of rates, but no significant change in the level of protection resulted from the Payne-Aldrich Tariff.[29] On the other hand, prior to convening Congress Taft aggressively used his leverage as newly elected President to obtain agreement of Republican leaders in Congress to eliminate duties on imports from the Philippines. To obtain this agreement, however, the President had to agree to absolute quotas limiting duty-free shipments of Philippine sugar and tobacco products to the United States and to duty-free entry of American exports to the colony.

Passage of the Payne-Aldrich Tariff carried an obvious threat to the revenues of the insular government by eliminating Philippine duties on imports from the United States, which accounted for one-sixth of all Philippine imports. This effect of mutual free trade was expected immediately to reduce annual revenues from the insular tariff by ₱1.6 to ₱2.5 million.[30] More important was the longer-term impact anticipated from mutual free trade. The Philippine tariff was designed to maximize revenues from foreign trade transactions. The rates of duty were sufficiently high, however, that imports from the United States, which would enter the Philippines free of duty after passage of the Payne-Aldrich Law, were expected to supplant imports from other countries, thus reducing revenues from the insular tariff.

Congress was concerned about the revenue loss the insular government would incur, and made two concessions in the Payne-Aldrich Law to minimize that loss. First, United States internal-revenue taxes collected on commodities imported from the Philippines, principally tobacco products, were turned over to the insular government. Congress also provided that proceeds of internal-revenue taxes shared between the insular and local governments "shall accrue intact to the central government . . . and shall only be allotted in accordance with future acts of the Philippine Legislature."[31] Subsequently, the legislature froze the amount of internal revenues going to local governments at the level of the allocations they received in fiscal year 1909. This level of funding, ₱1.6 million each to provincial and municipal governments, continued unchanged during the remaining period of American rule.

The War Department also sought to reassure the colonial administration that the impact of Payne-Aldrich on insular finances would be manageable by proposing that some $8 million of "unneeded" insular monetary reserves could be released for other purposes, if a crisis should arise.[32] The Commission also was assured that the Taft Administration would push legislation raising the debt limit of the insular government, and the War Department suggested that, under Taft's leadership, Congress would look with favor upon a measure calling for a direct American subvention to support public education in the colony.

The consequences of the Payne-Aldrich Tariff for the revenues of the colonial government materialized slowly. The Islands' economy had weathered the dislocation attending the Philippine revolution and war against the United States and the effects of the rural setbacks of 1902 and 1903 had been overcome, setting the stage for a surge in economic growth. During the three years ending with passage of the Payne-Aldrich Tariff, Philippine imports fluctuated narrowly around ₱60 million annually, and revenues from the insular tariff remained steady at ₱13.2 million (Table 3). In 1910, imports jumped to ₱99 million and, by 1912, they had more than doubled to ₱123 million. As expected, imports from the United States, which increased fourfold over the four years following 1909, accounted for virtually all the growth. Revenues from the insular tariff remained steady during 1910 and 1911 and increased by 10 percent in 1912, when partial failure of the rice crop led to a sharp increase in imports of rice, which were subject to a relatively high rate of duty. With recovery of rice production, revenues from the insular tariff declined in 1913 and, by 1914, were running below ₱10 million annually, a drop of 26 percent as compared to levels prevailing prior to passage of the Payne-Aldrich Tariff (Table 3).

Both the Washington Administration and the Commission were confident that the stimulus of duty-free access to the American market would accelerate economic development in the colony. They also were confident that the existing tax structure would generate sufficient revenues to replace tariff revenues lost and provide funds for "public improvements" and expanded governmental services needed to support further growth. The short-run challenge, however, was to bridge the period of fiscal stringency before economic expansion began to pay off in increased revenues. The immediate prospect worried the American administrators because the escalating confrontation between the Assembly and the American-dominated Commission made new taxes or major increases in existing tax rates unlikely.

The prospects of obtaining an increase in the borrowing power of the insular government were to fade with Taft's dwindling political fortunes. The major effort to double the debt limit of the colonial government occurred in the final session of the 61st Congress in the spring of 1911. The Republican leadership of the House, confident of passage of a bill that had received unanimous approval from the Philippine committees of both Houses, brought the measure to a vote

TABLE 3 Import Duties and Other Revenues of the Bureau of Customs, 1907–1920 (₱000)

Fiscal Year[b] Average	Import Duties	Export Duties	Wharfage Charges	Other Revenues	Total Revenues
1907–1909	13,213	1,830[a]	539	366	15,948
1910	13,408	1,580	808	640	16,436
1911	13,589	2,136	918	543	17,186
1912	14,800	2,143	1,082	488	18,513
1913	12,648	2,013	1,022	604	16,287
1914	9,548	n.a.	1,056	663	11,267
1915	10,724	n.a.	1,104	689	12,517
1916	9,872	n.a.	1,277	768	11,917
1917	11,184	n.a.	1,137	942	13,263
1918	13,480	n.a.	1,305	1,192	15,977
1919	10,975	n.a.	1,081	1,452	13,508
1920	13,786	n.a.	1,059	1,727	16,572

Source: GPI, Bureau of Customs, *Annual Reports of the Collector of Customs.*

[a] Unadjusted for drawback of export duty on shipments of Philippine products consumed in the United States in 1906.
[b] Prior to 1914, the Philippine fiscal year ended June 30, Beginning with 1914, the Philippine fiscal year ends December 31. Data for last 6 months of 1913 are not included.

with the "rules suspended" which required a two-thirds majority for passage. In a poorly attended session of the House, the Democrats mustered enough votes to defeat the bill.[33] Meanwhile, the congressional elections of 1910 increased the Democratic contingents in Congress and, when that Party organized the House in the new Congress, all prospects of enlarging the borrowing power of the insular government disappeared. Following 1909, the Commission repeatedly asked that $2 million be appropriated annually to support public education in the Islands, but Congress ignored these pleas.

The final years of the Taft era under Governor General Forbes were years of steady Philippine economic growth. Although the Legislature refused to enact new taxes or raise rates, the existing tax structure generated higher revenues both from internal taxes and taxes on foreign trade. By 1913, the share of internal revenues allocated to the insular government reached ₱10.3 million, as compared to an average of ₱5.4 million during 1907–1909 (Table 5). Taxes collected on foreign trade transactions—including export taxes, wharfage charges, and tonnage dues, as well as import duties—increased steadily, despite mutual free trade with the United States, until such revenues reached ₱18.5 million in 1912 (Table 3). As a result, the revenues available to the insular government in 1912 were one-third larger than in the three years prior to the initiation of mutual free trade (Table 5).

By the end of 1912, however, the impact of mutual free trade on insular revenues was beginning to be evident and, in 1913, revenues collected by the Bureau of Customs fell from ₱18.5 million to ₱16.3 million (Table 3). This fall in customs collections more than offset the small increase in internal revenues going to the insular government, and, for the first time since the launching of the colonial government, the revenues at the disposal of that government declined (Table 5).

When Woodrow Wilson took office in 1913, he also convened a special session of Congress to lower the tariff. The resulting Underwood-Simmons Tariff, the first thorough revision of the tariff since the Civil War, made deep cuts in duties across virtually the entire spectrum of American imports. The law promised to complicate the uncertain revenue situation facing the colonial government, however, as it prohibited taxation of Philippine exports which was producing revenues in excess of ₱2 million annually. Congress sought to replace this revenue loss by extending the United States income tax, the second major economic measure of the special session, to the Philippines and allowed the insular government to retain income taxes collected in the islands.

In the meantime, insular revenues were falling, and Forbes and Francis Burton Harrison, who became Governor General in the fall of 1913, struggled to weather the fiscal crisis which buffeted the colonial government with renewed vigor as collection of export taxes ceased. Forbes sought to maintain government expenditures on roads and other public works by drawing down the cumulative budgetary surplus of ₱4 million which was maintained in the treasury as a contingency reserve. The crisis worsened, however, and, by 1913, Forbes was sacrificing expenditures on public education and other priority services to maintain planned levels of road construction and other public works.

Harrison arrived in Manila in time to open the legislative session in October 1913, but the budget he submitted was that prepared by Forbes. Confronted by the fiscal crisis, Harrison urged the Assembly to consider new tax measures and to cut ₱6 million from the budget, imposed reductions in salaries at higher levels of the insular service, and required an across-the-board reduction in expenditures budgeted for bureaus and offices of the colonial government. The Legislature did amend the internal revenue law, but in doing so was more concerned with administrative changes than with Harrison's plea for new taxes.[34] The Legislature also cut Harrison's budget, not by the ₱6 million he proposed, but by ₱1 million.

THE IMPACT OF WORLD WAR I

Shortly after his arrival in the Islands, Harrison announced that it would be Democratic policy to extend Filipino participation in the insular government, and, as the first step under the new policy, a majority of Filipinos were named in forming the Commission. The Legislature reciprocated Harrison's overture by passing, for the first time in four years, a general governmental appropriations bill. The advent of an "era of good feeling" between American administrators and Filipino political leaders, however, did not solve the fiscal crisis, which worsened in 1914. The impact of the loss of export-tax revenues was reinforced following the outbreak of war in Europe in August, as shipping disappeared from normal trade routes and insular trade abruptly contracted. Economic activity in the Islands, traditionally led by the export sector, was hard hit and, for the first time since the establishment of the colonial government fourteen years earlier, revenues from internal sources declined. Much more severe was the fall in revenues of the Bureau of Customs, which dropped by ₱5 million from 1913 and by 39 percent as compared with the peak level of 1912 (Table 3). Total revenues available to the insular government fell in 1914 by ₱5.7 million or by one-fifth of revenues in 1913 (Table 5).

Belt tightening enabled the insular government to weather the revenue crisis during the first seven months of 1914. The dramatic impact on the island economy of the outbreak of war and the uncertain future confronting the Philippines, however, quickly disabused the leadership, both American and Filipino, of the hope that further economies might deal with the crisis. As a result, the Legislature convening in October 1914 enacted new taxes and substantially raised a number of existing taxes and, in the process, established a productive and responsive tax system that would endure with limited changes over the remainder of the American colonial period.

The major changes in the resulting Emergency Tax Law of 1915 included an increase of 200 percent in the percentage tax on the gross proceeds of merchants, manufacturers, and common carriers from 0.5 percent to 1.5 percent, and extension of the tax to public utilities, printers, publishers, hotels, and restaurants. In addition, the tax on insurance premiums was doubled; new excise taxes at relatively high rates were imposed on petroleum products, coal, and coke; and a new tax of 1.5 percent was imposed on the value of the output of mines.[35]

The next legislative session renewed the Emergency Tax Law through 1917, and, in the process, increased a number of excise tax rates and added new rates. Later in the same session, the

Legislature enacted the Administrative Code of 1916 which made permanent the taxes of the Emergency Tax Law. At the same time, the productive percentage tax on gross proceeds was extended to all consignments, which had the effect of bringing Philippine export shipments under the tax for the first time.[36]

Congress also made important contributions to the structure of taxes evolving in the colony under pressures of the revenue crisis. The first instance occurred when the excise tax on petroleum products was challenged in the insular courts, on the ground that these products were not produced in the Philippines and, therefore, the tax was not an excise tax but a duty on imports and could not be collected on petroleum products shipped from the United States. At this point, Congress settled the matter by adding a rider to an appropriation bill "legalizing and ratifying" the tax.[37] Similarly, when the gross proceeds tax was extended to export consignments, the tax was challenged in the insular courts as an export tax prohibited under the Underwood-Simmons Tariff, but again Congress passed legislation "legalizing and ratifying" the action of the Legislature.[38] Finally, in the midst of preparations for war in 1916, Congress raised the rates of the United States income tax which provided additional revenues for the insular government. Congress also made clear its intention to continue collecting the United States income tax in the Islands until the Legislature enacted such a tax. This occurred in 1919, when an income tax incorporating the exemptions and rates of the United States law was passed.[39]

The response of insular revenues to the Emergency Tax Law was prompt. Internal revenues increased by ₱4.8 million in 1915, virtually offsetting the previous year's decline in revenues available to the insular government (Table 5). Strong demand for Philippine exports was sustained during World War I and, as the shipping situation eased, exports increased in volume and earnings from shipments rose sharply as prices spiraled upward. New taxes and higher tax rates in conjunction with the economic expansion under way in the colony produced steady increase in internal revenues, which reached ₱50.7 million in 1920, as compared to an average of ₱11.2 million in 1907–1909 (Table 4). Receipts from the percentage tax on gross proceeds of businesses increased 13-fold as compared to 1907–

TABLE 4 Internal Revenue Collections, 1907–1920 (₱000)

Fiscal Year[a]	Excise Tax	Percentage Tax	Business Privilege Taxes[b]	Cedula	Income Tax	Other Taxes and Revenues	Total Internal Revenues
Average							
1907–1909	5,299	1,319	1,222	2,877	n.a.	445	11,162
1910	7.072	1,537	1,279	3,593	n.a.	1,120	14,601
1911	8,186	1,793	1,411	3,883	n.a.	797	16,070
1912	8,830	1,935	1,498	3,643	n.a.	1,264	17,170
1913	8,841	2,239	1,697	4,180	n.a.	1,524	18,481
1914	8,658	2,094	1,780	3,821	265	1,234	17,852
1915	9,866	5,051	2,026	4,007	430	1,247	22,627
1916	10,749	6,748	2,073	4,166	504	1,671	25,911
1917	12,923	9,529	2,632	4,717	1,178	1,375	32,354
1918	13,201	13,601	3,699	4,632	2,550	3,168	40,851
1919	14,179	13,731	4,360	4,435	3,406	4,239	44,350
1920	14,481	17,056	4,865	4,710	4,212	5,344	50,668

Source: GPI, Bureau of Internal Revenue, *Report on the Operation of the Bureau of Internal Revenue since its Organization in 1904.*

a See note b to Table 2.
b Includes internal-revenue taxes on manufacturers and dealers in alcoholic beverages and tobacco products.
c Includes franchise tax, documentary stamp tax, inheritance tax, U.S. internal revenue taxes on Philippine products, and revenue from public forests. Does not include fines and penalties and miscellaneous stamp collections.

TABLE 5 Distribution of Internal Revenue and Customs Revenue by Level of Government, 1907–1920 (₱000)

Fiscal Year[a]	Internal Revenue Collected	Internal Revenue to Local Governments[b]	Internal Revenue Retained by Insular Government	Customs Revenue	Total Tax Revenue of Insular Government
Average					
1907–1909	11,162	5,735	5,427	15,948	21,375
1910	14,501	7,257	7,244	16,436	23,680
1911	16,070	7,573	8,497	17,186	25,683
1912	17,170	7,484	9,686	18,513	28,199
1913	18,481	8,154	10,327	16,287	26,614
1914	17,852	8,197	9,655	11,267	20,922
1915	22,627	8,555	14,072	12,517	26,589
1916	25,911	8,736	17,175	11,917	29,092
1917	33,354	9,850	23,504	13,363	36,867
1918	40,851	9,816	31,035	15,977	47,012
1919	44,350	9,346	35,004	13,528	48,532
1920	50,668	9,900	40,768	16,572	57,340

Sources: See Table 2 and Table 3.

Notes: aSee note b to Table 2.
bGPI, Bureau of Internal Revenue, *Report of the Operation of the Bureau of Internal Revenue since its Organization in 1904*, Appendix B. Share allocated to local government is exclusive of city of Manila.

1909, and, by 1920, that tax generated one-third of all internal revenues. Excise taxes produced revenues of ₱14.5 million and, together with the percentage tax, accounted for three-fifths of internal revenues in 1920. The third most productive source of internal revenue was the range of business privilege levies, followed closely by the cedula and the income tax (Table 4).

Revenues collected by the Bureau of Customs on foreign-trade transactions and services remained stagnant through the war and postwar years, and in 1920 these revenues were only slightly in excess of average collections during 1907–1909 (Table 3). Bureau of Customs collections, which accounted for three-fourths of all revenues available to the insular government in 1907–1909, dwindled to less than one-third of such revenues over the three years ending with 1920 (Table 5).

THE SUMMING UP

American colonial administrators remained preoccupied with revenue problems over the first decade and a half of American rule. Like Secretary Root, they believed that American political development provided a valid model for the Philippines. Thus they found congenial his injunction that they provide adequate scope for the development of Filipino capabilities for self-government at the local level. As in America, they concluded, practice close to home would prepare people for the responsible conduct of representative government at the national level. The priority they maintained for this goal is evident in the taxes and other revenue sources they devised for local governments and the increasing share of internal revenues they diverted to local administrations.

Although the wartime fiscal crisis was weathered and revenues grew at an unprecedented rate following 1915, the priority maintained over the first decade of American rule for local government revenues was not restored. During 1907–1909, local governments received more than one-half of internal revenue collections, but, by 1920, their share had fallen to less than one-fifth (Table 5). As the revenues of the insular government continued to increase following 1915, Harrison and Rafael

Palma, his Secretary of the Interior, pleaded with the Legislature in each of their annual reports to increase the apportionment of internal revenues to local governments, but to no avail.

A second priority of the colonial administrators is evident in their persistent tinkering with the insular tariff over the first decade of American rule to maximize revenues from this source. By the end of this process, the insular tariff was producing virtually 60 percent more revenue from a given value of foreign trade than the tariff in effect at the end of the Spanish period.

The colonial administrators assigned a comparable priority to development of a structure of productive and flexible taxes on business activities of all kinds, which would ensure a constantly expanding pool of revenues as economic growth proceeded. Such a tax structure enabled the colonial administrators to provide the "public improvements" and government services required to sustain the economic growth under way.

The prolonged efforts of the American administrators to equip the Philippine colony with an appropriate revenue system was not a "labor" of Herculean dimensions; it was a modest accomplishment. American colonialism—like all other colonialisms—was done "on the cheap." Virtually every year was marked by an annual report produced in the insular government which included a tabulation of the annual per capita tax revenues, or per capita expenditures, or per capita debts of a range of countries and colonies.[40] We can assume that America's colonial administrators took pride in the appearance of the Philippine Islands at the bottom of these tabulations or they would not have updated them so assiduously. Such tables appeared widely in the reports and statistical publications of colonies because a low level of per capita tax revenues, expenditures, and public debt was, using the standards of the time, confirmation of the success of the stewardship of the administrators concerned.

Americans were not only convinced that their colonialism was more efficient, but also that it was more benign, in that it provided more services and material goods for its native beneficiaries than did other colonialisms. This internally inconsistent image was shattered in 1931 when Governor General Dwight Davis, in the course of a "goodwill" tour of Southeast Asia, discovered that the per capita revenues and expenditures of the insular government ranked below those of the governments of the Netherlands East Indies, the Federated Malay States, and Siam, and exceeded only those of French Indo-China. In the case of the Dutch colony, per capita revenues and expenditures were more than half again as large as those of America's colony, while, in the British colony, they were eight times higher.[41]

PART FOUR

Independence or Neocolonialism?

The Negotiation and Disposition of the Philippine War Damage Claims: A Study in Philippine-American Diplomacy, 1951-1972

BONIFACIO S. SALAMANCA

Philippine financial claims against the United States and Philippine-American trade relations were the two principal economic issues between the two countries during the 1950s. The financial claims included the unpaid balance of approved war damage claims in excess of $500, covered by the Philippine Rehabilitation Act of 1946. Estimated to total $80-$150 million, these war damage claims were lumped with other financial claims to constitute the Omnibus Claims. The matter was formally elevated to the diplomatic level by the Philippine Economic Mission to the United States in 1954.

In this chapter, Professor Bonifacio S. Salamanca of the University of the Philippines examines the background and the negotiation of the war damage claims and the channeling of the Special Fund for Education, which emanated from the claims, into various educational, cultural, and social projects in the Philippines. He suggests, on the basis of new evidence hitherto unavailable, that, although the war damage claims issue was not as sensitive a matter as the presence of U.S. military bases in the Philippines, it had become a significant irritant. Its resolution after a decade of formal and informal negotiations was a milestone in the post-colonial relations of the two nations.

On 21 March 1972, representatives of the Philippine and American Governments met in the Hall of Flags, Ministry of Foreign Affairs, at Padre Faura, Manila, and exchanged notes on the Fund for Assistance to the Philippine Agrarian Reform Education Program. In doing so, they wrote *finis* to a twenty-year-old issue of Philippine-America diplomacy—the Philippine War Damage Claims.

Technically, the negotiation of the Philippine War Damage Claims started in 1951 and ended with the enactment of the Philippine War Damage Act of 1962 by the American government. But an amendment to this act in 1963 creating the Special Fund for Education extended the life of the issue for almost a decade more, from the Macapagal-Johnson conversations in 1964 to the exchange of notes on 21 March 1972.

The War Damage Claims negotiations and the later discussions on the disposition of the Special Fund for Education had nothing of the excitement and emotionalism that characterized the renegotiation of the Military Bases Agreement of March 1947. This may have been due to the fact that, unlike the presence of American bases, the War Damage Claims and special fund issues were not "a matter of survival" for the Philippines, or "a question of life and death to the Filipino people."[1]

Still, as a facet of Philippine-American relations, the war damage claims issue and the succeeding issue of the Special Fund for Education are worth looking into, especially in light of hitherto unpublished materials which have recently become available to scholars.

FROM WAR DAMAGE FUND TO SPECIAL FUND FOR EDUCATION

The War Damage Claims issue may be traced directly to the Philippine Rehabilitation Act of 1946, which authorized $620 million for Philippine reconstruction and rehabilitation programs, both public and private.[2] Of this, $400 million was set aside for the "purpose of paying compensation for war damages sustained by private individuals, corporations and institutions arising out of the invasion and liberation of the Philippines." This figure was far below official and unofficial estimates of the value of private property losses, which ranged from $800 million to $1.2 billion. Realizing this, the U.S. Congress provided for full payment of only the first $500 of each valid claim; amounts beyond that were to be paid to a maximum of 75 percent.[3] In practice, the Philippine War Damage Commission (PWDC), after rejecting thousands of spurious claims and prudently, if unfairly, undervaluing approved ones, was able to pay only 52.5 percent of the value of claims in excess of $500. The remaining 22.5 percent it hoped to pay later through a supplemental appropriation of $80 million, which it had recommended to the Truman Administration in 1949.[4]

The Department of State initially endorsed the PWDC's request, which was promptly embodied in a bill (H.R. 7600) introduced by Representative George P. Miller of California, because it agreed with the Commission that the American government was "morally" obligated to pay the authorized maximum of 75 percent of all claims beyond $500. But, partly because the Office of the Budget and the Treasury Department were not receptive to additional payments, the State Department subsequently withdrew its support of HR 7600.

This was the situation when President Elipidio Quirino met with President Harry S. Truman on 4 February 1950. A few days earlier, Secretary of State Dean Acheson had advised President Truman that, should President Quirino raise the issue of additional war damage compensation, which turned out to be the case, Truman should inform Quirino that this was not possible. Acheson feared that additional war damage payments would remove a compelling reason for the Philippine Congress to enact much-needed but politically unpopular fiscal measures to stabilize the Philippine economy. Accordingly, pleading "fiscal restraint," Truman would tell Quirino that he could not recommend additional war damage payments to the American Congress "at present."[5]

Deprived of executive support, the Miller Bill died in committee; and so, when the PWDC completed its task at the end of March 1951, there remained an unpaid balance of between $80 million to $150 million. Thus arose the War Damage Claims issue—the 22.5 percent—against the United States.

President Quirino initiated what turned out to be a decade-long series of negotiations for additional war damage payments when he visited President Truman anew in September 1951, following medical treatment at Johns Hopkins Hospital. On that occasion:

The President said that as a matter of fact . . . he favored additional war damages, that he had originally recommended 500 million to the Congress, which had appropriated only 400 million, and that he thought the Philippines was entitled to the extra 100 million. He added, however, that in all frankness he should tell Mr. Quirino he did not think there was the slightest chance that Congress would agree.[6]

Truman was only being realistic. For, by that time, the report of the State Department's Economic Survey Mission to the Philippines—the *Bell Report*, after its Chairman—had been released; and its contention, that additional war damage payments would not contribute materially to Philippine economic development,[7] had become a strong argument against any war damage legislation.

The War Damage Claims issue temporarily receded into the background following the second Quirino-Truman conversations, as more important developments engaged the attention of the two countries. The Philippines was preoccupied with the Hukbalahap and Muslim problems; the senatorial and local elections of 1951 (spotlighted by the murder of Moises Padilla in Negros Occidental, home of sugar barons and rich millers who stood to gain most from additional war damage payments); and the critical presidential elections of 1953. Additionally, the Philippine economic picture had become brighter, ironically, through the economic assistance provided by the United States in spite of its disenchantment with the Quirino Administration. This robbed the War Damage Claims issue of a sense of urgency.[8] In the United States, where the war damage issue had never attracted a large constituency, the Korean War, then in its full fury, presidential primaries, state caucuses and conventions, rambunctious nominating conventions, and the electoral campaign of 1952 were more immediate concerns.

Hopes for additional war damage payments soared with the election of General Dwight Eisenhower as President in 1952. (Eisenhower had reportedly said when he visited Manila in 1946 that the extent of the city's destruction was second only to that of Warsaw.)[9] But, like his predecessor, President Eisenhower opposed additional war damage payments, and continued to do so until almost the expiration of his second term. In all likelihood, fiscal retrenchment—generally associated with Republican administrations—was the primary reason. The fighting in Korea, which did not end until July 1953, had been very costly, as was American rearmament.

The Eisenhower Administration's indifference had the effect of intensifying the Filipino claimants', and eventually the Philippine government's, determination to press for additional war damage payments. Earlier, in November 1951, Francisco Delgado, the Filipino member of the defunct PWDC, had been elected to the Senate, likewise now defunct. Predictably, he picked up the cudgels for private claimants, some of whom, like the sugar and manufacturing interests, were wealthy and politically influential. He and John A. O'Donnell, one of two American colleagues in the former PWDC, organized a Philippine War Damage Association,[10] with the latter as chief lobbyist in Washington. O'Donnell undertook his task with understandable alacrity; if successful in securing a war damage law, he could get a handsome fee or commission for assistance in filing claims later on. Senator Delgado's strategy was to convince Philippine officialdom, especially the President, to pick up the war damage issue. Toward this end, he encouraged other groups that had outstanding claims against the United States, such as war veterans and war widows, Philippine Scouts, and guerrillas, to act in concert. The more groups advancing claims, Delgado correctly assumed, the greater would be the pressure on the Philippine government, which also had its own pending claims, to negotiate with the American government. It was a classic demonstration of political mobilization.[11]

In 1954, Delgado's efforts finally bore fruit. Congressional prodding and the mounting clamor of interested groups eventually convinced President Ramon Magsaysay to instruct the Philippine Economic Mission to the United States (PEMUS), headed by wartime President Jose P. Laurel, which was then about to leave for the United States to renegotiate the Bell Trade Act of 1946, to prepare a thorough documentation of all outstanding Philippine claims against the United States—including, of course, the War Damage Claims—and to seek a satisfactory settlement.[12]

Presentation of these claims—lumped together as the "Omnibus Claims"—almost derailed the trade negotiations even before they could get started. The American panel, headed by James Langley, flatly refused to receive the Omnibus Claims, since it had no instructions or authority to deal with them. Since President Magsaysay did not wish to see the expensive PEMUS return empty-handed, he had to advise Senator Laurel to exclude the Omnibus Claims from the negotiations with the Langley Panel and settle instead for separate discussion.

While the PEMUS was successful in obtaining a slightly more favorable trade agreement, all that it could accomplish with respect to the claims was to document them—haphazardly in some cases—and discuss them with a Department of State Panel headed by Assistant Secretary of State William Robertson. The PEMUS, by then headed by Ambassador Melquiades Gamboa, Senator Laurel having returned to the Philippines in December 1954, discussed the Omnibus Claims with the Robertson Panel in ten fruitless sessions between January and April 1955. At one point, the Philippine Panel lost its composure when it was condescendingly informed that, while the American government would view the claims with sympathy and understanding, it would take time for experts to verify their validity and extent.[13] It was not an auspicious start.

The claims issue was kept alive by President Magsaysay. In March 1965, when Secretary of State John Foster Dulles visited Manila, Magsaysay handed him an *aide mémoire* on the omnibus claims. In his letter of transmittal, Magsaysay said that the Philippine government needed the money, to which it was "legally" entitled, for economic development.[14] But throughout the remainder of 1956, the American government kept silent; it evidently was not going to make a cursory review of the claims and rush into payment. Shortly before he perished in an airplane crash in March 1957, Magsaysay was urged by the Philippine Congress to send Senator Laurel back to Washington, "lest the U.S. might forego further negotiations." The American government, however, discouraged this; it would be "premature" to send a follow-up mission, it reportedly said, because the time was not yet ripe, its experts still immersed in verifying the claims.[15]

Recently declassified documents suggest that this, indeed, was the case.[16] But, by the middle of 1958, enough progress had been made to permit Dulles to inform President Carlos P. Garcia on 19 June that "President Eisenhower would recommend to Congress that it appropriate funds ... for the payment of the claim arising from the reduction of the weight of the gold dollar in 1934 ..."—one of the Omnibus Claims.[17]

Finally, on 4 August 1959, Acting Secretary of State C. Douglas Dillon handed the American reply on the entire Omnibus Claims to Ambassador Carlos P. Romulo.[18] It rejected all but three of the claims. As regards the War Damage Claims, the American note read:

... the executive branch of the United States Government will, at the next regular session of the Congress, and in connection with the legislative program for fiscal year 1961, request appropriate legislation enabling the settlement of this matter on the basis of $73 million, which amount reflects the statutory maximum of paid private claims according to the reports of the War Damage Commission.[19]

The American government also expressed its willingness "to discuss possible adjustments" in the amount of the Philippine obligation under the Romulo-Snyder Agreement of 6 November 1950. As will be mentioned presently, this proved to be crucial to the enactment of the war damage legislation.

The Philippine government was momentarily stunned by the American note, for it rejected—apparently finally—all the other claims. The Philippine government had hoped for "a full day in court," during which to argue the case for these claims and submit new ones whose documentation had been completed since the original presentation.[20] Its distress was exacerbated by the publication of the enclosures to the American reply.[21]

Nevertheless, the Philippine government expressed its "profound appreciation" for the promised $73 million.

There were, however, two problems. The first was that the United States intended to deduct from this $73 million roughly $24 million owed to it by the Philippine government in repayment of a loan made under the Romulo-Snyder Agreement of 1950. The net payment to the Philippines, therefore, would be only $49 million.[22] The other problem was the mode of payment. The American note promised a "direct settlement" with the Philippine government instead of direct payment to individual claimants; only under such a scheme would offsetting the Philippine obligation against the $73 million be feasible.

In a determined effort to settle its indebtedness, the Philippine government sent two special negotiators to the United States. But, before a satisfactory agreement could be reached, bills were introduced in both houses of Congress providing for payment of the War Damage Claims and deducting the Philippine government's obligation from any appropriation to satisfy the claims. One such bill, S.B. 3238, introduced by Senator J. William Fulbright, provided for direct payment to the Philippine government.[23]

With a view to forestalling both possibilities, because of their potential bearing on the forthcoming presidential electoral campaign in the Philippines, Ambassador Romulo sought a conference on 10 February, 1961 with U.S. Secretary of the Treasury Dillon, who, as Acting Secretary of State in 1959, had signed the American note. At this meeting, Romulo handed Dillon an *aide mémoire* that said, in part:

> This is an election year in the Philippines, and the recommendation of the Eisenhower administration that only $49,000,000 (and not $73,000,00) be allocated for the Philippine war damage legislation ... and $24,000,000 be retained to pay the Philippine obligation under the Romulo-Snyder Agreement, may be made the subject of criticism in the political campaign that has now started. This recommendation of Mr. Eisenhower has not been welcomed in the Philippines. The position of the Philippine Government on this matter has been that the Romulo-Snyder obligation is an obligation of the Philippine Government to the U.S. Government, while the war damage payments are intended for private individuals whose properties were damaged during the war. It would be unfair to the war

damage claimants if payments to them were reduced by an obligation of the Philippine Government.[24]

Romulo then suggested payment of the loan, but not the interest on unpaid annual installments since 1955, before final consideration of the War Damage Bill. This proposition was accepted and, in April 1961, the Philippine government finally paid $21,142,584.[25]

This gesture, however, did not lead to the enactment of the War Damage Bill during the remainder of the 1961 legislative session. The ostensible reason was "lack of time," although there were reports that many lawmakers were reluctant to endorse a War Damage Bill because of the view that the Garcia Administration was graft-ridden. President Kennedy informed a disappointed President Garcia that he would recommend enactment in 1962.[26]

By that time, a change in administration in the Philippines had taken place, President Garcia having lost the 1961 presidential election to Grand Alliance candidate Diosdado Macapagal. Since the latter had run with the unofficial "blessings" of the U.S. Embassy in Manila,[27] and was also attempting to rid the government of graft and corruption, hopes were high that the war damage bill would be favorably acted upon, even with only token support from the White House.

This turned out to be wishful thinking. Many congressmen were not convinced that the United States ought to pay the 22.5 percent of the War Damage Claims at all. Others thought that additional payments would only benefit a few corporations which did not need the money anyway. Still others preferred the money to be used for domestic purposes, while not a few simply assumed that war damage payments would encourage more graft in the Philippines.[28]

Ironically, one of President Macapagal's early moves to curb graft and corruption had the effect of increasing the ranks of the opponents of the War Damage Bill. This was his voiding of the importation of ₱70 million ($20 million at the average free exchange rate in 1962) worth of Virginia leaf tobacco, then awaiting unloading at the pier, which he assumed had been possible during his predecessor's term only because of the machinations of grafters. Congressmen from tobacco-producing states were incensed, despite the Philippine Supreme Court's eventually overruling President Macapagal. This patently adventitious circumstance and a complacent White House contributed to a convincing negative vote of 201–171, when the House of Representatives finally acted on the War Damage Bill on 9 May 1962.[29]

The defeat of the bill, after a decade of high expectations, touched off a series of reactions in the Philippines. War damage claimants were naturally indignant, labeling the action "callous" and an "act of betrayal." There was a national clamor for a "reexamination" of Philippine-American relations, with only a small minority of the national leadership counseling moderation. And, in an emotional nationwide address, President Macapagal announced that, on account of the "poisoned" atmosphere of Philippine-American relations, he was canceling his state visit to the United States already scheduled for the latter part of June. For good measure, he also would accept a hastily extended invitation from Generalissimo Francisco Franco to visit Spain, another "mother country."[30] Three days after the adverse vote on the War Damage Bill, he also issued Proclamation No. 28, changing the date of Philippine Independence from the traditional 4 July to 12 June 1898.[31] Philippine-American relations had suddenly deteriorated to a new low.

Acting quickly to defuse the situation, Kennedy now made the bill his own and assured Macapagal that it would be passed during the same legislative session.[32] With White House support, the House Foreign Affairs Committee favorably reported, anew, the Zablocki Bill;[33] the whole body acted on it with only 35 negative votes this time. The Senate, assured by Assistant Secretary of State for Far Eastern Affairs W. Averill Harriman that the transfer of the date of Philippine Independence was part of the Filipinos' continuing quest for national identity, something which would have taken place with or without the war damage issue,[34] then endorsed the House bill. On 30 August 1962, a beaming President Kennedy signed the Philippine War Damage Act, requesting Representative Miller to give General Romulo, who had in the meantime become President of the

University of the Philippines, one of the two pens he used in signing the bill.[35]

The long, patient wait was over. P.L. 87-616 was merely an enabling act, the money still to be appropriated, but the major step had been taken. Filipino-American relations returned to normal and the "special relationship" was unmistakably reaffirmed in outpourings of gratitude. The euphoria buried the affronts and insults, momentary lapses into bad manners, and veiled threats of terminating the "special ties" that had marked the conversations and negotiations from Quirino to Macapagal. So marked had these been that, in one sense, the appropriation of $73 million appeared anticlimactic.

The Philippine War Damage Act stipulated that only the unpaid balance of awards made by the former PWDC were to be considered; no new claims were to be entertained. Payments under other laws, such as the War Claims Act of 1948 and its amendment in 1956, were to be taken into account, so as to preclude multiple payments. Administration of the payments program was entrusted to the Foreign Claims Settlement Commission of the United States (FCSC). After the payment of approved claims and deduction of expenses incurred by the FCSC for implementing the Act, any unspent money was to be returned to the U.S. Treasury.

Meanwhile, the Senate Foreign Relations Committee had decided to inquire into the activities of obtrusive "lobbyists" in the United States.[36] O'Donnell was among fifty or so lobbyists subpoenaed by the Committee; he testified, in executive session, on 1 March 1963.[37] On the basis of O'Donnell's statements and the documents he was compelled to submit, the Committee came to the conclusion that O'Donnell and his clients had "subverted" the legislative process and deceived the Executive Branch as well, and that "a powerful moving force behind the passage of the Philippine War Damage Legislation Act of 1962 was private gain rather than public welfare" or "national security." The members of the Committee agreed that they would not have voted for the House measure had they known about O'Donnell's activities at the time; an amendment to the existing law—and soon—seemed only logical, before the FCSC started processing the claims.[38]

After some jockeying between the Senate and the House, an amendment was passed and signed into law by President Kennedy on 12 August 1963. It limited awards to a maximum of $25,000 for each claim and prohibited the use of any portion of the funds for direct or indirect payments to former employees of the Philippine War Damage Commission.[39]

The centerpiece of the amendment was the proviso that the surplus of all claims exceeding $25,000, which would have been payable were it not for the amendment, and after deducting administrative costs therefrom,

> ... shall be placed into a *special fund* in the United States Treasury to be used for the purpose of furthering educational exchange and other educational programs to the mutual advantage of the Republic of the Philippines and the United States in such manner as the Presidents of those two Republics shall from time to time determine.[40]

Thus was born the Special Fund for Education. It amounted to over $28 million, more than one-third of the entire war damage appropriations. Although the Philippine government was not totally free to decide on the uses of the money, since these had to be mutually agreed upon between itself and the American government, still the Fund was a windfall. One cannot tell whether the Philippine government was consulted about it in advance. Certainly, however, it would have been impolitic for the Macapagal Administration to have taken any credit for it, since 1963 was an election year for eight Senators and a host of provincial and municipal officials, and the Administration probably did not wish to alienate the support of private claimants who could have received more than $25,000 but for the amendment. Hence, there was no repetition of the official statements of gratitude that had greeted the original War Damage Bill.[41]

Turning now to the implementation of the War Damage Act, as amended, the FCSC's Manila office was swamped with 93,226 applications. Of these, only 78,929 were accepted for consideration on account of multiple filings and claims that were patently ghost claims; 2,678 were eventually denied for a "variety of reasons." Awards were issued on 76,250 adjudicated claims involving a total sum of $40,802,059, while $3,000,395 reverted to the U.S. Treasury.

The unawarded balance of meritorious and adjudicated claims beyond $25,000—the statutory ceiling for each claim—was $29,197,544.73. Since $1,065,000 had been incurred by the FCSC for administering the payments program, $28,132,544 was therefore available for the Special Fund for Education.

CHANNELING THE SPECIAL FUND FOR EDUCATION

Less than a month following the creation of the Special Fund for Education, and long before the exact amount would be officially known, alert Ateneo Jesuits began brainstorming on the possible uses of the Fund. Thus, Fr. John W. McCarron:

40 million dollars.
Who gets it [?]
1. *Suggest* . . . we get tough (not nasty) on this matter . . . that we go right to the top in Washington, not negotiate here . . . Are you interested?[43]

Ateneo de Manila University's restless Professor of Languages and Linguistics felt that prompt action was imperative, "lest the whole of $40,000,000 [*sic*] be turned over to *U.P.* or the Philippine Government."[44] So, in December 1963, he left for the United States in the naive hope of convincing the American government to consider using the Special Fund for upgrading higher education in the Philippines, about 90 percent of which was then being assumed by the private schools. He returned more than six months later, chastened somewhat by failure but all the more determined to work for private education's share of the Special Fund. His mission served as the unofficial backdrop, as it were, of the government-to-government negotiations on the disposition of the Special Fund for Education—soon to be initiated by President Macapagal and subsequently pursued successfully by his successor, President Ferdinand E. Marcos.

The "poisoned" atmosphere of Philippine-American relations created by the initial rejection of the war damage bill now a thing of the past, President Macapagal finally undertook his

American state visit in October 1964. He had with him—presumably—private education's appeal that he discuss with President Lyndon Johnson the possibility of setting aside at least $10 million of the Special Fund for the purpose of improving private higher education in the Philippines.[45] Macapagal, however, was not as keen on helping the private schools as on activating the Fund to support his land reform program. The "Joint Statement" issued after his talks with President Johnson attests:

Both Presidents discussed the disposition of the Special Fund for Education . . . . They *agreed* to consider plans including the possible formation of a joint committee which would ensure use of this fund to further educational programs to the mutual advantage of the Philippines and the United States, among which *educational programs pertaining to land reform would be eligible.*[46]

Macapagal's clear intent to channel a sizeable portion of the Special Fund into land reform education is borne out by his subsequent moves. On 17 October 1964, he designated the Chairman of the National Land Reform Council (NLRC) and concurrently Governor of the Land Reform Authority as the head of a Cabinet Technical Committee "to undertake a preliminary technical study for the *swift* implementation of the agreement on land reform education . . ." and to submit such a study to the Cabinet not later than 30 November 1964.[47] The Committee submitted its study, entitled "Philippine Land Reform Education Program: Tentative Program Design" (TPD), on 8 December 1964.[48] For some unknown reasons, Macapagal only approved the study about five months later, after being reminded of it by the NLRC Chairman.[49] He then requested the Department of Foreign Affairs to "find out the attitude of the United States Government for an early discussion of the subject." Informed of the availability of U.S. Embassy personnel for exploratory talks, he created, in July 1965, the Committee on Land Reform Education, also under the chairmanship of the NLRC Chairman, as the Philippine component of the "joint committee" mentioned in the Macapagal-Johnson "Joint Statement."[50]

The Committee then made representations with the U.S.

Embassy for an agreement to implement TPD.[51] In September 1965, President Johnson authorized the State Department to negotiate an agreement,[52] but the latter evidently balked at committing about two-thirds of the Special Fund for a single project—and land reform education at that—to the possible exclusion of other equally worthwhile and enduring educational programs. This was especially so since Philippine private education was frenetically lobbying for at least $10 million of the Fund. The State Department was also reluctant to deposit the Special Fund in Philippine banking institutions pending the Fund's "final disposition,"[53] preferring that disbursements be made from time to time based on a "mutually agreed schedule." Finally, it might be suggested that, 1965 being a presidential election year, with Macapagal running for reelection in hopes of breaking a jinx in Philippine politics,[54] the State Department did not relish the prospect of the American government's being dragged into the campaign through a release of a sizeable portion of the Special Fund—or the entire sum—at the time. Prudence dictated that agreement on the Philippine proposal and consequent monetary releases be held in abeyance until after the elections, which Macapagal lost.

Macapagal must have been quite disenchanted with the American attitude, which was tantamount to a turnabout, more so since he was running against a formidable challenger—Senate President Marcos; he most certainly would have wanted an agreement on the land reform education project, to endear himself further to the peasantry. But the Americans did not cooperate, and Macapagal's pet project was to be cavalierly treated for the next seventeen years. When, finally, the land reform education program received a share of the Fund in 1972, it was from the remaining portion thereof and an amount much, much less than what Macapagal had expected.

Perhaps it was all his fault. In trying to get the lion's share, as it were, of the Special Fund to support his land reform education program—by itself a laudable program—Macapagal led private educators to intensify their efforts to thwart his scheme. Their chief lobbyist, Fr. McCarron, wrote contacts in the United States who knew people close to President Johnson,[55] and he himself got in touch with U.S. Ambassador

Wm. McCormick Blair and other embassy personnel in Manila, to see to it that Macapagal did not get what he was asking for. And, even as he was assured that "the dumping of any large sums into the land reform movement [was] out,"[56] Fr. McCarron still deemed it necessary to undertake, in September 1965, another mission to Washington in behalf of private education.[57]

The first phase of the negotiations on the disposition of the Special Fund thus ended with Macapagal and his land reform education project suffering a major setback. The American government was probably relieved; in the fresh round of discussions with the new administration of President Marcos, it could look forward to insisting on more creative uses of the Special Fund and on staggered releases of funds. These *desiderata*, among others, were reflected in the first formal agreement between the two countries on the Special Fund signed on 26 April 1966,[58] which U.S. Ambassador Blair referred to as "a very significant step forward in the history of cooperation between our two countries."[59]

Determined to pursue the negotiations to their successful conclusion, President Marcos next created the Special Fund for Education Committee (more popularly known, and henceforth referred to, as the Education Assistance Committee), "to establish guidelines and to review project proposals screened by the Department of Education and to consult with the representatives of the United States Government on the projects to be financed under the Fund."[60] Assisting the Committee was a Secretariat headed by the Undersecretary of Education, Dr. Onofre D. Corpuz, who had been orally instructed by President Marcos to "take care" of the Special Fund.[61] After more discussions with American Embassy personnel, the Education Assistance Committee issued an "Information Bulletin on the War Damage Special Education Fund," inviting both public and private entities and agencies to submit proposals in accordance with a set of guidelines, among which was the "promotion of Filipino culture" (Guideline 2).[62] 15 October 1966 was set as the deadline for parties to submit project proposals.

A major impetus toward reaching agreements on the channeling of the Special Fund was President Marcos's state visit to the United States in September 1966. He and President Johnson

...agreed to put to effective and creative use the special fund for education. . . . They directed the joint panel established last Spring to accelerate [the] discussions already underway on project proposals and concurred in the rapid implementation of agreements as they are mutually agreed [upon].[63]

Seven project areas, including land reform education, were identified for assistance from the Special Fund. The formal project proposals, each cleared with the Office of the President, were submitted to the American Panel at varying intervals in late 1966 to 1967. The American Embassy studied the proposals and, after some modifications arrived at with the Education Assistance Committee, or its Secretariat, forwarded the same to the State Department. The latter, in turn, after clearing the proposals and amounts involved with the Office of the Budget and Treasury Department and securing the concurrence of key senators and congressmen, requested authority from the American President for the U.S. Ambassador in Manila to conclude project agreements, subject to final approval by the Secretary of State.[64]

The first project proposals to be developed were for the School Building Construction Project and the Textbook Production Project of the Philippine government. Authority to conclude agreements on these was granted by President Johnson on 22 March 1967;[65] the agreements were signed on 18 May 1967 and 26 June 1967, respectively.[66]

The proposal for the Cultural Development Project—the third, involving $3.5 million—was received by the American government on 24 February 1967. It was the subject of a specific memorandum from the State Department to the White House, no doubt because the project was "of close personal interest" to someone very special. To quote Secretary Dean Rusk:

President Marcos raised the question of Special Fund support for the National Cultural Center, a project of close personal interest to Mrs. Marcos, during his September 1966 state visit. At that time he was orally assured of U.S. willingness to see the Center supported by the Special Fund. . . .
The Philippine Government is particularly anxious to obtain early

agreement on the project. On March 3 [1967,] President Marcos stressed to Assistant Secretary [William P.] Bundy his high priority for the Cultural Fund proposal.[67]

The Rusk Memorandum was dated 17 June; three days later, the State Department was informed that President Johnson had approved it.[68] On 11 August 1967, the project agreement was signed in Manila.[69]

Approval of the next three proposals took longer, and negotiating the final agreements on them much longer still. The proposals for assistance to private education, the Philippine Science High School physical plant, and the Youth Development Program were submitted in March and April 1967. Rusk requested authority to conclude agreements in August,[70] but President Johnson took no action until January 1968, and at that time only to send the memorandum back to the State Department for modification.[71] White House approval was finally granted on 6 February,[72] but it took three leisurely years thereafter for agreements to be signed. Perhaps this was because the Philippine government desired agreement on these, according to Rusk, only "in the near future," whereas, in the case of the Cultural Development Project, it had been "particularly anxious" to conclude an "early agreement."

This is not to discount the delays occasioned by efforts to reconcile not only the two governments' contrasting viewpoints, but also the desire to accommodate suggestions emanating from vigilant non-governmental entities or parties. A case in point was the assistance to private education project proposal. As has been pointed out earlier, the private education sector was the first to develop tentative suggestions for the utilization of the Special Fund. Nothing had come out of this early effort because President Macapagal wanted prior agreement on his land reform education project.

In 1966, the private educators under the collective leadership of COCOPEA submitted a refined project proposal, entitled "A National Program for Upgrading Private Education in the Philippines."[73] This carefully conceptualized proposal sought $10 million of the Special Fund to be established as a trust fund, of which only the earnings were to be used to finance programs of assistance to private education. The Foundation for Private Education of the Philippines (FPEP), COCOPEA's creation, was to have been the trustee and administrator of the fund. Although endorsed by Undersecretary Corpuz to the Education Assistance Committee,[74] the latter submitted instead another project proposal, entitled "Government Assistance to Private Education" (GAPE), which sought to utilize ₱24 million ($6.1 million) of the Special Fund for low-interest, long-term institutional borrowing by private schools. The Fund was to be administered by the Development Bank of the Philippines, a government institution, instead of FPEP.

When COCOPEA leaders learned about this, they made strong representations to President Marcos to have the Philippine proposal drastically modified. The harmonization of different views took some time; finally, the compromise agreement— the Fund for Assistance to Private Education Project (FAPE)— was approved on 11 June 1968.[76] The amount of the trust fund—₱24 million—remained the same, but its trustee and administrator was neither a purely private foundation nor a government financing institution.

Agreement on the Philippine Science High School Building Project took place on 5 September 1969.[77] In the case of the project for assistance to the Youth Development Program, which became the Fund for Assistance to Students Project, agreement was not concluded until 30 March 1971.[78]

It therefore took almost five years from the exchange of notes on 26 April 1966 governing the channeling of the Fund for the Marcos Administration to conclude agreements with the United States on project proposals that were intrinsically its own. As for Macapagal's earlier proposal for land reform education, agreement was not reached until 1972, almost eight years from its inception! The reasons behind this unusual development can only be divined at this time. Perhaps, the Marcos Administration and the American government did not rate land reform education as a priority area. Indeed, the tentative guidelines suggested by a Philippine government inter-agency technical committee in June 1966 did not specifically mention land reform education as eligible for assistance; presumably, agrarian reform education* fell under the category of "non-formal education" (Guideline 1).[79] There also seemed to have been differences between the two governments on some features of the project proposal, including phraseology and terminology, especially since the National Land Reform Council had been replaced by the Department of Agrarian Reform before the formal agreement was signed. As late as December 1971, for instance, a representative of the U.S. Embassy was still getting in touch with Mrs. Angelina R. Muñoz of the Department of Agrarian Reform, asking whether the revised American draft reflected her "suggested changes." This was after the Philippine government had already been informally notified by the American Panel in October that its proposal had been accepted. Lastly, the agreement on the project proposal had to await the conclusion of the agreement on the Fund for Assistance to Students in 1971: the government had earmarked the "remaining balance" of the Special Fund to assist the agrarian reform education program of the Department of Agrarian Reform, and it wanted to have the exact figure before formalizing the agreement. The project agreement was finally signed on 21 March 1972.[81]

For the agrarian reform education project, therefore, it was a case of better late than never and better the remaining slice of the pie—not necessarily the smallest, by the way—than none at all. There was a double irony here. The project had received the first of White House blessings and was initially envisioned to receive $23 million, or 85 percent, of the $28 million Special Fund. But it was the last to be agreed upon and ultimately assigned only $1,282,051.28, or less than 5 percent of the Special Fund.

The War Damage Claims issue was one of several that grew out of the colonial era and remained to trouble the early years of Philippine independence. It had the possibility of disrupting and eroding friendly relations between the two countries soon

---

*The terminological change in this chapter parallels that in the Philippine government at this time. "Agrarian reform" replaced "land reform" in 1971 when the Code of Agrarian Reforms superseded the Agricultural Land Reform Code.

after the withdrawal of American sovereignty. The issue was eventually resolved in a mutually satisfactory manner after two decades of off-and-on negotiations and discussions, at times with private parties intruding themselves. The $28 million Special Fund was "creatively" channeled into seven projects. Whether it was wise to have done so—instead of confining assistance to just one or two—will never be convincingly demonstrated or proven. What is certain, however, is that the programs and projects supported by the Special Fund have had an appreciable impact on some sectors of Philippine society, and will most likely continue to do so. Continuing activities made possible through the four educational trust funds—the Fund for Cultural Development, the Fund for Assistance to Private Education, the Fund for Assistance to Students, and the Fund for Agrarian Reform Education—and the outcomes of the three "one-shot" projects, constitute visible monuments and constant reminders of Philippine-American collaboration and friendship.[82]

America's Philippine Policy in the Quirino Years (1948-1953): A Study in Patron-Client Diplomacy

RICHARD E. WELCH, JR.

The problems of a patron-client relationship have been the subject of several chapters of this book. Those problems did not end when the Republic of the Philippines achieved independence in 1946. Independence did not alter the comparative strength of the Philippines and the United States, and questions of dependency continued to plague their relations. The United States did not pursue a single-minded policy of neocolonialism, but its military security goals frequently clashed with Philippine nationalism. America wished to assist the Philippines, but only by instruments of its own choosing, and its emphasis on Philippine stability did not produce the long-term economic development of its Pacific ally.

In this essay, Professor Richard Welch of Lafayette College examines Philippine-American diplomatic relations during the presidency of Elpidio Quirino, 1948-1953. Those relations are examined primarily from the standpoint of policy-makers in Washington. He finds little economic imperialism but a great deal of ethnocentric insensitivity. His analysis emphasizes the contrasting perceptions and priorities of the American and Philippine negotiators and relates the revival of an interventionist mentality in the U.S. State Department to the established design of patron and client. At various points, the Quirino years appeared to offer the prospect of increased American respect for the demands of Philippine nationalism, but at their conclusion there was no fundamental change and a sustained dependence.

Elpidio Quirino succeeded to the presidency of the Republic of the Philippines in April 1948 with the death of Manuel Roxas. He secured a presidential term in his own right in the violent and corrupt election of 1949, and he was defeated four years later by his one-time protégé, Ramon Magsaysay. The Quirino years, 1948–1953, form a fairly distinct era in the domestic history of the troubled Philippine nation. They saw unsuccessful attempts at agricultural reform and more successful endeavors to increase national income, rescue the Philippine treasury from threatened bankruptcy, and improve the Philippine balance of payments. They witnessed as well increased ambition in foreign affairs. The Quirino Administration made abortive efforts to fashion a Pacific equivalent to NATO, establish a diplomatic alliance with Chiang Kai-shek, and assume a leadership role among the non-Communist nations of Asia. With more consistency, the Quirino Administration sought to take advantage of the value of Philippine military bases for United States Cold War strategy to obtain greater recognition from their former colonial master, though to little avail. For Philippine-American relations, the Quirino years offered the prospect of increased equality but saw no fundamental change and a sustained dependence. At their end, the "special relationship" between the United States and the Philippines remained that of patron and client.

The Quirino years find their significance in the diplomatic history of both nations, not because they witnessed greater recognition by the United States of the claims of the Philippines as a sovereign ally, but because they illustrate the difficulty for a small nation of obtaining political concessions from a major power while requesting increased economic assistance. Old ties and new fears assured the Philippines a measure of American generosity, but the effect of the Korean War was to give Japan and not the Philippines the central role in American Cold War strategy in the Pacific. The bargaining power of the Quirino Administration was restricted by that fact, and the evolving emphasis of United States Philippine policy from economics to stability and defense inspired a renaissance of interventionist mentality in the Department of State that lessened the possibility that the Philippine government could obtain meaningful concessions from the United States. Such issues as trade and tariff policy, the jurisdictional status of American forces in the Philippines, operational sovereignty in American military bases, and a regional security pact suffered American neglect.

On all these issues of Philippine-American relations, the Quirino years were years of postponement. A confusion of priorities in Manila and misperceptions and distractions in Washington diminished the chance of any fundamental correction in Philippine-American relations, and, though American policy by the end of 1953 witnessed limited acknowledgment of the military and economic requirements of Philippine nationalism, it witnessed as well a continued failure to recognize either the difficulties or accomplishments of Elpidio Quirino.

One of the more constant themes of American policy in these years was the tendency of American policy-makers to exaggerate the failures of Philippine political leadership and to deny its domestic accomplishments. Once the Korean War began, second-echelon officials in the U.S. State Department no longer plotted to remove Quirino, but to the end of his presidency they continued to judge him an embarrassment and an obstacle to Philippine stability and progress. The sufficiency of the domestic legislation of the Quirino Administration in behalf of fiscal stability and economic development may be debated, but unquestionable is the fact that, in the opinion of the Philippines and Southeast Asia Division of the State Department, Quirino was an unsatisfactory instrument for American military and economic policy in the western Pacific. In the perception of Washington, any improvement in the economic and military arrangements of the Philippines was the result of American aid and guidance alone and was achieved despite the vainglorious Quirino. That judgment, if inaccurate, was important and furnishes partial explanation for the fact that, though the Quirino years witnessed increased activity in the diplomatic relations between the Philippines and the United States and accelerated American economic and military assistance, they saw the patron-client character of those relations reaffirmed and strengthened. The correction of old grievances was postponed, opportunities for improved Philippine-American understanding and effective cooperation were missed, and the sensitivities of Filipino nationalism further aggravated.

U.S. PHILIPPINE POLICY, 1948–1949

The first two years of Quirino's presidency saw relatively little concern by the United States with developments in the Philippines. The State Department requested a report on the Hukbalahap from its Office of Intelligence Research;[1] interoffice memoranda were distributed by Far Eastern Desk officers bemoaning the political ineptitude of the Philippine administration and blaming that ineptitude for the revival of the Huks and the problems of the Philippine treasury; and the Chargé of the American Embassy periodically called for broader functions for the JUSMAG (Joint United States Military Assistance Group) mission in Manila,[2] but the "loss" of China had less impact on Philippine-American relations than might have been expected. The victory of Mao Tse-tung and the explosion of the first Russian atomic bomb had major impact on the course of Cold War diplomacy and measurable influence on American policy in Southeast Asia, but there was little sense of emergency in State Department memoranda respecting the economic and military vulnerability of the Philippine archipelago until the advent of the Korean War. There was, indeed, a belief on the part of some American diplomatic officials throughout the year 1949 that an enlarged American military presence in the Philippines could prove counterproductive by furnishing propaganda ammunition for the Huks.

The failure of Communist victory in China to increase the diplomatic leverage of the Philippines was revealed by the cool reception given Quirino's address to the United States Senate in August 1949 with its proposal for a collective defense system for the Pacific similar to the North Atlantic Treaty Organization. Still chillier was the State Department's response to

Quirino's surprise visit to Taipei and the vaguely bellicose joint communication that concluded his meeting with Chiang Kaishek.

U.S. PHILIPPINE POLICY, 1950-1951, AND THE IMPACT OF THE KOREAN WAR

The years 1950-1951 are in many ways the most important in an analysis of the relations of the United States with the Quirino Administration. It was in these years that the United States dispatched the Bell Mission, met the aggression of North Korea by force of arms, and signed a Mutual Defense Treaty with the Republic of the Philippines. They were years that gave promise of a significant evolution in Philippine-American relations and increased respect for the demands of Philippine nationalism. They saw increased aid and an expanded American military presence, but the demands of Philippine nationalism were postponed and frustrated.

The year 1950 began with another visit to Washington by the Philippine President. Quirino believed the time ripe to request both money and concessions from the Truman Administration. He wished increased economic assistance, explicit guarantees of American military protection, and revision of the Trade Act of 1946 and the Military Assistance Act of 1947. The reception he received demonstrated the arrogance of superior strength and the conviction of several Washington officials that they were negotiating not with an ally but with a self-serving and incompetent colonial.

In preparation for Quirino's visit, John F. Melby of the PSA division had drafted a memorandum listing the issues that would probably be raised by the Philippine President and suggesting the replies that might best be given by President Truman. This memorandum was sent to Secretary Dean Acheson on 31 January by Livingston T. Merchant, Deputy Assistant Secretary of State for Far Eastern Affairs, and, with minor revisions, submitted to President Truman on 2 February. Its tone was one of suspicion toward Quirino and impatience respecting the Filipinos and their "mismanagement of affairs since independence."

Truman was advised to tell Quirino that "Philippine performance" must precede considerations of additional American aid
if "the current trend of economic and financial deterioration"
was to be reversed. U.S. Ambassador Myron M. Cowen had
been urging Quirino to adopt certain fiscal and institutional reforms and, were the Administration to give unqualified promises
of aid, the influence of our Embassy would be undermined and
the "classical Philippine maneuver [of] playing off one part of
the American Government against another part" unwisely encouraged. Filipino demands for an ironclad pledge of American
military support in the event of attack were irrelevant. America
had made sufficiently clear its intention to protect the Philippines, and Quirino should concentrate on making the Filipino
army a more effective force for suppressing insurgency. His proposal for a Pacific regional organization was ill-timed, and the
United States should reserve judgment until its nature was
clarified and until the Filipinos had put their own house in
order. The principal problems confronting the Philippines were,
in any case, economic. Fiscal mismanagement had produced a
balance-of-trade deficit and a sharp reduction in Filipino dollar
reserves. Until the Philippine government took steps to reduce
unnecessary imports, reform its tax structure, and correct the
graft and corruption that robbed the treasury of needed revenue, Quirino should be given no promise of further American
aid. Philippine officials must be persuaded that they could not
"always count on the United States to bail them out" and that
further American aid would be effective only if it was preceded
by "drastic reforms undertaken by the Philippines itself."[3]

The Truman-Quirino conference of February proved predictably unsatisfactory for both parties, and State Department
dissatisfaction with Quirino increased over the next two months
as a result of the revived activity of the Huks and the exaggerated fears of some PSA officers that domestic opposition to
Quirino presaged a condition of political chaos that could lead
to a Communist takeover. Ambassador Cowen developed a
personal antipathy to Quirino and, together with John F. Melby
of the PSA, prepared to work secretly for his removal. In a
memorandum prepared by Melby and forwarded to Acheson by
Assistant Secretary of State Dean Rusk, "political factors" were

identified as a major cause of "the serious problems confronting the Philippines." Quirino's inability to gain public confidence was attributed to the fraud and violence that had accompanied his election and to his own vanity, arrogance, and incapacity. The "first and primary obstacle in the solution of the Philippine problem" was Elpidio Quirino, and, if there was "one lesson to be learned from the China debacle," it was that, when confronted "with an inadequate vehicle," American foreign policy should be directed toward discarding or immobilizing that vehicle in favor of "a more propitious one." To try to replace Quirino would be a potentially dangerous policy; were our intent to be generally known, it could "compromise the American moral position" throughout the world and be considered an example of "imperialistic interference in the affairs of a sovereign country." But the "emergency nature" of the situation demanded action. If political chaos opened the way to the eventual victory of the Huks, our influence throughout Asia would be crippled and the United States placed "in a highly embarrassing position vis-à-vis the British, French, and Dutch whom we have been persuading to recognize the realities and the legitimacy of Asiatic nationalism and self-determination." A possible course of action might be to request Senator Millard Tydings and some Republican senator of "comparable background and prestige in the Philippines" to undertake a special mission to Manila and try to persuade Quirino either to resign his office or share his presidential powers with other and more responsible leaders.[4]

Ambassador Cowen would continue, almost to the beginning of the Korean War, to urge the State Department to work for the replacement of Quirino. Cowen, a businessman with limited diplomatic experience, found Filipino politics and politicians distasteful. A self-assured exemplar of American efficiency and virtue, he displayed an ill-concealed aversion to Quirino, partially inspired by the latter's understandable reluctance to take Cowen into his confidence. In a letter to Rusk of 1 June, Cowen suggested that, though the corrupt nature of Philippine politics denied the possibility of an ideal solution, the best available answer would be the replacement of Quirino by the Vice-President, Fernando Lopez, a "likeable, unpretentious and apparently disingenuous man," possessed of a brainier brother—"the cold-blooded strategist," Eugenio Lopez.[5]

There is no evidence that these presumptuous schemes were ever seriously considered by either Acheson or Truman, but they offer an interesting contrast to the later conviction of the Philippines and Southeast Asia Division, during the Korean War, that American security interests in the Pacific required a renewed determination to support the Quirino Administration. When the threat of communism was translated from the phantom of a Huk takeover to the reality of Russian-trained North Korean soldiers, "the overweening vanity and arrogance of Quirino" shrank in importance. A "vehicle" subject to replacement became a client to be influenced. The impact of the Korean War on Philippine-American relations was quickly apparent, and that impact had the potential for promoting understanding as well as dependence.

The pivotal geographic position of the Philippines in an insular defense perimeter stretching from the Aleutians to New Zealand had been remarked in State and Defense Department documents prior to 25 June 1950, but it was given increased recognition when President Harry Truman ordered reinforcement of U.S. forces in the Philippines two days after the North Koreans stormed across the 38th parallel. By the end of June, the President announced that he was sending a special economic mission to the Philippines, headed by former Undersecretary of the Treasury Daniel W. Bell. Though Truman declared that he was acting in response to a request made by our ally during his visit to Washington, the form of the mission reflected not the wishes of Quirino but the determination of the Truman Administration to bolster the Philippine government, the better to assure its utility for American defenses in the Pacific. If the Communist victory in China had promoted the strategic value of the Philippines in the eyes of a few officials in the Defense Department, it was the Korean War that convinced the Truman Administration that the time had come for greater generosity, direction, and control. Military and economic aid would provide the instrument, and the budget crisis of the Philippine government would provide the opportunity.

The Philippine economy was, in fact, not in danger of imminent collapse. Its unfavorable balance of payments was in large part the result of the unrealistic official exchange rate of the peso and substantial outpayments for shipping and capital charges and profit remission to foreign investors.[6] Policy-makers in America, however, were convinced that the Philippine economy was in shambles and that primary blame could be attributed to domestic mismanagement. The exchange and import controls imposed early in 1950 were viewed with suspicion, and the bankrupt state of the Philippine treasury with alarm. The "fundamental fiscal and economic reforms" suggested in the Febuary memorandum to President Truman were, by the end of June, deemed essential.

The idea of a new economic survey mission to the Philippines had been the subject of office memoranda and dispute in the PSA Division for many months. Some PSA officials were reluctant to see the United States government assume responsibility for Quirino's "errors of judgment," while others favored "an intelligent and discreet United States mission" that would "handle the bridle, the carrot and the stick with utmost delicacy."[7] There was disagreement as well respecting the aims of a new mission. Should it be directed to the immediate fiscal crisis or to long-range Philippine economic developments? Should it demand undeviating fiscal austerity or recognize the discontent of Filipino tenant farmers and wage earners? Should it pressure the Philippine government to abandon exchange controls or emphasize such broader considerations as income distribution and improved productivity?[8]

The Bell Mission and Report

The instructions given the Bell Mission would better disguise than settle these disagreements, but the composition of the mission represented a clear defeat for President Quirino and his hopes that the instrument for increased American aid would be a "joint mission," composed of an equal number of American and Filipino representatives. Soon after his return in March from the Johns Hopkins Medical Center, Quirino had initiated a press campaign in behalf of a "joint mission." Whatever its internal divisions respecting the goals of an economic mission, the State Department was united in its opposition to what it saw as an attempt by Quirino to promote his own political power at the expense of "the integrity of the relations between the United States and the Philippines." Filipino representatives could only be obsequious agents of Quirino, and "any report prepared by a Joint Mission would not be worth the paper it was written on." The mission must be composed exclusively of American experts in order that its report be sufficiently objective to serve the purposes of economic reform in the Philippines and American security interests in the Pacific.[9]

The Bell Mission spent two months in the Philippines. Upon their return to Washington in September, Bell and Vice-Chairman Richard Marshall informed President Truman that the Philippines faced a dual crisis. The immediate problem was the Huk revolt, and this should be met by a government military offensive and social reforms that would lessen the appeal of the Communist insurgents for the tenant farmer. A more basic problem concerned the need to assure the fiscal stability and economic viability of the Islands. A major program of economic development and technical assistance was needed. Such a program would require $50 million in American aid annually for a five-year period and should be administered by an American mission of 200 persons. They would assume "direction of most of the Philippine Government activities."[10]

When the Bell Mission submitted its official report on 9 October, the Huk revolt was given little mention and emphasis was placed on "the generally unfavorable economic and political environment" in the Philippines. After describing the existing economic imbalances and their danger, the report rejected the adequacy of import and exchange controls to remedy "fundamental ills." Only concerted long-term efforts "to increase production and improve productive efficiency, to raise the level of wages and farm income, and to open new opportunities for work and for acquiring land" would provide a permanent solution. The finances of the Philippine government must be placed on a sound basis to avoid further inflation, the tax structure reformed to increase the proportion of taxes collected from high incomes and large property holdings, and a revised credit policy instituted that would encourage native and foreign investment. There should be an improvement of agricultural productivity with the introduction of new farming techniques and a program of land redistribution by means of government purchase for resale to small farmers and tenants. Accompanying these efforts, there must be administrative reforms to eliminate corruption and social reforms to improve public health, education, and living standards. The Philippine government must guarantee labor the right to organize trade unions and enact minimum-wage legislation for both agricultural and industrial workers.

For its part, the United States should provide loans and grants, on a project basis, and should send a technical mission to assist the Philippine government in implementing the recommended programs of economic development, public administration, and social welfare. Finally, the report recommended that the two governments complete negotiation of the long-delayed Treaty of Friendship, Commerce, and Navigation and suggested that the Trade Act of 1946 be reexamined "in the light of new conditions."[11]

It was the earnest wish of Quirino and the Philippine government that the Trade Act of 1946 be replaced by a new commercial agreement which would correct existing inequalities, particularly the requirement of "national treatment" for American businessmen in the development of Philippine natural resources and restrictions on Filipino currency management and export controls. The Foster-Quirino Agreement of 14 November 1950 would suggest but not require such revision.

The Foster-Quirino Agreement sought to give the recommendations of the Bell Report official and bilateral blessing. At a well-publicized meeting in Baguio, Quirino and William C. Foster, serving as the personal representative of President Truman, approved the text of a long and windy statement. They agreed to recommend to their respective governments a program covering "the nature and form of the assistance and cooperation" which the United States should extend to the Philippines to help solve "age-old social and economic problems ... [and] bring about a new Philippine era of progress and plenty." Quirino pledged on the part of the Philippine government "total economic mobilization" and guaranteed that the Philippine Council of State would immediately set to work to increase tax revenues and enact minimum-wage legislation for agricultural workers—as a first step toward improving the living conditions of all agricultural and industrial workers. In consideration of the determination of the Philippine government "to act boldly and promptly . . . to fulfill the aspirations of the Filipino people," the President of the United States would recommend to the Congress the appropriation of funds over a five-year period for an economic and technical assistance program.

The Economic Cooperation Administration would be the agency of the United States government for the distribution of American financial aid and technical assistance. Working with the Philippine Council for United States Aid, it would advise the Philippine government how best to implement the recommendations of the Bell Report and supervise the relations of the United States technical mission with the departments of the Philippine government.[12]

Although the Foster-Quirino Agreement contained a pledge that both governments would resume negotiations for a Treaty of Friendship, Commerce, and Navigation, it limited its discussion of a revision of the Trade Act to a brief and tentative forecast:

It is assumed that these negotiations will re-examine at the same time the provisions of the present Trade Agreement. It is realized that the Philippines needs special U.S. assistance in trade and privileges for several years.[13]

More than four years would pass before this assumption was validated, and the revision then accomplished would fail to meet the expectations of Philippine economic nationalism.

The Foster-Quirino Agreement proved indeed a disappointment for both nations. The supervisory functions of the United States Technical Mission that began operation in April 1951 could only irritate Filipino sensitivities, and the failure of American dollars to transform Filipino economic society would confirm the prejudices of American policy-makers conditioned to the more dramatic progress of the Marshall Plan nations.

Motives and Perceptions

The point to emphasize is not the accuracy of American judgments respecting Philippine economic conditions in 1950–1951, but the constancy of Washington's predictions of economic disaster unless the Filipinos accepted American advice with American aid. American policy was shaped by the perception that the Quirino Administration was ineffective. Some students of the Quirino presidency have challenged Washington's judgment of Quirino's capacity and accomplishments. For Professor Frank H. Golay, the Quirino years provided "an eventful period in postwar Philippine economic development" and witnessed important changes "which went far to solve the fiscal and balance of payments problems which had plagued the postwar Philippines," while making a significant contribution to improving the political and economic viability of the Republic.[14] One can argue that the economic history of the Philippine Islands over the next decade suggests that the effects of fiscal legislation in the Quirino years were not as salutary as Professor Golay implies and that this legislation did not provide a satisfactory basis for a long-term economic development, but the consequences of these tax and monetary reforms are in large measure irrelevant to an understanding of Philippine-American relations in 1950–1951. Those relations were shaped by contemporary American perceptions and Philippine vulnerability, not by the subsequent judgments of economic historians. Washington was convinced in the early 1950s that the Quirino Administration did not enjoy public confidence and that improvements in the reserve position of the Philippine treasury were the result of special demand conditions created by the Korean War.

The Bell Mission and the agreements that sought to implement its recommendations may be criticized for a confusion of motives and a failure to confront either the elitist structures of political power in the Philippines or the diplomatic frictions produced by continued Philippine economic dependence. They do not serve as an example of economic imperialism.[15] Rather, they provide a further illustration of America's longstanding effort to encourage the economic modernization of the Islands by means of foreign aid and direction. External aid is seldom a satisfactory instrument for domestic reform, and particularly is this true when the hopes of both contributor and recipient are exaggerated and financial assistance is limited in amount and inspired primarily by national-security considerations.[16]

Washington policy-makers displayed a measure of uncertainty in their attempt to conciliate and coerce the Filipino government.[17] Convinced that the Philippine government would accept the report of the Bell Mission because of a continuing hunger for American funds, they were nonetheless confounded by what they saw as the failure of the Filipinos to acknowledge the accomplishments of American aid. Persuaded that the Filipinos were greedy, they were surprised by the failure of the Filipinos to be grateful.[18]

A more central ambiguity concerns the State Department's determination to promote Philippine economic development as a political objective of the United States government. American political objectives in the Pacific were not necessarily antagonistic to the progress of the Philippine economy, but neither was it certain that measures that favored stability in the Philippines were most conducive to the expansion, diversification, and independence of its economy. One need not criticize the State Department for its emphasis on the political objectives of the United States; one can criticize the Department for its failure to consider the possibility that those objectives might not promote the economic development of the Philippines. Divisions among American policy-makers continued to be confined to disputes over the balancing of the carrot-and-stick technique and differing judgments respecting the best approach for persuading Congress to fund departmental recommendations.[19]

Some members of the PSA Division were indeed prepared to identify economic aid as "a bribe" made necessary by the requirement of America's more effective participation in Philippine affairs. They wished to see American funds directed primarily toward military assistance and the improvement of Philippine defense forces. The ability of the Philippine Congress to fulfill its obligations under the Foster-Quirino Agreement was judged dubious and a military assistance program likely to provide a better tool for dealing with the Philippine economic situation.[20] Their objections did not dictate American aid policy, but, in the wake of the Korean War, the United States demonstrated an increased concern for the military security of the Philippines.

When, on 27 June 1950, President Truman ordered United States air and sea forces to give cover and support to the South Korean army, he concurrently announced that American forces in the Philippines were to be strengthened and military assistance to the Philippine government accelerated.[21]

Military Assistance and Mutual Defense

Between 27 June 1950 and 30 August 1951, when the United States and the Philippines signed a formal Mutual Defense Treaty, there was a sizeable increase in the complement of the United States Army troops in the Philippines, particularly at Fort Stotsenberg and Clark Field, and the United States Navy enlarged its base facilities at Subic Bay, Zambales, Sangley Point, and Cavite.[22] Earlier concern over the adverse consequences of a larger American military presence in the Philippines was not so much overridden as forgotten, and by the Quirino Administration as well as the American State Department. Quirino appeared anxious, in the last months of 1950, to demonstrate the identity of Philippine and American security interests. Not only did he approve the increase of American soldiers stationed in the Philippines, but he applauded the announcement that the Seventh Fleet would protect Formosa from the Chinese Communists and agreed to send two Philippine battalion combat teams to fight in the Korean War under the UN-American command.

Though Quirino hoped that cooperation with American military strategy would lend strength to Philippine bargaining power in diplomatic relations with the United States, he was also inspired by a growing fear of the People's Republic of China. For both Quirino and the United States, the Korean War stimulated a fear of Communist expansion and subversion,[23] but, while the United States tended to see Soviet-directed international communism as the enemy to be contained, the Quirino Administration was more concerned with the ability of Red China to conquer Formosa and utilize the large Chinese community in the Philippines as a fifth column. American defense policy entertained considerable confusion respecting the role of the Philippines—whether they were part of an island chain that provided a strategic perimeter for the continental United States or part of "the entire structure of anti-Communist defenses in Southeast Asia"—but for Quirino the role of the United States was less ambiguous. The United States should give the Republic of the Philippines an ironclad guarantee that it would come to its immediate defense in case of external attack. Even before the entrance of Chinese troops in the Korean War, Quirino had determined that Red China posed the most likely source of attack and subversion.[24]

The determination of the Quirino Administration to strengthen its national security against domestic insurgents and external attack and the determination of the United States to thwart further Communist expansion in Asia complemented one another and assured a policy of increased American military assistance. The strengthening of American military bases and a widening advisory role for JUSMAG were matched by an expansion of the Philippine armed forces and an improvement in their equipment and efficiency. But increased appropriations and an expanded technical assistance program did not elevate the Republic of the Philippines from military dependent to diplomatic equal. United States policy-makers saw no need to make concessions respecting the status of military bases or Philippine jurisdiction over American armed forces. If the Filipinos had little reason to doubt the value of the bases for American defense strategy,[25] they could only be disappointed that the bargaining power they provided was confined to increased military aid and a mutual defense treaty. That treaty reflected not only a desire to conciliate Quirino but a determination to persuade the Philippine government to accept the new role of Japan in American defense planning.[26] A development that significantly affected the diplomatic leverage of the Republic of the Philippines was the evolving significance of Japan in the Cold War diplomacy of the United States.

The Role of Japan

Some months before the invasion of South Korea, Japan had begun to assume an important role in American containment strategy. No longer viewed as a vanquished enemy in need of redemption, Japan was recast as the central link in a defense perimeter directed against "further Communist aggression in Asia." Once the Korean War began, Japan provided the primary American base for troops and supplies, and its strategic value gained universal acknowledgment in Washington. The enhanced role of Japan in the American security system would not only anger many Filipinos who remembered the brutality of Japanese military occupation, but would serve to restrict the diplomatic influence of the Quirino Administration.

Anxious to gain Philippine acceptance of a Japanese peace treaty, the United States tried to allay Philippine apprehensions with reiterated assurances of the inability of Japan to remilitarize,[27] but the comparative importance of Japan and the Philippines in the eyes of American policy-makers was exhibited by their turnabout on the issue of Japanese reparations. Where once the United States had lent support to Philippine demands for a large indemnity from Japan, by the fall of 1950 it was anxious to scale down the Philippine reparation claim lest it hinder Japanese efforts at economic recovery and reduce the utility of Japan for American security policy in the Pacific. The Japanese Peace Treaty of 8 September 1951 contained no requirement for further Japanese reparation payments but only a carefully phrased acknowledgment that reparations were a suitable topic for bilateral negotiation.

The decisive impact of the Korean War was on the Japanese policy of the United States, not its Philippine policy. And the increased importance of Japan for American strategic planning in East Asia made unlikely a significant change in the accustomed pattern of Philippine-American relations.

The NSC Report

When the National Security Council finally approved a statement of policy respecting the Philippines and forwarded it to President Truman for his approval on 9 November 1950, one of the main arguments supporting the strategic importance of the Philippines was to the effect that, were the archipelago to fall within the orbit of Soviet domination, our "entire structure of anti-communist defenses in Southeast Asia and the offshore island chain, including Japan [would be jeopardized]."

That policy paper is illustrative of the American attitude toward the Philippines and the continuing limitations and ethnocentricity of United States policy.[28] The NSC made no pretense that its recommendations were directed toward the national pride and self-esteem of the Filipino people. United States policy had three major goals in the Philippines:

1. "An effective government which will preserve and strengthen the pro-U.S. orientation of its people."
2. "A military capability of restoring and maintaining internal security."
3. "A stable and self-supporting economy."

In accomplishing these objectives, the United States should urge the Philippine government to effect, without further delay, the political and economic reforms listed in the Bell Report; offer economic assistance, under United States supervision and control; extend military aid and guidance; and "continue to assume responsibility for the external defense of the Islands . . . prepared to commit United States forces, if necessary, to prevent communist control of the Philippines."

The independence of the Philippines was linked to its "pro-U.S. orientation." Were the Philippines to succumb to Communist influence, it would lose its independence, and the United States as sponsor of the Republic of the Philippines would consequently suffer a serious loss in prestige in Asia. The Philippines must not be viewed in isolation. Their development and defense was an essential feature of our Japanese policy. An anti-Communist and economically viable Japan was necessary to our defense posture in the Pacific, and the United States must favor "the establishment of friendly political and economic relations between Japan and the Philippines" because the "simultaneous sound development" of those nations would contribute to the stability of the Pacific area.

Philippines leaders must be persuaded of the necessity of "vigorous political and economic action." United States policy should take recognition of "the extreme sensitivity of Philippine officials," but it must not be inhibited from exerting a proper initiative and reasserting American influence:

The security interests of the United States require that the Philippines become and remain stable, anti-communist, pro-American, and an example for the rest of the world of the intention of the United States to encourage the establishment of progressive and responsible government. This entails the reassertion of U.S. influence to the extent required to eliminate prevalent corruption, provide efficient administrative services, and restore public faith in the concept of government in the best interests of the people.[29]

U.S. PHILIPPINE POLICY, 1952–1953

The last years of the Quirino presidency only confirmed the developments and policies of 1950–1951. Aid programs were continued; American guidance of those programs increased. But there was no settlement of the difficult issues of Philippine-American relations, only continued postponement.

The Mutual Defense Treaty of 1951 did not satisfy Filipino demands for a guarantee of automatic American support in case of attack,[30] nor did it give the Filipinos the participatory role in defense planning and base operations that they wished. The pact was itself the cause of much squabbling respecting the location and format of the signing ceremony and acrimonious debate over the question of whether ratifications should be exchanged before the Philippine Senate gave its assent to the Japanese peace treaty. The net result was that any sense of mutual cooperation and good will achieved by negotiation of the treaty had partially dissipated by the summer of 1952. The residue was soon consumed in needless bickering over the question of the establishment of a permanent Philippine-American Council as an instrument of implementation.[31]

The years 1952–1953 saw continued friction between the Department of State and the Quirino Administration over Philippine demands for a Pacific regional pact. Again, the result was exacerbation without resolution. Although the following year would see the United States eager to champion a regional security organization—convinced, after Dienbienphu, that bilateral treaties were inferior to a regional political arrangement for containing communism in Southeast Asia—the United

States throughout the Quirino presidency was reluctant to encourage Philippine proposals for an anti-Communist pact. There were various reasons for this reluctance. Not only did the State Department insist that Philippine ratification of the Japanese peace treaty and Philippine diplomatic recognition of the Associated States must precede preliminary discussions respecting a Pacific pact, but it was anxious that any regional organization embrace as many countries of mainland Asia as possible. Quirino had in mind an expansion of the ANZUS Pact to include the Philippines, the "Republic of China," and, possibly, Indonesia. Quirino was jealous of what he considered to be the more respectful arrangements of the United States with its ANZUS partners, and insisted that, were ANZUS to be absorbed in a larger Pacific organization, it would no longer be subject to Nacionalista criticism as an all-white, old-time-colonial club.[32]

Though the last years of Quirino's presidency saw no agreement on the composition, initiation, or specific obligations of a regional collective security organization, there was a temporary improvement in the social relations of the American Embassy and the Malacañan Palace, with the retirement of Myron Cowen and his replacement by the World War II naval hero Raymond A. Spruance in February 1952. Spruance did not entertain—at least initially—any personal animus toward Quirino and rather admired his desire "to play an active part in the fight against communism."[33] Yet, Spruance no more than his predecessor saw Quirino as the statesman-leader of a sovereign ally. And, in some measure, Quirino must share responsibility for this fact. In his efforts to obtain additional American military assistance, Quirino periodically adopted a posture not unlike that of an American Legionnaire. He assured Spruance that there were 100,000 Philippine youths of 20 years of age who, given American arms and training, would be of inestimable value "should any further outbreak of Chinese Communist aggression . . . require joint action," and he claimed that in his travels to other Asian countries he served not only as spokesman for the Philippine Republic and the Free World but for the democratic way and the United States of America.[34]

Quirino's services as unofficial American ambassador proved of little benefit when he continued to request the delimitation of the boundaries of American military bases and a revision of the 1947 agreement restricting Philippine jurisdiction over American military personnel. Both issues were brushed aside by the United States in 1952–1953 and for many years after.[35]

More disappointing for Quirino, however, was the continued refusal of the United States to begin negotiations on the revision of the Trade Act of 1946. Apart from a few indications that it might consider proposals for the revision of particular provisions, the United States made no effort to follow through on the promise of the Foster-Quirino Agreement. Quirino believed —and correctly—that the State Department wished to wait and negotiate with his successor. The years 1952–1953 saw no progress on such issues as the special privileges of American businessmen and investors in the Philippine economy, the power of the Philippine government to control the exchange rate of the peso, and the authority of that government to encourage economic diversification by selective taxation of American imports.[36]

SUMMARY: AN OLD PATTERN CONFIRMED

The relations of patrons and clients are seldom easy, and it would appear that there was a measure of validity in the expressions of dissatisfaction of both the Department of State and Elpidio Quirino. This mutual dissatisfaction reflected the stalemate quality of Philippine-American relations during the Quirino presidency and also echoed the imperial era. Similar expressions of grievance had been raised by American governors general and by leaders of the Philippine Assembly. Then, too, one party had sought to retain the initiative of the colonizer while the other had sought to make good the claims of political and psychological independence.

But Philippine-American diplomacy in the Quirino years is of interest for other than its nostalgic features. It was in these years that American direction and guidance shifted emphasis from economics to stability and defense; it was in these years that the rising importance of Japan in the Cold War strategy of the United States crippled the bargaining power of Philippine statesmen; it was in these years that there was a significant improvement in the balance-of-payments position of the Philippines and sustained economic dependence on the United States. The Quirino Administration sought increased recognition of the demands of Philippine economic and diplomatic nationalism, but the Quirino presidency saw a renaissance of interventionist mentality in the American State Department and the confirmation of a diplomatic relationship of patron and client.

Notes
Index

ABBREVIATIONS USED IN THE NOTES

BIA	Bureau of Insular Affairs, Record Group 350, U.S. National Archives
BP	Bandholtz Papers (Michigan Historical Collections, Bentley Historical Library, University of Michigan)
CEF	"The Christmas Eve Fiasco and a Brief Outline of the Ricarte and Similar Movements from the Time of the Breaking Up of the Insurrection of 1899–1901," in Artemio Ricarte, *Memoirs* (Manila, National Heroes Commission, 1963), Appendix N
COCOPEA	Coordinating Committee of Private Educational Associations
CRPC	Confidential Reports, Philippine Constabulary, mss., Bandholtz Collection (Bentley Library, University of Michigan)
FAPE	Fund for Assistance to Private Education
FARE	Fund for Agrarian Reform Education
FCSC	Foreign Claims Settlement Commission of the United States
FMP	Diary of Frederick M. Presher
HDP	Historical Data Papers (The National Library of the Philippines, on microfilm at the University of Michigan, Harlin Hatcher Library)
NLRC	National Land Reform Council
PACU	Philippine Association of Colleges and Universities
PEMUS	Philippine Economic Mission to the United States
PGH	Philippines General Hospital
RG 395	Records of the U.S. Army Overseas Operations and Commands
RPC	*Report of the Philippine Commission*
RPG	Report of the Governor General
SAW/Unit	Spanish-American War Survey/Specific unit in which soldier served
TPD	"Philippine Land Reform Education Program: Tentative Program Design"
WDAR	War Department Annual Report
WP	Worcester Papers (Bentley Historical Library, University of Michigan)
WPC	Worcester Philippine Collection (The Department of Rare Books and Special Collections, The University of Michigan Library)

Introduction by Peter W. Stanley

1. Ronald Robinson, "Non-European Foundations of European Imperialism: Sketch for a Theory of Collaboration," in Roger Owen and Bob Sutcliffe, eds., *Studies in the Theory of Imperialism,* (London, Longman, 1972).

2. Shiro Saito, comp. and ed., *Philippine-American Relations: A Guide to Manuscript Sources in the United States* (Westport, Greenwood Press, 1982).

Chapter 1. The American Soldier and the Conquest of the Philippines, by Stuart Creighton Miller

1. See, for example, William J. Pomeroy, *American Neo-Colonialism: Its Emergence in the Philippines and Asia* (New York, International Publishers, 1971); Daniel B. Schirmer, *Republic or Empire: American Resistance to the Philippine War* (Cambridge, Mass., Shenkman, 1972); Stuart C. Miller, "Our Mylai of 1900," *Trans-action*, September, 1970. Subsequent research has made me painfully aware of the superficiality of my own analogy. See Stuart Creighton Miller, *"Benevolent Assimilation": The American Conquest of the Philippines, 1899–1903* (New Haven, Yale University Press, 1982). Portions of this chapter closely parallel Chapter 10 of that book and are published here with the permission of the Yale University Press.

2. The most impressive single collection is in the U.S. Army Military History Research Collection, Carlisle Barracks, Carlisle, Pa. In addition, newspapers and the Anti Imperialist League published numerous fragments of letters from soldiers who fought in the Philippine War.

3. "Diary of Herman Dittner, Co. L, First Nebraska Volunteer Regiment," Dittner Papers, mss; William Christner to parents, 11 February 1899, Christner Papers, mss; Frederick Sladen, "Diary," entries for 30 October, 28 December 1898, Sladen Papers, mss, Carlisle Barracks.

4. Elwell S. Otis, *Official Report to the Adjutant General, U.S. Army* (Washington, D.C., 1899), pp. 90–96; *Sen. Doc.* 331, 57th Cong., 1st Sess., p. 884; *Sen. Doc.* 208, 56th Cong., 1st Sess., p. 25; *Manila Times,* 17 November 1899; *San Francisco Call,* 18 October 1899; Albert G. Robinson, *The Philippines: The War and the People* (New York, McClure, Phillips, 1901), pp. 58–60; R. B. Sheridan, *The Filipino Martyrs* (New York, J. Lane, 1900), pp. 90–92; James B. Blount, *The American Occupation of the Philippines* (New York, Putnam's, 1913), p. 101; *Collier's,* 29 October 1898; Christner to father, 22 September 1898 and 17 January 1899, mss. Carlisle Barracks.

5. Lt. William Connor to Sladen, 11 February 1899, Sladen, "Diary," entries for 7, 8 February 1899, both in Sladen Papers; William A. Kobbe, "Diary of Field Service in the Philippines, 1899–1901," typescript copy, p. 4, Carlisle Barracks.

6. Christner to parents, 11 February 1899; Sladen, "Diary," entry for 8 February 1899, Carlisle Barracks; William T. Sexton, *Soldiers in the Sun* (Harrisburg, Pa., Military Service Publishing Co., 1939) pp. 95–96.

7. Letters of Hugh Clapp, 11 February, 10 April, 1 May 1899, Clapp Papers, mss, Carlisle Barracks.

8. As published in the *Call,* 27 October 1899.

9. Ibid., 26 May 1899; *Literary Digest,* XVIII, 608 (27 May 1899).

10. Edward Atkinson, *The Anti-Imperialist* (Brookline, Mass., privately published by the author, 1899), pp. 32–39.

11. Ibid.; *Eighth Army Corps War Songs* (Manila, 1901), in Walter Cutter Papers, Carlisle Barracks.

12. *The Anti-Imperialist,* pp. 32–39.

13. *New York Evening Post,* 8 May 1899; *Omaha Bee,* 7 May 1899; *Call,* 24 April 1899; *Public Opinion,* XXVI, 499 (24 May 1899); *Literary Digest,* XVII, 499 (24 May 1899); *Arena,* XXII, 568 (1899). *Kansas City Times,* n.d., in clipping collection of Mrs. William James, Widener Library, Harvard University.

14. Kobbe, "Diary," mss, Michael Lanihan, "I Remember, I Remember," mss, Christner to father, 19 March 1899, mss, Carlisle Barracks.

15. Lyon to wife, 28 May–18 June, 11 October–12 November 1899, 30 January 1900, mss, Carlisle Barracks.

16. Lyon, "Notes on the Filipino Insurrection," mss, Carlisle Barracks.

17. *Sen. Doc.* 331, 57th Cong., 1st Sess., pp. 1443–1445; Matthew Batson to wife, n.d., bound typescript copy by Phillis Batson Davis, p. 78, mss; *The Soldier's Banner,* n.d., p. 38, in Cutter Papers, Carlisle Barracks.

18. *Call,* 4, 8, April 1900; Batson letters, 23 April–4 May, 24–31 March, 13, 16 September, 9 October, 13, 18 November 1899, in typescript copy pp. 34–35, 46–48, 113–114, 120–121, 148, mss, Carlisle Barracks.

19. Ibid.
20. Lyon to wife, 9 October 1899, 19 March, 12 April, 17 June 1900, mss, Carlisle Barracks.
21. Ibid., 13 January 1901.
22. Cutter, "Diary," pp. 18–19, *Soldier's Banner,* pp. 10–11, Carlisle Barracks.
23. Lyon to wife, 28 March 1900, mss, Carlisle Barracks.
24. Cutter, "Hank Harkins, Recruit," pp. 46–50, 56–61, "Diary," p. 18, mss, Carlisle Barracks.
25. Hambleton to father, 4, 27 March 1900, mss, Carlisle Barracks.
26. *Eighth Army Corps War Songs.* Actually the author was W.B. Emerson of the 50th Iowa.
27. Letters of Beverly Daley, 16 November 1900, Hambleton, 4 March 1900, Batson, 8 November 1900 (p. 48), mss. Carlisle Barracks.
28. The charge against Funston was made by several people, the most famous of whom was Charles Fox, a civilian teamster for the Kansas Regiment, because E. F. O'Brien, a former volunteer, published Fox's letter in his newspaper, *Freedom,* and was indicted for "treason and sedition" by Otis for this. Funston never denied it, but made a typical *ad hominem* attack on Fox instead, calling him "a worthless drunken camp follower." *Call,* 23 August, 15 September, 25 October, 30 December 1899. See also, *Literary Digest,* XIX, 486 (21 October 1899), and *Public Opinion,* XXVII, 484 (21 October 1899). For the July 4th caper, see Funston's *Memories of Two Wars: Cuba and the Philippines* (New York, Scribner's, 1911), p. 443.
29. *Soldiers' Letters, Being Materials for the History of a War of Criminal Aggression* (Boston, Anti Imperialist League, 1899), pp. 3–4, 6, 8, 10, 15; *Call,* 18 October 1899.
30. Ibid., pp. 3–15; Hambleton letter, 26 May 1900, mss, Carlisle Barracks. Jesse Peck, many years later, stated that the Filipinos "cut their penises off and stuffed them in their mouths." See his response to a 1968 questionnaire in the folder for the U.S. 32nd Volunteer Regiment, mss, Carlisle Barracks. For the other remarks, see *Omaha Bee,* 7 May 1899, *Call,* 24 April 1899, *Literary Digest,* XVIII, 499 (29 April 1899), *Public Opinion,* XXVI, 499 (24 May 1899).
31. *Call,* 6 March, 10 April 1900, 12 March, 11, 17 April 1902; *Sun,* 10 March 1902; *Sen. Doc.* 331, pp. 881–885; *Kingston* (New York) *Evening Post,* 8 May 1899, as cited in *Literary Digest,* XVIII, 601 (27 May 1894) *Soldier's Letters,* pp. 3, 15.
32. *Sen. Doc.* 331, pp. 637–639, 894–898. At one point, Otis also argued that the ratio was affected by the Filipinos carrying off their wounded as they retreated.
33. See dispatches from Otis in *Correspondence on the War With Spain* (Washington, D.C., 1902), II, 1001–1002, 1004–1005; Christner to parents, 13 March and 9 April 1899; *Eighth Army War Corps Songs,* Carlisle Barracks.
34. Guy Henry, Jr., "The Life of Guy Henry, Jr., " unpublished autobiography, pp. 26–27; *Soldier's Banner,* pp. 46–47, both at Carlisle Barracks. MacArthur insisted, however, that the drunkenness was no worse in the Philippines than among soldiers stationed in the United States. See *Correspondence,* II, 1150–1151, 1246–1247.

35. *Call,* 7 March, 7 April, 3, 5 November 1900; *Call Sunday Magazine,* 4 November 1900.
36. *Call,* 23 November 1899.
37. See *Call,* 26 August, 22, 28 November, 3 December 1899, 20 April 1900, 26 October 1901, *Call Sunday Magazine,* 9 September 1900; New York *Times,* 5, 7 January 1902; *Correspondence,* II, 1001, 1350; "Race Discrimination in the Philippines," *Independent,* LIV, 416–417 (13 February 1902); Willard Gatewood, *"Smoked Yankees" and the Struggle for Empire* (Chicago, University of Illinois Press, 1971), pp. 243–244.
38. "Negro Sentiment on Imperialism," *Call,* 29 September 1899; Gatewood, *"Smoked Yankees",* pp. 245–249, 288–290, 295–301, 306–309; Sexton, *Soldiers in the Sun,* p. 242; Richard Johnson, "My Life in the Army, 1899–1922," unpublished autobiography, pp. 20, 58, mss, Carlisle Barracks. See boxes for the "colored" regiments—24th, 25th, 48th, 49th Infantries and the 9th Cavalry at Carlisle for answers to the 1968 questionnaire, which reveal little difference between black veterans and their white comrades in looking back at the war in the Philippines. See also, Willard Gatewood's more recent *Black Americans and the White Man's Burden* (Urbana, University of Illinois Press, 1975), Chapter 8, for a different conclusion.
39. Lyon's letters to his wife, 16 August, 13, 18 November 1899, 7 January 1900, 18 November 1901. See also his brief essays, "Notes on the Philippine Insurrection," and "Philippine Sketches"; Kobbe, "Diary," pp. 46–47; William Carey Brown, "Diary," entries for 22, 23 January 1901; Connor to Sladen, 1 April 1899, Sladen papers, mss, all at Carlisle Barracks.
40. *Eighth Army Corps War Songs; Soldier's Banner,* pp. 38ff., Carlisle Barracks.
41. See Hall's speech in *Mass Meetings of Protest* (Boston, Anti Imperialist League, 1903); *Eighth Army Corps War Songs;* "The Flag of Destiny" (a brochure printed in Washington for the reunion of the 12th Minnesota Volunteer Regiment in 1922), Carlisle Barracks; *The New York Times,* 20 March 1960. For the tenacity of their patriotic view of the Philippine War, see the responses to the 1968 questionnaire filed by regiments at Carlisle. Hugh Clapp's daughter appended a note to his response, warning, "Father is a flag waver and would not like what is being written about the Philippine Insurrection."
42. The names of these soldiers, plus a few references to their "blood" or "heritage," indicate that a large proportion were of German and Scots-Irish descent, the two ethnic groups that not only once supplied most of the professional Indian fighters, but whose subcultures tended to stress a highly romantic, and often fiercely individualistic in the case of the latter, warrior mystique.

Chapter 2. *Private Presher and Sergeant Vergara: The Underside of the Philippine-American War, by Glenn A. May*

Reference Abbreviations:

FMP   Diary of Frederick M. Presher

RG 395   Records of the U.S. Army Overseas Operations and Commands

SAW/Unit   Spanish-American War Survey/Specific unit in which soldier served

1. I discuss other individuals whose experiences were similar to Presher's and Vergara's in another article, "Filipino Resistance to American Occupation: Batangas, 1899–1902," *Pacific Historical Review* 48: 531–556 (November 1979).
2. One might also argue that Vergara, like many interviewees, was likely to say what he thought the interviewer wanted to hear.
3. Diary entry of 1 May 1900, Diary of Frederick M. Presher (hereinafter cited as FMP) and Questionnaire of Frederick M. Presher, U.S. Army Military History Research Collection, Carlisle Barracks, Spanish-American War Survey, 1st Cavalry. (Hereinafter all references to items included in the Spanish-American War Survey, with the exception of the above-mentioned Diary of Frederick M. Presher, will be abbreviated as follows: SAW/Unit in which the soldier served.) Also see Enlistment Papers of Frederick M. Presher, U.S. National Archives, Record Group 94 (hereinafter cited as RG94).
4. Questionnaire of Frederick M. Presher, SAW/1st Cavalry; Solomon Kenyon, SAW/38th Infantry, Volunteers; William Allen, SAW/46th Infantry, Volunteers; Georges Le Vallée, SAW/6th Cavalry; Allen Mummery, SAW/30th Infantry, Volunteers. My description of the American soldier is based largely on the hundreds of questionnaires and other material contained in the SAW. It should be noted that the description applies, on the whole, to soldiers in both volunteer and regular units.
5. Diary entries of 1 May 1900 through 21 September 1900, FMP.
6. Manuel Sastrón, *Batangas y su provincia* (Malabong, Asilo de Huérfanos de Malabong, 1895), pp. 89–95; D. F. Allen to Adjutant, 38th Infantry, 16 May 1900, U.S. National Archives, Record Group 395 (Records of U.S. Army Overseas Operations and Commands; hereinafter cited as RG 395), File 2408; Fincas Urbanas, Batangas, Philippine National Archives, Manila; Libros de Matrícula de Facultad and Libros de Matrícula des Estudios Generales y de Aplicación de Segunda Enseñanza, 1866–1898, Archives of the University of Santo Tomas, Manila; Diary entry of 21 September 1900, FMP. On the wealthy of Bauan, a few examples may help document the above description. Ysidoro Amurao, for example, owned a house assessed in 1890 at 2,000 pesos; Sixto Martinez, one assessed at 1,300 pesos; and Eusebio Arquiza, one assessed at 1,000 pesos. On the education of the children of Bauan's economic elite, consider the following: In the school year 1874–1875, 28 children from Bauan were attending approved schools of secondary education; in 1884–1885, 48; in

1894–1895, 70. Furthermore, in that last-mentioned school year, 23 children from Bauan also attended the University of Santo Tomas.

7. U.S., War Department, *Annual Reports for the War Department for the Fiscal Year Ended June 30, 1900* (Washington, D.C., Government Printing Office, 1900), I, Part 5, 19–21, 51–57, 387, 395–398; *Columnas Volantes,* 2 July 1899; John L. Jordan to Mother, 23 January 1900, John L. Jordan Papers, Tennessee State Library and Archives.

8. Mariano Cabrera to Eliseo Claudio, 14 January 1900, Philippine Insurgent Records (microfilm), U.S. National Archives, Reel 56, Selected Document 936.7; Instructions of General Miguel Malvar, 27 October 1900, Philippine Insurgent Records, Reel 69, Selected Document 1132.4; Crisanto Borruel to Eliseo Claudio, 12 April 1900 and 30 April 1900, Philippine Revolutionary Papers, National Library of the Philippines, Manila, Box RL4, Claudio Folder. On the assistance provided by the civilian population of Bauan, see U.S. v. Florentino Panopio, U.S. v. Nicolas Cusafa, U.S. v. Leon Caringal, and U.S. v. Leon Generosa, RG 395, File 2398.

9. Diary entry of 7 December 1900, FMP.

10. Diary entry of 8 March 1900, Robert Lee Bullard Papers, Library of Congress, Manuscripts Division, Container 1, Supplement to Diary 1. See also C.J. Crane to Adjutant General, 2nd District, Department of Southern Luzon, 14 November 1900, RG 395, File 4134.

11. Diary entry of 21 January 1901, FMP. Many American soldiers—but not Presher—also referred to the enemy as "niggers." The following verse from a song entitled "The Water Cure in the P.I." appeared in the notebook of Albert E. Gardner (Troop B, First Cavalry):
Get the good old syringe boys and fill it to the brim.
We've caught another nigger and we'll operate on him.
Let someone take the handle who can work it with a vim
Shouting the battle cry of freedom.
See the Albert E. Gardner Papers, SAW/1st Cavalry.

12. Diary entries of 30 January 1901 through 5 May 1901, FMP; F. Ward to Adjutant General, 2nd District, Department of Southern Luzon, 5 May 1901, RG 395, File 3089.

13. Diary entry of 28 July 1901, FMP; F. Ward to Adjutant General, Department of Southern Luzon, 31 December 1900, J. Hartman to Adjutant General, Department of Southern Luzon, 27 July 1901 and Endorsement of J. Hartman, 22 January 1902, RG 395, File 3089.

14. Diary entries of 28 July 1901 and 31 July 1901, FMP; questionnaire of Homer V. Cook, SAW/1st Cavalry.

15. Diary entries of 28 September 1901 and 29 September 1901, FMP; F. Ward to Adjutant General, Batangas, 29 September 1901, and J. Hartman to Adjutant General, 3rd Separate Brigade, 4 January 1902, RG 395, File 3089.

16. Diary entry of 8 October 1901, FMP. As note 11 above implies, and as the diaries, letters, and questionnaires in the Spanish-American War Survey (SAW) make clear, the American soldiers themselves administered the water cure to Filipino suspects.

17. Questionnaire of Homer V. Cook, SAW/1st Cavalry; Records of

Summary Courts-Martial, Bauan, December 1900–April 1903, RG 395, File 3089.

18. Diary entry of 12 November 1901, FMP; J. Hartman to Adjutant General, 1st Cavalry, 12 November 1901 and 13 November 1901, RG 395, File 3089; A.B. Wells to Adjutant General, 3rd Separate Brigade, 19 November 1901, RG 395, File 4208.

19. Adna Chaffee to Henry Corbin, 5 November 1901 and 18 November 1901, Henry C. Corbin Papers, Library of Congress, Manuscripts Division, Container 1; U.S., Congress, Senate, Committee on the Philippines, *Hearings: Affairs in the Philippine Islands,* S. Doc. 331, 57th Cong., 1st sess., 1902, 2:1606–1608; transcript of an interview conducted by Don Rickey and James Steinbach with Clenard McLaughlin, 29 October 1971, Clenard McLaughlin Papers, U.S. Army Military History Research Collection, Carlisle Barracks.

20. Report of Operations of the Garrison of Bauan for the Month of December 1901, RG 395, File 2379; Diary entries of 13 December 1901 and 22 December 1901, FMP.

21. J. Hartman to Adjutant General, 3rd Separate Brigade, 26 December 1901, RG 395, File 3089.

22. Diary entries of 26 December 1901 and 28 December 1901, FMP.

23. J. Hartman to Adjutant General, 1st Cavalry, 29 January 1902, RG 395, File 4212; Report of Operations of the Garrison of Bauan for the month of January 1902, RG 395, File 2379.

24. Diary entry of 8 May 1902 and passim, FMP.

25. The following pages are based largely on my taped interview with Emilio Vergara in Mataasnakahoy on 27 July 1976. I have not, hereafter, included footnote references to that interview. The only notes for the remainder of this section refer to: (1) information I derived from other sources, and (2) material in other sources that corroborates (or relates to) statements made by Vergara.

   Also note that I have chosen to spell the place name, Mataasnakahoy, as it is currently spelled, rather than as it was spelled at the turn of the century (Mataasnacahoy).

26. Parish Census, Lipa, 1894, Lipa Cathedral, Lipa, Batangas.

27. Urban Property Assessment of Claro Recinto, November 1890, Fincas Urbanas, Batangas, Philippine National Archives, Manila.

28. Vergara's description of the battle can be corroborated in *Memoirs of General Artemio Ricarte* (Manila, National Heroes Commission, 1963), p. 19.

29. According to the Lipa parish census of 1894, Julian Recinto would have been 19 years old in 1896 (Parish Census, Lipa, 1894, Lipa Cathedral, Lipa, Batangas).

30. For a sampling of the literature on patron-client bonds, see Carl H. Landé, *Leaders, Factions, and Parties: The Structure of Philippine Politics* (New Haven, Yale Southeast Asia Studies, 1964); Benedict J. Kerkvliet, *The Huk Rebellion: A Study of Peasant Revolt in the Philippines* (Berkeley, University of California Press, 1977); and James C. Scott, "The Erosion of Patron-Client Bonds and Social Change in Rural Southeast Asia," *Journal of Asian Studies* 32:5–37 (November 1972).

31. May, "Filipino Resistance," p. 539; Reynaldo C. Ileto, *Pasyon and Revolution: Popular Movements in the Philippines, 1840-1910* (Quezon City, Ateneo de Manila University Press, 1979), pp. 95-209.
32. See, for example, Renato Constantino, *The Philippines: A Past Revisited*, 5th ed (Manila, Tala, 1979), pp. 161, 162, 171, 175, 233, 236, 246, 256.
33. Others also described the abandonment of Lipa by the townspeople (e.g. Diary entry of 24 January 1900, Robert Lee Bullard Papers, Library of Congress, Manuscripts Division, Container 1, Diary 1; John L. Jordan to Mother, 23 January 1900, John L. Jordan Papers, Tennessee State Library and Archives; Interview with Paz Luz Dimayuga, Lipa, Batangas, 5 July 1976).
34. In the documentary evidence, I have found three reports of attempted ambushes near San Jose that bear some resemblance to the one described by Vergara (J.W. Moore to Adjutant, 2nd Batt., Lipa, 28 April 1900, Letters Sent, Co. H, 38th Inf., U.S. Volunteers, RG 94; Robert Nolan to Adjutant, Lipa, 12 August 1900, Letters Sent, Co. G, 38th Inf., U.S. Volunteers, RG 94; and Robert Hall to Adjutant General, Department of Southern Luzon, 23 August 1900, RG 395, File 2405).
35. Other "veteranos" also indicated that a large number of soldiers were conscripted—unwillingly (e.g., Interview with Crisostomo Cuasay, San Luis, Batangas, 26 July 1976; and Interview with Damian Decipeda, San Luis, Batangas, 26 July 1976).
36. Urban Property Assessment of Florentino Mandigma, Fincas Urbanas, Batangas, Philippine National Archives, Manila; Libros de Matrícula de Estudios Generales y de Aplicación de Segunda Enseñanza for the school years 1886-1887 through 1891-1892.
37. See, for example, Files 2394, 2397, 2398, 4153, and 4229 in RG 395.
38. Report of Operations of the Garrison of Lipa for the Month of October 1901, RG 395, File 4147.
39. Endorsement of Loyd Wheaton, 21 February 1900, RG 395, File 2403.
40. The suffering in Lipa is also described in "Historical and Cultural Life of the City of Lipa," Historical Data Papers, Province of Batangas, National Library of the Philippines, Manila.
41. Jacob Kline to Adjutant General, 3rd Separate Brigade, 12 December 1901, RG 395, File 4134.
42. George Anderson to J. F. Bell, 6 February 1902, RG 395, File 4134. See also File 4151 of RG 395.
43. John M. Gates, *Schoolbooks and Krags: The United States Army in the Philippines, 1898-1902* (Westport, Greenwood Press, 1973), pp. 256-263, 270-290.

Chapter 3. *The Politics of Collaboration in Tayabas Province: The Early Political Career of Manuel Luis Quezon, 1903–1906,* by Michael Cullinane

I would like to thank the following people for encouragement and helpful suggestions in preparing this chapter: Fe Susan Go, Morton J. Netzorg, Norman G. Owen, and Peter W. Stanley.

Reference Abbreviations

BP	Bandholtz Papers (Michigan Historical Collections, Bentley Historical Library, University of Michigan)
HDP	Historical Data Papers (The National Library of the Philippines, on microfilm at the University of Michigan Harlin Hatcher Library)
RPC	Report of the Philippine Commission
WDAR	War Department Annual Report

1. These Americans, most notably Harry H. Bandholtz, Arlington U. Betts, Peter Borseth, and Charles A. Reynolds, personally engaged with some success in electoral politics during the earliest elections under the civil government. For information on these men, see Norman G. Owen, "Winding down the war in Albay, 1900–1903," *Pacific Historical Review* 48:557–589 (November 1979); Louis E. Gleeck, Jr., *Americans on the Philippine Frontiers* (Manila, Carmelo and Bauermann, Inc., 1974), pp. 24–29; *Recollections of the American Regime* (Manila, Historical Conservation Society, 1973, Publication no. 24), pp. 3–44.
2. See, for example, John A. Larkin, *The Pampangans: Colonial Society in a Philippine Province* (Berkeley, University of California Press, 1972), p. 141.
3. William C. Forbes, *The Philippine Islands* (Boston, Houghton Mifflin, 1928), I, 161.
4. For a brief account of the Federalistas of Pampanga, see Larkin, p. 142.
5. Information on the political activities in Cebu is based on research in the early twentieth-century newspapers of Cebu City, especially *El Pueblo, Ang Suga,* and *Tingog sa Lungsod.*
6. For a concise account of Bandholtz's early career, see Frank E. Jackson, *The Representative Men of the Philippines* (Manila, E. C. McCullough & Co., 1906), p. 41. Some of the political activities and accomplishments of Bandholtz will be discussed later in this chapter. The phrase, "play the game," was commonly used by Americans in their correspondence and implied that the individual "playing the game" was a loyal collaborator with the colonial government. Dean C. Worcester, for one, found it inappropriate for Bandholtz to have so "extremely intimate" a relationship with a native politician; see his letter to William H. Taft opposing Bandholtz's appointment as Director of the Bureau of Insular Affairs, 2 May 1912, Dean C. Worcester Papers, Michigan Historical Collections, Box 1, folder 13. The rise of William C. Forbes in conjunction with his close links with Sergio Osmeña have already been suggested by Peter W. Stanley, *A Nation in the Making:*

the *Philippines and the United States, 1899–1921* (Cambridge, Harvard University Press, 1974), pp. 133–134.

7. For an excellent discussion of the collaborative relationship, see Peter W. Stanley's introductory essay in this volume.

8. Carlos Quirino, *Quezon: Paladin of Philippine Freedom* (Manila, Filipiniana Book Guild, 1971), pp. 72, 78.

9. I first suggested some of these problems in the biography of Quezon in a review of Quirino's 1971 account in the *Journal of Asian Studies* 31:995–997 (August 1972). The term "meteoric" is used by Teodoro A. Agoncillo, "The aristocrat of Philippine politics: Manuel Quezon as symbol and reality welded Filipinos," *Archipelago* 1:8 (August 1974). Regardless of any support from the masses, Quezon's entry into politics was determined by the elite of Tayabas, who monopolized the electorate throughout the period under discussion here.

10. These three paragraphs are based on the following sources: *Census of the Philippine Islands: taken under the direction of the Philippine Commission in the year 1903* (Washington, Government Printing Office, 1905), II, 123, 132; IV, 210, 214, 219, 220, 250, 259, 266, 275; Frederick L. Wernstedt and Joseph E. Spencer, *The Philippine Island World: A Physical, Cultural, and Regional Geography* (Berkeley, University of California Press, 1967), pp. 397–399, 406–407, 421–427; U.S. Bureau of Insular Affairs, *A Pronouncing Gazetteer and Geographical Dictionary of the Philippine Islands* (Washington, Government Printing Office, 1902), pp. 882–885; Manuel Luis Quezon, *The Good Fight* (New York, Appleton-Century, 1946), p. 91; "Report of Colonel Cornelius Gardener, Civil Governor of Tayabas," *The Philippine Review* 2:218–219 (May 1902); U.S., War Department, Bureau of Insular Affairs, Philippine Commission, *Report of the Philippine Commission to the Secretary of War . . . 1905* (Washington, Government Printing Office, 1906), I, 422–423 (hereinafter cited as *RPC* 1905); *RPC* 1906, I, 461, where Quezon, at the time Governor of Tayabas, stated that "the directing class is in the majority, if not wholly, composed of rich agriculturalists."

11. These two paragraphs are based on the following sources: John R.M. Taylor, *The Philippine Insurrection against the United States: A Compilation of Documents with Notes and Introduction* (facsimile edition, Pasay City, Lopez Memorial Museum, 1971), II, 44, 70, 95, 121, 265–267, 287–288, 292, 366; Quirino, p. 65; "Report of Colonel Cornelius Gardener," pp. 218–221; Teodoro A. Agoncillo, *Malolos: The Crisis of the Republic* (Quezon City, University of the Philippines Press, 1960), p. 789; *RPC* 1902, I, 211; Historical Data Papers, Quezon Province, The National Library of the Philippines (hereinafter cited as HDP) (microfilm copies available at the University of Michigan Harlin Hatcher Libarary, reels 38–40); U.S., War Department, *Annual Report . . . 1900* (hereinafter cited as WDAR 1900), I, pt. 5, 404–411, 508–514.

12. All of the above quotations are from "Report of Colonel Cornelius Gardener," pp. 221, 223.

13. WDAR 1900, I, pt. 5, 508–510; WDAR 1902, IX, 230–231, 235, 274;

Taylor, II, 265-267; "Report of Colonel Cornelius Gardener," pp. 218-224.

14. Taylor, II, 366, 368-371; WDAR 1902, IX, 230-231; HDP, Quezon Province (towns of Tiaong and Dolores); "Memorandum," 8 July 1904, in the Harry H. Bandholtz papers (hereinafter BP), Michigan Historical Collections, Box 1; U.S., Congress, Senate, *Affairs in the Philippine Islands. Hearings before the Committee on the Philippines,* 57th Congress, 1st Session, 1902, pp. 65, 138 (testimony of William H. Taft).

15. HDP, Quezon Province (town of Sariaya), p. 4.

16. "Report of Colonel Cornelius Gardener," p. 217; see also WDAR 1900, I, pt. 5, 508-510.

17. "Notes and documents," Worcester's Philippine Collection, Department of Rare Books and Special Collections, University of Michigan Harlin Hatcher Library, pp. 227, 231; *RPC* 1901, II, 49-60. Aside from Sofio Alandy, the Commission was also greeted in Lucena and Tayabas by two other prominent men of the revolution: 'Eleuterio Marasigan of Atimonan (ex-General under Aguinaldo) and Quirino Eleazar of Lucban (ex-Governor of Tayabas under the Republic).

18. "Report of Colonel Cornelius Gardener," p. 220. One of the cases upon which Gardener's fears were based is described in U.S., Congress, Senate, *Courts-Martial in the Philippine Islands,* 57th Congress, 2nd Session, 1902, pp. 34-43. The case involved the torture of two Filipinos by an American lieutenant less than a month before Gardener's report.

19. U.S., Congress, Senate, *Affairs in the Philippine Islands: Hearings before the Committee on the Philippines,* 57th Congress, 1st Session, 1902, pp. 65, 138; *Official Gazette,* I, 67 (1 January 1903).

20. Jackson, p. 41; see also, *Who's Who in America* (Chicago, Marquis, 1910), 87; *Manila Times,* 8 April 1903.

21. Most of the biographical information presented in this essay is drawn from Quezon, *The Good Fight,* and Quirino, *Quezon.* Other useful works on Quezon's career are: Vicente Albano Pacis, *President Sergio Osmeña: a fully-documented biography,* 2 vols. (Quezon City, Phoenix Press, 1971); Peter W. Stanley, "Manuel Luis Quezon," *Dictionary of American Biography,* supplement 3, 1941-1945 (New York, Scribner's, 1973), pp. 613-615; Carlos Quirino, "The Paladin of Freedom," *Bulletin of the American Historical Collection,* 6:7-12 (July/September 1978); Agoncillo, "The Aristocrat of Philippine Politics"; Frank L. Jenista, "Problems of the Colonial Civil Service: An Illustration from the Career of Manuel L. Quezon," *Southeast Asia: An International Quarterly,* 3:809-829 (Spring 1974): "Quezon and Osmeña, a Joint Biography of Two Providential Leaders," in *Official Program and Souvenir Book of the Inauguration of the Commonwealth Government, November 15, 1935* (Manila, [1935]).

22. *A Pronouncing Gazetteer,* p. 766.

23. Quezon, p. 87.

24. Ibid, p. 6.

25. Quirino, p. 4.

26. Quezon, pp. 6-7, 87.
27. The first two quotations are from Quezon, pp. 88-89, 91; the third is from *Messages of the President* (Manila, Bureau of Printing, 1939), IV, pt. 1, 59.
28. Linebarger remained in the Philippines until 1907. After living for some time in Mexico, he returned to his native Wisconsin and in 1910 ran for Congress. Following his defeat in the congressional race, he became intimately identified with the Chinese Nationalist movement and its leader, Sun Yat Sen. He lived for many years in China, wrote several books and was involved in at least two periodicals on contemporary Chinese affairs, and eventually obtained his doctorate at Johns Hopkins with a dissertation on Dr. Sun's "political doctrines" (1936). *Who's Who in America, 1916-1917*, p. 1656; ibid., 1918-1940. In Bandholtz to Linebarger, 12 August 1910, BP, Box 3, reference is made to "your Filipino friends" and the "delightful days spent in your company in old Tayabas province."
29. For general biographical information, see Jackson, p. 41; *Manila Times*, 8 April 1903; *Who's Who in America, 1910-1911* to *1926-1927*. Bandholtz's work for the Philippine Commission is referred to in RPC 1901, II, 65; "Notes and documents," Worcester's Philippine Collection, Department of Rare Books and Special Collections, University of Michigan Harlin Hatcher Library, p. 244. Some of his military activities in Marinduque and Tayabas are mentioned in WDAR 1901, I, pt. 2, 39, 42; I, pt. 3, 475, 482; I, pt. 5, 413, 418, 426; 1902, IX, 136, 156, 307.
30. Quezon, pp. 88-89.
31. Jackson, p. 41; *The Manila Times*, 10, 26 September, 6, 19 October, 19, 21 November 1903. Bandholtz had earlier received acclaim for his pacification of Tayabas and the quelling of the "Rios band" of that province; *Manila Times*, 8 April 1903. Owen, "Winding down the war in Albay," the best account of the Ola surrender and its aftermath, suggests the political implications of the negotiations, which "smacked of opportunism all around."
32. Quezon, p. 98, remarked that men like Bandholtz "were rare exceptions."
33. Dean C. Worcester to William H. Taft, 2 May 1912, in the Dean C. Worcester papers, Michigan Historical Collections, Box 1, folder 13.
34. The terms "Bandholtz regime" and "despot" were used by Bandholtz's replacement at Lucena, James G. Harbord, who was greatly impressed by the hold Bandholtz maintained over his people in Tayabas province ("You and your wife certainly live in the hearts of the people here"). Harbord to Bandholtz, 31 October 1905 and 13 March 1907, BP, Box 1. For a brief report of a Bandholtz affair, see *Manila Times*, 7 July 1903; he and his wife, other Constabulary officers, and the Lucena Municipal Council organized a huge celebration for the 4th of July with six bands and two orchestras playing all day until 4 a.m. the next morning!
35. See BP in general, 1905-1907; see specifically, Bandholtz to Judge John S. Powell, 25 March, and 4 April 1907; Powell to Bandholtz, 30 March 1907. In his 4 April 1907 letter to Judge Powell, Band-

holtz explained that his giving advice to judges was nothing new, for he was just proceeding as he always had done with previous judges; he named Carson, Trent, McCabe, and Linebarger.

36. Ricardo Parás was born in 1861 in Mindoro, but, while he was still young, his family migrated to Marinduque, residing in the capital at Boac. Parás was an *ilustrado,* having graduated from the Ateneo Municipal; he became a *maestro* in the final years of Spanish rule. Though he remained loyal to the Spanish during the 1896-1897 Revolution, in 1898-1899 he emerged as an elected representative from Marinduque at the Malolos Assembly. He did not take part in the fighting against the Americans. In 1901, however, he was appointed Governor of Marinduque and Mindoro by the Taft Commission. By this time (but probably before this) he became closely associated with Bandholtz, who was campaigning in Marinduque with his headquarters in Boac and had been named chairman of a committee responsible for setting up municipal governments on that island. During Bandholtz's administration as Governor of Tayabas (1902-1903), Marinduque and Mindoro were incorporated into Tayabas, and it is quite likely that Bandholtz brought Parás to Lucena at this time in some capacity. Subsequently, Parás was named Acting Governor (May 1903) when Bandholtz resigned, and was elected Governor in February 1904 as a Federalista. E. Arsenio Manuel, *Dictionary of Philippine Biography* (Quezon City, Filipiniana Publications, 1955), II, 295-297; RPC 1901, II, 188-192; sources cited in note 29 above. The close relationship between Bandholtz and Parás is verified later when, after retiring as Governor in 1906, Parás served as Bandholtz's secretary until 1913, and thereafter as a Constabulary translator until his death in 1938.

37. Quezon, p. 88.

38. Ibid., pp. 91-93; Jenista, p. 811, who gives the date of his appointment as 22 September 1903.

39. Quezon, p. 92: "Soon after I had met [Bandholtz], I came to the conclusion that the Americans were not as bad as I thought them to be"; *Messages of the President,* IV, pt. 1, 59.

40. The details and implications of these charges are the subject of Jenista's article.

41. Quezon was transferred to Tayabas when the then Fiscal of Tayabas, Sofio Alandy, Quezon's later political rival, was accused of "extra legal dealings" and transferred to Mindoro; Jenista, pp. 812-814; Quezon, p. 93.

42. Quezon, p. 93.

43. Ibid., pp. 94, 116.

44. Ibid., pp. 94-99; Jenista, p. 812.

45. Quezon, pp. 94, 100.

46. These charges were apparently dropped upon Quezon's resignation; Jenista, pp. 812-813. Even at this early date, some kind of arrangement must have been made to allow Quezon to avoid a trial, which, if the charges were valid, should have occurred. The fact that the case was subsequently buried and never, to my knowledge, given much attention within the inner circles of high officialdom (except by

Worcester, who meticulously copied and saved all the related documents), indicates that someone, most likely Bandholtz and/or Linebarger, managed to have it suppressed. Three years later (1907), an undercurrent of criticism against Bandholtz's backing of Quezon was surfacing among some Americans. The thrust of the criticism was that it was Bandholtz's support of the "rascally Quezon" that had kept the latter out of prison. Bandholtz was furious and replied to one of the participants, "Personally, I know of absolutely nothing that [Quezon] has done along the lines you indicate." Bandholtz to Louis T. Grant, 10 September 1907, BP, Box 1.

With some understanding of Bandholtz, it can be assumed that, after reading the transcript of the charges against Quezon, he would have concluded that they were a combination of politically motivated lies and/or exaggerations and some unfortunate errors of judgment by a well-meaning but young and impulsive Fiscal, who, nonetheless, had great potential. Quezon, as Bandholtz often remarked later, simply required careful watching by a concerned patron, like himself, who could keep him out of trouble. He later informed Harbord, "I do not consider [Quezon's Mindoro trouble] to have been of a very serious nature." Bandholtz to Harbord ("Memoranda"), [27 October 1905], BP, Box 1. A similar attitude was expressed at the time by the senior inspector of the Constabulary in Tayabas, William C. Rivers, the subordinate and colleague of Bandholtz. Stressing that Quezon's fault was one of a lack of diligence (rather than of a criminal or moral nature), Rivers recommended the young lawyer: "I can only say that Quezon has borne a very good name here [in Tayabas] and that his ability and energy qualify him for the place of Fiscal . . . On the whole, I would say that the interests of the Government would not suffer by his reappointment." A copy of Rivers's recommendation, dated 10 November 1904, can be found in BP, Box 1. Five years later, in a letter to President Taft, Governor General Forbes referred to the incident in the midst of an exceedingly praiseworthy recommendation of Quezon: "As fiscal of the Province of Mindoro while very young, his record is bad. He is said to have used that position to further his personal ends and to have been extremely loose morally in his relations with women, using his position to assist him in his desires." Nevertheless, even Forbes seems to have attributed Quezon's mistakes to his youth and quickly added: "As governor of his province, on the contrary he did most excellent work." Forbes to Taft, 13 November 1909, copy in the William Cameron Forbes papers, Houghton Library, Harvard University, Confidential Letter Book, I.

47. See, for example, Quirino, p. 71.
48. Jackson, p. 27; Quezon, p. 100.
49. Quezon, p. 100; Quirino, p. 71.
50. Quezon, p. 101.
51. Ibid.
52. The first quotation is from Claro M. Recto, "The Political Philosophy of Manuel L. Quezon" (1953), appendix in Quirino, p. 391; the second is from Quezon, pp. 102, 106. The best accounts of Quezon's personality and political character, especially in his later career, are

Theodore Friend, "Manuel Quezon: charismatic conservative," *Philippine Historical Review*, 1:153-169 (1965), and Claude A. Buss, "Charismatic leadership in Southeast Asia: Manuel Luis Quezon," *Solidarity* 1:3-8 (July/September 1966). In his autobiography, Quezon covered all his activities between 1905 and 1907 in 7 pages (100-107), with only slight references to his involvement in politics. Quirino, who devotes more space to politics, mentions (on p. 72) Quezon's victory in an election for the provincial board in January 1905, and his resignation a month later. No other sources exist for this fact: Quirino himself cites no source for this statement; Quezon does not mention it; and, until 1907, all posts on the boards, besides governor, were appointive. If Quezon served briefly as a board member, he would surely have been appointed, and not elected.

53. Jackson, p. 41. Up to this time, Bandholtz had controlled Tayabas on a face-to-face basis, leaving us very few sources for his early years in the province. After he moved to Manila, our information on Tayabas increases considerably, for, from this time on, much of his intervention in the affairs of Tayabas was carried out by correspondence.

54. Quezon, p. 102. It is essential to point out that, at the time this statement was made by Quezon, Bandholtz was dead and Harbord was a powerful executive in the Radio Corporation of America and its many subsidiaries. *Who's Who in America*, 1944-1945, p. 881; see also his laudatory speech presented to Harbord in *Messages of the President*, IV, pt. 1, 58-62.

55. Bandholtz to Harbord, 27 October 1905; "Memoranda for Colonel Harbord. Tayabas Province," [27 October 1905]. The term *faction* here is used in the sense of "patron-client network" as described by Carl Landé and James G. Scott in *Friends, Followers and Factions: A Reader in Political Clientelism* (Berkeley, University of California Press, 1977), pp. 75-99, 123-146. The factions in Tayabas in 1905 consisted primarily of members of the municipal elites. Presumably, the three main faction leaders could draw broad support from their three respective municipalities: Lucena (Carmona), Atimonan (Castro) and Tayabas (Alandy), and, as in the case of Castro, could control the votes of councilors and other elites from neighboring municipalities, probably due to their economic influence. It is not entirely clear why Bandholtz considered Alandy a "fanatic." There are several reasons, however, for Alandy to resist the Bandholtz-Quezon takeover of Tayabas. Prior to the coming of the Americans, Alandy was the most prominent member of Tayabas's leading family. At the outset, the Americans moved the provincial capital from his home town of Tayabas to Lucena. His protests against this were assuaged by his appointment as Fiscal of Tayabas. Meanwhile, the province fell into the hands of outsiders (Bandholtz and Parás). His first encounter with another outsider, Quezon, was also negative; in late 1903, Quezon successfully defended the then Mayor of Tayabas against the Alandy family. To add insult to injury, Alandy, after getting involved in another family-related squabble, was transferred to Mindoro and had to relinquish his post in Tayabas to Quezon (late 1904). It may be that his "fanatical" reputation began in Mindoro, where one of his first successful tasks was the preparation of the government's case

against Quezon. Regardless of the facade of friendship between the two, Quezon was surely not pleased with the "accurate, intelligent and very helpful" assistance Alandy provided the investigating attorney. There is ample evidence to suggest a smoldering feud between Quezon and Alandy. Bandholtz's opposition to Alandy, however, appears to have been directed less against Alandy himself than against his followers, that is, his relatives and friends in Tayabas town; Alandy was not a bad sort, but was too susceptible to the bad influences of the "Tayabas clique." It seems that Bandholtz's main objection to Alandy was that he was "a trifle weak." RPC 1901, II, 60; Quirino, p. 65; Jenista, pp. 812–814; Bandholtz to Harbord ("Memoranda"), [27 October 1905]; Bandholtz to Harbord, 20 January 1906, BP, Box 1.

56. "Memoranda for Colonel Harbord."
57. Harbord to Bandholtz, 31 October 1905, BP, Box 1.
58. Ibid.
59. Ibid.
60. The quotation is from Recto in Quirino, p. 394. For an unfavorable contemporary assessment of Quezon as a leader and an orator ("He is undoubtedly a clever and fluent speaker, but his oratory is flowery and superficial"), see V. Albert's comments and analysis dated 31 July 1907 in "Politics in the Philippines," *The Boston Evening Transcript, ?* August 1907, in Worcester's Philippine Collection, clippings, Department of Rare Books and Special Collections, University of Michigan Harlin Hatcher Library.
61. Alfredo de Castro to Bandholtz, 23 November 1905, BP, Box 1 (translation from the original Spanish); see also Bandholtz to Harbord, 10 November 1905, BP, Box 1.
62. Bandholtz to Henry T. Allen, 24 November 1905, BP, Box 1.
63. Harbord to Bandholtz, 3 December 1905; Henry H. Balch to Bandholtz, 27 December, 1905; R.H. Wardall to Bandholtz, 7 December 1905 and 21 January 1907, all in BP, Box 1. It is evident from the Balch letter that *modernos* referred in part to the corps of American teachers and other minor officials in the province of Tayabas, who apparently had been active in Bandholtz's election as Governor in 1902 (and most likely that of Parás in 1904). It is not entirely clear, however, who else made up the *modernos*.
64. Bandholtz to W.W. Weston, 14 December 1905, BP, Box 1. Reference here to the "clique of Tayabas town" not only suggests the opposition to the Alandy faction, but also suggests a continuing feud between the elite of this town and that of Lucena, which apparently grew out of the decision of the Taft Commission in 1901 to transfer the capital to Lucena.
65. Harbord to Bandholtz, 3 December 1905, BP, Box 1.
66. Ibid.; Wardall to Bandholtz, 7 December 1905, BP, Box 1, who stated that Carmona was pressured into withdrawing his candidacy.
67. Weston to Bandholtz, 11 December 1905; Balch to Bandholtz, 27 December 1905, BP, Box 1; Quirino, p. 72.
68. Harbord to Bandholtz, 3 December 1905, BP, Box 1; for a later version of the situation by Quezon himself, see *Messages of the President,*

IV, pt. 1, 58-60. Although never specified, Wardall's opposition to Quezon and his criticism of his personal character probably derive from information circulating about Quezon's conduct in Mindoro, as well as his many amorous activities in Tayabas.

69. Wardall to Bandholtz, 7 December 1905, BP, Box 1.
70. Bandholtz to Wardall, 15 December 1905, BP, Box 1.
71. Ibid. Wardall later informed Bandholtz that his communication with David Barrows, Director of Education, denied the assertion made by Bandholtz regarding the distinction between teachers and Constabulary officers involving themselves in politics, and, in fact, said the true situation was the reverse of what Bandholtz alleged. Wardall cited the law restricting Constabulary members from engaging in politics; see Wardall to Bandholtz, 21 January 1907, BP, Box 1. Article 86 of the *Manual for the Philippine Constabulary, 1907* (Manila, Bureau of Printing, 1906), p. 23, states, "All members of the Constabulary are forbidden to interfer in any way with any election held in their province."
72. Harbord to Bandholtz, 3 December 1905; Bandholtz to Wardall, 15 December 1905; Bandholtz to J.C. Muerman, 16 December 1905; Bandholtz to Harbord, 16 December 1905; Bandholtz to Harbord, 1 September 1906; Bandholtz to Wardall, 9 January and 10 February 1907, BP, Box 1.
73. There is some doubt that the candidates themselves were left to transport their supporters. An official account of the 1902 election for governor in Cebu, for example, reports that "the Provincial Board arranged for a steamer to transport" the electors to the capital. It may be, however, that the procedures varied in these early elections. Frederick S. Young and J.G. Holcolme to the Executive Secretary, 11 February 1902, in the United States National Archives, Bureau of Insular Affairs, Record Group 350, pp. 3015-3019. This 5-page document is also a concise description of how these early elections were conducted.
74. Quirino, p. 73. Quirino's account is based on Quezon's own version in a 1938 speech reproduced in *Messages of the President*, IV, pt. 1, 60.
75. Ibid. In the event that the transport of electors was a legally authorized government service (see note 73 above), it is likely that Quezon cleverly made the authorized act appear as government favor toward his candidacy.
76. *Messasges of the President*, IV, pt. 1, 60.
77. Eugene Garnett to Bandholtz, 21 February 1906, BP, Box 1.
78. Bandholtz to Garnett, 27 February 1906, BP, Box 1.
79. Quirino, p. 73.
80. Bandholtz to Harbord, 7 February 1906, BP, Box 1. One of the actions Quezon seems to have taken to facilitate his election was to run simultaneously for municipal councilor of Tayabas; holding this post would have made him a voting member of the assembly that selected the governor and allow him to have a closer working relationship with the municipal councilors. Alandy, whose civil service position precluded his running for any municipal post, must have been even more disturbed to learn that Quezon had built up a constituency

within his own town; one report suggested that Quezon was even ally-
ing himself with members of the Alandy faction in the Tayabas municipal election. The knowledge of Quezon's dealings with the "Tayabas
clique" did not seem to bother Bandholtz, who probably realized that
politics makes strange bedfellows. Although there is no mention of
Quezon's involvement in municipal politics in Tayabas in either his
autobiography or in Quirino, at least two other sources refer to this:
Zoilo M. Galang, ed., *Encyclopedia of the Philippines* (Manila, Exe-
quiel Floro, 1950), IV, 29; and the introductory materials and "Biographical Note" preceding the microfilm copies of Quezon's "general
correspondence" file; the latter source, prepared by the staff of
The National Library of the Philippines, states that Quezon was
elected municipal councilor of Tayabas on 15 January 1906. Information on Quezon's political activities in Tayabas at this time comes
from Balch to Bandholtz, 27 December 1905, BP, Box 1.

81. Harbord to Bandholtz (telegram), 11 February 1906, BP, Box 1.
82. Bandholtz to Garnett, 27 February 1906, BP, Box 1.
83. *The Manila Times,* 26 February 1906.
84. Bandholtz to Garnett, 27 February 1906, BP, Box 1.
85. Stanley, *Reappraising an Empire,* p. 5.
86. Stanley, "Manuel Luis Quezon," p. 615; Bandholtz to Clarence Ed-
    wards, 17 May 1909, BP, Box 2; Bandholtz in introducing Quezon
    to Edwards wrote: "We consider him over here to be one of the best
    assets of the Government."
87. Stanley, *Reappraising an Empire,* p. 5.

*Chapter 4. Orators and the Crowd: Philippine Independence
Politics, 1910–1914, by Reynaldo C. Ileto*

Reference Abbreviations

BIA   Bureau of Insular Affairs, Record Group 350, U.S. National
        Archives.
BP   H.H. Bandholtz Papers, Bandholtz Collection.
CEF   "The Christmas Eve Fiasco and a Brief Outline of the Ricarte
        and Similar Movements from the Time of the Breaking up of the
        Insurrection of 1899–1901," in Artemio Ricarte, *Memoirs,*
        Manila: National Heroes Commission, 1963, Appendix N.
CRPC   Confidential Reports, Philippine Constabulary, mss., Bandholtz
        Collection, Bentley Library, Univ. of Michigan. Records are ar-
        ranged and cited chronologically.
I wish to thank Bernardita R. Churchill, Michael Cullinane, and Brian
Fegan for lending me some materials used in this essay.

1. Hermenegildo Cruz was co-founder, with Dominador Gomez, of the
   Union Obrera Democratica de Filipinas; President of the Union del
   Trabajo in 1911 and first President, in May 1913, of the Congreso
   Obrero. In 1911, he was also Secretary-General of the Liga Popular
   Nacionalista. Patricio Dionisio, *Fact Finding Report,* Bureau of Labor,
   Philippine Islands, 1936, ms., American Historical Collection, Manila;
   CRPC, February 13, May 5 1910.

2. Various members of the Cadeliña, Nañagas, and Eleazar families are mentioned, including the Presidente, Gregorio Cadeliña; unsigned letter, Lucban, Tayabas, 31 May 1911, w/CRPC. The municipal officials, elected by a small fraction of the populace, wanted at most to be free from control and supervision by the provincial and central governments, where Americans still occupied key positions. Populist appeals naturally threatened their very existence. See Glenn A. May, *Social Engineering in the Philippines* (Westport, Greenwood Press, 1980), Chapter 3.

3. CRPC, Lucena, Tayabas, 22 April 1912. Another sign of impending "trouble" in 1912 was the wearing of the *rayadillo*—the military uniform of the Spanish *casadores,* adopted by the Filipino revolutionaries—by many men in and around Pitogo.

4. Rafael Crame, Confidential Memorandum, Manila, 2 July 1914, BIA 4865-109. CRPC, 21 June, 25 June, 25 July 1912.

5. Cited in Peter W. Stanley, *A Nation in the Making* (Cambridge, Harvard University Press, 1974), p. 175.

6. Crame, Confidential Memorandum; CEF, pp. 157–126.

7. Stanley, p. 218; Goodman, "General Artemio Ricarte and Japan," *Journal of Southeast Asian History,* 7.2:52 (1966).

8. Bandholtz to Rivers, Manila, 17 October 1911, BP. Ignacio Velasco, Ricarte's "Primer jefe en las Islas Filipinas" and "Inspector General" of the "New Katipunan," was a Constabulary agent. He had gained Ricarte's confidence while an employee at Bilibid Prison; CRPC, "Confidential Memo for Col. Rivers," Laoag, 22 May 1913; CRPC, 30 October 1912.

9. CRPC, 30 September 1912; Brian Fegan, "Light in the East: Continuities in Central Luzon Peasant Movements," unpublished paper, 1979; Taylor to Riggs, 8 July 1914, BIA 4865-108.

10. "Compadre (ritual co-parent) colonialism" refers to the symbiotic relationship between the U.S. administration and Filipino nationalist leaders from the wealthy and educated class (*ilustrado*). The theme is developed by Norman Owen, ed., and Michael Cullinane in *Compadre Colonialism: Studies on the Philippines under American Rule* (Ann Arbor, Michigan Papers on South and Southeast Asia, no. 3, 1971).

11. Manila *Cablenews-American,* 29 December 1914, w/BIA 4865-110. Drilling in baseball grounds and parks at night was common, even in some Visayan towns. It was justified as "amusement" or as part of the activities of Boy Scouts and other registered bodies that regularly participated in parades and festivals. The Union de Marinos, led by a Lieutenant Colonel in Ricarte's army, had a municipal permit "to organize as a military body, which it used as a cloak to screen its true operations." After the 1914 uprisings, the Constabulary limited the time allowed for drilling and banned the use of wooden guns; this may have led to the popularity of *escrima,* fencing with wooden swords. (CEF, 169; *Cablenews-American,* 29 December 1914; CRPC, 12 May 1910; Memo to Constabulary Chief, Visayas, 8 March 1915, w/BIA 4865-134a; Confidential Memo for Quezon, 10 September 1915, pp. 9–10, in Box 45, Harrison Papers, U.S. Library of Congress; Fegan, pp. 17–18).

12. Stanley, pp. 145, 155–156, 162. See also May, Chapter 4.
13. Stanley, p. 183.
14. Charles B. Elliott, *The Philippines to the End of the Commission Government* (Indianapolis, Bobbs-Merrill, 1917), pp. 411–412.
15. Usha Mahajani, *Philippine Nationalism; External Challenge and Filipino Response, 1565–1946* (St. Lucia, University of Queensland, 1971), pp. 243–244; also Renato Constantino, "Veneration without Understanding," in *Dissent and Counterconsciousness* (Manila, Erehwon, 1970), pp. 125–146.
16. See Reynaldo Ileto, "Rizal and the Underside of Philippine History," in D.K. Wyatt and A.B. Woodside, eds., *Moral Order and the Question of Change: Essays in Southeast Asian Thought* (New Haven, Yale Southeast Asia Series, 1982).
17. CRPC, Conversation with Emilio Aguinaldo and Attorney Ferrer, 12 September 1911. The form of the prophecy is from Rizal's novel *El Filibusterismo*. The news article was signed by M.P. Leuterio, a director of the Liga Popular Nacionalista and an Aglipayan; CRPC, 3 January 1910.
18. CRPC, 3 January 1910. On the significance of the image, see Reynaldo Ileto, *Pasyon and Revolution; Popular Movements in the Philippines, 1840–1910* (Quezon City, Ateneo de Manila, 1979), pp. 61–62, 195.
19. CRPC, summaries of patriotic speeches delivered in Calle Raxa Matanda, Tondo, 30 December 1909ff., 3 January 1910. In Calle Bascarlegui, Padre Mariano Sevilla was heard speaking in the same vein; CRPC, 31 December 1910.
20. CRPC, 28, 31 December 1911. Wooden guns were used by companies parading on Rizal Day 1914 in Iloilo; Memo to Chief of Constabulary, Visayas, 8 March 1915, w/BIA 4865–134a.
21. Bandholtz to Quezon, 2 January 1913, BP. Trinidad refused to sign the official waiver.
22. CRPC, 1 January 1913. The principal who reported the "Tiaong incident" noted that Hermenegildo Cruz's speech was similar to one he had heard Buencamino deliver in Manila. However, the latter's reputation as an *ilustrado* capitulationist during the revolution was not forgotten. During a speech on 30 April 1910 (Labor Day) Buencamino was booed by some: "Away with traitors!"; "Away with the assassin of Cabanatuan!"; "Away with the assissin of General Luna," CRPC, 5 May 1910.
23. Confidential memorandum for Quezon, 10 September 1915, pp. 13–14. Fourth of July and, to a lesser extent, Washington's birthday came to be celebrated "with great fervor, but chiefly because of what was supposed to be the significance of these commemorations toward insular freedom"; Charles E. Russel, *The Outlook for the Philippines* (New York, 1922), p. 323.
24. Teodoro Agoncillo has set the record straight on this: the cry of defiance actually happened on the 23rd, at Pugadlawin; *Revolt of the Masses* (Quezon City, 1956), pp. 146–150.
25. Manila *Cablenews-American*, 29 December 1914, w/ BIA 4865–110.

26. Bandholtz to Rivers, Manila, 17 October 1911, BP.
27. CRPC, 4 September 1911, nos. 1471 and 1473.
28. CRPC, 5 September 1912.
29. CRPC, conference between Patricio Belen and Santiago Alvarez (Makabuhay Society), 5 September 1912; Annual Report of the Director of Constabulary, Manila, 1913, w/ BIA 1184-124; CRPC, 23 March 1913; Bandholtz to Quezon, 19 December 1912, BP. Santos, known for his socialist novel *Banaag at Sikat,* was elected Governore of Rizal province in 1909.
30. Wallace Taylor (acting Chief of Constabulary) to Riggs, Manila, 8 July 1914, BIA 4865-108; "Childish Fears and Sedition—Imaginary," *El Ideal,* 28 August 1914, w/ BIA 4865-105; Ricarte to Herminio, Hong Kong, 8 March 1912, in CRPC; letter of Mrs. Thomas Carey Welch, 28 December 1914, in Worcester Papers, Vol. 5, University of Michigan library.
31. Manila *Cablenews-American,* 29 December 1914, w/ BIA 4865-110. The so-called Flag Law made it illegal for Katipunan flags and insignia to be displayed publicly.
32. Bandholtz to Rivers, 17 October 1911, BP; Bandholtz to Quezon, 18 December 1912, BP. On the special relationship between Quezon and Bandholtz, see Michael Cullinane's chapter in this book.
33. Elliott, p. 447; *Washington Post,* 12 January 1913, in BIA 4865-69, citing information furnished by the BIA.
34. Taylor to Riggs, 8 July 1914, BIA 4865-108. Former revolutionary General Teodoro Sandiko, during his term as Governor of Bulacan (wherein he promised to implement "socialist" policies), waged a campaign from 1906 on to eradicate Felipe Salvador's peasant movement, the Santa Iglesia, even threatening to reconcentrate the populace; see Ileto, *Pasyon,* pp. 150-151, 250, 278-279. Fegan (p. 22) explains why Sandiko nevertheless won votes: "Sandiko was a popular orator. His fiery speeches calling for immediate and total independence and the rights of the common man won large crowds in Bulacan, where old men recall travelling to listen to him." As early as December 1910, Sandiko is reported to have given a speech at Masantol, Pampanga, in which, alluding to the Katipunan, he suggested that people "prepare bolos and lances, as the only means to secure independence"; CRPC, 10 January 1911.
35. The continued influence of novenas and prayerbooks on popular thinking is described, with typical *ilustrado* disdain, in T. H. Pardo de Tavera, *The Legacy of Ignorantism (Ignorantismo)* (Manila, 1921). On Tagalog ideas of *panahon,* see Robert Love, "The *Samahan* of Papa God: Tradition and Conversion in a Tagalog Peasant Religious Movement" (PhD dissertation, Cornell University, 1977).
36. See Ileto, *Pasyon,* pp. 127, 158, and passim.
37. CRPC, popular reactions to news reports, 23 May 1913.
38. CRPC, 14 February 1910.
39. CRPC, popular reactions to nationwide speeches in praise of Quezon's work, 27 July 1910.
40. Stanley, p. 184.

41. Bandholtz to McCabe, 21 February 1913; Bandholtz to Wood, 21 February 1913, BP. The extent of the unrest generated by the event is suggested by Bandholtz's comment to a U.S. Congressman: "I have not seen since 1903 [when Ricarte managed to slip in from exile] so much activity in our secret service division"; Bandholtz to Curry, 20 January 1913, BP.

42. Stanley, p. 204; Mahajani, p. 252. The style is reminiscent of Gen. Douglas MacArthur's well-known announcement of his return in 1945; see Alfred McCoy, "The Philippines: Independence without Decolonization," in R. Jeffrey, ed., *Asia: The Winning of Independence* (London, MacMillan, 1982).

43. Elliot, p. 410.

44. CRPC, 19, 20 November 1909.

45. Preface to Vol. II of Constabulary Reports, 19 November 1909, CRPC.

46. Fegan, pp. 13–14; Harrison to Secretary of War, 31 December 1914, BIA 4865–124.

47. CRPC, 9 September, 10 November 1909; 6 February, 15 April 1910. A student wrote in 1916 that the *espiritista* movement was "widespread and growing," particularly in provinces around Manila. Its basis is the belief that "the spirits of their ancestors hover around ready to respond whenever called." Ramona Tirona, "The Kolorum and the Spiritismo," Beyer Collection, Tagalog Ethnography I, paper 41, Australian National Library. One attraction of these predictions must have been their familiarity: In 1896, prophets and mediums also predicted a conflict, and continued to give advice throughout the war; the Katipunan "made all the poor people believe that arms would come from Japan"; statues of Christ and various saints (apparently manipulated by revolutionaries) ordered devotees to fight against Spain and the U.S. CRPC, 10 November 1909, 23 February, 1910; Ileto, *Pasyon,* pp. 94–95, 208; William Freer, *The Philippine Experiences of an American Teacher* (New York, 1906), pp. 10–11. In the Beyer Papers, there are accounts of how the Virgin helped certain towns against Spanish onslaughts. In similar fashion, the "Taytay Affair" of 1914 was attributed to the "fanaticism of the majority of its inhabitants who were devotees of the "alleged miraculous image" of Nuestra Señora de la Paz y Buen Viaje in Antipolo. This may have contributed to the cancellation of the annual pilgrimage to Antipolo in May 1913. (CEF, 212; CRPC, 12 May 1913).

48. CRPC, 22 May 1910; see Ileto, *Pasyon,* p. 298.

49. *The Return of Halley's Comet and Popular Apprehensions* (Manila, Bureau of Printing, 1910).

50. CRPC, 30 April 1910; Ileto, *Pasyon,* p. 302.

51. CRPC, 12 May 1910. Isabelo de los Reyes, in his speeches in late 1910, was also saying that "the hour of redemption is approaching"; CRPC, 10 November 1910.

52. Goodman, p. 52.

53. Stanley, p. 143; Goodman, p. 52.

54. CRPC, 18 May 1910. Not that many Filipinos of Adriatico's stature really cared about the *ladrones* in Bilibid. Villafuerte and Carreon,

officers in Sakay's Katipunan, had been betrayed in 1906 by politician and labor leader Dominador Gomez.

55. CEF, December 1914, p. 159. There also seems to have been a policy of recruiting from such ranks. When a leader of a 1914 Nueva Ecija uprising was asked why "none but the ignorant" took part in it, the reply was that their instructions from Ricarte were "not to approach any intelligent men for enlistment or to sell them commissions as officers of the army of liberation, as the intelligent men do not desire independence" (*Cablenews-American*, 29 December 1914).

56. *Social Problems in the Philippines*, (1929), p. 408. Macaraig's comments suggest that, because of his absence, Ricarte became a mythical hero, replacing the characters of *awit* and *corrido*, emulated by leaders of youth gangs (*barkada*). This may explain why some Ricartista groups had a large composition of men 18 to 28 years of age, belonging to the same neighborhood ("List of persons connected with the revolutionary army of the Philippines," w/ Harrison Papers, Box 45, U.S. Library of Congress). One quality of a leader was possession of unusual powers. The celebrated cases of two top Ricartista leaders, Timoteo Cariaga and Bartolome de la Rosa, who "carried their enthusiasm for anting-anting to the extent of inflicting self injury or murder," indicates their leadership style. (CRPC, 30 June 1912, 24 March 1913; *Renacimiento Filipino*, Vol. 3, 28 March, 7 April 1913.) Brian Fegan's fine description of Huk leader Andron de Guzman should be applicable here; see "The Social History of a Central Luzon Barrio," in A. McCoy and E. de Jesus, eds., *Philippine Social History* (Quezon City, Ateneo de Manila, 1982), p. 115.

57. CRPC, 17 October 1910. This rumor was concomitant with that of impending war between Japan and America.

58. CRPC, 29 May 1911. Ilocano support for Ricarte is not surprising, since he hailed from Batac, Ilocos Norte.

59. CRPC, 6 October 1911. It seems that Belen himself came to be perceived as a redeemer. Two Dimas-Alang leaders who admitted that they turned collections of monthly dues to Belen are quoted as saying that he "is working and sacrificing himself for the society and . . . is the Moses who is to save the Israelites" (CRPC, 30 September 1912).

60. CRPC, 19 May 1913.

61. *Rizal's Correspondence with Fellow Reformists* (Manila, National Heroes Commission, 1963), pp. 344–345; Jose Arcilla, S.J., ed., "Documents Concerning the Calamba Deportations of 1891," *Philippine Studies*, 18:617 (1970).

62. Carlos Ronquillo, "Ilang Talata Tungkol sa Paghihimagsik Nang 1896-7" (Some Notes on the Revolution of 1896-7; Hong Kong, 1898), ms., University of the Philippines Library, 21.

63. Isabelo Artacho, *Declaration, Letter, and Proclamation*, orig. in Spanish (Hong Kong, October 1899).

64. Fegan, p. 17. A contrary, and orthodox, view is held by Maria Pilar Luna, who calls the Ricartista movement "truly nationalistic" and not millenarian or agrarian; "General Artemio Ricarte y Garcia, a Filipino Nationalist," *Asian Studies*, 9:229 (1971).

65. CEF, p. 181. Ricarte's letters are full of Biblical allusions; in one, he styles himself as the banished leader suffering for the sake of a "Holy Ideal" (w/ CRPC, 26 February, 4 March, 15 April 1912).
66. CRPC, 5 September 1911. Villarino, like Ricarte, was a revolutionary veteran, deported to Guam, and convicted of sedition. After conferring with Ricarte in Hong Kong, he returned in 1911 to organize an armed force. He was also a labor organizer, having been General Secretary of the Union Obrera Democratica under Lope K. Santos's leadership (Crame to Director of Constabulary, 8 February 1911, CRPC; Dionisio, 79).
67. CRPC, 26 October 1909. At about that time there was a Tagalog drama *Ang Dakilang Martir sa Corregidor* (The noble martyr at Corregidor) which portrayed Gomez as a suffering patriot; summary and audience reaction in CRPC, 10 January 1910.
68. Senior Inspector to Chief, District of Central Luzon, Iba, 24 June 1914, BIA 4865-138a.
69. Crame to Bandholtz, 27 December 1912, CRPC.
70. CRPC, 17 May 1912.
71. See manifestos, translated from the Tagalog, in "Statement of Timoteo Cariaga y Visco ..." 25 October 1915, BIA 4865-138a; and CEF, pp. 169-170. Fegan (pp. 15-16) has pieced together a more complex myth, based on conversations with Ricartista/Tanggulan/Sakdal veterans in San Miguel, Bulacan, which accounts for Japan's presence. Constabulary records from 1909-1913 confirm the main contours of the myth but suggest that Japan's role was still unclear.
72. Bonifacio's appeals follow a more basic pattern which can be delineated in popular religious texts. The notion of *dayà* (deception) rests on the disjunction between *loób* (inner) and *labás* (outer), the sign of moral decay; see Ileto, *Pasyon*, pp. 102-109.
73. CRPC, 15 November 1912; Memo to Bandholtz, 21 April 1913, CRPC. Another orator, the dramatist Aurelio Tolentino, said he still had hope in the Democrats, but called for armed struggle should the United States fail to grant independence.
74. Stanley, p. 217; CRPC, 11 April 1912.
75. "A Political Letter from General Ricarte to a Municipal President," Hong Kong, 13 February 1911, translation in CRPC.
76. Confidential Memo for Bandholtz, 12 February 1913, CRPC; CEF, p. 159.
77. CRPC, 18 May 1910. This is the same rally, at San Miguel de Mayumo, mentioned by Stanley, p. 156.
78. Stanley, p. 218.
79. CRPC, 10 May, 8 December 1911. Old associates of Bonifacio were still reminding people of how Aguinaldo ordered the former's execution. These observations were made by Daniel Tirona, who had been very much a part of the 1897 event.
80. CRPC, 12 November 1911.
81. We can add to this the report of Daniel Tirona, who toured Manila, Bulacan, Pampanga, and the Ilokos in 1911, and discovered how much talk there was of Quezon's waste of effort and expense abroad (CRPC, 8 December 1911).

82. "A Political Letter"; Ricarte, prior to his capture in 1904, had been "attacking almost everyone of his former co-revolucionarios as having sold out to the Americans and giving a low estimate of the value of their political parties." Bonifacio Salamanca, *Filipino Reaction to American Rule, 1901–1913* (New Haven, Shoe String Press, 1968), p. 181.

83. Report of Governor Mariano Melendres, Pasig, 28 December 1914, in CEF, pp. 161–163.

84. He had worked with the original Katipunan, joined the chorus of Cavite *principales* that denounced Bonifacio and his secret society methods, and risen to become one of Aguinaldo's most trusted officers. Having experienced the social tensions that plagued the revolution, he felt, while working for the Constabulary in 1911, that again "civil war was inevitable." Tirona, alias Mariano Nicolas, expressed his own sentiments to his superior, Col. Crame, at the end of a report dated 30 January 1911, PCR; see Ileto, *Pasyon,* Chapter 4; Milagros Guerrero, "Provincial Elites during the Philippine Revolution," in McCoy and de Jesus.

85. Salamanca, p. 175. The latter disputes Forbes's claim because it is based on the assumption that "anarchy had prevailed during the shortlived Philippine Republic," which Teodoro Agoncillo's book *Malolos: The Crisis of the Republic* (Quezon City, 1960) has shown to be false. However, more recent scholarship, beginning with David Sturtevant's *Popular Uprisings in the Philippines* (Ithaca, Cornell University Press, 1976) seems to prove Forbes right.

86. Chas. Cohn to the Hon. Newton Gilbert, 2 January 1915, in Worcester Collection, documents and papers, Vol. 5.

87. CRPC, 27 March 1913. Victorino was a carpenter, some kind of Protestant preacher, and Ricarte's "Sub-Inspector General of Arms." Convicted of conspiracy, he served a 2-year prison term from November 1905. Arrested for sedition in Tarlac in August 1914, he was again imprisoned (CRPC, 7 November 1910; "List of names of persons connected with the Revolutionary Army").

88. Goodman, p. 52; CEF, p. 171; CRPC, 17 September 1911, 12 November 1911, 30 September 1912, 19 May 1913. On the meanings of *kalayaan,* see Ileto, *Pasyon,* esp. pp. 144–146, 233–235, 257.

89. *A Handbook of the Philippines* (3rd ed., Chicago, 1909). Wright presents a hypothetical case based on several cases that he knew of.

90. Stanley, p. 218.

91. Confidential Report to Chief of District of Visayas, Iloilo, 8 March 1915, BIA 4865-134a: ". . . it being pertinent to add that the lower classes, here throughout the Visayas as well as Luzon, are generally more fanatic in their desire for independence than the educated class itself."

92. Dapen Liang, *The Development of Philippine Political Parties* (Hong Kong, 1939), p. 106.

Chapter 5. "The Voice of Worcester is the Voice of God": How One American Found Fulfillment in the Philippines, by Peter W. Stanley

Reference Abbreviations

BIA　Bureau of Insular Affairs

PGH　Philippines General Hospital

WP　Worcester Papers, Bentley Historical Library, University of Michigan

WPC　Worcester Philippine Collection, The Department of Rare Books and Special Collections, The University of Michigan Library

1. Ralston Hayden, "Biographical Sketch," in Dean C. Worcester, *The Philippines Past and Present,* ed. Hayden (New York, Macmillan, 1930). The photograph is opposite p. 42.

2. Not only did Worcester use words like "fight," "struggle," and "have a row" to describe normal differences of opinion, but so did others when talking about their dealings with him. "I had a pitched battle with Commissioner Worcester," wrote Bishop Charles H. Brent to Mercer G. Johnston, 9 January 1909 (Brent Papers, box 8, Manuscript Division, Library of Congress). "Bandholtz came in, and Worcester immediately went after his hide," Charles B. Elliott recorded in his diary entry for 19 January 1912 (Elliott Papers, Manuscript Division, Library of Congress). "I went after him [Worcester] pretty roughly, and we had some pretty sharp words." See also Worcester's recurrent use of the word "desperation" in many forms: "Building is a desperately slow business here" (Worcester to Jacob E. Reighard, 23 April 1903, Reighard Papers, Michigan Historical Collections, Bentley Historical Library, University of Michigan). Like practically all Americans in the Islands, he spoke often of "playing the game," but Worcester more typically emphasized the competitive implications of this figure of speech than the element of teamwork.

3. Charles H. Brent to W.C. Rivers, 21 October 1912, Brent Papers.

4. *Philippines Free Press,* 29 January 1910. A less objective observer, Dr. John R. McDill, a victim of Worcester's wrath, wrote to Senator John C. Spooner that Worcester was "universally detested" (Copy in Bureau of Insular Affairs, National Archives, 5543-39).

5. Worcester's BIA personnel file is number 5543; see esp. entry 6. Hayden, "Biographical Sketch," Chapter 1 and pp. 75-76.

6. Worcester, *Philippines Past and Present,* Chapter 1; Hayden, "Biographical Sketch," Chapter 2.

7. Worcester to Jacob E. Reighard, 30 August 1898, Reighard Papers. See also the collection of Worcester's magazine articles in the Worcester Papers, Michigan Historical Collections, Bentley Historical Library. The University of Michigan has two Worcester collections. That housed in the Bentley Historical Library will hereafter be designated WP. The Worcester Philippine Collection in the Department of Rare Books and Special Collections of the University of Michigan Library will be designated WPC.

8. Worcester, *The Philippine Islands and Their People* (New York, Macmillan, 1898), pp. 75 and 57, respectively.
9. Memorandum of questions to ask the President, WPC, DS 685.W9, XVII, 51. Margaret Leech, *In the Days of McKinley* (New York, Harper, 1959), p. 351.
10. Concerning salary and perquisites, see, for example, John Hay to Worcester, 20 January 1900, WPC, DS 685.W9, XVII, 295; A.W. Fergusson to Chief, Bureau of Insular Affairs, 22 June 1903, BIA 5543-10; L.H. Nutting to Clarence R. Edwards, 16 November 1903, BIA 5543-33; Worcester to Edwards, 31 August 1903, and reply 1 September 1903, BIA 5543-14. The 1899 lecture series may be followed in WPC, DS 685.W9, vol. XVII.
11. Worcester to Reighard, 30 August 1898, Reighard Papers, box 1.
12. Reighard to Worcester, 9 March 1901, Reighard Papers, box 3.
13. Worcester to Reighard, 5 May 1901, Reighard Papers, box 3.
14. Worcester to Reighard, 23 April 1903, Reighard Papers, box 4. "The heads of our bureaus here," he added, "are for the most part, bigger and broader men in their way than is the average member of the faculty of the University of Michigan." Reighard expressed at least some interest in taking the job.
15. Elliott, who was open about his own aspirations, recorded the progress of others, especially Gilbert, in his diary. See, for example, the entries of 25 August and 31 October 1911, along with the chronicle of his repeated attempts to get a place for himself on the Philippine delegation to the Republican National Convention in 1912. Concerning Worcester's leave, see Worcester to Frank McIntyre, 19 November 1912, BIA 5543-19. Worcester attributed his decision to remain permanently in the Islands to concern over his health. He doubted he could survive a cold climate after his numerous tropical diseases; Worcester to Miss C.E. Worcester, 5 February 1908, WP, box 1. This is not persuasive, since he did live in the United States during the winters of 1913 and 1914 while engaged in lecturing and preparing for his business ventures in the Philippines. While Filipinos never forgave his polemical role in the years of his political power, many came to respect him as a model foreign businessman. See the obituary editorial in *El Debate,* praising him for "affording the highest example of labor, of efficiency, and administration which an American industrialist, a progressive business man, could give to the country, without attempting ever to play politics" (3 May 1924). For more on Worcester's business career after leaving office, see Ronald K. Edgerton's chapter in this book.
16. See, for example, Worcester's account of the Schurman Commission's journey to Manila, WPC, DS 685.W9, Vol. XVI, letters of 27 January and 23 February 1899.
17. Like many of his American contemporaries in the Philippines, Worcester used the child metaphor repeatedly when describing Filipinos. See, for example, his reference to Mateo, his one-time guide, whom he had known in the Philippines and America for over 10 years, as "the boy" (WPC, DS 685.W9, Vol. XVI, 10 April 1899); his characterization of General Gregorio del Pilar, then 22 and only about

11 years younger than himself, as "only a boy" who amused himself "playing with my typewriter" (WPC, DS 685.W9, Vol. XVI, 26 May 1899); and his dismissal of the views of an emissary from Aguinaldo as "perfectly childish" (WPC, DS 685.W9, Vol. XVI, 8 March 1899). For persistence and offensiveness, however, no one could match the unctuous Episcopal bishop of the Philippines, who once said of the Filipino people, "You cannot treat children as though they were grown men without spoiling them" (Brent to Bishop Hall, Maundy Thursday 1904, Brent Papers, box 6).

18. This composite statement of Worcester's views is drawn from WPC, DS 685.W9, Vol. XVI, letters of 14 February, 8 March, 30 March, and 27 April 1899.

19. Bourns to his family, 23 August, 1898, copy in WPC, DS 685.W9, Vol. XVII; Bourns to Worcester, 13 February 1899, ibid.; Bourns, testimony before the Schurman Commission, *Report of the Philippine Commission* (1900), II, 352; Worcester letter of 27 April 1899, WPC, DS 685.W9, Vol. XVI.

20. Bourns to Worcester, 25 June 1899, WPC, DS 685.W9, Vol. XVII; Worcester, letters of 17 April and 22 July 1899, ibid., Vol. XVI, and letter of 18 June 1899, ibid., Vol. XVII. For more on Schurman, see Kenneth E. Hendrickson, Jr., "Reluctant Expansionist—Jacob Gould Schurman and the Philippine Question," *Pacific Historical Review*, 36:405–421 (November 1967).

21. Worcester, letter of 13 June 1899, WPC DS 685.W9, Vol. XVI.

22. The quotations are from Worcester's letters of 8 March and 30 March 1899, WPC, DS 685.W9, Vol. XVI.

23. "Strange as it may seem," he wrote, "the two people that are running the political, and influencing the war end of this thing are Frank and myself"; Worcester, letter of 26 May 1899, WPC, DS 685.W9, Vol. XVI.

24. Although Worcester felt that Otis lacked vigor in prosecuting the war, he defended the General and the Army against critics of the war itself. One such defense, a public telegram to the Chicago *Times Herald*, not only pleased Otis, but strengthened Worcester's position with the McKinley Administration at home. See Worcester's letters of 3 June and 25 July 1899, WPC, DS 685.W9, Vol. XVI.

25. Worcester, letters of 17 April, 26 May, 19 June, and 9 July 1899, WPC, DS 685.W9, Vol. XVI. See esp. the second of these: "We fill [Otis] full of good ideas, and he communicates them to others as though they were his own." Hayden, "Biographical Sketch," Chapter 3, emphasizes Worcester's struggle to assert the Commission's power and legitimacy against Otis. This remained a problem, no matter how closely allied the two men were in their opposition to Schurman. See, for example, Worcester's letter of 24 August 1899, WPC, DS 685.W9, Vol. XVI.

26. As Schurman lost power, Worcester's condescension toward him grew. "I have never been more angered or disgusted in my life than I was with Schurman's harangue," he wrote to his family, "but you would be surprised to see how sweetly I have learned to smile when disgusted to the bottom of my soul. I simply rode around on the gentle-

man's back, figuratively speaking, until he was convinced that his plan offered some serious difficulties"; Worcester, letter of 26 May 1899, WPC, DS 685.W9, Vol. XVI.

27. Worcester, letters of 14 March, and 1 May 1899, WPC, DS 685.W9, Vol. XVI.

28. Pardo to Worcester, 9 July 1899; Pardo to Bourns, 3 September 1899; Pardo to Worcester, 9 October 1899, all WPC, DS 685.W9, Vol. XVII.

29. Worcester to Mrs. Henry W. Lawton, 16 June 1900, and Worcester to Mrs. E.H. Worcester, 10 July 1901, copy with his letter to Mrs. Lawton, 11 July 1901, all in Henry W. Lawton Papers, Manuscript Division, Library of Congress.

30. See, for example, the indictment of him in *Philippines Free Press,* 28 September 1912, BIA 5543-138. Worcester's neglect of the PGH for the first year of its operation, when administrative and ethical irregularities took root, is implicitly admitted in his report on corrective measures; Worcester to Vice-Governor, 10 November 1911, WPC, DS 685.W9, Vol. XX.

31. Forbes to Taft, 19 August 1909, BIA 12940-12.

32. *Philippines Free Press,* 28 September 1912, BIA 5543-138; Worcester to McIntyre, 19 November 1912, and McIntyre to Worcester, 13 January 1913, BIA 5543-139; Forbes to Secretary of War, cable, 24 February 1913, BIA 5543-144. Worcester had earlier broached this possibility when there were rumors Taft might fire him; Worcester to Taft, 27 January 1908, WP, box 1.

33. Worcester, letter of 21 December 1899, WPC, DS 685.W9, Vol. XVI.

34. Worcester Journal, WPC DS 685.W912, pp. 79 ff. Worcester to Mrs. Lawton, 10 October 1900, Lawton Papers. This emphasis on healthfulness overshadowed the other typical first reaction of Americans when seeing Benguet, a sense of awe before its beauty. See, for example, Brent to Mrs. Monks, 16 February 1903, Brent Papers, box 6: "In all my travels I have struck nothing more varied or grander." Frank Jenista maintains that Americans drawn deeply and lastingly to the mountain people usually were attracted first by the awesome terrain; Jenista, "The White Apos: Ifugao and American Perceptions of Colonial Rule" (PhD dissertation, University of Michigan, 1978), pp. 390-391, 438.

35. This collaboration is described in my *A Nation in the Making: The Philippines and the United States, 1899-1921* (Cambridge, Harvard University Press, 1974), passim, esp. Chapters 3-6 and conclusion. It is the same phenomenon identified as a "modus vivendi" and a "tacit agreement between *ilustrados* and Commissioners" in Norman G. Owen's perceptive introductory essay to Owen, ed., *Compadre Colonialism: Studies on the Philippines under American Rule* (Ann Arbor, Michigan Papers on South and Southeast Asia, no. 3, 1971). See Michael Cullinane's chapter in this book for a case study of great significance.

36. He told the story himself in *The Philippines Past and Present,* 2 vols. (New York, Macmillan, 1914), esp. Chapters 20-23. See also Karl L. Hutterer, "Dean C. Worcester and Philippine Anthropology," in

Philippine Quarterly of Culture and Society, 6:125–156; and Jenista, "The White Apos," passim, esp. pp. 168–169, 443–446.

37. See, for example, Worcester to Reighard, 11 July 1910, Reighard Papers, box 6: "Just before starting for Palawan I made a trip through [Nueva Vizcaya and Mountain Province], in the course of which I traveled more than 700 miles, mostly on horseback, riding regularly twenty to thirty-five miles a day . . . . Three army officers accompanied me on this trip. Two were obliged to drop out before it was finished, and the third, although he got through to Aparri, was sick for a month afterwards, and the hardest riding and hiking of the trip was done after he left us. I arrived at Baguio quite ready to continue the march if necessary, and my saddle horse . . . was the only horse in the outfit that came in without a sore back." Life on the trail was not one of raw testing, however. Mrs. Worcester's diary of a trip through Mountain province in 1909 with her husband, several friends, 3 Filipino major domos, and 30 cargadores records that, along with some danger and unhygienic conditions, there was much fun and lots of good eating. One trail lunch, for example, consisted of soup, stewed chicken with dumplings, roast beef, potatoes, peas, and two kinds of freshly baked pies! (p. 14).

38. Concerning the word *apo,* see Nanon Leas Worcester's trail diary, 1909, WP, and Jenista, "White Apos," passim, esp. pp. 29, 108, 125, 167, 433. Worcester to Frank Carpenter, 7 August 1914, WP, box 1.

39. Worcester, text of speech introducing Secretary of War Jacob M. Dickinson at Bontoc in 1910, BIA 3833–25.

40. Worcester to Reighard, 26 March 1909, Reighard Papers, box 5.

41. See, for example, Worcester's denunciation of General H. H. Bandholtz, chief of the Constabulary, and certain of his officers in Mountain Province over charges made against one of Worcester's lieutenant governors, Walter F. Hale; his 5-page paste-up of criticisms of Bandholtz; and his comments on the encroachment of both General Pershing and the Christian Filipinos on part of his Mindanao fief in the Lewis-Fortich cases, 18 May 1911, all in WPC, DS 685.W9, Vol. XXI. Jenista argues that "isolation," "independence of action," an "irresistible element of romance," and fear of encroachment by rivals and superiors motivated the white apos of Ifugao ("White Apos," pp. 391–392).

42. On Worcester and the friar land "scandal," see Hayden, "Biographical Sketch," Chapter 5. The episode is related to larger issues in Philippine-American relations in Stanley, *A Nation in the Making,* pp. 157–163. For Worcester's side of the *El Renacimiento* case, see Hayden, "Biographical Sketch," Chapter 6; Jenista, "White Apos," p. 23.

43. Edwards to Dickinson, 29 November 1909, BIA 6257–30.

44. See, for example, Worcester's letters of 19 June 1899, and 9 July 1899, WPC, DS 685.W9, Vol. XVI; and Worcester's journal, 11 January 1901, WPC DS 685.W912.

45. Worcester to McIntyre, 19 November 1912, BIA 5543–139.

46. Report by the Secretary of the Interior on the Lewis-Fortich Matter, 18 May 1911, WPC, DS 685.W9, Vol. XXI, part 2.

47. See, for example, Worcester's contribution to the successful effort

to prevent General H.H. Bandholtz's appointment as chief of the Bureau of Insular Affairs, WPC, DS 685.W9, Vol. XXI, part 1.

48. Worcester to Forbes, 22 October 1911, WPC, DS 685.W9, Vol. XXI, part 1. When Forbes tried to prevent Worcester from pressing this investigation, Worcester threatened to resign before the day was out. Forbes relented and transferred Dr. Gregg to a different government hospital, outside Worcester's control. Elliott diary, 23 October 1911, and 27 January 1912, Elliott Papers.

49. Unsigned typescript dated Calapan, Mindoro, 3 March 1906, WPC, DS 685.W9, Vol. XXI, part 2. Frank Jenista calls this document a "letter of notation" and attributes it to Worcester, a judgment that seems very credible in view of the syntax and style of the document; Jenista, "Problems of the Colonial Civil Service: An Illustration from the Career of Manuel L. Quezon," *Southeast Asia: An International Quarterly,* 3:809–829 (Spring 1974).

50. Worcester to Vice-Governor, 10 November 1911, WPC, DS 685.W9, Vol. XX. Worcester also made much of the accusation that another doctor—with whom he was involved in a heated conflict over the treatment of a cholera epidemic—had continued to examine and certify the health of prostitutes after having been forbidden to do so. See BIA file 6257.

51. Worcester to Smith, 13 May 1908, BIA 2223-112.

52. Worcester to Reighard, 26 February 1900, and 5 May 1901, Reighard Papers, box 2 and 3, respectively. Cf. the expectation of martyrdom that characterized Bishop Brent's early approach to the Philippines: "There would be a few years of earnest work with all the anxieties that belong to the workman without tools, then would come broken health; and the end,—for a man must face the fact, as I have faced (and accepted) it, that missionary life in the Philippines means an early death for a son of the North." Draft of letter to be circulated to several other Episcopal bishops requesting funds, 26 October 1901, Brent Papers, box 5. It is useful to compare these melodramatic, self-serving predictions with the reality: Though controversial, Worcester became famous, powerful, and at least relatively affluent; Brent lived to the age of 67, dying finally in 1929, 11 years after leaving the Philippines.

53. Worcester to Taft, 27 January 1908, WP, box 1; Worcester, text of introductory remarks at Bontoc in 1910, BIA 3833-25. See also Worcester to Reighard, 23 April 1903, Reighard Papers: "I have been at times somewhat in the fix of the soldier who is hired to be shot at. The results may be bad for his constitution but he has to discharge the duties that he is paid for."

54. Worcester to Taft, 27 January 1908, WP, box 1. See also the citations in note 32 above.

55. Worcester to Carpenter, 17 August 1914, WP, box 1; Worcester, introductory remarks at Bontoc, BIA 3833-25; Worcester to Reighard, 23 April 1903, Reighard Papers, box 4. See also his criticism of Bandholtz—politician, bureaucrat, trimmer—in WPC, DS 685W9 Vol. XXI, for a profile of the qualities he abhorred in a government official and sought to avoid in his own life.

56. Worcester, introductory remarks at Bontoc, BIA 3833–25.
57. Elliott diary, 1 August 1911, Elliott Papers. See also note 38 above. Most of the "White Apos," Worcester's subordinates in the tribal regions, invoked either royal or divine metaphors for their role (Jenista, "White Apos," pp. 392, 433). This was the Philippine variant of a not uncommon phenomenon among whites living amidst native people in the nineteenth century. "We are like little kings among them," said the Rev. John Williams of his ministry on the island of Raiatea in the South Pacific. (Quoted in Gavan Daws, *A Dream of Islands: Voyages of Self-Discovery in the South Seas,* [New York, Norton, 1980], p. 34.)

Chapter 6. *Protestant Missionaries and American Colonialism in the Philippines, 1899–1916: Attitudes, Perceptions, Involvement, by Kenton J. Clymer*

Reference Abbreviations
BIA Bureau of Insular Affairs
1. Charles W. Briggs, *The Progressing Philippines* (Philadelphia, Griffith and Rowland, 1913), p. 135.
2. An investigation of the Protestant missions in the Philippines is perhaps best begun by perusing the relevant portion of Kenneth Scott Latourette, *A History of the Expansion of Christianity,* Vol. V, *The Great Century in the Americas, Australia, Asia and Africa A.D. 1800–A.D. 1914* (New York and London, Harper, 1943). A more complete introduction is Peter G. Gowing, *Islands Under the Cross: The Story of the Church in the Philippines* (Manila, National Council of Churches in the Philippines, 1967). Arthur Leonard Tuggy, *The Philippine Church: Growth in a Changing Society* (Grand Rapids, Eerdmans, 1971) is a brief account. Camilo Osias and Avelina Lorenzana, *Evangelical Christianity in the Philippines* (Dayton, United Brethren Publishing House, 1931) is an older account by two important Filipino converts.
   More specialized accounts not written by participants include Mariano C. Apilado, "Revolution, Colonialism, and Mission: A Study of the Role of the Protestant Churches in the United States' Rule of the Philippines, 1898–1928" (PhD dissertation, Vanderbilt University, 1976), one of the few studies based on extensive archival investigation; Donald Dean Parker, "Church and State in the Philippines 1896–1906" (PhD dissertation, Divinity School, University of Chicago, 1936), which is weak on analysis but which contains much valuable information; some of the contributions to Gerald H. Anderson's fine edited collection of essays, *Studies in Philippine Church History* (Ithaca and London, Cornell University Press, 1969); Richard L. Deats, *Nationalism and Christianity in the Philippines* (Dallas, Southern Methodist University Press, 1967). I have written several articles on various aspects of the early Protestant mission experience: "The Methodist Response to Philippine Nationalism, 1899–1916," *Church History,* 47:421–434 (December 1978); "Methodist Missionaries and American Colonialism in the Philippines, 1899–1913,

Pacific Historical Review, 49:29-60 (February 1980); "The Limits of Comity: Presbyterian-Baptist Relations in the Philippines, 1900-1925," *Kabar Seberang,* 10-11:76-84 (December 1982); "Methodist Missionaries and Roman Catholicism in the Philippines, 1899-1916," *Methodist History,* 18:171-178 (April 1980); and "The Episcopalian Encounter with Roman Catholicism in the Philippines, 1910-1916," *Philippine Studies* 28:86-97 (1980).

There are also some important studies of individual missions, including David L. Rambo, "The Christian and Missionary Alliance in the Philippines, 1901-70" (PhD dissertation, New York University School of Education, 1974); Elmer A. Fridell, *Baptists in Thailand and the Philippines* (Philadelphia, Judson [1956]); F.V. Stipp, "The Disciples of Christ in the Philippines" (DD Thesis, Yale Divinity School, 1927); Lee Donald Warren's account of the Seventh-day Adventist mission, *Isles of Opportunity: Progress and Possibilities in the Philippines* (Washington, D.C., Review and Herald Publishing Association, 1928); Walter N. Roberts, *The Filipino Church: The Story of the Development of an Indigenous Evangelical Church in the Philippine Islands as revealed in the work of The Church in the United Brethren in Christ* (Dayton, The Foreign Missionary Society and the Women's Missionary Association, United Brethren in Christ, 1936). Methodist work is examined in Richard L. Deats, *The Story of Methodism in the Philippines* (Manila, Published for Union Theological Seminary by the National Council of Churches in the Philippines, 1964); Dionisio D. Alejandro, *From Darkness to Light: A Brief Chronicle of the Beginnings and Spread of Methodism in the Philippines* ([Manila?] Philippine Central Conference, Board of Communications and Publications, United Methodist Church, 1974); and J. Tremayne Copplestone, *History of Methodist Missions,* Vol. IV, *Twentieth-Century Perspectives (The Methodist Episcopal Church, 1896-1939)* (New York, Board of Missions of the United Methodist Church, 1973), pp. 170-239. On the Episcopalian undertaking, see William Henry Scott, "Staunton of Sagada: Christian Civilizer," *Historical Magazine of the Protestant Episcopal Church,* 31:305-339 (December 1962); and Alexander C. Zabriskie, *Bishop Brent: Crusader for Christian Unity* (Philadelphia, Westminster, 1948).

Among the general accounts by the missionaries themselves (or their close associates), the most valuable is Frank C. Laubach, *The People of the Philippines: Their Religious Progress and Preparation for Spiritual Leadership in the Far East* (New York, Doran, 1925). Other accounts include John B. Devins, *An Observer in the Philippines* (Boston, American Tract Society, 1905); Briggs, *The Progressing Philippines;* Homer C. Stuntz, *The Philippines and the Far East* (Cincinnati, Jennings and Pye, 1904); William F. Oldham, *India, Malaysia, and the Philippines: A Practical Study in Missions* (New York, Eaton & Mains, 1914); Arthur J. Brown, *The New Era in the Philippines* (New York, Fleming H. Revell, 1903). The best account of the Baptist mission is by an early missionary, H.W. Munger, *Christ and the Filipino Soul: A History of the Philippine Baptists* (n.p., 1967). James B. Rodgers, *Forty Years in the Philippines: A History of the Philippine Mission of the Presbyterian Church in the United States of America, 1899-1939* (New York, Board of Foreign Missions of the Presbyterian Church in the United States of America, 1940) is a good account. Elmer K. Higdon and I.W. Higdon, *From Carabao to Clipper* (New York, Friendship Press, 1941) is a very fine account of the Disciples mission, though the book concentrates on the period after 1916.

3. See, for example, Gerald H. Anderson and Peter G. Gowing, "The Philippines," in Gerald H. Anderson, ed., *Christ and Crisis in Southeast Asia* (New York, Friendship Press, 1968), p. 153. It should also be noted that some Protestant influences were at work in the formation of the Philippine Independent Church (Iglesia Filipina Independiente), which at its height claimed the allegiance of as many as one-third of the population. Today the church has 3 or 4 percent; it maintains a connection with the Episcopal church.

4. Hermogenes Cera, "The Impact of Evangelical Faith Upon Philippine Culture" (BD Thesis, Union Theological Seminary, Dasmarinas, Cavite, Philippines), especially pp. 58-61. Anthropological studies of the effects of Protestantism in specific areas of the Philippines include F. Landa Jocano, "Conversion and the Patterning of Christian Experience In Malitbog, Central Panay, Philippines," in Peter G. Gowing and William Henry Scott, eds., *Acculturation in the Philippines: Essays on Changing Societies (A Selection of Papers Presented at the Baguio Religious Acculturation Conference from 1958 to 1968)* (Quezon City, New Day Publishers, 1971), pp. 43-72; and John J. Carroll, "Magic and Religion," in John J. Carroll et al., eds., *Philippine Institutions* (Manila, Solidaridad Publishing House, 1970), pp. 40-74.

5. "Biography of H.W. Widdoes" (unpublished typescript), United Brethren in Christ records, United Methodist Archives, Lake Junaluska, N.C. (hereafter cited as United Brethren records), p. 25; Clymer, "Methodist Missionaries and American Colonialism in the Philippines, 1899-1913."

6. Bishop Matthew Simpson, quoted in Philip D. Jordan, "Immigrants, Methodists, and a 'Conservative' Social Gospel, 1865-1908," *Methodist History,* 17:16 (October 1978).

7. Cyrus Foss, quoted in ibid., p. 17.

8. Gerald H. Anderson, "Providence and Politics behind Protestant Missionary Beginnings in the Philippines," in Anderson, ed., *Studies in Philippine Church History,* p. 289.

9. Ray Allen Billington, *The Far Western Frontier 1830-1860* (New York and Evanston, Harper & Row, 1956), p. 83.

10. R. Pierce Beaver, *Church, State, and the American Indians: Two and a Half Centuries of Partnership Between Protestant Churches and Government* (St. Louis, Concordia Publishing House, 1966), pp. 122-176; Sydney F. Ahlstrom, *A Religous History of the American People* (New Haven and London, Yale University Press, 1972), p. 861.

11. Jordan, "Immigrants, Methodists, and a 'Conservative' Social Gospel," p. 37. In 1882, the Society declared that the "work of the missionary and the patriot is one."

12. Quoted in *The Report of the Philippines Mission of the Presbyterian*

Mission of the Presbyterian Church in the U.S.A. 1904; Together with Short Sketches of the Work of its Several Stations from the Inception of the Mission in 1899 (Manila, Methodist Publishing House, 1905), p. 5.

13. Arthur J. Brown, *Report of a Visitation of the Philippine Mission of the Presbyterian Church in the United States of America* (New York, Board of Foreign Missions of the Presbyterian Church in the United States of America, 1902), p. 10.

14. Quoted in Cornelia Moots, *Pioneer 'Americanas' or first Methodist Missionaries in the Philippines* (n.p., 1903), p. 13.

15. William F. Oldham and James B. Rodgers for the Evangelical Union, 25 March 1905, Presbyterian Church in the U.S.A. Board of Foreign Missions. Missions Correspondence and Reports, microfilm reel 288, Presbyterian Historical Society, Philadelphia. (References to the Presbyterian Mission Correspondence and Reports available on microfilm will hereafter be cited as Presbyterian Mission Correspondence, reel ---).

16. Charles Henry Brent to William Howard Taft, 14 April 1902, William Howard Taft Papers, Manuscript Division, Library of Congress, microfilm reel 35.

17. Brent to W.A. Leonard, 26 October 1901, Charles Henry Brent Papers, Manuscript Division, Library of Congress. The following year Brent wrote, "For God and Country is the watchword of this outpost of the Church's work." Brent to John W. Wood, 20 September 1902, Philippine Mission Correspondence, Archives and Historical Collections of the Episcopal Church, Episcopal Theological Seminary of the Southwest, Austin, Texas (hereafter cited as Episcopal Mission Correspondence).

18. Homer C. Stuntz to Taft, 27 July 1906, Taft Papers, reel 602.

19. [Bruce L. Kershner], "The Mission and the Government" (unpublished manuscript), read 31 December 1907, at the seventh annual conference of the Philippine Mission of the Disciples of Christ. Bruce L. Kershner Papers, Disciples of Christ Historical Society, Nashville.

20. George F. Pentecost, "Protestantism in the Philippines," Preached at Manila, P.I., December 21, 1902 (printed sermon), p. 14. Copy in the Presbyterian Historical Society.

21. H.H. Steinmetz, "Vacation Ramblings," *Pearl of the Orient*, 11:5–6 (July 1914). Missionary communications emphasized the possibilities of improvement under American and Protestant tutelage, suggesting that the perceived deficiencies were cultural ones. But it is sometimes difficult to distinguish between deficiencies perceived as purely cultural and those deemed to derive, in part, from inherent racial incapacities. In 1928, the prominent missionary spokesman Sherwood Eddy reflected on the attitude of optimistic certainty that pervaded the turn-of-the-century missionary outburst and assumed that racial superiority commonly entered into that attitude. "Then," he recalled, "we felt called to take up 'the white man's burden' and go out from our 'superior' race to the backward peoples of the world." G. Sherwood Eddy, "Can We Still Believe in Foreign Missions?" in Gordon Poteat, ed., *Students and the Future of Christian Missions* (New York, Student Volunteer Movement for Foreign Missions, 1928), p. 78.

22. J. Andrew Hall, "Philippine Life and Character" (unpublished manuscript), pp. 1, 3–4, Presbyterian Historical Society.
23. J[ames] H. Thoburn, *India and Malaysia* (Cincinnati, Cranston & Curts, 1892), p. 504.
24. See, for example, Stuntz, *The Philippines and the Far East*, p. 86; and Ernest J. Pace to Samuel S. Hough, 12 September 1909, United Brethren Records. The Episcopalian mission represents something of an exception to these generalizations, for it was more sympathetic to Roman Catholic theology and therefore generally refused to establish work among the Catholic population. Nevertheless, Episcopalian correspondence contains numerous denunciations of Roman Catholic corruption in the Philippines and indicates a strong resentment of Catholic methods.
25. "Civilization Dangers to Backward Peoples," *Philippine Presbyterian*, 11:2 (August 1911).
26. Brent to John W. Wood, 15 July 1904, Episcopal Mission Correspondence. Walter C. Clapp, *Bontoc Bulletin*, #3, Epiphanytide, 1905, ibid.
27. One Episcopalian missionary, for example, while aware of "the vices of the civilized West," wrote that it was not until the "Americans appeared on the scene as the great civilizing, elevating power" that there had "been a semblance of safety or a lessening of the profound suspicion of the savage." Irving Spencer, "Bagobo Land," *Spirit of Missions*, 70:387 (May 1905).
28. "Liberties Unappreciated," *Philippine Christian Advocate*, 8:[3] (November, 1908).
29. John McKee, "Alliance Missions," *Christian and Missionary Alliance*, 31:303 (31 October 1903); Paul Doltz, "The American Volunteer" (unpublished manuscript), Paul Doltz Correspondence, Presbyterian Historical Society.
30. This theme was a common one. See, for example, "Bishop Thoburn's Instructive Words," *Christian Advocate*, 76:1056 (29 August 1905); Eric Lund to Henry C. Mabie, 4 October 1900, American Baptist Mission Correspondence, Baptist Historical Society, Rochester, microfilm reel 80 (hereafter cited as Baptist Mission Correspondence) Bessie White, "God's Providence in the Entering of the Philippines," *Christian and Missionary Alliance*, 25:119 (1 September 1900); and Charles W. Briggs to E.R. Merriam, 11 April 1901, Baptist Mission Correspondence, reel 181.
31. Homer C. Stuntz, *The Philippine Mission of the Methodist Episcopal Church* (New York, Missionary Society of the Methodist Episcopal Church, n.d.), p. 16. See also, *"A Missionary for the Philippines,"* *Christian and Missionary Alliance*, 22:145 (April 1899).
32. Brown, *Report of a Visitation*, p. 85.
33. Presbyterian David S. Hibbard, for example, wrote, "If things are as 'eminently satisfactory'" as General Otis claimed, "it does not require much to satisfy the General." In Panay, Hibbard added, the Filipino soldiers were disciplined and had "the sympathy of almost all the natives." Hibbard to F.F. Ellinwood, 24 July 1900, Presbyterian Mission Correspondence, reel 287. See also Bessie White, "The Philip-

pines from a Missionary Standpoint," *Christian and Missionary Alliance,* 24:1 (24 March 1900).

34. Stuntz, *The Philippines and the Far East,* p. 135.

35. Charles Henry Brent, "American Democracy in the Orient" (manuscript article), enclosed in Brent to Taft, 6 April 1905, Records of the Bureau of Insular Affairs Relating to the Philippine Islands, National Archives, Washington, D.C., file 12848. (Hereafter cited as BIA file - - - -). At least one missionary, Presbyterian Leonard P. Davidson, did use the term "American-Filipino war." Quoted in Alice Byram Condict, *Old Glory and the Gospel in the Philippines: Notes Gathered during Professional and Missionary Work* (Chicago, New York, and Toronto, Fleming H. Revell, 1902), p. 65.

36. Charles W. Briggs to - - - -, 7 March 1902, Baptist Mission Correspondence, reel 181.

37. Bishop Brent and an Episcopalian nurse, Ellen T. Hicks, were invited to inspect the reconcentration camp at Bacoor. They found nothing amiss. See Charles Henry Brent, "Various Notes on Matters Philippine" (manuscript article), 24 October 1905, Episcopal Mission Correspondence; Ellen T. Hicks, "An Experiment in Nursing: A Belated Story," *Spirit of Missions,* 71:320–321 (April 1905); and Journal of W. Cameron Forbes (5 vols., unpublished), I, 272–273 (entry for 4 August 1905), W. Cameron Forbes Papers, Houghton Library, Harvard University.

38. Z[erah] C. Collins, "With the Y.M.C.A. in the Spanish-American War in the Philippines" (unpublished manuscript), Collins biographical file, Y.M.C.A. Historical Library, New York.

39. James B. Rodgers to Ellinwood, 28 August 1899, Presbyterian Mission Correspondence, reel 287. Stuntz, *The Philippines and the Far East,* p. 136. Anti-imperialist critics who publicized atrocities, wrote Stuntz, possessed minds that "forever miss currents, and get caught in eddies."

40. David S. Hibbard to Ellinwood, 24 July 1900, Presbyterian Mission Correspondence, reel 287.

41. J. Andrew Hall to Ellinwood, 1 November 1900, ibid. Hibbard had complained that the Army had been "carefully feeding and housing the prisoners and making them as comfortable as they are in their own homes." Hibbard to Ellinwood, 23 October 1900, ibid.

42. Rodgers to Ellinwood, 21 January 1901, ibid., reel 288.

43. Peter G. Gowing, *Mandate in Moroland: The American Government of Muslim Filipinos 1899–1920* (Quezon City, Philippine Center of Advanced Studies, 1977), pp. 35, 36.

44. Rodgers to Ellinwood, 11 January 1900, Presbyterian Mission Correspondence, reel 287; Jonathan McKee, "Alliance Missions," *Christian and Missionary Alliance* 31:303–304 (31 October 1903). The Alliance supported its missionary, and urged that the agreement, "which, instead of bringing peace, can only bring more bitter misunderstanding and evil," be overturned. Ibid., 29:106 (23 August 1902). When the Bates agreement was abrogated unilaterally in 1904, the missionaries were presumably gratified.

45. For a contrary view contending that the military viewed Protestant

Missions as an unsettling factor and preferred to cultivate relations with the Catholics, see Donald Dean Parker, "Church and State in the Philippines 1898–1906" (PhD dissertation, University of Chicago, 1936), pp. 195, 262–263; and John Marvin Dean, *The Cross of Christ in Bolo-land* (Chicago and New York, Fleming H. Revell, 1902), pp. 49–50.

46. "Bishop Thoburn's Instructive Words," *Christian Advocate*, 74:1056 (6 July 1899).

47. Apilado, "Revolution, Colonialism, and Mission," p. 129.

48. Gowing, *Mandate in Moroland*, pp. 141–225 passim.

49. Newspaper clipping, "Sees Pagans in Fifth Avenue as in Luzon," penciled *New York Tribune*, 18 October 1913, BIA file 12848. All that the Moro had learned from Western nations, Brent wrote shortly thereafter, was "that we are able to kill him." Copy, Brent to Henry L. Higginson, 3 February 1914, Brent Papers. Brent attempted, apparently without success, to get Congressional support for better medical services for the Moros. So devoted did he become in later years to humanitarian work among the Muslim Filipinos that he directed that any memorial gifts received upon his death be used to assist such efforts. Copy, Brent to Mabel T. Boardman, 26 March 1914, Brent Papers; copy, Senator G.H. Hitchcock to Boardman, 13 May 1914, ibid.; Zabriskie, *Brent*, p. 73.

50. E.H. Gates, in the *Advent Review and Sabbath Herald*, 83:11 (10 May 1906).

51. Cited in Rodgers to F.M. Bond, 16 March 1904, Presbyterian Mission Correspondence, reel 288.

52. Stealy B. Rossiter, "The Philippines Before and After the Occupation, May 1, 1898" (unpublished manuscript) ibid., reel 289; L.V. Finster to A.G. Daniells, 23 August 1911, Record Group 11 (Presidential), Incoming Letters 1911–F, Seventh-day Adventist Archives, Washington, D.C.

53. Henry W. Warren, "The United States in the Philippines," *Christian Advocate*, 79:2032 (15 December 1904). For other comments lauding American efforts to improve public health, see Rodgers to Ellinwood, 26 March 1902, Presbyterian Mission Correspondence, and Robert W. Carter to Arthur J. Brown, 27 October 1907, ibid., reel 289.

54. J.M. Groves to W.D. Murray, 30 June 1909, Y.M.C.A. Historical Library. "Publish nothing which may compromise the administration or officials," a Y.M.C.A. official admonished John R. Mott. [W.A. Tener] to John R. Mott, 1 September 1908, ibid.

55. Samuel S. Hough, quoted in "Biography of H.W. Widdoes," p. 249.

56. *Eighty-Sixth Annual Report of the Missionary Society of the Methodist Episcopal Church for the Year 1904* (New York, Board of Foreign Missions of the Methodist Episcopal Church, 1905), p. 273.

57. Alex A. Pieters to Ellinwood, 29 April 1903, Presbyterian Mission Correspondence, reel 288.

58. Charles W. Briggs, "The Pulahanes in Panay," *Missionary Review of the World*, 34:515 (July 1911).

59. For example, Arthur W. Prautch, "A Crime, Not a Blunder" (unpub-

lished manuscript), Record Group 74–11, Philippine Islands Correspondence (Prautch folder), Records of the Methodist Episcopal Missionary Society, United Methodist Archives (hereafter cited as R. G. 74–11, United Methodist Archives). Arthur W. Prautch, "Marriage Question in the Philippines" (unpublished manuscript), 28 December 1899, ibid. David S. Hibbard to F. F. Ellinwood, 29 December 1899, Presbyterian Mission Correspondence, reel 287. Dean, *Cross of Christ in Bolo-land*, pp. 49–50. On the questionable validity of the criticism, see Rodgers to Ellinwood, 6 February 1900, Presbyterian Mission Correspondence, and Donald Dean Parker, "Church and State in the Philippines, 1896–1906," *Philippine Social Science Review*, 10:381–382 (1938).

60. Journal of W. Cameron Forbes, V, 174 (entry for 14 January 1913).
61. Walter C. Clapp to John W. Wood, 9 July 1908, Episcopal Mission Correspondence; Brent to John W. Wood, 21 November 1908, ibid.
62. J. H. Groves to Sherwood Eddy, 29 June 1914, Y.M.C.A. Historical Library. Worcester's reputation changed, however, at least in some important Protestant circles. No one doubted his intellectual abilities, and, by 1912, even Brent felt that the Commissioner had "a genuine and self sacrificing love for the primitive folk." Brent to W.C. Rivers, 21 October 1912, Brent Papers. See also Frank C. Laubach to J.L. Barton, 27 March 1916, Philippine Mission Records, American Board of Commissioners for Foreign Missions, Houghton Library, Harvard University (hereafter cited as American Board Mission Correspondence).

Worcester, for his part, counted Brent among his friends, and in 1914 he endorsed the Bishop's efforts to organize a non-denominational "Christian peace work" among the Moros. Dean C. Worcester, *The Philippines Past and Present* (2 vols., New York, Macmillan, 1914), II, 643. Worcester's endorsement is referred to in Edward H. Fallows to Hamilton Holt, 18 August 1914, a copy of which is in the Brent Papers. When the Commissioner resigned in 1913, the publication of the Disciples mission observed, surely incorrectly, that Americans reacted with "almost universal regret." "This and That," *Philippine Christian*, 13:1 (10 September 1913).

63. G. A. Irwin, "Malay Peninsula and the Philippines," *Advent Review and Sabbath Herald*, 82:14 (15 June 1905).
64. Peter G. Gowing, "The White Man and the Moro: A Comparison of Spanish and American Policies Toward Muslim Filipinos," *Solidarity*, 6:40 (March 1971).
65. Robert F. Black to Judson Smith, 14 May 1903, American Board Mission Correspondence. A favor that must have been especially meaningful to the missionary involved Colonel Harbord's decision to order a Constabulary physician to remain in Davao to assist with the birth of Black's child. The physician may well have saved Mrs. Black's life. Black to Smith, 3 July 1905, ibid.
66. "Address by Major Henry Gilheuser, Governor of the District of Davao, October 13, 1911" (unpublished manuscript), ibid.
67. Laubach to James L. Barton, 28 December 1915, ibid.; Laubach to Enoch F. Bell, 6 January 1916, ibid.

68. Brent to John W. Wood, 8 August 1903, Episcopal Mission Correspondence; Irving Spencer to Wood, 15 May 1904, ibid.; Brent to Wood, 8 August 1903, ibid.
69. Perhaps Bruce Kershner of the Disciples mission expressed most persuasively the advantages missions brought to the government. At a time "when the premonition of Oriental power and invasion" was "creeping like a chill up the spine of the West," he wrote in a reflective paper, it behooved the missionary community to foster conservative change only. As the promoters of carefully controlled change, Kershner thought, the missionary and the government were surely allies. For, like the government, the missionary was "holding back the billows which may break with desolating power upon his own people . . . . He feels that he is the one whose hand is upon the balance wheel of a nation and his influence is the same as kings, emperors or presidents." Bruce L. Kershner, "Missionary Inspiration" (unpublished manuscript), n.d. [1911?], given to Stephen J. Cory, Kershner Papers.
70. See, for example, James B. Rodgers to Taft, 22 March 1905, and Taft to Rodgers, 10 February 1906, BIA file 12662.
71. Charles Henry Brent, "The Church in the Philippine Islands: A Trip through Northern Luzon," *Spirit of Missions*, 68:792 (November 1903).
72. Homer C. Stuntz, "Governor William Howard Taft, of the Philippines," *Christian Advocate*, 76:1380 (29 August 1901).
73. Stuntz to Adna B. Leonard, 24 December 1903, R.G. 74–11 (Stuntz folder), United Methodist Archives.
74. Clymer, "Methodist Missionaries and American Colonialism."
75. Stephen Neill, *Colonialism and Christian Missions* (New York, McGraw-Hill, 1966), p. 93.
76. Robert T. Handy, *A Christian America: Protestant Hopes and Historical Realities* (New York, Oxford University Press, 1971), pp. 38–40, 101–105. The quotation is on p. 101.
77. George W. Wright to Arthur J. Brown, 13 April 1905, Presbyterian Mission Correspondence, reel 288. Charles N. Magill to Brown, 7 July 1910, ibid., reel 289.
78. Laubach to J.L. Barton, 6 May 1915, American Board Mission Correspondence.
79. Report of Charles W. Briggs (unpublished), 16 January 1907, Baptist Mission Correspondence, reel 181.
80. Marvin Rader to Adna B. Leonard, 17 March 1911, R.G. 43, file 66–12 (Rader folder), United Methodist Archives.
81. Rodgers to F.F. Ellinwood, 5 March 1899, Presbyterian Mission Correspondence, reel 287.
82. Walter O. McIntyre to Arthur J. Brown, 21 October 1903, ibid., reel 288.
83. Charles L. Maxfield to Miss MacLaurin, 27 December 1904, Baptist Mission Correspondence, reel 194. "Private Journal of Harry Farmer: Beginnings of Methodism in the Agno Valley Area, the Philippines, 1904–1907" (unpublished), 8 May 1904; 9 December 1905; 26 Au-

gust 1905, pp. 21-22, 95-96, 143; United Methodist Church national office, Manila.

84. Stuntz to Roosevelt, 2 February 1907, BIA file 4213-1. The BIA, which investigated Stuntz's "rather bitter complaint," found it to be without substance. Unsigned BIA memorandum, ibid.

85. W.H. Hanna, "Religious Liberty in the Philippines," *Christian Evangelist*, 45:1161 (10 September 1908). David O. Lund, quoted in Elizabeth White Jansen, "A Visit to Zamboanga, Philippines," *Christian and Missionary Alliance*, 8 May 1909, p. 90.

86. Laubach to J.L. Barton, 6 May 1915, American Board Mission Correspondence.

87. See, for example, Leon C. Hills to F.F. Ellinwood, 13 January 1902, Presbyterian Mission Correspondence, reel 288.

88. Copy, L.B. Hilles to Dr. Sauber, 20 August 1903, ibid. If such a policy ever existed, it was quickly rescinded or ignored, for, during their travels, missionaries regularly lodged with American schoolteachers. See, for example, "The Journal of Harry Farmer," passim.

89. *Eighty-Sixth Annual Report of the Missionary Society of the Methodist Episcopal Church for the Year 1904*, p. 273. It seems likely that Atkinson was not very sympathetic with Protestant missionary work, for he once wrote that "The prospects as to Protestant work . . . are not very encouraging." Fred W. Atkinson, *The Philippine Islands* (Boston, Ginn, 1905), p. 225.

90. *Pearl of the Orient*, 3:38 (October 1906).

91. H.W. Langheim to Arthur J. Brown, 26 May 1909, Presbyterian Mission Correspondence, reel 289.

92. Robert W. Carter to Dr. Halsey, 5 October 1909, ibid.

93. Brown, *Report of a Visitation*, p. 54.

94. Laubach to James L. Barton, 6 May 1915, American Board Mission Correspondence. For similar expressions, see Rader to A.B. Leonard, 17 March 1911, R.G. 43, file 66-12 (Rader file), United Methodist Archives; Charles Maxfield to "Dear Friends," 2 February 1912, Baptist Mission Correspondence, reel 198; and Eric Lund, "Schools in the Philippines" (unpublished manuscript) enclosed in Lund to Thomas S. Barbour, 28 March 1906, Baptist Mission Correspondence, reel 197.

95. George W. Wright strongly defended the government's school policy and claimed that relationships with the teachers were "most cordial and happy" (Wright to Brown, 18 May 1909, Presbyterian Mission Correspondence, reel 289), whereas H.W. Langheim and Charles Hamilton disagreed. They felt that the policy was enforced only in cases involving Protestant teachers and, in any event, raised serious constitutional problems (Langheim to Brown, 26 May 1909, ibid.; Hamilton to Brown, 20 August 1909, ibid).

96. "Philippine [Mission] Minutes, 1910," (unpublished) ibid., reel 290.

97. For example, Laubach, *People of the Philippines*, pp. 333-334.

98. Charles Maxfield to "Dear Friends," 2 February 1912, Baptist Mission Correspondence, reel 198; galley proofs of J.L. McLaughlin's report of April 1907, to the American Bible Society, enclosed in William I. Haven to Taft, 3 April 1907, BIA file 1158.

99. For example, "Journal of Harry Farmer," 7 February 1906, pp. 176-177; Robert W. Carter to Arthur J. Brown, 27 October 1907, Presbyterian Mission Correspondence, reel 289. Carter noted the "active opposition" to Protestant work "from government officials."

100. Stuntz to Roosevelt, 4 December 1904, BIA file 11980.

101. Copy, Bruce L. Kershner to W.H. Hanna, 9 October 1907, Kershner Papers, J.L. McElhany, in *Advent Review and Sabbath Herald,* 84:19-20 (12 December 1907). The missions were also angered a few years later when the government helped reconstruct the town of Antipolo. See "This and That," *Philippine Christian,* 8:[1] (10 October 1913).

102. Clipping, Charles W. Briggs to the editor, 21 May 1908, "Unjust and Perilous Favoritism," *The Examiner,* 9 July [1908], BIA file 2396. James A. Graham to Arthur J. Brown, 18 December 1907, Presbyterian Mission Correspondence, reel 289.

103. Harry Farmer to William F. Oldham, 5 October 1908, file 43, box 339 (Mrs. Harry Farmer), United Methodist Archives.

104. I have dealt with this matter in more detail in "Methodist Missionaries and American Colonialism."

105. "Philippine [Mission] Minutes," January 1910 and December 1910, Presbyterian Mission Correspondence, reel 290.

106. Report of Bohol Station, Presbyterian Philippine Mission, received 29 December 1911; and Report of Camarines Station, Presbyterian Philippine Mission, received 29 December 1911; both in United Presbyterian Church in the United States of America, Philippine Mission Correspondence, 1911-1921, Record Group 85, box 1, file 2, Presbyterian Historical Society.

107. Statements on file in BIA file 2396. The statements were made in August and September 1902.

108. Walter C. Clapp to Arthur S. Lloyd, 12 August 1902, Episcopal Mission Correspondence; Brent to E.F. Baldwin, 24 July 1903, Brent Papers.

109. Zabriskie, *Brent,* pp. 54-55.

110. Adolph Wislizenus to Brent, 31 January 1910, Brent Papers; Brent to Wislizenus, 21 February 1910, ibid.

111. Memorandum, James M. Thoburn, "Opium Monopoly in the Philippines," (memorandum of a hearing of 9 July 1903, before Elihu Root), BIA file 1023-44. For other protests, see Methodist Episcopal Mission of the Philippine Islands to Wilbur Crafts, 2 May 1903, BIA file 1023-17, and Report of the American Church in Manila of the [Presbyterian] Philippine Mission, 1903, Presbyterian Mission Correspondence, reel 290.

112. Telegram, Roosevelt to Taft, 9 June 1903, BIA file 1023-24.

113. *Official Journal of the Second Annual Session of the Philippine Islands Mission Conference of the Methodist Episcopal Church* [1906] (Manila, Methodist Publishing House, 1906), p. 48. See also Parker, "Church and State," (dissertation) pp. 271-272.

114. "The Moral Progress League in Manila," *Christian Advocate,* 80:1319 (30 August 1906).

115. Brent's endorsement of the Moral Progress League was not unqualified. It tended to be overly emotional, he thought, and did not provide constructive alternatives. Still, the Bishop concluded, "The Spirit of God is in it." *Manila Times,* 16 July 1906, pp. 1-2. Although Forbes was a good friend of Brent, he resented the Bishop's position in this instance. See Journal of W. Cameron Forbes, II, 60, 62 (entries for 3 July and 2 August 1906).

116. Unidentified clipping, "The Government and Gambling in the Philippines," enclosed in Mrs. Stephen L. Baldwin to Roosevelt, 31 July 1908, BIA file 6633.

117. Ibid.; Journal of W. Cameron Forbes, II, 402 (entry for 21 February 1908).

118. Telegram, Evangelical Union to Roosevelt, 15 February 1908, BIA file 6633; Mercer G. Johnston, "A Covenant with Death, An Agreement with Hell" (printed sermon), preached in the Cathedral of St. Mary and St. John, Manila, 23 February 1908, copy in BIA file 6633. Johnston also cabled Roosevelt directly; see Johnston to Roosevelt, received 24 February 1908, BIA file 6633.

119. Journal of W. Cameron Forbes, II, 408 (entry for 3 March 1908).

120. Ibid., II, 396 (entry for 5 February 1908).

121. Clarence Edwards, "Memorandum for the Secretary of War: In Re: Concession for a Cockpit During a Carnival at Manila," 24 February 1908, BIA file 6633.

122. Journal of W. Cameron Forbes, II, 403 (entry for 21 February 1908).

123. *Missions in the Philippines* (Boston, American Baptist Missionary Union, [1906]), p. 40.

124. H.H. Steinmetz, "A Social Gospel for the Philippines," *Pearl of the Orient,* 10:3-8 (July 1913). Methodist Harry Farmer also surmised that the government had lost interest in helping the poor. See Harry Farmer, "Contending for Religious Liberty," *Philippine Christian Advocate,* 7:6-8 (July 1908).

125. For example, copy, Brent to W.C. Rivers, 25 November 1907, Brent Papers.

126. The debate can be followed in the *Manila Times* during October and November 1907, and in Rossiter's correspondence with the mission board during the same period. Presbyterian Mission Correspondence, reel 289.

127. For missionary involvement in the Philippine Society, see BIA file 16654; issues of the *Philippine Bulletin* (published by the Philippine Society), copies in ibid.; Apilado, "Revolution, Colonialism, and Mission," pp. 269-274; and Clymer, "The Methodist Response to Philippine Nationalism," pp. 431-432.

128. Copy, C.L. Pickett to Bruce Kershner, 12 March 1914, Kershner Papers; Kershner to D.O. Cunningham, 12 September 1914, ibid.

129. W.F. Oldham, "The Profits and Peril of Philippine Autonomy—At This Time," *Report of the Thirty-first Annual Lake Mohonk Conference of Friends of the Indian and Other Dependent Peoples, October*

22d, 23d, and 24th, 1913, p. 129; "Philippine Society Banquet," *The Philippine Bulletin*, 1:3 (July, 1913). For the changes in missionary thought, see Valentin H. Rabe, *The Home Base of American China Missions, 1880-1920* (Cambridge, Council on East Asian Studies, Harvard University, 1978), pp. 173-191, and Paul A. Varg, *Missionaries, Chinese, and Diplomats: The American Protestant Missionary Movement in China, 1890-1958* (Princeton, Princeton University Press, 1958), pp. 99-104, and Chapter 9.

130. Walter C. Clapp to John W. Wood, 22 May 1904, Episcopal Mission Correspondence.

131. Brent, quoted in the *Manila Times*, 16 November 1907, p. 3, col. 3, citing the *Washington Post* of 9 October 1907. President Roosevelt was so disturbed by the Bishop's criticism that in private he questioned Brent's veracity, suggested that his knowledge of history was sadly deficient, and complained that his analogies were inept, his arguments absurd, and that he had given aid and comfort to the anti-imperialists. "Surely he must be suffering from some great mental strain," the President conjectured. Roosevelt to Silas McBee, 27 August 1907, in Elting E. Morison, ed., *The Letters of Theodore Roosevelt* (8 vols., Cambridge, Harvard University Press, 1951-1954), V, 772-775. In spite of this temporary falling out, the two men remained good friends.

132. [Arthur Seldon] Lloyd, "To Bontoc and Back Again," *Spirit of Missions*, 72:367 (May 1907).

133. Steinmetz, "A Social Gospel for the Philippines," pp. 3-8.

134. Copy, Brent to Mrs. George Monks, 27 April 1907, Brent Papers.

135. Quoted in Daniel R. Williams, *The Odyssey of the Philippine Commission* (Chicago, A.C. McClurg, 1913), p. 350.

136. See, for example, Michael V. Metallo, "American Missionaries, Sun Yat-sen, and the Chinese Revolution," *Pacific Historical Review*, 47:266 (May 1978).

137. Apilado, "Revolution, Colonialism, and Mission," pp. 254-286; Clymer, "The Methodist Response to Philippine Nationalism," pp. 424-427; Richard L. Deats, "Nicolas Zamora: Religious Nationalist," in Anderson, ed., *Studies in Philippine Church History*, pp. 325-336.

138. Cornelio M. Ferrer, "How to Survive in the Ministry" (typescript), p. 63, Cornelio M. Ferrer Papers, United Methodist Archives.

139. Alejandro, *From Darkness to Light*, p. 16; Cornelio M. Ferrer and Paul Locke A. Granadosin, "The Episcopal Address: Philippine Central Conference, The United Methodist Church, November 29, 1972" (mimeographed), Ferrer Papers.

140. Robert L. Youngblood, "The Protestant Church in the Philippines' New Society," *Bulletin of Concerned Asian Scholars*, 12:19-29 (July-September 1980). Youngblood discusses Roman Catholic attitudes toward martial law in "Church Opposition to Martial Law in the Philippines," *Asian Survey*, 58:505-520 (May 1978).

Chapter 7. *Americans, Cowboys, and Cattlemen on the Mindanao Frontier*, by Ronald K. Edgerton

1. *Cablenews-American,* 29 January 1907, in Houghton Library, Harvard University, W. Cameron Forbes MSS, Vol. II of Philippine Data—Departmental (fms AM 1192.3); and 29 August 1911 entry, Forbes Journal, V, 18, Forbes MSS, fms AM 1365.
2. 29 August 1911 entry, Forbes Journal, V, 18, Forbes MSS, fms AM 1365.
3. Population figures for the plateau area in the nineteenth century are estimates at best. The figure cited here is from D. Agustin de la Cavada, y Mendez de Vigo, *Historia Geografica, Geologica y Estadistica de Filipinas* (Manila, Imp. de Ramirez y Girandier, 1876), II, 197. As Bukidnon Province was not created until the twentieth century, the figure is for the "Monteses and Manobos" and "Moros" in Misamis Province which then encompassed the plateau. Other estimates suggest that this figure was reasonably accurate. José Maria Clotet, S.J., estimated "more than 13,000" Bukidnons in 1889. His letter of 11 May 1889 has been translated and edited by Frank Lynch, "The Bukidnon of North-Central Mindanao in 1889," *Philippine Studies* 15.3:466 (July 1967). The 1903 Census estimated the "pagan" population of Misamis Province to be 21,163. Republic of the Philippines, National Census and Statistics Office, *1975 Integrated Census of the Population and Its Economic Activities: Population, Bukidnon* (Manila, National Census and Statistics Office, 1975), p. 1.
4. Most of this plateau is known as Bukidnon Province today, a province that covers a total of 829,378 hectares. The highest point is Mt. Kitanglad (or Katanglad) which rises to 2,938 meters (9,639 feet). See Republic of the Philippines, National Census and Statistics Office, *1971 Census of Agriculture, Bukidnon* (Manila, National Census and Statistics Office, 1974), p. xxii. See also Francis C. Madigan, S.J., *Mindanao's Inland Province: A Socio-Economic Survey of Bukidnon,* (Cagayan de Oro, Xavier University, Research Institute for Mindanao Culture, 1969), I, 55; and Juan A. Mariano, *Soil Survey of Bukidnon Province Philippines,* Soil Report 21 (Manila, Department of Agriculture and Natural Resources, 1955), pp. 4–5. Mariano estimates the height of Mt. Kitanglad to be 2,380 meters, but more recent estimates have corrected this. The average height of the plateau is approximately 500 meters (about 1,600 feet), but it rises to at least 800 meters (about 2,600 feet) at Dalwangan, the watershed just north of Malaybalay between the Tagoloan River which flows north and the Sawaga River which flows south. Map No. NC 51-52, U.S. Army Map Services (PV), Corps of Engineers, 1956–1957, 1:1,000,000.
5. In this chapter, no distinction will be made between Bukidnon and Higaonon people. Although the Presidential Assistant on National Minorities (PANAMIN) regards these as different groups, this writer tends to agree with William E. Biernatzki that Higaonon denotes the same group as the Bukidnon, at least within the boundaries of Bukidnon Province. See Biernatzki, "Bukidnon Datuship in the Upper

Pulangi River Valley," *Bukidnon Politics and Religion,* ed. Alfonso de Guzman II and Esther M. Pacheco, IPC (Institute of Philippine Culture) Papers No. 11 (Quezon City, Ateneo de Manila, 1973), p. 16. For more detailed studies of the Manobo and Bukidnon, see John Garvan, *The Manobos of Mindanao,* in *National Academy of Science Memoirs,* 23:1 (Washington, U.S. Government Printing Office, 1931), and Fay-Cooper Cole, *The Bukidnon of Mindanao,* in *Fieldiana: Anthropology,* Vol. XLVI (Chicago, Chicago Natural History Museum, 1956). The fact that most Bukidnons lived along the Tagoloan and Cagayan Rivers, both of which flow north, helps explain why most of them developed closer ties to the north coast than to the Moslem south.

6. Cole spent 7 months in Bukidnon in 1910. By that time, there was no recognized leader higher than local village headmen in the Cagayan River valley. But among Bukidnons living in central Bukidnon, Cole concluded that there might have been more organization. His informants there told him that "before the coming of the Spaniards they had a principal ruler or *datu* who had the same power as is now exercised by the American governor—'when he gave orders all people obeyed.'" Below this ruler he was told that there had been petty *datus* who had lived in large houses in which there also lived "a considerable number of retainers and fighting men." Cole, *The Bukidnon of Mindanao,* pp. 18, 79-80. Cole did not study the Bukidnons living along the upper Pulangi in the northeast corner of the province. Biernatzki, studying this group in the late 1960s, concluded that the "high datu (*datu-datuon*)" of northeastern Bukidnon, who possessed a *giling* or "black stick the length of one's forearm and hand," enjoyed territorial jurisdiction over "all or portions of several river valleys occupied by the bands of subordinate datus." "Bukidnon Datuship in the Upper Pulangi River Valley," pp. 15-16, 19.

7. Biernatzki, "Bukidnon Datuship," pp. 30-33. There was usually a chief *datu* of the settlement and then lesser *datus* who were men on whom that title was bestowed by their tribesmen who looked to them for mediation in disputes.

8. Cole, *The Bukidnon of Mindanao,* p. 34.

9. The date for Kalasungay is in Manuel Buzeta and Felipe Bravo, *Diccionario Geográfico, Estadístico, Histórico, de las Islas Filipinas* (Madrid, 1850), I, 460. The date for the other pueblos may be found in the National Archives of the Philippines, "Ereccion de Pueblos—Misamis." Austin Dowd, S.J., states that the Recollects came to Bukidnon in 1867. "Questionnaire of the History of San Isidro Church, Malaybalay," 7 April 1938, Ateneo de Manila University, Jesuit Archives, VIII, 10. Another source comments that "northern Bukidnon was evangelized by the Augustinian Recollect Missionaries as early as 1830. Malitbog was settled in 1848." However, Jesuit visits to the plateau settlements did not begin until the 1870s. *Catholic Directory of the Philippines* (Manila, Catholic Trade, Inc., 1976), p. 551. It is my belief that the Jesuits became active on the plateau itself after they set up a parish at Tagoloan in 1888.

10. *Catalogus Provinciae Aragoniae Societatis Jesu* (Manila, IHS Matriti,

1859–1920). Concerning the Sumilao parish, there is today a "very large bronze church bell" in the nearby barrio of Impasugong which "gives the date 1880–Sumilao, and the Patron del Pilar," suggesting that Sumilao was at least a *visita* for the Jesuits from the coast by that time. Vincent G. Cullen, S.J., letter to me, 2 October 1978. Concerning Linabo, this parish was officially called Sevilla at first. But Sevilla, the Spanish name for Mailag, proved to be too small a settlement so that the mission came to be located in Linabo instead. See The Society of Jesus in the Philippines, *El Archipiélago Filipino* (Washington, Government Printing Office, 1900), I, 128.

11. Cole, *The Bukidnon of Mindanao*, p. 36.

12. *Cartas de los Padres de la Compañía de Jesus de la Misión de Filipinas* (Manila, M. Perez, Hijo, 1892), IX, 677.

13. Frederick Henfling, S.J., "A Short History of the Parish of Sumilao, Bukidnon," 28 June 1938, Ateneo de Manila University, Jesuit Archives, VIII, 15. The number 4,992, based upon the Sumilao parish records begun in 1890, may not include baptisms in the Sevilla parish before it was absorbed into Sumilao in 1896. In the same letter, Henfling comments that "fifty years ago the Priests from the Jasa-an parish often visited the Province of Bukidnon and during their visits they baptized almost 10,000."

14. The outpost was set up in Bugcaon in 1888–1889. P. Pablo Pastells, S.J., "Informe sobre la Isla de Mindanao presentado al Exaño por Governador Gral. de las Islas Filipinas, D. Valeriano Weyler, por el R.R. Superior de la Misión de la Companía de Jesus," 15 August 1888, Ateneo de Manila, Jesuit Archives, VII; and the Secretary of the Governor General to the Superior, S.J., 4 October 1889, Ateneo de Manila, Jesuit Archives, VIII, 9.

15. The Governor General to the Superior, S.J., 20 August 1894, Ateneo de Manila, Jesuit Archives, VIII, 9; and Thomas B. Cannon, S.J., "History of the Jesuits in the Philippines," Woodstock Letters (Woodstock, Maryland, Woodstock College Press, 1872–1951), LXVII, 145–146.

16. "Information furnished by Col. Cristobal de Aguilar, Spanish Chief of Staff for Mindanao," Appendix 19 to "Report of Major General J.C. Bates, U.S.V. of an Expedition to Northern Mindanao, P.I., March 20 to April 2, 1900," in *Annual Reports of the War Department, Fiscal Year Ended June 30, 1900*, I:Part 6 (Washington, Government Printing Office, 1900), p. 705. Information on the export of abaca is taken from Cavada, *Historia Geografica*, II, 201. He indicates that, in 1870, 30,243 piculs, valued at 128,532 pesos fs., were exported from Misamis, and most of this amount probably came from the interior. Abaca was second in export value only to palay (210,000 cavanes valued at 210,000 pesos fs.) for the province of Misamis, and corn was third (140,000 cavanes valued at 80,000 pesos fs.). Clotet remarked in 1889 that "among the Bukidnon there is widespread interest in the harvesting of abaca, for they know the high price this fiber brings in the market." He also noted that "they smoke tobacco which they grow themselves, and it is rated as top quality. They sell it in large quantity at Cagayan, in exchange for clothing." Finally, he

mentioned that "they engage in agriculture, and make extensive plantings of corn . . . [which] is not only their ordinary food, but their cash crop as well." He confirms that salt was among the commodities most desired by Bukidnons in return for their crops. Clotet, "The Bukidnon of North-Central Mindanao in 1889," in *Philippine Studies*, 15.3:476-77 (July 1967). Dean C. Worcester, in his manuscript entitled "The Non-Christian Tribes of the Philippine Islands and What the United States Has Done for Them," claimed that "the Bukidnon . . . harvest all of the gutta-percha, and grow nearly all of the hemp, coffee, and cacao shipped from Misamis." The University of Michigan, Worcester's Philippine Collection, Documents and Papers, VI:40, p. 36.

17. Clotet noted that "the most commonly used weapon [among the Bukidnon] is the balarao, which varies in value, and is obtained in trade from the Manobos of the Agusan River in exchange for cloth, corn, camotes, salt, etc." This indicates that Bukidnons may well have been middlemen in a trade between Manobos and Bisayans. "The Bukidnon of North-Central Mindanao in 1889," p. 474.

18. Fay-Cooper Cole, "Cultural Relations between Mindanao Regions and Islands to the South," in *Papers Read at the Mindanao Conference*, University of Chicago, Philippine Studies Program (Chicago, University of Chicago, Philippine Studies Program, 1955), pp. 13-14.

19. Fisher H. Nesmith to the Governor-General, 29 April 1911; and Eugene Barton to W. Cameron Forbes, 12 December 1910, Worcester's Philippine Collection, Documents and Papers, XXI: Part 2.

20. Worcester came to despise the Bartons when, in 1910, it was discovered that their farm in Mailag was south of the border of Bukidnon sub-province, then fixed at the 8th parallel. This meant that the Bartons and (more important) the splendid Mailag valley would be taken from the administrative control of Worcester and placed within Moro Province, then directed by John J. Pershing. When word spread that the valley would come under the jurisdiction of Moro Province, the Bukidnon and Manobo people living there fled to Malaybalay. At the same time, a group of Manobos surrounded the Barton store, claiming that Barton had cheated them in paying for lumber they had supplied. Worcester's appointees in Bukidnon—Frederick Lewis and Manuel Fortich—were slow to come to the Bartons' rescue, arguing that Mailag was no longer in their jurisdiction. Barton attempted to retaliate against both Lewis and Fortich, but, when they were cleared of wrongdoing, he, his wife, and his brother felt compelled to leave Mailag for good. See Worcester's Philippine Collection, Documents and Papers, XXI: Part 2, for extensive documentation collected by Worcester on this issue.

21. Jesus D. del Rosario, former chief-cowboy of the Gearharts, interview, Sante Fe, Bukidnon, 3 March 1977.

22. Teofilo Madula, former cowboy under Lewis, interview, Manolo Fortich, Bukidnon, 3 March 1977.

23. 7 July 1911 entry, Forbes Journal, IV, 419.

24. Worcester to Frank Carpenter, 7 August 1914, Michigan Historical

Collections, Worcester Papers, Box 1, Folder marked "Correspondence, July–December 1914," italics his.

25. In the 1820s and 1830s, Rev. Samuel Austin Worcester fought for the rights of Cherokee Indians in Georgia, going to jail rather than accepting a pardon for his actions. Joseph Ralston Hayden tells the story in his biographical sketch of Worcester in Dean C. Worcester, *The Philippines Past and Present* (New York, Macmillan, 1930), pp. 3–4.

26. Worcester to William Howard Taft, 27 January 1908, Michigan Historical Collections, Worcester Papers, Box 1, Folder marked "Correspondence, 1907–11."

27. Dean C. Worcester, "The Non-Christian Tribes of the Philippine Islands and What the United States Has Done for Them," manuscript, Worcester's Philippine Collection, Documents and Papers, IV:40, pp. 36, 44–45.

28. Dean C. Worcester, "Report of the Secretary of the Interior," in U.S., Philippine Commission, *Report of the Philippine Commission to the Secretary of War for the Year ended June 30, 1910*, Senate Document No. 869, 61st Congress, 3rd session (Washington, Government Printing Office, 1911), p. 71.

29. Forbes Journal, III, 446, footnote 145. Also see Act No. 1693, 20 August 1907, *Official Gazette*, V, 39:568–569 (25 September 1907), creating the province of Agusan and the sub-provinces of Bukidnon and Butuan. This was done in accord with the Special Provincial Government Act of September 1905 (Act No. 1396), which mandated that provinces inhabited by "non-Christian" and non-Moslem peoples would be governed directly by officials appointed by the American Governor General upon the advice of the Philippine Commission and especially of the Secretary of the Interior. A good summary of these acts can be found in Worcester's "The Non-Christian Tribes of the Philippine Islands and What the United States Has Done for Them," pp. 28–30.

30. Act No. 2408, 23 July 1914, made Bukidnon into a full province. Worcester mentions "the ambition of Pershing to establish Moro provincial control over territory . . . previously . . . administered by Bukidnon" in his letter to Frank Carpenter, 7 August 1914, Michigan Historical Collections, Worcester Papers, Box 1, Folder marked "Correspondence, July–Dec., 1914." In this same letter Worcester gave vent to his anger at having his stepchildren, Agusan and Bukidnon, taken out of the Interior Department's jurisdiction. In February 1920, these provinces reverted once again to the control of the Interior Department, this time coming under the jurisdiction of that department's Bureau of Non-Christian Tribes.

31. Carpenter to Worcester, 13 May 1914, quoting his cablegram to Worcester, Michigan Historical Collections, Worcester Papers, Box 1, Folder marked "Correspondence, Jan–June, 1914."

32. Ibid.

33. Worcester to Carpenter, 7 August 1914. Worcester followed this remark with the words: "The above is a joke." Clearly, though, it was

not meant entirely in jest, for later in the same letter he insulted Carpenter for seeking to avoid making decisions involving grave responsibility, and berated him again and again for betraying the minority tribes and their American protectors in order to curry favor with the Filipino politicians.

34. Carpenter to Worcester, 13 May 1914. This letter is a response to a letter dated 17 February, which Worcester sent Carpenter but which has been lost.

35. Information on homestead applications for Bukidnon and Cotabato is from José Sanvictores, "Plan of Land Settlement for the Philippines," 10 June 1924, Philippine National Library, Manuel Quezon MSS, Box 163, Folder marked "Bureau of Non-Christian Tribes." Information on pre-war homestead patents for Bukidnon is from the Registry of Deeds, Malaybalay, Bukidnon. At most, 369 of the 598 homestead patents were issued for land on the plateau rather than near the north coast. It should be noted that Worcester had nothing against farming on the plateau so long as it was not dominated by thousands of migrant settlers. He had nothing against pineapple-plantation farming by Americans or against small-scale farming by Bukidnons. Thus, he was the strongest supporter and publicizer of the Bukidnon Agricultural School, which taught new agricultural techniques to Bukidnon boys.

36. Karl J. Pelzer, *Pioneer Settlement in the Asiatic Tropics* (New York, American Geographical Society, 1945), pp. 104–106. In the Constitution of the Philippines ratified in May 1935, the amount of grazing land individuals or corporations were permitted to lease was increased to 2,000 hectares.

37. Worcester to Carpenter, 7 August 1914.

38. Cesar Fortich, interview, Cagayan de Oro, 17 November 1976, and Cesar and Manuel Fortich, Jr., interview, Cagayan de Oro, 26 March 1977.

39. Carlos O. Fortich, interview Dabongdabong, Bukidnon, 14 November 1976.

40. Information on the extension of fence lines is taken from José G. Sanvictores, interview, Quezon City, 17 June 1977. Manuel Fortich was the most dominant pre-war figure in Bukidnon. He became Acting Lieutenant Governor of the sub-province on 5 March 1911, and then continued as Lieutenant Governor and (after 1914) full Governor until 1922, when, upon his recommendation, Antonio Rubin became Governor. Both men were, as we shall see, enthusiastic ranchers.

41. Information on PPC (Philippine Packing Corporation) subleases from the Navy and the National Development Company is from Cesar Fortich, interview, Cagayan de Oro, 17 November 1976, and Cesar and Manuel Fortich, Jr., interview, Cagayan de Oro, 26 March 1977.

42. José Fortich, interview, Quezon, Bukidnon, 6 May 1977.

43. A list of 67 ranches is provided in Antonio Rubin, "Annual Report, Office of the Provincial Governor, Bukidnon," 31 December 1933, Michigan Historical Collections, Joseph Ralston Hayden Papers, Box 27, Folder 27. Concerning cattle counts for Bukidnon, in 1911 Lieutenant Governor Manuel Fortich gave the number as 159 in his

"Annual Report of Bukidnon Sub-Province," 15 July 1911, National Archives and Records Service, RG 350, Philippine Commission Manuscript Reports, 1911, Vol. II. By 1929 this number had increased to 39,472, according to the Bureau of Animal Industry, *Annual Report of the Bureau of Animal Industry, 1930* (Manila, Bureau of Printing, 1931), p. 229. For the estimate on good grazing land, see Frank Gearhart's report on cattle in Mindanao, mentioned in F.W. Taylor, memorandum, 16 November 1912, Worcester's Philippine Collection, Documents and Papers, I, 2. Manuel Fortich, Jr., interview, Cagayan de Oro, 13 March 1977, recalled that "all was cattle" from north to south by 1941.

44. "Report of the Director of Animal Industry," *Philippine Journal of Animal Industry*, 1.6:486–487 (November–December 1934). This report gives the following figures:

	No. killed, 1932/	Wt., 1932	No. killed, 1933/	Wt., 1933
Bukidnon	4,879	680,820 kilos	6,539	854,794
Batangas	4,391	643,873	4,655	690,647
Masbate	7,752	727,662	8,180	780,213

To this day, Bukidnon is first among the provinces in the number of cattle on "commercial farms" as opposed to those owned by "backyard raisers." Bureau of Animal Industry, "Cattle and Carabao Population as of 1 January 1976, by province and by region, Philippines," unpublished report in the Bureau of Animal Industry, Manila. This counts 69,980 cattle in Bukidnon in 1975. It is widely believed among ranchers in Bukidnon today that the figures on cattle are underreported and always have been.

45. Cavada, *Historia Geografica*, I, 378; II, 351. In the 1870s, the provinces with the largest cattle populations were Batangas, 85,673; Cebu, 52,788; Negros, 47,323; and then Iloilo, 42,878.

46. Colonel H.R. Andreas, "Harking Back," *American Oldtimer*, 2.1:24 (November 1934).

47. Ibid.

48. "Compilation of Notes and Reports on the Condition of Agriculture in the Philippine Islands," in U.S., War Department, Bureau of Insular Affairs, *Seventh Annual Report of the Philippine Commission* (Washington, Government Printing Office, 1907), VII, 745.

49. Andreas, "Harking Back," *American Oldtimer*, 2.6:18–19 (April 1935).

50. Manuel Fortich, "Annual Report of Bukidnon Sub-Province," 15 July 1911, NARS, RG 350, Philippine Commission Manuscript Reports, 1911, Vol. II; and Dean Worcester to C.E. Worcester (his sister), 5 February 1908, Michigan Historical Collections, Worcester Papers, Box 1, Folder marked "Correspondence, 1907-11."

51. For Worcester's and Forbes's interest in eliminating the disease, see *Cablenews-American*, 30 January 1910; *The Manila Daily Bulletin*, 23 May 1910; and *Manila Times*, 20 July 1910, in Forbes MSS, Vol. I of Philippine Data—Executive (FMS AM 1192.3). Also see "Is Rinderpest Stamped Out?" *Manila Times*, 20 February 1913. When the disease began to spread again after Worcester's retirement, he blamed it on the Harrison Administration's Filipinization program. Worcester to the Wood-Forbes Mission, 4 August 1921, Michigan Historical

Collections, Worcester Papers, box 1, Folder marked "Papers, 1921–22, concerning the Wood-Forbes Mission."

52. Worcester's and Forbes's vigorous efforts on behalf of Connor are documented in Worcester's Philippine Collection, Documents and Papers, I, 2. Connor is said to have been a former member of the Australian Parliament. See *The Manila Daily Bulletin,* 3 January 1913. The same article reported that "a party of American capitalists, said to be ex-Congressman J. Sloat Fassett and his associates, are understood to be in negotiation . . . for a large tract of this [Bukidnon] territory to stock with cattle."

53. Remedios Ozamis Fortich, interview, Dabongdabong, Bukidnon, 18 February 1977.

54. Joseph Ralston Hayden in Dean C. Worcester, *The Philippines Past and Present,* pp. 71–72.

55. For information on Worcester's connection with the American-Philippine Company, see ibid., pp. 70–71. The figure of 6,000 is taken from a promotional pamphlet entitled "Bukidnon: The Great Grazing Province of Mindanao," n.d., but dated 1920 on the record card, NARS, RG 350, Bureau of Insular Affairs, File marked "Bukidnon."

56. Carlos O. Fortich, interview, Dabongdabong, Bukidnon, 14 November 1976; and Cesar and Manuel Fortich, Jr., interview, Cagayan de Oro, 26 March 1977.

57. Jesus D. del Rosario, interview, Santa Fe, Bukidnon, 3 March 1977.

58. Worcester's respect for Fortich is expressed in *The Philippines Past and Present,* pp. 483–488. Also, see Worcester to Forbes, 18 May 1911, Worcester's Philippine Collection, Documents and Papers, XXI:2.

59. Cesar and Manuel Fortich, Jr., interview, Cagayan de Oro, 26 March 1977.

60. Information on the ranch itself is taken from the pamphlet entitled "Bukidnon: The Great Grazing Province of Mindanao," n.d., but dated 1920 on the record card, NARS, RG 350, Bureau of Insular Affairs, File marked "Bukidnon." The government, according to this, owned 51% of the stock. Information on the dividends was provided by Cesar Fortich, interview together with Manuel Fortich, Jr., Cagayan de Oro, 26 March 1977.

61. Dean Worcester to the Wood-Forbes Mission, 4 August 1921, Michigan Historical Collections, Worcester Papers, Box 1, Folder marked "Papers, 1921–22, concerning the Wood-Forbes Mission."

62. Estimates on the sizes of these pre-war herds vary greatly. Roces's herd, for example, was estimated by some to have been 11,000, by others to have been 27,000. I have chosen as a rule the more conservative estimates. Sources are: Manuel Fortich, Jr., interview, Cagayan de Oro, 13 March 1977; Cesar and Manuel Fortich, Jr., interview, Cagayan de Oro, 26 March 1977; Carlos O. and Remedios Fortich, interview, Dabongdabong, Bukidnon, 18 February 1977; and José Sanvictores, interview, Quezon City, 17 June 1977.

63. Escaño and Ozamis were related to the Fortich family. Mrs. Escaño was the first cousin of Manuel Fortich, whose son Carlos married one of José Ozamis's daughters, Remedios.

64. The north-coast families with whom the Fortiches became linked by marriage were the Ozamis, Lluch, Neri, and Hojas families.
65. Information on selling cattle in Bukidnon is from Manuel Fortich, Jr., interview, Cagayan de Oro, 13 March 1977. His estimate of 10 centavos a kilo was substantiated by José Sanvictores, who said that a rancher could expect to get a maximum of ₱35.00 per head. Interview, Quezon City, 17 June 1977. Roberto Montalvan, a rancher in Bukidnon today, remarked that even now the average 3-year-old Bukidnon-raised steer weighs 300 kilos. Interview, Quezon, Bukidnon, 28 April 1977.
66. Dr. Stanton Youngberg, Director of the Bureau of Animal Husbandry, quoted in *The American Chamber of Commerce Journal*, 14.2:10 (February 1934).
67. Information on wholesale prices in 1927, on the average dressed weight of Bukidnon cattle, and on charges and costs is from "Trends in the Philippine Cattle Industry," *The American Chamber of Commerce Journal*, 12.9:9–12 (September 1932). Information on the wholesale prices for "Indian grade" cattle in 1933 is from "Report of the Director of Animal Industry," *Philippine Journal of Animal Industry* 1.6:495–496 (November–December 1934).
68. *The American Chamber of Commerce Journal*, 8.4:9 (April 1928).
69. "Trends in the Philippine Cattle Industry," p. 9.
70. Information on cattle-boat owners is taken from interviews with Carlos O. Fortich, Dabongdabong, 18 February 1977; and Mineheart Cudal, Malaybalay, Bukidnon, 6 March 1977. Other boats were owned by Vicente Madrigal, Ramon Fernandez, and the Tabacalera Corporation. It should be noted that, for other wealthy ranchers like Roces, ranching remained just a small sideline to his principal business interests, so that he was able to ride out the most depressed years without debilitating losses. José Sanvictores, interview, Quezon City, 17 June 1977, estimated Alejandro Roces's investment in cattle as amounting to ₱100,000 at most.
71. Antonio Rubin, "Annual Report, Office of the Provincial Governor, Bukidnon," 31 December 1933, Michigan Historical Collections, Joseph Ralston Hayden Papers, Box 27, Folder 27. The sale of 7,038 cattle for ₱175,950 represents an average of ₱25.00 per carcass in 1933. This is less per carcass than the estimates for the same year made by the Director of Animal Industry (see note 67 above), in which the average carcass of 135 kilos sold (at 35 centavos a kilo) for ₱47.25. This ₱47.25, minus ₱17.75 in costs, becomes ₱29.50 per carcass profit. The discrepancy between ₱29.50 and ₱25.00 can perhaps be explained by under-reporting of profits by cattlemen in their reports to the provincial governor.
72. Ibid.
73. Lewis Atherton, *The Cattle Kings* (Bloomington, Indiana University Press, 1961), p. 243. Also see Joe B. Frantz and Julian E. Choate, Jr., *The American Cowboy: The Myth and the Reality* (Norman, University of Oklahoma Press, 1955).
74. Manuel Fortich, Jr., interview, Cagayan de Oro, 12 May 1977.
75. José Sanvictores, interview, Quezon City, 17 June 1977. Pay varied

according to skill. One former rancher recalls that his chief cowboy received 25 pesos a month, and ranch hands got 20-23 pesos. Domingo Limbo, interview, Malaybalay, 11 August 1981.
76. Jesus D. del Rosario, interview, Santa Fe, Bukidnon, 3 March 1977.
77. Teofilo Madula, interview, Manolo Fortich, Bukidnon, 3 March 1977.
78. José Fortich made the distinction between "real" and "tenant cowboys" in an interview, Quezon, Bukidnon, 6 May 1977. Manuel Fortich, Jr. made mention of the patron-client relationship that developed, interview, Cagayan de Oro, 12 May 1977.
79. José Sanvictores, interview, Quezon City, 17 June 1977.
80. José Fortich, interview, Quezon, Bukidnon, 6 May 1977.
81. Teofilo Madula, interview, 3 March 1977; and Manuel Fortich, Jr., interview, 13 March 1977.
82. Salvador Albarece, interview, Manolo Fortich, Bukidnon, 3 March 1977.
83. José Fortich, interview, 6 May 1977.
84. Interviews with Manuel Fortich, Jr., 13 March 1977; Teofilo Madula, 3 March 1977; Carlos O. and Remedios Fortich, 18 February 1977; and José Fortich, 6 May 1977. The Fortich herd, despite Manuel's attentions, was reduced from about 1,500 to 400 on that ranch, but that was still the biggest herd in the province in 1945.
85. Cesar Fortich, interview, Dalirig, Bukidnon, 17 November 1976.
86. Marcela Abello Cudal, interview, Malaybalay, Bukidnon. Mrs. Cudal was one of many Bukidnons for whom Fortich paid school tuition, in her case to the Philippine Normal College in Manila.
87. The cowboy, Pedro Anihan, was sentenced to one month and one day in jail and required to repay the 7 pesos. Case No. 185, Proceedings of the Justice of the Peace Court, Malaybalay, Bukidnon, 20 May 1931.
88. Lorenzo Dinlayon, former Mayor of Malaybalay, interview, Malaybalay, 25 January 1977, was one of many who confirmed that the Fortiches traditionally received the Bukidnons' vote.
89. Remedios Ozamis Fortich, interview, 18 February 1977, used the word "obliged" to describe Don Manolo's persuasive powers.
90. Marcela Abello Cudal, interview, Malaybalay.
91. Mineheart Cudal, interview, Malaybalay, 6 March 1977.
92. Winlove Cudal, interview, Manila, 15 June 1977.
93. Marcela Abello Cudal, interview.
94. Ibid. It is conjectured by his wife that Santos Cudal may have been murdered by Manobos because of the strict obedience to contract he demanded of his Manobo cowboys.
95. Interviews with Guillermo Tabios, Jr., Malaybalay, 26 April 1977, and Benjamin Tabios, Manila, 19 June 1977.
96. Cesar and Manuel Fortich, Jr., interview, 26 March 1977.
97. Julian P. Rubio and Mrs. Adelmira Micayabas Rubio, interview, Malaybalay, 27 April 1977.
98. Edilberto Mamawag and Mrs. Mamawag, interview, Malaybalay, 17 May 1977.

99. Bartoleme and Adoracion Rubin Mendoza, interview, Pasig, Rizal, 25 June 1977; and Domingo and Patricia Mendoza Limbo, interview, Malaybalay, 11 August 1981.
100. These families are listed among the 67 ranchers in Antonio Rubin, "Annual Report, Office of the Provincial Governor, Bukidnon," 31 December 1933, Michigan Historical Collections, Joseph Ralston Hayden Papers, Box 27, Folder 27.
101. Information on moving cattle from the range to Manila is taken from interviews with Carlos O. and Remedios Fortich, 18 February 1977; Cesar and Manuel Fortich, Jr., 26 March 1977; Mineheart Cudal, 6 March 1977; and Benjamin Tabios, 19 June 1977.
102. It should be emphasized that even these people did not eulogize the cowboy ethic purely for its own sake. Rather, they adapted it in such a way that it would enhance their already noteworthy opportunities for success.
103. José Fortich, interview, 6 May 1977.

Chapter 8. Americans in the Abaca Trade: Peele, Hubbell & Co., 1856–1875, by Norman G. Owen

1. Frederick Emory Foster (FEF) to William H. Foster [Sr.], 17 February 1869, F.E. Foster Papers, Lopez Memorial Museum, Pasay City. There were 226 male foreigners (and 40 female) in Manila in 1870, according to Agustín de la Cavada y Méndez de Vigo, *Historia geográfica, geológica, y estadística de Filipinas* (Manila, Ramírez y Giraudier, 1876), I, 49.
2. "Foreign Trade, Economic Change, and Entrepreneurship in the Nineteenth-Century Philippines" (PhD dissertation, Harvard University, 1955); "American Entrepreneurs in the 19th Century Philippines," *Bulletin of the American Historical Collection* [Manila] 1:25–52 (1972) (originally published in *Explorations in Entrepreneurial History*, 9 [1957]).
3. Norman G. Owen, *Prosperity Without Progress: Manila Hemp and Material Life in the Colonial Philippines* (Berkeley, University of California Press, 1984), pp. 107–110. Other major studies of the provincial Philippines in this period include John A. Larkin, *The Pampangans: Colonial Society in a Philippine Province* (Berkeley, University of California Press, 1972), Chapters 3–4; Robert Bruce Cruikshank, "A History of Samar Island, the Philippines, 1768–1898" (PhD dissertation, University of Wisconsin, 1975); and Alfred W. McCoy, "Ylo-ilo: Factional Conflict in a Colonial Economy, Iloilo Province, Philippines, 1937–1955" (PhD dissertation, Yale University, 1977), Chapter 1.
4. F.E. Foster Papers (Cat. 3309–3312), Lopez Memorial Museum, Pasay City; Peirce Family Papers, Stanford University Libraries; Richard Dalton Tucker Papers, Peabody Museum, Salem. I am grateful to the staffs of these three institutions for assistance in using these papers, and to Mrs. Elizabeth P. Kincade, Mrs. Carolyn Peirce Brown, the Lopez Memorial Museum (Celso G. Cabrera,

Director), and the Peabody Museum (Barbara B. Edkins, Librarian) for permission to quote from them.

Records for other houses and other periods are generally much more sparse. Legarda has utilized the available sources on the early days (1820s–1840s) of both PHC and the other American agency house, Russell & Sturgis, but for the later period he was limited to one major source each on PHC (the Tucker Papers) and Russell & Sturgis ("Estate of Jonathan Russell," Baker Library, Harvard University). The Baker Library also has the papers of H.W. Peabody & Co., who had an agent in Manila during the 1890s. Incidental information on American merchants is also contained in the *Despatches from United States Consuls in Manila, 1817–1899* (Microfilm, Washington, National Archives, 1955).

The British houses—Smith, Bell & Co., Ker & Co., Macleod & Co., Martin Dyce & Co., Holliday, Wise & Co., Findlay, Richardson & Co., Jackson, French & Co., etc.—seem to have left no such collections of nineteenth-century records, though a few important documents have survived, such as John Wise, "Account of the Philippine Islands" (1837), in *Centenary of Wise and Company in the Philippines: 1826–1926* ([Manila, 1926?]). *Under Four Flags: The Story of Smith, Bell & Company in the Philippines* ([Manila, 1974?]) reflects the fragmentary nature of the surviving documentation for that firm. Nicholas Tarling, "Some Aspects of British Trade in the Philippines in the Nineteenth Century," *Journal of History* (Manila) 11:287–327 (September–December 1963), is based primarily on the correspondence of Manila houses (including Russell & Sturgis) with Jardine Matheson in China, 1820s–1860s. The brief pamphlet by Frank Hodsoll, "Britain in the Philippines" ([Manila, 1954?]), seems to derive from various company traditions, often unreliable.

5. Legarda, "American Entrepreneurs," pp. 28–29. PHC did, however, do business with Hubbell, Stone & Co. of New York (?) until the failure of that firm in 1867; Ogden Ellery Edwards (OEE) to George Henry Peirce (GHP), 8 December 1867, and Peirce Family Papers, passim.

6. The nominal capitalization of PHC was altered every 3–6 years with the creation of a new partnership; correspondence leading up to, and copies of, the partnership agreements are scattered through the Peirce Family Papers and the Tucker Papers. Balance sheets and 1881 export figures are found in the Tucker Papers; prices and total Philippine exports come from Legarda, "Foreign Trade." On Peirce's purchase of one-third of the abaca supply, see GHP to Charles Wyman, 25 August 1862, 13 April 1863, 9 January 1864, Peirce Family Papers. Abaca (*musa textilis*) was a natural monopoly of the Philippines until the twentieth century. On the world market it competed with botanically different but technologically similar fibers such as hemp (*cannabis sativa*) from Russia, henequen or sisal (*agave rigida*) from Yucatan, and "New Zealand flax" (*phormium tenax*), to all of which it was generally reckoned superior; Owen, pp. 44–49.

7. Some 35 partners and clerks of PHC, 1856–1873, can be identified by family name. Of these, apparently at least 18 were American,

6 were Spanish, and 5 were English, leaving 6 (Cryder, Deblois, Genton, Greenough, Herschel, and Thorne) of unknown origin. Among the Americans, partners W. Peirce, Palmer, Tucker, G. Peirce, and Foster were from New England, as were clerks F.C. Eaton, William D. Huntington, and Stone. From New York came Edwards (of an old western Massachusetts family) and clerks J.J. Comstock, V.B. Downs, E.D. Edwards, Joseph and Columbus Tyler, and Edward Young. Arthur Marvin was a "kinsman" of Edwards, presumably from either New York or New England; OEE to GHP, 20 July 1869, Peirce Family Papers. J.B. (?) Endicott (Jr.?) came from a Massachusetts family heavily involved in the China trade, and may actually have been born in China; FEF to OEE and Tucker (RDT), 29 September 1874, Tucker Papers; FEF to C.E. Endicott, 11 December 1874, Foster Papers; cf. Archivo Histórico Nacional (Madrid), Sección de Ultramar, Legajo 1404, Expediente 180, report of Leonardo Castelló y Castro, 19 November 1870; Wayne Altree, personal letter to author, 25 July 1979. Lane's background is unknown to me, but when he returned to the United States in 1887 he was seen in New York; OEE to RDT, 6 September 1887, 30 November 1887, Tucker Papers.

Russell & Sturgis, though also heavily "Yankee" in personnel, had one clerk (R. Schuyler) from Mobile, Alabama; GHP to Wyman, 10 June 1865, Peirce Family Papers.
8. OEE to GHP, 27 September 1866, Peirce Family Papers; cf. OEE to GHP, 17 December 1866, 31 July 1868, Peirce Family Papers.
9. Henry K. Bibby was a former employee of Ker & Co.; Frank Heald was related to "old" Heald and to the Coates brothers, all Manila traders; Foster and Endicott had worked for China houses; and Downs and Young were relatives of American importers. Other family connections to Asian trade include George Peirce's grandfather (a shipmaster in the India trade) and father (trading in Macao and Hong Kong), Foster's brother (with Russell & Co. in Hong Kong), and several relatives of Endicott (trading in China). In addition, there may have been some relationship between PHC's clerk Stone and the importers Hubbell, Stone & Co., and it may be significant that J.J. Comstock is referred to as "the son of Captain Comstock of New York"; E.D. Edwards to GHP, 31 January 1866. (Although F.C. Eaton had the same family name as George Peirce's wife, he was not related to her; GHP to RDT, 9 September 1869, Tucker Papers.)
10. OEE to GHP, 8 May 1864, Peirce Family Papers. This comment accompanied a request for a frank appraisal of E.D. Edwards (Ogden's brother), who left PHC less than two years later for reasons of health. Among those clerks fired by PHC in this period were Comstock (1869, for marrying a Spanish woman), Stone (1872), and Downs (1874). Charles W. Nicholson, a young British bookkeeper hired by PHC in 1872, was fired almost at once when his "vice" (unspecified) was discovered; OEE to GHP, 2 July 1872, Peirce Family Papers.
11. GHP to Wyman, 20 March 1860, 19 May 1862 (quotation), 6 March 1865, 23 January 1886; OEE to GHP, 26 August 1863 (quotation), 19 October 1865, Peirce Family Papers; cf. Legarda, "American Entrepreneurs," p. 35. Ironically, most of the partners in PHC did

not realize their original ambitions to return to a comfortable life in their home towns. Edwards lived for a time in Savannah, Georgia, and Tunbridge Wells, England, before returning to Manila; Palmer also returned to Manila regularly before his death in Great Britain in 1889; Foster went back to the China trade; and George Peirce died in Cairo on his way home to the United States. Lane's eventual destiny is unknown. Only Tucker and William Peirce made it home in peace (to Salem), though both were poorer than they had hoped to be and had once been.

12. "For nearly all of my operations I am indebted to the kindness and good will of the gentlemen here for means." GHP to Wyman, 6 January 1861, Peirce Family Papers.

13. GHP to Wyman, 20 June 1862, 9 May 1864, 11 September 1865, 21 March 1867 (quotation); OEE to GHP, 25 November 1860, 30 August 1865, Peirce Family Papers. These papers also contain Peirce's account books, from which further computations might be made.

14. OEE to GHP, 27 November 1865, 21 January 1873, Peirce Family Papers. By contrast Russell & Stugis gave only 8% interest to its partners; see 1872 partnership agreement in "Estate of Jonathan Russell," Baker Library.

15. See, for example, OEE to GHP, 9 December 1869, 6 February 1870, 15 June 1870, 13 July 1870, 21 January 1873, 6 June 1873, Peirce Family Papers; Palmer (HNP) (?) to RDT, 10 January 1870, Tucker Papers.

The partners in Russell & Sturgis were probably worth even more than those in PHC. Edwards was astounded that Charles Griswold left an estate of only £30,000 (roughly $150,000) at his death in 1868, and reported a rumor that Josias Burr Pearson took $500,000 out of the firm when he retired in 1872; OEE to GHP, 19 June 1868, 7 March 1872, Peirce Family Papers. On the worth of Edward Henry Green and Jonathan Russell, see "Estate of Jonathan Russell," Baker Library.

16. OEE to GHP, 1859-1873 passim (8 May 1864 on his 11-year totals); William Peirce to GHP, 18 May 1858, 18 April 1859; RDT to GHP, ? November 1858; HNP to GHP, 2 March 1859, Peirce Family Papers; Foster letterbooks, 1874-1875 passim, Foster Papers; minutes of meeting of creditors of PHC (Manila, 8 November 1875); undated notes on PHC losses, 1872-1874; OEE to RDT, 24 May 1887, Tucker Papers, and passim.

17. The depression of the late 1850s forced the winding-up of the short-lived American firm Fred Baker & Co. as well as the bankruptcy of one partner (J.K. Chandler); in 1874 Samuel Getty Downs of W.F. Weld & Co. also went bankrupt; HNP to GHP, 2 March 1859, 30 March 1859, Peirce Family Papers; FEF to RDT, September-November 1874 passim, Tucker Papers.

18. Even those who escaped were not entirely unaffected by the losses of their former firms. Green was still owed money by Russell & Sturgis when it went bankrupt, while Foster tried to get Palmer to assume some of PHC's losses due to defalcations which had occurred prior to

1873, but were only discovered in 1874. "Estate of Jonathan Russell," Baker Library; FEF to HNP, 3 March 1875, 9 July 1875, Foster Papers.

19. The deaths were those of PHC men Huntington (1868, of smallpox), E.D. Edwards (1868, after leaving the Philippines in 1866 with lung trouble), G. Peirce (1874, en route home, of "overwork"), and Deblois (1875, of sunstroke), and Russell & Sturgis's Abbot Kinsman (1864, of cholera), Rollins Torrey (1865), H. Cutler (1871) and S.G. Downs (1876). Another PHC employee (1872–1887), Joseph Tyler, died in Manila in 1890. With regard to the hardships of the survivors, it should be noted that Edwards, Tucker, and V.B. Downs all lost brothers in the Philippine trade (E.D. Edwards, Huntington, and S.G. Downs, respectively) and that Endicott became a very heavy drinker, sometimes to the point of apoplexy or paralysis. Information on these misfortunes, as well as some minor ailments, is scattered through the Foster Papers, the Peirce Family Papers, the Tucker Papers, and the consular *Despatches.*

20. Such "liberal" sentiments were not free of racism and condescension, however; in 1865, Edwards claimed he favored suffrage for the "darkies" only as the least evil option, and in 1868 he made plans to move to the south to start a farm and contribute to the real *"Reconstruction"* there "through schools and roads and the example of a civilized family life." OEE to GHP, 23 August 1865, 17 July 1868, Peirce Family Papers. On politics in general, see OEE to GHP, 1860–1865 passim, and GHP to Wyman, 1860–1865 passim, Peirce Family Papers.

21. Lydia Eaton [later Lydia Eaton Peirce] to GHP, 1856–1866 passim; OEE to GHP, 12 March 1859; Peirce Family Papers. Some years after he first retired from Manila, Edwards took to reading the Stoic philosophers; OEE to GHP, 10 April 1871, 14 June 1871, September 1871, Peirce Family Papers.

22. Edwards felt a deep moral obligation to pay off the debts his father had owed his employees at the time of his death (1848), even though it took him almost twenty years to get the money together, but he mentions no specifically religious dimension to this obligation; OEE to GHP, 9 December 1867, Peirce Family Papers.

23. OEE to GHP, 25 February 1872 and passim, Peirce Family Papers.

24. Peirce, as an adolescent, had been one of the founders of the "Franklin Literary Association" in Boston, and often wrote to Wyman about F.L.A. business, while lamenting his lack of opportunity for literary composition in the Philippines. His correspondence with Edwards's wife includes, besides Manila gossip, some discussion of Thomas Carlyle. GHP to Wyman, 1856–1859 passim; Mrs. Ogden E. Edwards to GHP, 1858–1864 passim, Peirce Family Papers. In 1876, Foster wrote a number of descriptive articles on the Philippines (intended for newspaper publication) which show some signs of a "literary" bent; Foster Papers. Edwards, however, after leaving Manila, admitted that his years there had not been entirely barren: "The opportunities for culture . . . are very great, and one learns to see things from many points of view and to understand how many sided every question really is." OEE to GHP, 25 February 1868, Peirce Family Papers.

25. GHP to Wyman, 10 December 1858, Peirce Family Papers; cf. Percival Spear, *A History of India* (Baltimore, Penguin, 1965), II, 131: "The Victorian seriously believed he was five times as good as other people because he travelled five times as fast." The interest of the American merchants in technology is reflected in their correspondence about hemp-stripping machines and steamships (and in George Peirce's fond recollections of the Massachusetts Mechanics Fair); their identification of technology with cultural superiority is suggested by Edwards's comment that "the natives of Albay are not civilized enough to use anything so complicated" as a hemp-stripping machine; OEE to GHP, 10 June 1863; GHP to Wyman, 22 February 1864, Peirce Family Papers.

26. GHP to Wyman, 15 April 1859, 17 June 1859, 18 November 1859, 11 November 1862, Peirce Family Papers; FEF to OEE, 12 April 1872, Foster Papers: "For agricultural undertakings, this country affords only two elements; which are the two footed caribao (the indian) and the four footed indian (the caribao). The latter is perhaps more reliable than the former."

27. GHP to Wyman, 5 December 1858, 15 April 1859, 17 June 1859, 3 September 1860, 22 July 1862, 25 August 1862, 9 November 1863, 8 December 1865; OEE to GHP, 6 August 1871, Peirce Family Papers; FEF to OEE, 14 August 1871, Foster Papers.

28. OEE to GHP, 25 May 1859, 8 March 1863, 19 October 1868, 25 September 1868, 3 September 1869, 31 October 1871, 1 February 1873, 9 February 1873, Peirce Family Papers. Many of Edwards's most cutting remarks were reserved for American importers (such as Banker, Barnard, and Weld) he regarded as "sharpers"; it seems he expected higher standards from them than from Spaniards and Filipinos in the abaca trade—"men destitute of common honesty"; OEE to GHP, 12 October 1864, Peirce Family Papers.

29. From 1817 to 1883, the post of American consul in Manila was held by resident merchants rather than by professional diplomats or domestic politicians; during the first forty years, the consulship went often to partners in PHC, ending with brief interim appointments of William Peirce, Palmer, and Edwards, 1853–1856, after which the post passed to partners in Russell & Sturgis for the next twenty years; *Despatches,* passim. Occasionally, American merchants served as consuls for other countries (Edwards was Danish consul in 1862, and Lane was the "dean" of foreign consuls by 1886), and they also hosted such European travelers as the German naturalists Semper and Jagor; Mrs. OEE to GHP, 9 February 1859, 10 August 1859; GHP to Wyman, 7 November 1860; OEE to GHP, 16 July 1862, Peirce Family Papers; Lane to RDT, 30 August 1886, Tucker Papers. For testimony of former associates of PHC before the Schurman Commission, see *Report of the Philippine Commission to the President* (Washington, G.P.O., 1900), II, 1–19, 27–50, 160–175, 182–201; cf. *Under Four Flags,* p. 28.

30. William Peirce to GHP, 14 June 1856; GHP to Wyman, 5 December 1858, Peirce Family Papers.

31. GHP to Wyman, 17 June 1859, 26 October 1862, 9 November 1863;

OEE to GHP, 6 December 1865; E.D. Edwards to GHP, 1863–1866 passim, Peirce Family Papers. On the question of the jackets, the British and the Americans, who favored white, stood together against the Spanish, who insisted on black; when the former lost, they left the "Casino" together.

32. OEE to GHP, 1858–1865 passim, Peirce Family Papers; Foster Papers, 1869–1875 passim; Manila Jockey Club, programs of 1886 and 1887 race meetings, Tucker Papers. Among the officials of the Jockey Club were E.H. Warner, C.I. Barnes, and Tucker himself.

33. OEE to GHP, 27 April 1864, 4 May 1864, 22 June 1864, 26 April 1865, 17 May 1865, 14 June 1865, 4 October 1865, 11 October 1865, 1 November 1865, 15 November 1865, 6 December 1865, 6 August 1871 (quotation), Peirce Family Papers. The favored Spanish officials included José Feced y Temprado (Governor, Camarines Sur, 1864–1866, Albay, 1866–1868); José Fociños y Armada (Treasurer, Camarines, 1858–1870); Marceliano Hidalgo (Governor, Albay, 1865); and Antonio Gutiérrez Salazar (Treasurer, Albay, 1862?–1869). Salazar's daughter was married to Schuyler, of Russell & Sturgis. On Salazar's trial for embezzlement and other grave misconduct in office—in which PHC and Russell & Sturgis supported him—see Archivo Histórico National (Madrid), Ultramar, Legajo 1404, Expediente 180.

34. William P. Peirce to GHP, 7 September 1858, 9 November 1858, Peirce Family Papers. Similar attitudes are suggested in Tucker's admission that he preferred (Manila) Spaniards to (London) Englishmen; Edwards's description of Palmer as "a thorough Filipino" in his tastes; and Edwards's comment that he was buying a house in Savannah because that city was friendly, like Manila. RDT to GHP, 18 April 1862, OEE to GHP, 6 August 1865, 12 April 1869, Peirce Family Papers.

35. GHP to Wyman, 28 May 1858, Mrs. OEE to GHP, 23 February 1859, OEE to GHP, 31 July 1868, Peirce Family Papers; GHP to RDT, 9 September 1869, Tucker Papers; FEF to William H. Foster [Jr.], 10 April 1869, Foster Papers. Similarly, Edwards advised Peirce to hire a "European" rather than a Spanish woman to care for his infant children; OEE to GHP, 27 September 1866, Peirce Family Papers.

36. An important effort to restore to the Spaniards their place in nineteenth-century Philippine economic history is Clarita T. Nolasco, "The Creoles in Spanish Philippines," *Far Eastern University Journal* 15:1–201 (1970), esp. pp. 36–68. Although nominally limited to the creoles or *españoles-filipinos* (Spaniards born in the Philippines), this study also deals with those *peninsulares* (born in Spain) whose children became creoles. The traditional view of Spanish enterprise was most forcefully expressed by British Consul W. Gifford Palgrave in 1887: "Spanish capitalists here are none" (quoted in Legarda, "Foreign Trade," p. 313).

37. The Spanish agents of PHC in Albay were Juan Emeterio Roco (Legazpi, 1855–1859), Felix Dayot (Tabaco, 1857?–1872), and José Crespo (Legazpi, 1859–1862). In 1862, Russell & Sturgis, whose

agent in Albay (Eulogio Gonzales) was probably also Spanish, formed a "joint account" with PHC in abaca buying. For the 13 years it lasted, the "joint account's" agents in Albay were Americans (beginning with George Peirce), but in Leyte (1871?–1875) the "joint account" employed Ramón Arlegui, a Spaniard, later sent by PHC to Albay to clear up the mess left there after the collapse of Russell & Sturgis. PHC's Spanish *personeros* in Kabikolan included Dionisio Bordenabe, Felipe Estevez, Mariano Garchitorena (the only identified *español-filipino*), Antonio Menchaca, Antonio Pujol, Vicente and Joaquín Roco (brothers of Juan Emeterio), Eugenio Martínez Santos, and José Suarez. Independent Spanish hemp brokers were Ceferino Aramburu and his associate (and brother-in-law?) García, José Aznar, Manuel Caldera, Miquel Riú, and the Zumalabe brothers. The principal associates of Muñoz were José Montero and Aguirre. For the Spanish officials dabbling in province trade in these years, see note 33 above; the priests, both seculars, were José Azada and Pedro Manrique. Other abaca brokers in Albay whose associations suggest that they were Spanish, but for whom no direct evidence of nationality has been found, include Manuel Arteaga, Jímenez, José Lizaso, Molís, and Andrés Pobe. Except in a few cases where the PHC correspondents note nationality, identification as Spaniards has been based on Spanish colonial sources, chiefly the notarial records (*Protocolos*) of Albay in the Philippine National Archives. It should be noted that, although legally the term *español-filipino* referred to a person of pure Spanish blood born in the Islands, at times it was also applied to the children of Spanish fathers and Filipina mothers; Nolasco, pp. 8–10.

38. Owen, pp. 66–71, 83–84, 97–103.

39. Spanish mestizos were *personeros* Ceferino Bautista and Canuto Fuentebella, and perhaps also Alejo Rodriguez; Joaquín Anson, though only a minor *personero* of PHC, was among the leaders of a significant community of Chinese mestizos from Iloilo living in Albay; Rufino Soler of Manila, also a *personero,* was probably a Tagalog; Tomás Borondía was probably a Bikolano. The "Vera" with whom PHC dealt in Tabaco may have been either the Spaniard Valentín de Vera or the Bikolano Vicente de Vera. There was even one French abaca broker in the region, Edouard Demia.

40. The most important of these were Francisco de P. "Quicoy" Cembrano, Lorenzo Margati, Francisco Reyes, and Antonio V. Barretto. Legarda says that the Barrettos were of Portuguese and Indian ancestry, but Nolasco regards them as Spaniards, as did PHC. Legarda, "Foreign Trade," pp. 387–388; Nolasco, pp. 57–59, 181; FEF to William H. Foster [Jr.], 7 January 1869, 10 April 1869, Foster Papers.

41. Peirce once indicated a vague desire to learn "the Indian's language" at some later date, but there is no evidence that he ever did so; GHP to Wyman, 5 December 1858, Peirce Family Papers.

42. OEE to GHP, 20 January 1864, 13 December 1871, Peirce Family Papers.

43. FEF ("Forastero"), "Letter descriptive of a visit to the Hemp producing districts of the Philippine Islands," 24 March 1876; FEF to C.R. Blair Pickford, 28 October 1875, Foster Papers. Foster had expressed

the same sentiment to Pickford in almost identical terms three weeks earlier (8 October 1875) just prior to his departure for the "Hemp producing districts"; clearly he learned from his visit only what he expected to learn. On the process of abaca stripping, see Owen, pp. 75-78.

44. GHP to Wyman, 5 December 1858, Peirce Family Papers.

45. Others in this category include Cayetano Arellano, Manuel Xerez Burgos, Felipe González Calderón, Benito Legarda, José de Loyzaga, José Luís de Luzuriaga, and Trinidad H. Pardo de Tavera. (In addition, the Commission heard testimony from *peninsulares* Manuel Sastrón, Venancio Balbas, Santiago Payo, Miguel Saderra, and Pedro Torre. I have not been able to ascertain the ethnic background of Dr. Enrique López, Dr. José Albert, Angel Fabié, Arcadio Zialcito, José Camps, and other witnesses.) Sources vary as to what proportion of Filipino blood (if any) each of these men had, but agree that all at least had Spanish fathers. *Report of the Philippine Commission,* II, 19-27, 60-70, 116-127, 176-182, 190, 257-266, 368-422; Nolasco, pp. 49, 59, 67, 178-184; E. Arsenio Manuel, *Dictionary of Philippine Biography,* 2 vols. (Quezon City, Filipiniana Publications, 1955 and 1970), I, 317, II, 62; Gregorio F. Zaide, *Great Filipinos in History* (Manila, Verde Book Store, 1970), pp. 67, 130, 378.

46. Between 1890 and 1895, the American importers H.W. Peabody & Co. sent agents to the Philippines to buy abaca. From their correspondence with the home firm, it appears that their circle of business contacts within Manila was almost identical with that of PHC twenty years earlier—other foreign houses, Spanish merchants, and Chinese hemp brokers. Unlike PHC and other foreign houses, Peabody deliberately chose to establish no "connections in the Provinces." H.W. Peabody Papers (Baker Library), HE-A, Private fibres-letters 1890-1897.

47. Elias M. Ataviado, *The Philippine Revolution in the Bicol Region,* tr. Juan T. Ataviado (Manila, 1953), I, 69-70; Ataviado, *Lucha y Libertad (conmonitorio de la revolución filipina en las tierras albayanas)* (Manila, 1941), II, 7-11.

48. Legarda, "Foreign Trade," pp. 361-362.

49. There are partial runs and miscellaneous individual copies of these circulars in a number of places around the world: Baker Library (separate, also in Augustine Heard and Appleton/Dexter papers); Cambridge University Libraries (in Jardine Matheson Papers); *Despatches;* Tucker Papers; and the office of Warner, Barnes & Co., Manila (microfilm only).

50. In 1869-1872, there was some talk among the leading abaca exporters of raising the standard commission to 5%, but it was eventually agreed to leave it at 2.5%, OEE to GHP, 18 May 1869, 27 September 1871, 13 November 1871, 4 January 1872, Peirce Family Papers.

51. Among the partners of Baring Brothers, 1851-1882, was Russell Sturgis, formerly of Russell & Sturgis in Manila; Ralph W. Hidy, *The House of Baring in American Trade and Finance* (Cambridge, Harvard University Press, 1949), pp. 395, 579-580.

52. Decisions on how much of what to export and whether to seek

commission business or to venture "own account" voyages were always left in the hands of the PHC partner(s) resident in Manila. Partners in the United States or Europe could solicit orders or advise and admonish the managing partner, but could not supersede his decisions except by returning to Manila to do so. As the managing partner was often junior to the partners at home or in Europe (since Manila was considered a hardship post, to be escaped whenever possible) and, therefore, more inclined to take risks (having more to gain and less to lose), PHC's policy was often more "gambling" than its principal owners would have preferred. Despite the friction and occasional recriminations this produced, the partners in PHC remained remarkably friendly over a span of more than thirty years, even in bankruptcy.

53. OEE to GHP, 29 April 1863, Peirce Family Papers. (The limits were apparently based not on Manila prices, but on prices to arrive in Britain or the United States, c.i.f., leaving the Manila merchants to make the necessary adjustments for exchange and freight; OEE to GHP, 25 February 1863, Peirce Family Papers.) Foster kept complaining that "mere commission" was an inadequate basis for business, though even he was eventually driven to admit that the world market in the 1870s was so bad that PHC might have to learn to live on commissions; FEF to Pickford, 18 January 1876, Foster Papers.

54. Legarda, "American Entrepreneurs," pp. 38–43; FEF to RDT, 28 September 1874, Tucker Papers. On PHC indebtedness, see trial balance sheets, 1871–1875, Tucker Papers.

55. Owen, pp. 74–76, 81–88.

56. RDT to GHP, 1 November 1862, 9 April 1863, 25 September 1863, 2 March 1864; GHP to Wyman, 9 February 1863, 18 August 1863, 26 September 1864; OEE to GHP, 10 June 1863, 24 February 1864, 16 April 1864, 31 August 1864, Peirce Family Papers; Owen, p. 76. The "knife" (*cuchilla*) was actually a simple machine in which strips of abaca were drawn between a hardwood bar and a blade pressing down on it.

57. OEE and HNP to GHP, November 1858–May 1859 passim, Peirce Family Papers.

58. Owen, pp. 96–98. Estimates of shipping volume are derived from the daily listing of arrivals in the Manila newspaper *El Comercio*.

59. HNP to GHP, 17 November 1858 and 1859 passim, Peirce Family Papers; FEF to Captain Lewes, 21 December 1874, Foster Papers; *El Comercio*, 1872, 1876, 1881. By 1886, the two Spanish firms of Aldecoa and Muñoz accounted for almost two-thirds of all voyages from the region arriving in Manila.

Americans were responsible for one further technological innovation in the abaca industry, the establishment in mid-century of a steam-powered rope mill at Santa Mesa, a suburb of Manila; Legarda, "American Entrepreneurs," pp. 45–48; Owen, p. 160. For various reasons, however, including tariff barriers in the industrial West, Philippine cordage manufacture did not become a major industry and never accounted for more than 5–10% of total abaca utilization.

60. OEE, HNP, and RDT to GHP, 1858–1859 passim, Peirce Family Papers; FEF to HNP, 26 November 1874, 3 March 1875, to James

Methven, 22 December 1874, 10 March 1875, 18 March 1975, Foster Papers; Philippine National Archives, Protocolos, Albay.

61. Owen, pp. 84-85, 102-104, 192-202. José Montero y Vidal, *Historia general de Filipinas*, 3 vols. (Madrid, 1887-1895), III, 490.

62. OEE to GHP, 16 March 1859, GHP to Wyman, 9 November 1863, Peirce Family Papers. A translation of an 1873 coffee contract of PHC (with Antonio Enriques) appears in Legarda, "Foreign Trade," p. 440.

63. See *Cordage Trade Journal* (New York), 1 May 1895, 15 April 1897, 17 February 1898, 16 February 1899, etc. On the nineteenth-century American cordage industry, see also Owen, pp. 44-51; Arthur S. Dewing, *A History of the National Cordage Company* (Cambridge, Harvard University Press, 1913); Samuel Eliot Morison, *The Ropemakers of Plymouth* (Boston, Houghton Mifflin, 1950). The effort to "rationalize" business through a reduction in competition (by any means possible) was typical of nineteenth-century America; cf. Gabriel Kolko, *Railroads and Regulation, 1877-1916* (Princeton, Princeton University Press, 1965).

64. OEE to GHP, 25 February 1868; cf. William Peirce to GHP, 1 March 1858 (complaining of "the Combination among Hemp buyers" in the United States), Peirce Family Papers.

65. Russell & Sturgis circulars, 25 March 1844, 31 March 1844 (quotation), 16 December 1844; Legarda, "American Entrepreneurs," p. 44.

66. GHP to Wyman, 29 September 1857; RDT to GHP, 14 June 1865, Peirce Family Papers.

67. OEE to GHP, 11 July 1860, 24 July 1860, 3 March 1861, 23 July 1861, 21 January 1873, Peirce Family Papers. The letter of 23 July 1861 suggests the thinking behind the "joint account"; Edwards believed the two firms "should try to make some arrangement which would make the business more safe & profitable. . . . Together we can be pretty independent of Ker & Co. even if they should decline to join us."

68. FEF to OEE, 19 December 1871, 8 July 1872, Foster Papers. There had been an earlier threat of Smith, Bell & Co. involvement in the province when Spanish hemp-broker Ceferino Aramburu decided to break off his arrangement with PHC and shop for a better deal elsewhere. But Smith, Bell & Co., advised by PHC that Aramburu was unreliable and still owed them considerable sums "advanced" to him, eventually decided not to get involved with him. OEE to GHP, 30 May 1865, 7 June 1865, 4 October 1865, 11 October 1865, 18 October 1865, 1 November 1865, Peirce Family Papers.

69. The earliest reference that I have seen to the Muñoz brothers in Albay dates from 1854, when Antonio, who had arrived in the Philippines in November 1852, was said to be living and trading there; Archivo Histórico Nacional, Ultramar, Legajo 5165, Expediente 2 y 13 [*sic*]. The family had earlier connections with the Philippines, for between 1800 and 1816 one Fernando Muñoz de Bustillo, native of Santander, was living in Manila, and rose to be First Consul of the Tribunal of the Consulado before he asked permission to return to Spain; Archivo General de Indias [Seville], Sección de Ultramar, Legajo 661. As soon as PHC's American agents arrived in Albay in

1858, the Muñoz family appears in their letters, and, by January 1859, "enmity" was noted. Besides whatever nationalistic or cultural prejudices the Muñoz brothers may have had, they clearly resented PHC efforts to expand abaca purchases from local brokers previously selling to them. HNP to GHP, 18 November 1858, 16 February 1859; OEE to GHP, 12 January 1859, Peirce Family Papers.

On the political clout of the Muñoz family—exercised through influence on the governor and interference in local elections—see RDT to GHP, 15 November 1865, Peirce Family Papers; Philippine National Archives, Eleccion de Gobernadorcillo, Albay, V, particularly the Bacacay election of 1889.

70. OEE to GHP, 28 October 1863, 15 February 1864, 24 February 1864, 14 June 1865, 21 June 1865, 28 June 1865, 6 September 1865; RDT to GHP, 24 August 1864, 11 October 1865, 18 October 1865, 25 October 1865, 28 December 1865, Peirce Family Papers.

71. Huntington to RDT, 2 September 1867, 15 October 1867, 17 February 1868, Tucker Papers; OEE to GHP, 10 February 1867; RDT to GHP, 21 April 1868 (quotation), Peirce Family Papers; FEF to Methven, 11 February 1875, 10 March 1875, 21 April 1875, 13 May 1875, to Pickford, 12 April 1875, 22 May 1875, to Niemann, 24 May 1875, to Arlegui, 24 May 1875, Foster Papers. In 1869, Jardine, of Ker & Co., was reported to have said that no arrangement would ever work in Albay, but in Leyte there was nothing "to prevent all working together to keep prices down to a moderate level." OEE to GHP, 11 February 1869, Peirce Family Papers.

72. HNP to GHP, 6 April 1859, Peirce Family Papers. Other references to PHC trying to force down province prices include HNP to GHP, 5 January 1859, 12 January 1859; OEE to GHP, 30 July 1862, Peirce Family Papers; FEF to Methven, 11 February 1875, to Pickford, 28 October 1875, Foster Papers. At other times—occasionally even at the same time—the provincial agents were instructed to buy all the hemp they could, "following price" or even raising it if necessary! A monopsony would clearly obviate the contradiction here, as the partners realized.

73. RDT to GHP, 24 June 1862, Peirce Family Papers; FEF to Methven, 10 March 1875, to Pickford, 27 March 1875, Foster Papers; Barretto to RDT, 8 April 1861, Tucker Papers. "Strict classification" refers to the effort by the exporters to upgrade the quality of abaca and reject inferior lots; such efforts always accompanied a falling market. For references to calculations of the costs of abaca production, see note 90 below.

74. FEF to HNP, 19 December 1871, Foster Papers.

75. Legarda, "American Entrepreneurs," pp. 39–40; Tarling, p. 307; Owen, p. 90.

76. OEE to GHP, 30 July 1862, 28 September 1864, 21 January 1873, Peirce Family Papers; "Estate of Jonathan Russell," Baker Library. Two plausible assumptions are involved in the estimates of abaca advances in the 1870s—that PHC's advances were identical with those of Russell & Sturgis, under the "joint account" arrangement, and that advances in Albay were roughly three times those in Leyte. Calcula-

lations of the total worth of Albay abaca are based on the "receipts" in Manila, as listed in U.S., War Department, Bureau of Insular Affairs, *A Pronouncing Gazetteer and Geographical Dictionary of the Philippine Islands* . . . (Washington, G.P.O., 1902), p. 279, multiplied by median Manila export prices, computed from PHC circulars.

77. Edwards showed occasional concern about the legal anomalies of this practice, but there is no indication that any importers ever pursued the point; OEE to GHP, 3 January 1868, 30 December 1868, 18 January 1872, 13 April 1873, Peirce Family Papers.

78. G.L. Gonggrijp, quoted in *Indonesian Economics* (The Hague, W. van Hoeve, 1961), p. 31.

79. Two observers claimed that abaca advances made "slaves" of those who received them; F[edor] Jagor, *Travels in the Philippines* (London, Chapman & Hall, 1875), p. 316n; William A. Daland, testimony in *Report of the Philippine Commission*, II,171. The weight of the contemporary evidence, however, particularly as it pertains to the higher levels of the provincial trade, indicates that it was the prospective borrowers who usually clamored for advances and compelled even reluctant merchants to provide them.

80. Owen, pp. 107-109, 202-207, 212-214, 228-229. Owen, "The Principalia in Philippine History: Kabikolan, 1790-1898," *Philippine Studies*, 22:309-311, 319-322 (1974); Philippine National Archives, Protocolos, Albay.

81. Foreman, *The Philippine Islands*, 2nd ed. (London, Samson Low, Marston & Co., 1899), pp. 180 (quotation), 314, 335, 338.

82. Francisco Enríquez (Governor of Camarines Sur) to Governor General, 15 March 1845, in Philippine National Archives, Ereccion de Pueblos, Camarines Sur, II. On general Southeast Asian principles of equity, see Maria Cristina Blanc Szanton, *A Right to Survive* (University Park, Pennsylvania State University Press, 1972), and James C. Scott, *The Moral Economy of the Peasant* (New Haven, Yale University Press, 1976).

83. The extent of PHC's obligation towards its *personeros* is discussed in OEE to GHP, 22 March 1859, Peirce Family Papers. The willingness of the firm to fire old employees and close old accounts is most evident in Foster's letters, e.g., to OEE, 14 August 1871, to HNP, 19 December 1871, to Heald, 8 March 1875, 27 September 1875, Foster Papers. One of those fired, Felix Dayot, had been an agent of the firm since the 1850s; he was fired in 1872 and was still being sued by PHC in 1875.

84. OEE to GHP, 21 January 1873, Peirce Family Papers.

85. William Peirce to GHP, 7 January 1859 (quotation); HNP to GHP, 5 December 1858, 19 January 1859, 16 February 1859, 30 March 1859, Peirce Family Papers.

86. OEE to GHP, 21 September 1864, 28 September 1864, 12 October 1864, Peirce Family Papers.

87. OEE to GHP, 31 July 1868, 29 January 1871, 27 September 1871, 31 October 1871, Peirce Family Papers; FEF to OEE, 14 August 1871, Foster Papers.

88. FEF to HNP, 26 November 1874, to Eaton, 7 April 1875, to Luch-

singer, 12 April 1875 ("The advance system is ruinous" actually refers to Iloilo sugar); cf. FEF to Arlegui, 12 November 1874, to Methven, 22 December 1874, 30 January 1875, 13 May 1875, to Greenough, 22 March 1875, Foster Papers. On the pointlessness of trying to sue "the small backward debtors" in Albay, see OEE to GHP, 1 December 1872, Peirce Family Papers.

89. HNP to GHP, 8 December 1858, OEE to GHP, 7 March 1872, Peirce Family Papers. See also the PHC partnership agreement for 1874–1879 (signed 31 December 1873), allocating 8% of the net profits every year to cover the "Province Advances account"; Peirce Family Papers. Twenty-five years later, in drawing up a typical budget for a hemp plantation, Foreman suggested that ₱10 per worker be set aside for "unrecoverable advances"; Foreman, p. 333.

90. For examples of PHC estimates as to what the price of abaca had to be to insure its steady production (in other words, how low could the price fall before it no longer paid the workers to harvest it?) see PHC circular, 16 August 1849; Barretto to RDT, 8 April 1861, Tucker Papers; OEE to GHP, 29 June 1859, 6 April 1864, 15 June 1864, 3 March 1871; GHP to Wyman, 6 March 1861, 6 November 1861, 16 December 1862, 8 June 1863, Peirce Family Papers; FEF to Neil Macleod, 14 January 1875, to Methven, 10 March 1875, to Pickford, 27 March 1875, 24 July 1875, to H.W. Ferd Neimann, 13 September 1875, Foster Papers; Marcos Zubeldía to OEE, 22 January 1882, Tucker Papers.

91. Owen, *Prosperity*, pp. 212-220.

92. HNP to GHP, 8 December 1858, 19 January 1859; OEE to GHP, 17 August 1864, 24 August 1864, 31 August 1864, 7 September 1864, Peirce Family Papers; FEF to OEE and RDT, 1 September 1874; OEE to RDT, 25 January 1875, Tucker Papers; Owen, "Kabikolan," pp. 285-286.

93. Owen, *Prosperity*, pp. 96-98, 189-190, 209.

94. See Owen, *Prosperity*, pp. 232-253.

95. Tucker Papers, 1886–1887 passim; quotation from HNP to RDT, 21 February 1887. Legarda, "American Entrepreneurs," pp. 49-50, also used the Tucker Papers in discussing the collapse of PHC. Little is known of Blodgett, who in 1896 left Warner, Blodgett & Co. (which then became Warner, Barnes & Co.); see *Cordage Trade Journal*, 15 August 1896; Hodsoll, p. 31.

96. OEE to RDT, 8 June 1886, 5 November 1886, 13 January 1887, cf. HNP to RDT, 14 January 1887, 13 June 1887, Tucker Papers. Edwards always suspected the competence—and occasionally the integrity—of import brokers in the United States and England; see his comments on American brokers Barnard, Gardner, Stone, Weld, and Youngs, 1865-1873 passim, Peirce Family Papers, and on the British broker Neimann, 1867-1868 passim, Peirce Family Papers, and 1881-1882 passim, Tucker Papers.

97. Stephen C. Lockwood, *Augustine Heard and Company, 1858-1862: American Merchants in China* (Cambridge, East Asian Research Center, Harvard University, 1971), pp. 103-119; "Commerce: The Old China Trade" in James C. Thomson, Jr., Peter W. Stanley, and John

Curtis Perry, *Sentimental Imperialists: The American Experience in East Asia* (New York, Harper & Row, 1981), Chapter 3, esp. pp. 38-42. The progenitors of many Manila houses (though not PHC itself) were the American and British houses in China; the Manila merchants often referred to the structural arrangements and business practices of the China houses for precedents in discussions of how an agency house ought to operate, though they were aware that it was the Philippine market, not that of China, in which they ultimately had to make their own way; OEE to GHP, 27 September 1865, 19 October 1865, 11 February 1869, 14 August 1870, Peirce Family Papers; cf. Legarda, "American Entrepreneurs," pp. 30-34; *Under Four Flags*, pp. 1-4; Tarling, pp. 293-303, 308-309.

98. OEE to GHP, 13 October 1871, 31 October 1871, 18 January 1872, Peirce Family Papers; FEF to (?) Forbes, 18 September 1875, Foster Papers.

99. Antonio M. Regidor y Jurado and J. Warren T. Mason, *Commercial Progress in the Philippine Islands* (London, Dunn and Chidgey, 1905), pp. 29-30; Compton MacKenzie, *Realms of Silver: One Hundred Years of Banking in the East* (London, Routledge & Kegan Paul, 1954), p. 133; Maurice Collis, *Wayfoong: The Hongkong and Shanghai Banking Corporation* (London, Faber and Faber, 1965), pp. 98-101; cf. Legarda, "Foreign Trade," p. 354; *Under Four Flags*, p. 21.

100. FEF to James Grieg, 27 October 1874, Foster Papers; OEE to GHP, 13 April 1873, Peirce Family Papers; Legarda, "American Entrepreneurs," pp. 49-50. PHC, while under the management of George Peirce, had been speculating in exchange operations for several years. Edwards never felt the profits (0.5%-1% per transaction?) were worth the risk; OEE to GHP, May 1868-July 1873 passim, Peirce Family Papers.

101. FEF to Pickford, 8 October 1875, Foster Papers; cf. FEF to Forbes, 18 September 1875, Foster Papers, blaming "Bankers & the telegraph" for helping "men of straw" inflate commodity prices.

102. Compare minutes of PHC creditors' meeting, 8 November 1875, with the statement of PHC's assets and liabilities, 1887, both in Tucker Papers. By the latter date, the Hongkong & Shanghai Bank held over 45% of PHC's total liabilities. In 1898 the Bank's branch in Manila would make $500,000 in profits; Collis, p. 101. (Legarda, "American Entrepreneurs," pp. 49-50, is apparently in error in speculating that it was "probably the Chartered Bank" to whom PHC was indebted in 1875; Foster had earlier indicated that the Hongkong Bank handled all PHC's business—"we always expect to be squeezed by that institution"; FEF to William H. Foster [Jr.], 3 May 1869, Foster Papers.)

103. OEE to RDT, 14 June 1886, 4 September 1886, Tucker Papers; cf. Thomson, Stanley, and Perry, *Sentimental Imperialists,* cited in note 97 above; Owen, *Prosperity*, pp. 65-70, 102-103. *El Comercio,* 1886.

104. FEF to Pickford, 22 April 1875, to Forbes, 31 July 1875, to Niemann, 13 September 1875 and 21 January 1876, to Cembrano,

15 September 1875, Foster Papers; OEE to RDT, 4 September 1886, 18 October 1886, Tucker Papers; Collis, pp. 98-99. For later allegations of British conspiracy against American trade, see Regidor and Mason, pp. 29-31; cf. *Cordage Trade Journal*, 15 August 1896.

Relations between British and American merchants in Manila were always a curious mixture of comradeship and competition. As business rivals, they fought for export orders and for supplies of abaca from the provinces. But they showed solidarity not only against Spanish society (as in the "Casino" affair) but against bureaucratic red tape in the Philippines and even against pressure by fiber importers in the United States and England; see the letter from PHC, Russell & Sturgis, Ker & Co., Smith, Bell & Co., and Tillson, Herrmann & Co., 1 November 1861, responding to a circular from the "Manufacturers of Manila Hemp in the United States," January 1861, copy in James Duncan Phillips Library, Essex Institute, Salem. And despite its preference for "Yankees," PHC also hired British clerks and bookkeepers such as Bibby, Heald, Methven, Warner, Nicholson, and Frederic Parker. PHC seems to have had an implicit hierarchy of preference in the Philippines: first the firm itself, of course, then other Americans, then the "John Bulls," then the Spaniards, and at the bottom the "Indians."

105. Owen, *Prosperity*, pp. 69-70, 102-103, 184-187; Edgar Wickberg, *The Chinese in Philippine Life, 1850-1898* (New Haven, Yale University Press, 1965), pp. 62-63, 94-108.

Chapter 9. The Search for Revenues, by Frank H. Golay

Reference Abbreviations:

RPC   Report of the Philippine Commission
RGG   Report of the Governor General

1. 56th Congress, 2nd Session, *Message of the President*, House Document No. 1, pp. 34-35.
2. 56th Congress, 2nd Session, *The Insular Cases*, House Document No. 509.
3. 56th Congress, 2nd Session, *Message of the President*, House Document No. 1, pp. 35, 36.
4. Act 82 of 1/31/1901. The installation of municipal governments by the Commission continued a policy initiated by the Military Government, which created participatory local governments as American control was extended by the Expeditionary Army. Act 183 of 7/31/1901 imposed a tax of 2% on the assessed value of the land and improvements in Manila.
5. Act 230 of 9/17/1901. Congress "ratified and legalized" the insular tariff in Public Law (PL) 28, 3/8/1902, 32 Stat. L. 54, Sec. 1.
6. PL 141, 3/3/1905, 33 Stat. L. 928, PL 27, 2/26/1906, 34 Stat. L. 24; and PL 7, 8/5/1909, 36 Stat. L. 130.
7. 56th Congress, 1st. Session, S. 2355; PL 118, 3/2/1901, 31 Stat. L. 895.

8. Root to Taft, 3/5/1901, National Archives, Bureau of Insular Affairs, BIA–141–44 1/2.
9. *Report of the Philippine Commission (RPC)*, 1901, I, 148–150.
10. 57th Congress, 1st Session, *Affairs in the Philippines*, Sen. Doc. No. 331 (1), pp. 141, 149.
11. Ibid., p. 142.
12. PL 235, 7/1/1902, 32 Stat. L. 691 and PL 28, 3/8/1902, 32 Stat. L. 54.
13. *Report of the War Department*, 1900, XV, 32–34. Under the Spanish cedula, the adult male population was divided into 13 classes taxed at rates ranging from ₽0.5 to ₽37.5 per year.
14. PL 141, 3/3/1905, 33 Stat. L. 928. The ban on imports of opium went into effect 3/3/1908.
15. Act 1189 of 7/2/1904.
16. Taft to Wright, 8/18/1904; Honorary Commission to Taft, 8/10/1904; Cruz Herrera, Pres., Federal Party to Taft, 4/14/1904 and 4/22/1904, BIA–1228-items 27, 30, 15, 20.
17. Taft to Wright, 8/18/1904; Wright to Taft, 8/21/1904; Taft to Wright, 10/27/1905, BIA–1228-items 27, 28, 39.
18. As a concession to their Filipino colleagues, the Americans on the Commission set the excise taxes on liquors and tobacco manufactures at rates somewhat below the maximum authorized in the law.
19. Act 1511 of 7/13/1906.
20. W. Cameron Forbes, *Journal*, II, 46 (7/13/1906) Forbes Papers, Houghton Library, Harvard University.
21. Act 1652 of 5/18/1907 and Act of 1688 of 8/17/1907.
22. W. Cameron Forbes, *The Philippine Islands* (Boston, Houghton Mifflin, 1928), I, 372.
23. Forbes, *Philippine Islands*, I, 255; Smith to SecWar, 1/14/1907, BIA–1973–1; Act 1578, 12/18/1906; *RPC 1907*, I, 53.
24. *RPC 1907*, I, 11 and *RPC 1908*, I, 13.
25. Taft to Wright, 10/27/1905 and 11/4/1905, BIA–1228-items 39 and 41; Act 1455 of 2/19/1906.
26. Act 1579 of 12/20/1906; Act 1713 of 9/18/1907.
27. A second general reassessment of land values was made in 1913-1914 and, thereafter, assessments were revised annually. The taxable value of real property increased 6-fold from ₽302 million in 1913 to ₽1.8 billion in 1935, and revenue from the land tax increased proportionately from ₽2.8 million to ₽17 million.
28. For analysis of the confrontation between the Commission and the Assembly over tax measures, see Arthur R. Williams, "Politics and Purse: Fiscal Politics in the Philippines from 1907 to 1916," *Bulletin of the American Historical Collection*, 7:46–52 (April-June 1979).
29. Frank W. Taussig, *The Tariff History of the United States*, 8th rev. ed. (New York, 1931), pp. 407–408.
30. Smith to SecWar, 3/19/1909 and 4/18/1909, BIA-C1250-items 72 and 90.
31. PL 5, 8/5/1909, 36 Stat. L. 11, Sec. 5. United States internal revenue collections returned to the insular government averaged less than

₱0.5 million annually during 1910–1916. Thereafter, excise tax rates were raised, and collections returned to the insular government averaged ₱2.5 million annually for the 3 years ending with 1920.
32. Edwards to Smith, 4/17/1909, BIA-C1250-after 89.
33. 61st Congress, 3rd Session, S. 7400. This legislative defeat for Taft was engineered by Representative Francis Burton Harrison (N.Y.) who was floor manager of the Democratic opposition to the bill.
34. Act 2339 of 2/27/1914.
35. Act 2432 of 12/23/1914.
36. Act 2541 of 12/21/1915 and Act 2657 of 7/1/1916. The Administrative Code was reenacted as Act 2711 of 3/10/1917.
37. Harrison to SecWar, 2/16/1915. Library of Congress, Harrison Papers, Cablebook 1915; PL 296, 3/4/1915, 38 Stat. L. 1138.
38. Harrison to SecWar, 12/7/1917 and 1/7/1918, Cablebooks 1917 and 1918; PL 164, 6/4/1918, 40 Stat. L. 594.
39. Act 2833 of 3/7/1919.
40. For example, *RPC 1908*, p. 45, *RPC 1910*, p. 17, *RPC 1911*, p. 9, *Report of the Governor General (RGG), 1919*, p. 16, *RGG 1922*, p. 36. Bureau of Commerce and Industry, *Statistical Bulletin*, 1919, II, 173.
41. *RGG 1931*, p. 55.

Chapter 10. The Negotiation and Disposition of the Philippine War Damage Claims: A Study in Philippine-American Diplomacy, 1951–1972, by Bonifacio S. Salamanca

Reference Abbreviations:
COCOPEA   Coordinating Committee of Private Educational Associations
FAPE   Fund for Assistance to Private Education
FARE   Fund for Agrarian Reform Education
FPE(P)   Foundation for Private Education of the Philippines
NLRC   National Land Reform Council
PACU   Philippine Association of Colleges and and Universities
1. See "A Matter of Survival," address delivered before the University of the Philippines Law Alumni Association, 16 April 1975, in Ferdinand E. Marcos, *Presidential Speeches*, V, 295–305.
2. Public, No. 370, 79th Cong., 2nd Sess.; 60 Stat. 128.
3. Limiting payment of claims to the first $500 was related to the similar provision of the Bell Trade Act, enacted at the same time as the Rehabilitation Act, which withheld payment of rehabilitation funds beyond that amount until the Filipino people had amended their constitution to allow Americans in the Philippines to do business as if they were Filipino citizens—the so-called "parity rights" amendment. Parity rights ended with the expiration of the Laurel-Langley Agreement on 3 July 1974. For the Bell Trade Act [Public, No. 371, 79th Cong., 2nd Sess.], see 60 Stat. 141. The Laurel-Langley Agreement is in *Philippine Treaty Series*, III, 471–479.
4. Foreign Claims Settlement Commission of the United States, *Twenty-*

First Semiannual Report to the Congress for the Period Ending December 31, 1964 (hereinafter 21 FCSC Semiannual Report, July-
December 1964), p. 11.

5. "Memorandum from the Secretary of State to the President," 2 February 1950, in U.S. Department of State, *Foreign Relations of the
United States: Diplomatic Papers, 1950*, VI, Part 2, 1409. Acheson's
memorandum also discusses the withdrawal of the State Department's
initial support of HR 7600. The Memorandum on the Truman-Quirino
Conversations, by Secretary Acheson, is in ibid., pp. 1412-1416.

6. *Foreign Relations, 1951:VI-Asia and the Pacific*, Part 2, p. 1563.

7. U.S. Economic Survey Mission to the Philippines, *Report to the President of the United States*, Washington, G.P.O., 9 October 1950, p. 103.

8. Nicholas O. Berry, "Representation and Decision Making: A Case
Study of the Philippine American War Claims" (PhD dissertation, University of Pittsburgh, 1967), pp. 61-62. Several documents not available to Berry have since been published, and archival sources not then
open have been declassified.

9. See Mamerto S. Ventura, *United States-Philippine Cooperation and
Cross-Purposes: Philippine Post-War Recovery and Reform* (Quezon
City, Filipiniana Publications, 1974), p. 52.

10. In his testimony before the U.S. Senate Foreign Relations Committee
on 1 March 1963, O'Donnell said that the Philippine War Damage Association was nothing but a "figment of the imagination, because it
was just Delgado's idea of having an association there in case, to win
some support or try to get a retainer . . . to prosecute this [war damage]
bill . . . there really was no such a thing as an association of claimants,
as such. *We just called ourselves that.*" (Emphasis supplied) U.S.
Senate Committee on Foreign Relations, *Hearing on Activities of
Nondiplomatic Representatives of Foreign Principals in the United
States*, 88th *Cong.*, 1st Sess., Part 2, p. 199.

11. So claims Berry, pp. 79-87.

12. Laurel to Dulles, 26 October 1954, copy in Miguel Cuaderno Papers,
PEMUS, Box 4, Folder 4-4, Doc. 49. The Miguel Cuaderno Papers,
deposited at the University of the Philippines Library, Diliman, Quezon City, are described in detail in Aurelio B. Calderon, *The Laurel-
Langley Agreement: A Critically Annotated and Selected Bibliography* (Manila, De Salle University Research Council, 1979). Delgado
chaired the subcommittee on War Damage Claims of the PEMUS
Claims Committee.

13. Berry, pp. 98-109.

14. See Republic of the Philippines, *Official Gazette*, LII, clxxiv-clxxv
(April 1956). A more thorough documentation of the Omnibus Claims
was presented by President Ramon Magsaysay in the *aide-mémoire* to
Secretary Dulles (pp. 1909-1910); this was released on 12 April 1956.

15. *Philippines Herald*, 13 February 1957 and 17 February 1957.

16. See inter-office memoranda on the Omnibus Claims within the Treasury Department, in Treasury Files, Phi 2.201.00, presently deposited
in the Washington National Records Center, Suitland, Maryland. Also
Miscellaneous memoranda in Philippine Embassy File 295.2. I have
xeroxed copies of some of these documents.

17. Acting Secretary of State C. Douglas Dillon to Ambassador Carlos P. Romulo, 4 August 1959, in Philippine Embassy File 295.2. A xeroxed copy of the original is in my possession. Apparently, the determination of the amount of unpaid War Damage Claims had yet to be made at the time of the Garcia State Visit in June 1958; hence the Eisenhower-Garcia Joint Communiqué silence on the matter of Philippine War Damage Claims. As of 24 February 1959, Ambassador Romulo could only surmise that the new American Ambassador to the Philippines, Charles E. "Chip" Bohlen, "carries instructions to the effect that the State Department will support the $130 million additional war damage claims"; Romulo to Garcia, 24 February 1959, in Carlos P. Garcia Papers, National Library, Manila. See, specifically, John H. Henricksen to R.S. Watshon, 15 June 1959 (Memo on the Philippine claim for additional war damage compensation), Treasury Files, Phi2.201.00.
18. Romulo to Felixberto Serrano, Secretary of Foreign Affairs, 5 August 1959, in Philippine Embassy File 295.2.
19. Dillon to Romulo, 4 August 1959.
20. Secretary of Foreign Affairs Felixberto Serrano to Secretary of State Christian Herter, 10 December 1959, in Philippine Embassy File 295.2. A xeroxed copy of a carbon copy of this long letter is in my possession.
21. The Philippine government's reaction to the publication was expressed in the opening sentence of Foreign Affairs Secretary Felixberto Serrano's cablegram to Ambassador Romulo, 9 October 1959: "URGENT PLEASE CONVEY STATE DEPARTMENT DISSATISFACTION OF PHILIPPINE GOVERNMENT OVER UNTIMELY PUBLICATIONS DETAILS STATDEPT REPLY TO PHILIPPINE OMNIBUS CLAIM." Serrano insinuated that, because of clamor by "groups adversely affected," a situation could develop that "might call for the disclosure [of] multifarious documents which are still classified for security reasons." Ambassador Romulo forthwith wrote Secretary Christian A. Herter in the same vein. The latter admitted that the documents accompanying the American note had indeed been declassified, but these "have not been released to the press by my government." He also said that the American government shared the Philippine government's concern over the probable repercussions of the documents' premature publication. Serrano to AmbaPhil, Romulo to Herter and Herter to Romulo—all dated 9 October 1959, and copies of which are in Philippine Embassy File 295.2. See, also, Minister Mauro Calingo's memorandum of his conversation with Director J. Gordon Mein of the State Department's South Pacific Affairs Office [to whom he handed Romulo's letter to Herter], 9 October 1959, in Philippine Embassy File 295.2.
22. The Romulo-Snyder Agreement of 6 November 1950 provided for a loan of about $35,000,000. Annual amortizations plus 2.5% interest were paid from 1951 to 1954. However, because of a court injunction and disagreement as to the exact amount of the loan, the annual payments were suspended beginning in 1955. By 1960, when the loan had matured, the interest alone amounted to $3,150,000. See Romulo's

aide-mémoire handed during his meeting with Secretary of the Treasury Dillon on 10 February 1961, a copy of which was forwarded to President Garcia. Romulo to Garcia, 11 February 1961, in Philippine Embassy File 295.2. Dillon to Anderson, 20 May 1959, in Treasury Files, Phi 2.201.00.

23. This was filed by Senator Fulbright, then chairman of the Senate Foreign Relations Committee, on 21 March 1960, at the request of the Eisenhower Administration. See Fulbright's statement, in *Activities of Nondiplomatic Representatives,* p. 231.

24. Romulo to President Carlos P. Garcia, 11 February 1961, copy in Philippine Embassy File 295.2. Romulo, *aide-mémoire,* 10 February 1961, in Philippine Embassy File 295.2.

25. The correspondence on the settlement of the Romulo-Snyder obligation is in Philippine Embassy File 295.2.

26. Berry, "Representation and Decision-Making," p. 204.

27. The unofficial U.S. role in at least the formation of the Grand Alliance is described in detail in Joseph B. Smith, *Portrait of a Cold Warrior: Second Thoughts of a Top CIA Agent* (New York, Putnam's, 1976), esp. Chapter 17.

28. *U.S. Code, Congressional and Administrative News,* 88th Cong., 1st Sess., pp. 794–803. This gives a brief legislative history of the War Damage Act and its amendment. See, also, Berry, citing contemporaneous congressional records.

29. Ibid.; see, also, *Manila Times,* 11 May 1962.

30. Diosdado Macapagal, *A Stone for the Edifice: Memoirs of a President* (Quezon City, Mac Publishing House, 1968), pp. 298–299, 341. See, also, *Manila Times,* 14 May 1962.

31. Proclamation No. 28, 12 May 1962. It is probably too facile to attribute a causal relationship between the rejection of the War Damage Bill and Proclamation No. 28, for, as early as 1959, there had developed a strong clamor, especially by Filipino historians and surviving *revolucionarios*—particularly General Emilio Aguinaldo—for changing the date of Philippine Independence, something which could not be ignored for long. But the timing gave the impression that there was such a causal relationship.

32. Kennedy to Macapagal, 28 May 1962, in Macapagal, *A Stone for the Edifice,* Appendix T. In a way, Macapagal and Kennedy were reenacting history. During the colonial period, if the Filipino leadership made a loud enough noise against American "high-handedness," or lack of *simpatica,* or policies they did not like, they always managed to get what they wanted. This was particularly true during the first decades of American rule. See Peter W. Stanley, *A Nation in the Making: The Philippines and the United States, 1899–1921* (Cambridge, Harvard University Press, 1974).

33. U.S. Congress, House Report No. 1715 [To accompany H.R. 11721: The Zablocki Bill], 87th Cong., 2nd Sess.; *Manila Times,* 3 August 1962.

34. U.S. Congress, Senate, Committee on Foreign Relations, *Hearings: Philippine War Damage Claims,* 87th Cong., 2nd Sess., p. 11. By coincidence, Harriman appeared before the Committee on 12 June 1962.

See, also, U.S. Congress, *Senate Report 1882: Philippine War Damage Claims,* 87th Cong., 2nd Sess. This constitutes a legislative history of the War Damage Bill.

35. Public Law 87-616; 76 Stat. 411; *Manila Times,* 31 August 1962 and 1 September 1962. General Romulo eventually got both pens. President Kennedy gave Speaker John W. McCormack the second pen, but the Speaker sent his to General Romulo also. For Speaker McCormack's touching letter of transmittal, see the *Philippine Collegian* (student organ at the University of the Philippines) for 18 September 1962.

36. Pursuant to Senate Resolutions 362 (87th Cong., 2nd Sess.) and 26 (88th Cong., 1st Sess.); texts in *Activities of Nondiplomatic Representatives,* pp. 190–191.

37. O'Donnell's testimony is printed in *Activities of Nondiplomatic Representatives,* pp. 189–250. It was revealed that he had disbursed $18,000 as contributions to several Congressmen and Senators who were in favor of additional war damage payments, and that the money had been given to him by the Philippine Sugar Association through the Philippine Embassy in Washington.

38. *Activities of Nondiplomatic Representatives,* pp. 262–263 and passim.

39. Public Law 88-94. This is also referred to as the Fulbright-Hays Amendment, Fulbright being the chairman of the Senate Foreign Relations Committee and Wayne L. Hays, the chairman of the House Foreign Affairs Committee. A high official of the FCSC told me in Washington, D.C., November 1978, that O'Donnell suffered a heart attack and almost died when the amendment was passed.

40. Emphasis supplied.

41. Understandably, Amelito Mutac, then Philippine Ambassador in Washington, hailed the enactment of P.L. 88–94. See *Manila Times,* 15 August 1963.

42. There were a few appeals to the FCSC. See its *Decisions and Annotations* (Washington, G.P.O., a.p.). As of 1978, the decision on the Madrigal appeal was still pending. Interview with Mr. Paul McClelland, FCSC General Counsel, 1 December 1978. *21 FCSC Semi-Annual Report, July–December 1964,* p. 13.

43. McCarron to Paulino D. Garcia, 3 September 1964, in John W. McCarron Papers, Ateneo de Manila University Archives, Quezon City. Emphasis is McCarron's. There is only one box of the Papers. Garcia was then Ateneo's Vice-President for Research and Development. The two other prominent Jesuits were Fr. Pacifico A. Ortiz, then Regent of the Ateneo Graduate School, and Fr. Thomas R. Fitzpatrick, Ateneo Treasurer.

44. McCarron to John A. Hurley, S.J., 8 October 1963, in McCarron Papers.

45. Sixto K. Roxas III to Macapagal, 3 October 1964. A copy of this letter with an accompanying memorandum is in Philippine Association of Colleges and Universities (PACU) Files, Foundation for Private Education (FPE) Folder, generously lent me by Dr. Amado C. Dizon, PACU Executive Vice-President.

46. "Joint Statement following Discussions with the President of the

Philippines, 6 October 1964," in *Public Papers of the Presidents of the United States: Lyndon B. Johnson . . . 1963–1964.* (Washington, G.P.O., 1965), Bk. II, p. 1214. Emphasis added. See, also, *Manila Times* for 8 October 1964.

47. Juan Cancio, Assistant Executive Secretary, to Benjamin Gozon, Chairman, NLRC, 17 October 1964, in Ministry of Agrarian Reform, Fund for Agrarian Reform Education (FARE) Files.

48. Gozon to Macapagal, 8 December 1964, FARE Files.

49. Gozon to Macapagal, 20 April 1965, FARE Files.

50. Administrative Order No. 127, 1 July 1965, in *Official Gazette,* LXI, 4397–4398. Besides the NLRC Chairman, the members of the Committee were the secretaries of Foreign Affairs and Agriculture and Natural Resources and the Director-General of the Program Implementation Agency.

51. Secretary of Foreign Affairs Mauro Mendez to AMBAPHIL, Washington, D.C. (Cablegram), 11 August 1965, copy in FARE Files, 70 SFE-Land Reform Education Program. The amount being requested for TPD was ₱70 million (approximately $23 million), "without precluding consideration other eduction projects to be submitted later by public and private sectors." Mendez also requested that representations be made for the United States to appoint other members of its panel in addition to the American Ambassador.

52. Dean Rusk to President Johnson (Memorandum), 17 June 1967, in Department of State Files, EDU 9 PHIL 166. For information on this document, see note 64 below. See, also, the undated mimeographed summary history of the NLRC's efforts to tap the Special Fund, in FARE Files.

53. This was stipulated in Paragraph III of a confidential draft project agreement, which was probably submitted with TPD to the U.S. Embassy. A carbon copy is in FARE Files: 70 SFE-Land Reform Education Project.

54. Since the first presidential elections after World War II, no one had been reelected to a second term until President Marcos's reelection in 1969.

55. Among these were Fr. Hurley of Loyola Seminary in New York and especially Rev. Frederick McGuire, CM, who was based in Washington and knew Vice-President Hubert H. Humphrey, Jack Valenti, and Representative Cornelius Gallagher of New Jersey personally. "Can you think of a bigger rathole down which to pour good money?" McCarron wrote fellow Jesuit Hurley (McCarron to Hurley, 20 July 1965, McCarron Papers). "Just pray Macapagal does not spend this money before we can get to him," he would also write the same correspondent (3 October 1965).

56. McGuire to McCarron, 30 August 1965, McCarron Papers.

57. McCarron undertook the mission to make sure that private education was specifically identified as a recipient of the Special Fund; to him the view that the private sector would "not be excluded" was not sufficient. He wrote thus: "All I can say is that this is damn nice of the bureaucrats in Washington. Hence, within 2 or 3 days I shall be

off to Washington to become *not* excluded but *included*." (McCarron to Hurley, 20 September 1965, McCarron Papers. Emphases are McCarron's.) McCarron was evidently successful as he reported upon his return that: "The people in Washington [White House staff, State Department personnel, and key congressional leaders] indicated not only willingness to help the private sector but they seem eager to do so. The present climate could hardly be better. Washington seems to await the merest suggestion from the Philippines side that they, the Philippines side, are willing that at least one half of this money [i.e., of $28,132,544.73] be deposited in the Foundation for Private Education." See, "Re: Report to the Education Committee of the Educational Associations . . . November 30, 1965," mimeographed copy in Papers of Fr. Thomas R. Fitzpatrick, Folder on FAPE. This was lent by Fr. Fitzpatrick to FAPE.

58. Exchange of Notes . . . Regarding the Special Fund for Education under the War Damage Act, as Amended, Manila, 26 April 1966, in *United Nations Treaty Series,* DCCVI, 110–113.

59. As quoted in the *Manila Daily Bulletin,* 27 April 1966.

60. Administrative Order No. 11, 13 May 1966, in *Official Gazette,* LXII, 4533. The members of the Committee were: the Secretary of Foreign Affairs, or his representative, as Chairman; and the Secretaries of Education, Finance, and Agriculture and National Resources; and the Chairmen of the National Economic Council and National Land Reform Council, or their representatives. Administrative Order No. 11 also dissolved the Committee on Land Reform Education earlier created by President Macapagal.

61. Author's interview with Dr. Onofre D. Corpuz, 31 August 1978.

62. This guideline made it possible for the Cultural Center of the Philippines, under the First Lady Mrs. Imelda Romualdez-Marcos, to qualify for assistance; as will be seen presently, proposal for the Cultural Development Project was a high-priority project. A copy of the "Information Bulletin . . ." is in PACU Files, FPE Folder.

63. I have used the mimeographed text of the Marcos-Johnson Communiqué in the Department of Foreign Affairs Archives, Comminqué Files. Presidents Marcos and Johnson held their talks on 14–15 September 1966.

64. I have reconstructed this procedure on the basis of an interview with Dr. Corpuz (31 August 1978) and on a few documents from the Department of State Files (EDU 9 PHIL, Nos. 166, 177 and 185) declassified for me under the Freedom of Information Act (E.O. 12065). See Beverly Zweiben (Director of Freedom of Information, National Security Council) to me, 20 November 1979.

65. Rusk to Johnson [Memorandum], 14 August 1967, Department of State Files, EDU 9 PHIL 177. See the preceding footnote.

66. "Exchange of Notes Constituting an Agreement Between the United States of America and the Philippines on the Use of the Special Fund for Education for the School Building Construction Project, 1967–1968, May 18, 1967" and "Exchange of Notes Constituting an Agreement . . . on the Use of the Special Fund for Education on the Fund for Textbook Production Project, 1967–1968, June 26, 1967," in

UN Treaty Series, DCCVI, 57–113, 115–137. The amounts involved were $13,077,000 and $2,564,103, respectively.

67. Rusk to Johnson [Memorandum on the Cultural Development Fund Project], 17 June 1967, Department of State Files, EDU 9 PHIL 166.

68. Typed notation on page 1 of Rusk to Johnson, 17 June 1967.

69. "Exchange of Notes Constituting an Agreement . . . on the Use of the Special Fund for Education for the Cultural Development Project, Manila, August 11, 1967," *UN Treaty Series,* DCCVI, 139–163. The amount involved was $3.5 million.

70. Rusk to Johnson [Memorandum], 14 August 1967.

71. Scribbled on top of page 1 of above: "WH will return to State for *Redo,* 1/18/68."

72. Marshall Wright to Robert G. Houdek, 1 February 1968, Department of State Files, EDU 9 PHIL 185. The following appears on the top of the page: "Memo approved and cleared by Marshall Wright, White House, and approved by the President, per telcon Alice Caubert, WH, and P. Brannigan, 2/6/68."

73. I have discussed in greater detail the dogged efforts of the private-education sector to secure a portion of the Special Fund in *FAPE: The First Decade* (Metro Manila, Fund for Assistance to Private Education, 1981), especially Chapters 2 and 3. COCOPEA stands for Coordinating Committee of Private Educational Associations.

74. A carbon copy of Corpuz's indorsement, dated 26 September 1966, is in Fitzpatrick Papers: FAPE Folder.

75. A comparison of the texts of "A National Program . . ." and "GAPE" reveals striking similarities. This is because both documents were written by the same person—former U.P. English professor and columnist Josefina D. Constantino, now Sister Theresa of the Carmelite Order. Miss Constantino was the unpaid Executive Secretary of the FPEP, while at the same time an assistant to a top executive of the Development Bank of the Philippines, which had proposed GAPE to the Education Assistance Committee. Constantino to me, 5 October 1978.

76. "Exchange of Notes Constituting an Agreement . . . on the Use of the Special Fund for Education for the Fund for Assistance to Private Education Project, Manila, June 11, 1968," *UN Treaty Series,* Vol. DCCVI. The amount involved was $6,154,000. For details, see Salamanca, *FAPE: The First Decade,* Chapter 3.

77. "Exchange of Notes Constituting an Agreement . . . on the Use of the Special Fund for Education for the Philippine Science High School Project, Manila, September 5, 1969," *UN Treaty Series,* DCCXXIII, 243–252. The amount involved was $950,507.

78. The texts of the Notes and Agreements are in United States, *Treaties and other International Agreements,* Vol. XXII, 1971, Part 1, pp. 501–506. The amount involved was $605,000.

79. [Juan] Manuel to Corpuz [Memorandum], 22 June 1966, copy in Fitzpatrick Papers, FAPE Folder.

80. Jason Parker to Muñoz, 11 December 1971, in FARE Files.

81. The texts of the Notes and Agreements on the Fund for Assistance to the Agrarian Reform Education Project, Manila, 21 March 1972,

are in United States, *Treaties and Other International Agreements* (1972), Vol. XXIII, Pt. 1, pp. 251–256.

82. The notes conveying American approval of each project proposal enjoined the Philippine government to identify the programs undertaken under such projects as "the contribution of the Special Fund for Education, which was made available by the people of the United States in recognition of the common efforts of the Philippines and the United States during World War II."

Chapter 11. *America's Philippine Policy in the Quirino Years (1948–1953): A Study in Patron-Client Diplomacy, by Richard E. Welch, Jr.*

1. This OIR Report was not completed until September 1950, but its conclusions reflected State Department thinking in the pre-Korean War period. Though proclaiming the Huks "the army of Philippine Communism," the report spent much of its time denouncing Philippine government efforts as "notably ineffective." The problem of the Huks was "inextricably connected with larger problems of government viability," and the ineffectuality of the government's military measures "stems directly from the corruption, abuse of public authority, and incompetence that characterize the Philippine Government's activities in other fields." It was well within the capacity of a reformed Philippine government to suppress the Huks by correcting the conditions that fostered their continued support in Central Luzon:

   Given the will . . . the government could do much to promote stability through a coordinated program of enforcement of already existing agrarian legislation, resettlement of the excess population of Central Luzon, promotion of improved techniques of cultivation, elimination of corruption in the government, drastic revision of military tactics . . . and better discipline of government troops in relations with the peasant population.

   OIR Report No. 5209, "The Hukbalahaps," 27 September 1950. Declassified by request but with "sensitive information deleted."

2. See Vinton Chapin, Embassy Chargé, to Secretary of State, 7 April 1950, *Foreign Relations, 1950*, VI, 1433–1438. Chapin, a man inclined to gloomy forecasts, believed that Quirino's "inability" to suppress the Huks might require the United States in the near future "to conduct in the Philippines an operation similar to that which we carried out in Greece."

3. *Foreign Relations, 1950*, VI, 1403–1410.

4. Draft memorandum by Secretary of State to President, 20 April 1950, *Foreign Relations, 1950*, IV, 1440–1444.

   In his forwarding letter, Rusk counseled delay in sending this memorandum to Manila. It was never formally submitted by Acheson to the President but only used as a basis for his "oral briefing of the President" on Philippine developments in the last days of April.

Richard Ely was, with Melby, one of the more caustic critics of
Quirino's ability. See his office memorandum to Livingston Merchant
of the Far East Division, 9 October 1949, Records of the Philippines
& Southeast Asia Division, Country File, Box 17, RG 59.
5. Cowen to Rusk, 1 June 1950, *Foreign Relations, 1950,* VI, 1453-
1456.
6. Frank H. Golay, *The Philippines: Public Policy and National Economic Development* (Ithaca, Cornell University Press, 1961), especially, pp. 74-77.
7. See, for example, memoranda of Charles Shehan to Ely, 10 November 1949, and Ely to Butterworth and Merchant, 30 November 1949,
PSA Records, Box 17.
8. See memoranda to "MN" from Richard Ely, 31 January 1950, ibid.,
and Mamerto S. Ventura, *United States-Philippine Cooperation and
Cross-Purposes: Philippine Post-War Recovery and Reform* (Quezon
City, Filipiniana Publications, 1974), pp. 119-144.
9. Acting Secretary of State to Embassy in the Philippines, 26 May
1950: Butterworth memorandum to Secretary of State, 23 March
1950, *Foreign Relations, 1950,* VI, 934, 1424.
10. Memorandum of conversation by Secretary of State, 11 September
1950, *Foreign Relations,* 1950, VI, 1483. Acheson recorded that "the
President... was horrified at the situation they reported [and] indicated general agreement with the lines of their thought."
11. "Report to the President by the United States Economic Survey
Mission to the Philippines," *Foreign Relations, 1950,* VI, 1497-1502.
See also Department of State Publications #4010, 9 October 1950.
The Bell Report recommended that the distribution of American aid
be conditional upon the enactment by the Philippine legislature of
tax legislation and "other urgent reforms" and coordinated with the
expenditure of peso counterpart funds.
For an interesting contemporary evaluation of the Bell Report and
its failure to recognize "political realities," see Shirley Jenkins, "Philippine White Paper," *Far Eastern Survey,* 20:1-6 (10 January 1951).
See also memorandum from Michael J. Deutch to "Mr. Checchi,"
23 November 1950, PSA Division Records (declassified by request).
12. Memorandum from Michael J. Deutch to "Mr. Checchi," 23 November 1950, PSA Division Records; *Foreign Relations, 1950,* VI, 1521-
1523.
13. *Foreign Relations, 1950,* VI, 1522.
14. Golay cites, in particular, tax-reform legislation of 1951 which raised
corporate income taxes and imposed a special tax on sales of foreign
exchange, asserting that the increased tax revenues permitted "rapid
expansion in social investment and welfare expenditures," in conjunction with a new commercial policy that helped stimulate Philippine in-
dustrialization. The establishment of a Central Bank and Monetary
Board are seen as further examples of "effective economic statesman-
ship," and the years 1950-1953 characterized as a period of increasing
Philippine foreign exchange reserves, internal monetary stability, and
"steady economic expansion superimposed on far-reaching institutional changes." Golay, pp. 77-78. See also Benito Legarda, Jr., and

Roberto Y. Garcia, "Economic Collaboration: The Trading Relationship," *The United States and the Philippines* (Englewood Cliffs, Prentice-Hall, 1968), pp. 144–145.

15. For a strained effort to depict the Foster-Quirino Agreement as the epitome of American neocolonialism and a concerted effort to prevent Philippine industrial development, see William J. Pomeroy, *An American Made Tragedy: Neo-colonialism & Dictatorship in the Philippines* (New York, International, 1974), pp. 24–37.

16. Some advisors to the PSA Division suggested at the time that the goals of the Foster-Quirino Agreement were vague and exaggerated. See Deutch to Melby, 9 December 1950, PSA Division Records (declassified by request).

   For a variable evaluation of the American economic assistance program, see Sung Yong Kim, *United States-Philippine Relations, 1946–1956* (Washington, Public Affairs Press, 1968), p. 7.

17. The summer of 1950 saw not only the promise of increased financial aid for the Philippines but relief from certain prospective demands. Prior to America's deepening involvement in the Korean War, a memorandum had been circulated about the Far Eastern Division of the State Department which suggested that the appropriation for the final U.S. payment for Philippine war damages be shifted to the account for future Philippine development projects, and the Filipinos required to establish a peso counterpart fund for payment of the remaining war damage claims. This proposal, once warmly endorsed by Undersecretary Dean Rusk, had been shelved by the late summer. The increased strategic importance of the Philippines helped persuade American policy-makers that such an arrangement would aggravate the budgetary difficulties of the Philippine government and make more difficult its financing of "the internal costs" of the programs recommended by the Bell Mission. See memorandum of conversation dated 5 July 1950, drafted by R.W. Barnett, PSA Division Records (declassified by request); State Department office memorandum, Clay to Rusk and Merchant, 13 July 1950, ibid.

18. See memorandum from Conrad Bekker to Jack Lydman, 29 August 1950, PSA Division Records (declassified by request); Richard R. Ely to William S.B. Lacy, 29 September 1950, ibid.; Samuel T. Parelman to "Mr. Tyson," 29 November 1950, ibid.

19. See, for example, Parelman to Melby, 26 January 1951, PSA Division Records (declassified by request); Wanamaker to Silver, 8 February 1951, ibid.; "Conversation on Philippine ECY FY 1952 Budget," 15 March 1951, ibid.; Melby to Parelman, 15 March 1951, ibid.

   For a perceptive if veiled reference to the stimulating effect of the Korean War on private American investment in the Philippines and the relevance of expanded investment to the continuation of special tax privileges for American businessmen, see Carlos P. Romulo, "Philippine-American Economic Collaboration," Department of Foreign Affairs [RP] *Quarterly Review*, 1:49–54 (August 1950).

20. See Shehan to Lacy, 12 January 1951, PSA Division Records (declassified by request).

21. *Foreign Relations, 1950*, VII, 187. The Russian Deputy Foreign

Minister, A. A. Gromyko, declared that Truman's statement offered proof that the United States still considered the Philippines to be its colony, and that the purpose of military reinforcement was to manipulate domestic affairs in the Philippines and incite "internal struggle." Statement of Deputy Foreign Minister on American Intervention in Korea, *USSR Information Bulletin* 10:420–423 (28 July 1950).

22. A supplementary Mutual Defense Assistance appropriation of September 1950 provided $303 million for Southeast Asia and the Philippines. For the recommendations of a U.S. survey team (headed by John Melby) on the need for increased military assistance to the Philippines, see *Foreign Relations, 1950,* VI, 1495–1496. Melby recommended the reestablishment of the Philippine Scouts, funds for a Philippine National Intelligence Coordinating Agency (for anti-Huk covert activities), and an increase of Philippine ground forces to the equivalent of two U.S. divisions.

23. See *Foreign Relations, 1950,* VII, 349, 358, 403, 466, 1292.

24. JCS to Secretary of Defense, 6 September 1950, *Foreign Relations, 1950,* VI, 1485–1487; Alejandro M. Fernandez, *The Philippines and the United States: The Forging of New Relations* (Quezon City, NSDP-UP, 1977), pp. 244–245.

25. George E. Taylor, *The Philippines and the United States: Problems of Partnership* (N.Y., Praeger, 1964), p. 150.

26. American determination to "prevent Communist seizure of the islands," even in the last resort by "direct United States military intervention in the Philippines," had been the subject of a detailed, top-secret memorandum from the Joint Chiefs of Staff to the Secretary of Defense and the National Security Council in September 1950. For the JCS, the most likely dangers were the Soviet Union and the Huks in their role as Soviet agents. "The situation in the Philippines" could not be viewed as a local problem "since Soviet domination over these islands would endanger the United States military position in the Western Pacific and the Far East." Leadership of the Huks had been assumed by "disciplined Communists who conduct their operations in accordance with direction from the Far Eastern Cominform." So far as Red China was concerned, the chief danger lay in the potential ability of the Chinese Communists to "influence" the large Chinese population in the Philippines and encourage subversive activity. "The threat to the United States position in the Far East now magnified by events in Korea" required "an integrated plan" of military assistance and "remedial political and economic measures." *Foreign Relations, 1950,* VI, 1184, 1485–1487.

27. At the Japanese Peace Treaty Conference in September 1951, Carlos P. Romulo would publicly announce his government's continued fear of Japanese militarism and its determination to obtain reparations, "any provision of the treaty notwithstanding." It is doubtful that the Philippines would have given even its conditional assent to the treaty had not the Philippine-American Mutual Defense Treaty been initialed nine days earlier.

28. Originally requested by President Truman in May 1950, the NSC policy paper was the subject of considerable delay and revision. For

an earlier and pre-Korean War draft, see *Foreign Relations, 1950,* VI, 1461–1464. That draft placed comparatively less stress on the need for American supervision and support of the Philippine military and comparatively more emphasis on weaknesses of political leadership, foreign exchange problems, and corruption.

29. *Foreign Relations, 1950,* VI, 1514–1520.
30. Article IV of the Mutual Defense Treaty of August 1951 offered the following pledge: "Each Party recognizes that an armed attack in the Pacific area on either of the Parties would be dangerous to its own peace and safety and declares that it would act to meet the common danger in accordance with its constitutional processes." Department of State *Bulletin,* 27 August 1951, XXVI, 335.
31. See Webb (Acting Secretary) to American Embassy, Manila, 18 August 1951; Spruance to Department of State, 14 May 1952; Spruance to Acheson, 23 August 1952, 9 September 1952, 28 October 1952; Bonsal and Day to Temple Wanamaker, 9 February 1953; transcript of "Mutual Defense Conference Called by His Excellency President Elpidio Quirino . . . Malacañan Palace . . . 27 October 1952," PSA Division Records (all declassified by request).

   Only with the establishment of a joint security council in September 1954, the dispatch of an "explanatory note" by Secretary John Foster Dulles to the Philippine Foreign Minister in the same month, and the formation of the Philippine-United States Mutual Defense Board in 1959 did the Philippine government consider the Mutual Defense Treaty properly implemented.
32. See Acheson to American Embassy, Manila, 16 April 1951; Spruance to Acheson, 9 September 1952, 12 September 1952; Acheson to Spruance, 4 September 1952, PSA Division Records (all declassified by request).

   Although Quirino's successor, Ramon Magsaysay, willingly served as host for the Manila Conference in 1954, that conference, the SEATO treaty, and Manila Charter were all products of United States initiative. Carlos Romulo made a gallant but pointless effort to describe the Manila Charter as an example of the new Asian leadership role of the Philippine government. Equally doubtful was Romulo's belief that the SEATO treaty signified the increased importance of the Philippines in the military strategy of the United States. By the mid-1950s, the military importance of the Philippines for the United States was increasingly associated with its regional setting. Fernandez, pp. 334–335.
33. Spruance to Acheson, 28 October 1952, PSA Division Records (declassified by request). By 1953, Spruance considered that Quirino was corrupt as well as inefficient, and the United States Embassy worked surreptitiously to assure Magsaysay's victory in the presidential election of 1953. Thomas B. Buell, *The Quiet Warrior: A Biography of Admiral Raymond A. Spruance.* (Boston, Little, Brown, 1974), pp. 404–422.
34. Spruance to Acheson, 28 October 1952; transcript of "Mutual Defense Conference . . . October 27, 1952," PSA Division Records.

35. The controversy concerning the jurisdictional rights of the Republic of the Philippines over criminal acts committed by American troops lasted until 10 August 1965. A source of considerable bitterness, it saw American negotiators confusing ends and means with consistent stupidity. The Bohlen-Serrano Agreement of 1959, restricting and defining the boundaries of American bases, and the status of forces agreement of 1965 could have been negotiated by the Truman Administration in 1950 or earlier. Ventura, p. 243; Taylor, p. 88; Fernandez, pp. 246–248.

36. The trade-tariff-monetary grievances of the Philippines that were brushed aside in 1952–1953 were only partially settled by the Laurel-Langley Trade Agreement of 15 December 1954. That agreement, which took effect 1 January 1956, did not end the privileged position and "parity rights" of Americans in the Philippines but gave the Filipino capitalist equal access to investment opportunities in the United States—a concession of some psychological if little economic benefit. The Philippine government was given control over its own currency, and the prohibition against the imposition of Philippine export taxes was eliminated. The agreement allowed reciprocal quantitative restrictions by the Philippine government on American exports and eliminated most of the "absolute quotas" on Filipino exports. Most important, it provided that tariff preferences for United States articles entering the Philippines be reduced more quickly and at a steeper rate than tariff preferences for Philippine articles entering the United States.

This agreement was not without importance insofar as it encouraged the diversification of Philippine export markets and provided for a more satisfactory transition period while the Philippine economy sought to adjust to the end of tariff preferences over an eighteen-year period. But it would not be accurate to claim—as did a Department of State publicist—that the Laurel-Langley Agreement assured "mutually beneficial ... economic relations between the two peoples." State Department *Bulletin,* 27 December 1954 (Volume XXI, No. 809); Armand V. Babella & Terrell E. Arnold, "The Philippine-U.S. Relationship: Economics," *The Philippine-American Relationship: Sixth Annual Seminar for Student Leaders* (Manila, 1974), pp. 194–195; Frank H. Golay, "The Philippine-U.S. Relationship: Trade," ibid., pp. 243–245.